Challenging Authority

Social Movements, Protest, and Contention

Series Editor: Bert Klandermans, Free University, Amsterdam

Associate Editors: Sidney G. Tarrow, Cornell University
Verta A. Taylor, The Ohio State University

Challenging Authority

The Historical Study of Contentious Politics

Michael P. Hanagan, Leslie Page Moch, and Wayne te Brake, editors

Social Movements, Protest, and Contention
Volume 7

University of Minnesota Press
Minneapolis • London

For Charles Tilly
Scholar, teacher, friend

Published by the University of Minnesota Press
111 Third Avenue South, Suite 290
Minneapolis, MN 55401-2520
http://www.upress.umn.edu

Printed in the United States of America on acid-free paper

Library of Congress Cataloging-in-Publication Data

Challenging authority : the historical study of contentious politics / Michael P. Hanagan,
    Leslie Page Moch, Wayne te Brake, editors.
        p. cm. — (Social movements, protest, and contention ; v. 7)
    Includes bibliographical references and index.
    ISBN 0-8166-3108-5 (alk. paper). — ISBN 0-8166-3109-3 (pbk. : alk. paper)
        1. Revolutions. 2. Social movements. 3. Political participation. I. Hanagan,
    Michael P., 1947–   . II. Moch, Leslie Page. III. Brake, Wayne te. IV. Series.
JC491.C444   1998
322.4′4—dc21   98-21178

The University of Minnesota is an equal-opportunity educator and employer.

10 09 08 07 06 05 04 03 02 01 00 99 98   10 9 8 7 6 5 4 3 2 1

Contents

Preface

The work published in this volume was first commissioned for and discussed at a conference entitled "Structure, Identity, and Power: The Past and Future of Collective Action," organized by the editors and held in Amsterdam, June 2–4, 1995. We gratefully acknowledge the support of a large number of individuals and institutions who contributed to the success of the conference and helped us in the preparation of this volume.

From the very beginning, three people—Louise A. Tilly, Ira Katznelson, and Maurice Aymard, none of whom as it turned out was able to attend the conference—allowed us to tap into their considerable networks within the international scholarly community as we moved from an interesting idea to an actual project proposal. All three not only helped us to recruit the participants and contributors, but they facilitated contacts with potential sources of funding. At an early stage, Wim Blokmans and Hans Medick also helped us to sharpen our ideas on both themes and participants, while Abram de Swaan and Jan Lucassen helped us to complete the funding package when our original plans collapsed, joined us on the organizing committee, and served as our hosts in Amsterdam.

Eventually the conference brought together some fifty scholars, from ten countries on three continents, for three long days of camaraderie and exceptionally rich debate that easily transcended disciplinary differences and regional specialties. The considerable funding required to transport, house, and feed all these participants came from an unusual collaboration among a variety of institutions in three different countries. In France, the Maison des Science de l'Homme, under the direction of Maurice Aymard, provided the seed money that allowed us to get started and to fund a portion of the conference's costs. In the Netherlands, the Amsterdam School for Social Science

Research and the International Institute of Social History provided major funding as well as infrastructural support; indeed, two very able administrative assistants, Jose Komen of the Amsterdam School and Annmarie Woudstra of the International Institute, actually made the practical, organizational details seem easy. In the United States, the Russell Sage Foundation, under the direction of Eric Waner, generously subsidized the travel to and within Europe of the North and South American participants, while the New School for Social Research and Purchase College, SUNY, provided both financial and material support. Judith Friedlander, dean of the Graduate Faculty at the New School, and Deborah McTigue, her assistant, generously facilitated our organizational work on this side of the Atlantic.

The remarkable success of the conference itself was due in no small measure to the impressively large number of very gifted people who were willing to serve as discussion moderators and commentators for the relatively small number of papers we had commissioned and distributed in advance. Thus we would especially like to thank Rod Aya, Wim Blokmans, Bernard Ebbinghaus, David Fasenfest, Eric Hobsbawm, Bert Klandermans, Lynn Lees, Yves Lequin, M. J. Maynes, Doug McAdam, John Merriman, Michelle Perrot, Bill Roy, Salvador Sandoval, James C. Scott, and Olivier Zunz. The energy and creativity of the debates are amply reflected in the revisions to the individual papers as well as in our collective introduction.

During the preparation of this volume, we have benefited especially from the commentary and advice of Marco Giugni, John Merriman, Francesca Polletta, Sidney Tarrow, Mayer Zald, and two anonymous reviewers for the Russell Sage Foundation. And in the end, when we were in the truly awkward position of having to choose between two contracts for publication, the Russell Sage Foundation graciously relinquished its prior claim and allowed us to publish this work in the University of Minnesota Press series Social Movements, Protest, and Contention.

Most of all, we three, speaking we trust on behalf of his many students and colleagues around the world, would like to thank Charles Tilly—a truly extraordinary scholar, an invaluable teacher, and always a generous friend—in whose honor we organized the conference and to whom we now dedicate this modest collective action.

Michael P. Hanagan
Leslie Page Moch
Wayne te Brake
May 1, 1997

Introduction

Challenging Authority: The Historical Study of Contentious Politics

Michael P. Hanagan, Leslie Page Moch, and Wayne te Brake

As long as there have been formal governments, there has been political contention. At bottom, political contention involves the interaction between those who occupy positions of governmental authority, that is, the rulers of a political domain, and those who are effectively subject to their authority, the subjects or citizens of that domain. These interactions between rulers and subjects can, of course, take an enormous variety of both routine and exceptional forms; they entail a complex interplay of political claims and counterclaims, involve difficult choices ranging from compliance to resistance, and betray a variety of attitudes including cooperation, resignation, condescension, and resentment. Traditionally, those who have studied politics as such have been principally concerned with the actions and aspirations of those who ruled, while those who focused on the actions and aspirations of subjects and citizens were said to be studying something else, like popular resistance or collective action or social movements. To focus on just one or the other, however, is to risk missing the essential drama of the political interaction.

The chapters in this volume direct our attention to the interaction as the heart of the story of contentious politics. They introduce us to a variety of popular political actors: to peasants and workers, to tax resisters and religious visionaries, to bandits and revolutionaries. But to say that all of them were in one way or another *challenging authority* is also to underscore the essentially political context in which they acted and to introduce us to the variety of rulers who claimed authority over them. To be sure, the specific objects of study in these chapters vary considerably in time and place: They take us from Brazil to Beijing and from the late Middle Ages to the present. Still, they converge in their focus on the drama of political interaction, and we believe that in the end they present a coherent and fundamentally relational approach to the study of contentious politics. The purpose of this introduction is to explicate the central features of this convergence and to locate our common approach within the larger body of literature on political contention.

To begin, it is important to highlight the dual sense in which the chapters in this volume represent a distinctly *historical* approach to the study of contentious politics even though their individual authors represent a variety of academic disciplines. In the most obvious sense, these chapters are historical in their concern with reconstructing narratives of political conflict and contention for power. Each seeks to describe and account for the course of political contention in a specific time and place and in so doing to relate the resulting narratives to other equally historical narratives regarding, for example, the consolidation or disintegration of state power and the expansion or contraction of capitalist economic relations. The different levels of narrative abstraction from the routines of daily life are, of course, unequally represented in the individual chapters, yet despite the chapters' obvious differences in scale and approach all of the authors are struggling with the specific problems of historical reconstruction on the basis of often difficult source material.

An equally important historical dimension of these chapters is their treatment of both subjects and rulers as historical actors. Thus, the authors of this volume not only locate subjects and rulers in specific historical circumstances and situate their histories within larger historical processes, but they treat all actors, subjects and rulers alike, as creative and potent participants in a larger interactive process. To do so is to give them both a past and a future—not only a past that renders them explicable but a future that reveals them to be consequential. On the whole, the analysts of popular collective action, in particular, have been most adept at situating popular politics within precise historical contexts so as to explain both their incidence and their changing character, but by situating popular collective action within the larger drama of contentious politics, the chapters in this volume demonstrate how we can move toward more precise descriptions and accounts of the highly contingent consequences or outcomes of popular collective action.

The Structuralist Tradition and Its Critics

This kind of historical study of contentious politics has a history of its own; indeed, examining this history by way of introduction will help us to clarify the specific contributions of our collective effort. As a point of departure, it is useful to see the chapters in this volume as part of a larger structuralist tradition in the analysis of contentious politics. In the 1960s and 1970s, one or another brand of structuralism dominated the practice of social history and historical sociology. The most important characteristics of this structuralism can be quickly summarized: It interpreted behavior in terms of structural constraints rather than in terms of voluntaristic, individual goals; it focused on the relations between units instead of on inner attributes of these units; and it emphasized patterned relationships among multiple units as influencing individual behavior in place of an interaction between the individual and larger units (Wellman 1988). Typically, both historical sociologists and social historians employed quantitative methods to locate social structures and predicted behavior from structural positions.

In the historical study of collective action, structuralism was represented by the work of William Gamson and Charles Tilly, both loosely associated with an approach to the study of social conflict known as the resource mobilization school. Gamson and Tilly emphasized that although social movements usually involve feelings of deprivation, such feelings do not explain the differences between situations in which participants feel grieved but act collectively and similar situations in which they do not. Organizational factors explain why deprived people turn to protest, especially the resources participants are able to collectively mobilize to engage in collective action. For both Gamson and Tilly, social movements arose on the foundations of preexisting social solidarities. Gamson (1990) labeled these preexisting social networks "solidarity groups," and Tilly (1978), drawing on an idea of the American sociologist Harrison White, called these primitive solidarities "catnets," a term derived from a combination of "category" and "network." Catnets are based on a combination of (1) some generally recognized commonality that members possess (category) and (2) interpersonal linkages among members (network). Industrial workers who work together in the same factory or who live next door to one another are members of a catnet. For Tilly, catnets were the basic building blocks for mobilization in collective action. Whatever the nomenclature, preexisting networks were seen as providing the core resources for social movements, and they did so because movements represented the interests of these groups.

In opposition to the dominant social psychological approaches, Gamson's and Tilly's emphasis on social protestors as representatives of well-defined and preexisting interest groups is understandable. Gamson criticized the pervasive pluralism dominating U.S. social theory in the 1950s and early 1960s. U.S. pluralists such as E. E. Schattschneider and Gabriel Almond emphasized the diversity of groups operating within the U.S. political system and portrayed the state as a neutral regulator of political quarrels. Violence and mass action were judged "irrational" and morally reprehensible in a democratic society like the United States. By contrast, Gamson argued that political influence was limited by the ability of groups to mobilize and that mobilization was restricted by the unequal possession of resources; moreover, Gamson's historical analysis of U.S. protest (1965) demonstrated that violence had often been effective in gaining political recognition.

Tilly's response to his theoretical opponents also led him in the same direction. Such prominent scholars as Chalmers Johnson and Neil Smelser saw protestors as frustrated anomic individuals whose explicit political claims could be ignored because they were only symptomatic of the protestors' own inability to adapt to modern society. Tilly's emphasis on the rationality of protestors portrayed them as less lonely and enraged than solidary and purposeful. At the same time, however, Tilly also opposed those who sought to blur the identity of protestors into a shapeless and amorphously defined group called the "neighborhood" or the "community." Instead, in his classic 1964 study of the peasant rebellion in the Vendée region of France in 1793, Tilly emphasized the importance of historically specific linkages and social ties as well as the need to understand the ways in which such large-scale processes as proletarianization, urbanization, and state making affected the identity and interests of different groups.

The stress on the interests underlying collective action deepened as resource mobilization theory became more influential and concentrated on contemporary events. In the mid-1970s less historically oriented but more central figures in the resource mobilization school, John D. McCarthy and Mayer N. Zald, argued that the future of social movements and U.S. social protest lay with professional movement spokesmen and that bureaucratized public lobbies as social movements evolved in the direction of interest groups (McCarthy and Zald 1973). Professionalized organizations would increasingly come to articulate the views of broadly based constituencies interested in efficiently obtaining favorable political outcomes (McCarthy, Britt, and Wolfson 1991). Such predictions, however, were not generally borne out. The influence of professionalized social movement organizations increased, but they did not succeed in capturing the allegiance of most activists or the loyalty of the broad strata of the population concerned with their issues. Though the high level of protest of the late 1960s and early 1970s declined, U.S. protest activity continued to follow the patterns of sporadic mass mobilization, mainly of middle-class students and professionals. These mobilizations were often quite powerful but rarely exhibited much staying power. The diverse ad hoc social movements that sprang up in the 1970s, competing with one another and quar reling internally, proved unable to provide shelter for political causes that found themselves increasingly on the defensive (Epstein 1991).

However much we might be sympathetic to Gamson's and Tilly's criticism of reigning scholarly opinion, their portrayal of the stability and continuity of the interests and identities of protestors opened their position to attack, and the historical study of social movements has undergone great change over the last two decades as a consequence. The "new social history" sought to ground social protest in structural terms, often class terms, and to stress the relationship between social conflict and the ability of diverse groups to mobilize resources to achieve defined goals, but much of this program was challenged by a self-styled poststructuralism or by a culturalism composed of strands of cultural criticism, social constructionism, semiotics, discourse analysis, and postmodernism. All of these strands drew attention to the fluid quality of identity and challenged the very notion of structure. To label some-one a "worker" was to ignore gender, race, or sexual orientation, and in the late 1970s and 1980s it seemed to many that these identities often proved more politically conspicuous than class identity. By the late 1980s many European scholars had come to share the same sense of skepticism about stable identities, particularly class identities, that was developing in the Unit-ed States. In both Europe and the United States a suspicious generation of historians studied great historical processes such as the French Revolution, and many found no trace of a "bourgeoisie" or a "nobility" acting in a coherent way over the course of these events (Furet 1981; Reddy 1987; cf. Knight 1992). Only portions of these larger social groups could be found in concrete historical situations, and even then they often behaved in ways that did not reflect their assumed interests. Though the intellectual critique of these cul-tural approaches proved effective, critics were unable to present an alterna-tive interpretation; indeed, they eschewed such interpretations in principle. Too often, cultural historians, influenced by this poststructuralist mood, im-plied that the task of studying past events was fruitless and that only the in-terpretation of glosses on past events was fit work for historians (Cohen 1988).

Like structuralism, poststructuralism and culturalism encompass a wide variety of arguments and social thinkers but share a number of common char-acteristics. In general, culturalists and poststructuralists are wary of general-izations and suspect that Western reason suppresses particularities in its ef-fort to construct stable identities. They assert the malleability of identity and celebrate diversity and heterogeneity, particularly of those excluded from so-ciety (Mcgowan 1991, 1–30). The later works of Michel Foucault played a key role in the elaboration of cultural approaches. Foucault dismissed a politics that centered on trying to influence or gain control over the state and argued that real power was diffused through the entire institutional and cultural framework of society. Rather than constructing a new order of repression, Foucault argued that freedom came only by revealing and rejecting efforts to impose order (1980, 78–108). In the hands of culturalist interpreters, identity formation developed into an almost arbitrary, individual process that increasingly was seen as subjectivist and relativist. Today the Althusserian structuralist turned postmodernist Jacques Rancière (1994) altogether denies the possibility of attributing collective identity.

In the study of collective action in particular, "new social movements" theory has been strongly influenced by poststructuralist intellectual currents. Although one early prominent advocate, Jürgen Habermas, with his commitment to a communicative ideal, remains resolutely opposed to poststructuralism, some of its most prominent recent champions have moved in this direction. Proponents like Alain Touraine (1988) often assume that orthodox Marxism was roughly right for the nineteenth and early twentieth centuries. At some vaguely specified time in the twentieth century, however, perhaps after 1950, a fundamentally new pattern developed, characterized by the emergence of a new type of social movement. In contrast to traditional Marxist orientations, these movements were not only anticapitalist but also resolutely antimodernist. Breaking with the assumptions of socialists and communists, they denounced economic growth and engaged in collective action, favoring small-scale, decentralized, antihierarchical organizations run through direct democracy (see Klandermans and Tarrow 1988; Cohen 1985; Larana, Johnston, and Gusfield 1994).

Early on, new social movement theorists often insisted that the identities of movement participants were based on more deeply personal conceptions of self and of nature than those of Marxist conceptions. Whereas class originated in a conception of rational collective interest, these new movements were based on characteristics inscribed in the intimate terrain of the "life world." In their view, a person might *choose* to identify with a class, but he or she does not choose to be gay or straight, female or male, child or adult; these are basic characteristics of the individual's life world, not matters of choice. Instead of raising demands for a new society, new social movement theorists portrayed themselves as defending a private sphere increasingly threatened by the intrusion of the welfare state, environmental pollution, and nuclear war. As the theory developed, some of its prominent advocates, such as Alberto Melucci, abandoned the conception of such a primal identity. Gender, race, and environmental concerns began to be seen not only as social constructions but as constructions ex nihilo (Melucci 1989). At the limit, Ernesto Laclau and Chantal Mouffe proclaimed the arbitrary character of all identity. There was room, it turned out, for an infinite number of new social movements, and Laclau and Mouffe proclaimed the need for a democratic citizenship whose constituents shared only one belief: that they were, each and every one, utterly different from one another (Laclau 1990; Mouffe 1992).

Recently, the claims of new social movement theorists have been reevaluated in the light of more thoroughgoing investigations and systematic international comparisons of modern European social movements. New studies have examined both the formation of movements' identities and their relations with political power and questioned the theorists' tendency to separate cultural and political forces, presenting culture as defining identities and political structure as hindering or facilitating the growth of these identities (Johnson and Klandermans 1995). In opposition to the separation of the cultural from the political, scholars like Jan Willem Duyvendak have insisted that "by polarizing power and culture one cannot adequately understand the *power* orientation of some *identity*-oriented movements" (1995, 9; emphasis in the original). Duyvendak reminds us that the tactics of many social movements flow less from the requirements of identity than from an "instrumental" consideration of the tactics required to accomplish their common goals. According to Duyvendak, this should not surprise us because, deprived of an instrumental logic, social movements either disappear or evolve into "a subcultural phenomenon, a club, a psychotherapeutic sect, or a religious movement organization" (29; see also Kriesi et al. 1995).

In the meantime, current events have let much of the air out of the new social movement balloon. Exactly at the time that Laclau and Mouffe began to celebrate the infinite diversity of libertarian social movements, those movements began to lose some of their vigor. Though summoned by their theorists, a whole series of new progressive social movements did not arise. Moreover, such new social movements as the protests against migrants, the growth of conservative regionalism, and attacks on multiculturalism were authoritarian and intolerant of diversity. New social movement theorists offered little explanation for the decline of left-wing and the rise of right-wing social movements.

A New Interactional Structuralism

Against this backdrop, the chapters in this collection represent a structuralist riposte to the poststructuralists of the 1980s and 1990s, but it is a structuralism that has undergone a major linguistic turn. Taken together, these chapters clearly demonstrate that the relationship between mobilization for collective action and identity formation is a perennial and recurrent problem for protest groups and that the historical study of contentious politics—with its focus on political interaction—can shed much light on that relationship. Our specific approach to political interaction nevertheless owes a very considerable debt to the major reformulations of social movement theory by such pioneers as Charles Tilly and William Gamson, as well as to the work of Sidney Tarrow.

Doug McAdam, whose work exemplifies a "political process" approach that is shared by many of our authors, locates the emergence of social protest in "a combination of expanding political opportunities and indigenous organization, as mediated through a process of collective attributions" (1982, 2). Dealing with this problem of "collective attributions," in particular, has reinvigorated the study of collective action and helps to explain the convergence of the recent work of Tilly, Gamson, and Tarrow on the linguistic ties binding groups together and relating them to other groups. In his recent book *Talking Politics* (1992), Gamson uses frame analysis to show how groups use information from the press and media to develop their own political orientations or "frames," which are often quite different from those found in their journalistic sources. Gamson has argued that framing should be seen as a factor in creating political opportunities as well as a response to shifts in political opportunities (Gamson and Meyer 1996).

In contrast to Gamson, Tarrow and Tilly have focused more attention on the role of change in repertoires and in the mobilization process in relation to shifting political opportunity. Both have stressed that in times of political crisis, routine identities based on networks rarely mobilize smoothly or enter directly into contention. Tarrow's insight that a social movement is typically part of a whole family of related movements is important here, as is his idea of a "cycle of protest." A cycle of protest is defined as "a rapid diffusion of collective action from more mobilized to less mobilized sectors; a quickened pace of innovation in the forms of contention; new or transformed collective action frames; a combination of organized and unorganized participation; and sequences of intensified interaction between challengers and authorities which can end in reform, repression and sometimes revolution" (1994, 153; see also Tarrow 1989, 1992). During a cycle of protest, movements grow with political encounters in which contending organizations try to win the support of all available networks. The identity of a network and of the organization or spokespersons claiming to speak in its name is, however, seldom complete.

During cycles of protest, coalitions are formed and reformed, and contingent political events have enduring consequences. Unlikely allies sometimes discover more in common than seemed possible. Innovative forms of protest are transmitted rapidly from capital city to region and across national boundaries. The political process is less a matter of political organizations smoothly mobilizing networks and is more like a U.S. presidential debate in which each debater tries to appeal to uncommitted constituencies. More often than not, the rhetoric used by political organizations does not consist solely of slogans but employs the symbolic language of demonstrations, strikes, and barricades. Success is dependent not simply upon one's own rhetoric but on taking advantages of the rhetorical blunders and failed gambits of one's opponent. Typically, movement success comes through rallying a heterogeneous array of sections of catnets behind a common rhetoric. If appeals to an initially heterogeneous collection of groups is successful and sustained, then, in time, the coalition itself becomes a new catnet (McAdam, Tarrow, and Tilly 1996).

Historians of contentious politics will find Tilly's "linguistic turn" especially relevant. Tilly's concept of a "repertoire of contention" is a specifically action-oriented concept rather than a set of beliefs. For the study of history, where our records of collective action are more complete than our records of collective belief, such an approach has a clear pragmatic appeal; it is more useful for research than other approaches. More important, whereas the concept of framing represents a collective perspective held by one group, a repertoire is constituted by the interaction between at least two contending groups. "Framing" is the preparation of a group monologue; a "repertoire" emerges from encounters or conversations among contending groups. Although "framing" may give us a fuller understanding of the motives that draw groups into protest, "repertoire" provides a better understanding of the interactions that produce actual contentious events and their outcomes.

At bottom, political contention is a kind of conversation or exchange among groups.[1] Like any conversation, the collective actions that Tilly studies, even the most violent, are complexes of signs, complexes that are communicative and directed; they use symbols to present the claims of one group to another group. Like conversation, contention occurs within an existing framework of conventions but allows leeway for the expression of new ideas and the forging of new conventions. Established groups often reject the efforts of protesting groups to communicate with them and even deny that these protests represent attempts at communication. While it does happen that rulers may fail to understand some contentious collective actions as protest, typically such responses are a refusal to consider the claims of a group. "They're not protestors, they're common criminals" is usually a formula for dismissing intelligible but unacceptable political claims.

Over time, claim-making groups establish a well-known repertoire of contention whose implications are understood by everyone. Repertoires change as shifts in political opportunities bring new groups into contention or as they alter the relationship between established groups. A handful of great revolutions provide the best examples of dramatic changes in repertoires (Tilly 1982). At the height of such "revolutionary situations," when conflicting groups find support for mutually incompatible claims to state power, every group in society finds its position in question. With state power at stake, groups must reevaluate their ties to existing governments; they must consider the advisability of strengthening their claims on the existing state or of entering into negotiations with its rivals. Not surprisingly, such circumstances bring a host of new social interactions and are particularly fertile in the production of new repertoires. But revolutions are not the only means for creating repertoires (Sewell 1994; Tarrow 1997); revolution is only the most dramatic of the many types of shifts in political opportunity that provide the occasion for presenting new kinds of claims. Serious political differences within political establishments provide chances for organized groups excluded from power to make allies among the powerful and to win at least some recognition for their demands.

The important point that needs to be emphasized is that however partial or incomplete the recognition of a right to claim making based on an identity of citizenship, nationality, or class, recognizing the right to make a claim also helps to stabilize and secure that identity. To acknowledge the claims of a national minority may help moderate its claims, but such acknowledgment also grants it a measure of legitimacy. To the extent that claims by organized groups are recognized, those who belong to the same category as a successful claimant may launch similar claims. Other groups will consider whether their situation is sufficiently similar to warrant the assertion of similar claims. Successful struggles for civil rights for African Americans, for example, have not only inspired other groups to make claims but have profoundly influenced the *kinds of* claims made by Native Americans, Hispanics, women, and gays.

Successful claim making gives new meaning to a particular identity. In many cases, to strengthen acquired positions on their way to asserting new claims, organizations often assert the antiquity of the network they claim to represent or assert the depth and extent of their support among members of the network. No groups assert the antiquity of their traditions more fervently than nascent national minorities first asserting their own claims (Hobsbawm and Ranger 1983; Kiberd 1988). The underlying assumption is that if the group has endured for thousands of years with the same demands, sooner or later these will have to be met. Socialists and communists spoke as representatives of ordinary factory workers and miners, and feminists claim to speak for all women. At the first sign that political groups can find backers, their claims to represent the previously unarticulated needs of significant sections of the population is taken seriously in democratic societies.

Networks, Repertoires, and Political Opportunities

From a relational perspective, then, the task of reconstructing the history of contentious politics highlights three interrelated areas of research: the complex relationship of social networks to identities and claim making, the shifting repertoires of contention by means of which rulers and subjects interact, and the changing constellations of political opportunity that channel the political action of subjects and rulers alike. These are the principal concerns of the chapters in this collection. Using a relational prism to view each of these problems, we examine the interrelationship and dialogic interaction between contending groups and authorities. Thus a new relational structuralism emerges in this volume as a whole, though not in equal measure in each of the individual chapters. This new structuralism insists that changing configurations of networks cannot be understood without analyzing their spatial, temporal, *and linguistic* aspects because these are inseparably connected elements of network change.

To explore different dimensions of the problem of historical reconstruction as well as the specific contributions of the individual chapters, we have grouped them in terms of the larger research themes. It will nevertheless be obvious to the reader that most of the chapters address more than one of the themes.

Networks, Identities, and Claim Making

The first part includes five chapters—by Charles Tilly, Marc W. Steinberg, Roger V. Gould, Andrew G. Walder, and Risto Alapuro—that illuminate from a variety of angles the complex relationship between ever changing social networks and the identities and claim making of political actors. Charles Tilly provides an exceptionally well balanced depiction of how rights and identities are molded through political contention, but he deepens our understanding of changing nineteenth-century British protest, in particular, by focusing on the shift in network configurations as groups reoriented themselves toward national politics. Reconstructing the story of political contention in Preston, near Manchester, Tilly shows us that at the beginning of the nineteenth century political protest was parochial, particular, and bifurcated, but by the 1830s it had become cosmopolitan, modular, and autonomous. As local political actors began to orient themselves toward the national state, they shed their old networks of mobilization, including neighbors, friends, or fellow parishioners, and identified themselves with new categories of political actors: electors and their supporters. This new identity also called for a fundamental reorientation of protest action. Grievances formerly expressed in local festivals, food riots, and Rough Music were now articulated at election rallies and as part of political campaigns. To a surprising extent, the authorities accepted these new assertions. Their decision to remove the army and allow mass participation while keeping firm control over the Preston elections was in fact an important compromise that inched forward toward popular participation.

Like Charles Tilly, Marc Steinberg focuses his study of the forms of social protest on early-nineteenth-century England and also explores how changes in the form of protest were related to the content of protestors' claims and the identity of protestors. Whereas Tilly emphasizes how protestors gained new rights by reshaping their political identities, Steinberg considers the losses. The transformation that Steinberg portrays is the movement away from a traditional carnivalesque celebration, the Riding of the Black Lad, that provided an opportunity for shaming those who had violated established codes of behavior. It was succeeded by the "turnout," a precursor to the strike in which workers emptied out of one factory and then proceeded to other factories, soliciting workers in other factories to join them. In both the Riding of the Black Lad and the turnout, local working-class communities expressed their grievances against individuals or groups whom they labeled oppressors. To explore what was lost and what was won in the change, Steinberg focuses on the locational and gender aspects of the different protests. Although Steinberg is not able to describe specific networks in the transformation of protest, network assumptions are central to his analysis. Basically, he describes a market-based series of ties that included women and contrasts it to work-based networks focused on factories that privileged ties among male factory workers, and thus he reminds us that every change in repertoire benefits some groups and disfranchises others.

More than any other chapter, Roger Gould's study of the 1794 Whiskey Rebellion in western Pennsylvania explicitly explores the relationship between networks and contention (cf. Gould 1995a). Gould gives us a fascinating picture of the way that clearly defining networks and analyzing their changing relationships can help us understand a regional rebellion. He begins with a decentralized federal government whose influence in peripheral areas of the young American republic was mediated by powerful local authorities who personally profited from their positions. These local authorities had considerable leeway in law enforcement and did not enforce a tax on whiskey that brought them much unpopularity and little profit. As the power of the young republic was consolidated, however, federal authorities began to directly enforce federal law, including the excise tax, on the periphery. Direct federal intervention threatened the autonomy of local elites, who played an ambiguous if crucial role in fomenting rebellion while all the time trying to avoid a direct confrontation with federal authorities. In this changing context, Gould shows how networks constitute (rather than merely constrain) the rebels' interests and identities. Indeed, what at first blush might seem a strange and mysterious conglomeration of rebels makes sense when we see that government actions impinged on the drinking habits of small farmers and the political autonomy of powerful local men.

Whereas Gould specifically concentrates on the network aspect of contention and Steinberg focuses on its claim-making aspects, Andrew Walder's study of mobilization in Beijing in 1989, like Tilly's study of Preston, skillfully balances both aspects of contention. Walder describes Chinese rulers who, paralyzed by factionalism, ceased to provide leadership for the military, the party, industrial managers, or the administration. During a few weeks in the spring of 1989 the Chinese bureaucracy, uncertain which of several contending factions would win, was too confused to use its customary tactics of repression; some party factions even encouraged popular groups to form and express their opinion. Within a few days and almost from scratch, elements of popular mobilization began to appear. Based on his interviews with participants, Walder distinguishes four citizen groups: self-defense organizations, "protest brigades," political associations, and "workers' autonomous federations." Most of these groups seem to have formed during the events of the spring of 1989, but they clearly had preexisting roots in factory, neighborhood, and school networks. Although all of these groups felt themselves to be part of a common pro-democracy movement and although most of them were composed of urban industrial workers, nonetheless the protestors employed a variety of rhetorics, each of which could have evoked a favorable response from the government. By tolerating some of the mass popular movements and outlawing others, the Chinese government could have played a role in shaping the identity of its opposition and defining the means it would employ. As it happened, however, the most important factions of the Chinese bureaucracy were able to unite and to repress the tide of popular mobilization before it was completely out of control.

Finally, Risto Alapuro's local study of a Finnish country town between 1900 and 1918 underscores the importance of existing networks and political organizations in the context of a dramatic shift in political opportunities. Finland was a relatively developed and autonomous province within a backward Russian Empire, but beginning in the 1890s the empire, in its efforts to modernize, began to centralize and to strengthen its hold over Finland (cf. Alapuro 1988). As the Russian Empire hurtled toward revolution, Finnish politics began to center on opposition to a tsarist autocracy. Then, suddenly, in 1917, with hardly any Finnish efforts, the dominant state power collapsed because of a revolution in the heartlands, and the Finns found themselves faced with the utterly unexpected task of ruling their country. Alapuro looks at how ordinary Finns adapted to this new constellation of political opportunities, focusing on the Social Democratic leadership in the commune of Huittinen. With the tsarist regime gone, the local Social Democrats quickly mobilized through their established networks and organizations to build the foundations for the democratic Finland that they had long advocated. They seized formal control over many of the voluntary organizations that they had long dominated, but local politics quickly polarized and community solidarity quickly gave way to a sharper and clearer sense of distinct and conflicting local identities. In response to growing tension, the Social Democrats organized their own security squads to deal with violence, and when the Social Democrats were overthrown nationally, they led local Social Democratic militants in an uprising in defense of local democracy in January 1918. Unfortunately, this uprising led to the military conquest of Huittinen and the execution of twenty-seven men and women associated with the Social Democratic regime in the city.

All of the chapters in part I remind us that political contention, even the most revolutionary, establishes a relationship between networks of protestors and powerholders. As social confrontation mounts, members of both established and outsider networks attempt to raise support. Such efforts to win allies often involve a significant reshaping of political identities; indeed, the success or failure of efforts to win allies (and thereby some measure of state recognition) can permanently change both the networks and their identities.

Repertoires of Political Contention

The second part consists of five chapters—by Anton Blok, William A. Christian Jr., Robert M. Schwartz, Kim Voss, and R. Bin Wong—that illuminate in a variety of contexts the origins, the historically specific character, and the gradual transformation of the repertoires of contention through which rulers and subjects interact. In some ways the most curious set of political actors in this volume is the series of robber bands in the Lower Meuse between 1730 and 1778, whose experiences Anton Blok has reconstructed. Just as Roger Gould showed the importance of networks in understanding contentious action in western Pennsylvania, so Blok reveals how networks can help in studying the evolution of repertoires. Indeed, without a clear understanding of the bandits' origins, it might not be apparent that their actions were part of a repertoire of protest at all. According to Blok, the outcast social position of the network of skinners who constituted the core of the robber bands helps to explain the extreme violence and ritual mockery in the robbers' actions. By means of ceremonies mocking sacred religious rituals and initiation rites that involved the profanation of sacred symbols, the so-called *Bokkeryders* (Goat Riders) made fun of the society that spurned them by inverting society's symbols of community. Yet it is clear that the public officials in this border region recognized this challenge and responded in kind. Indeed, as Blok demonstrates, the authorities overcame the initial disadvantages of their fragmented jurisdictions and punished the bandits with an extraordinary savagery that mirrored the symbolic language of the rebels.

Even though the means of social expression open to professed sinners was limited in the early-modern period, the options available to potential saints were not much wider. In another chapter that clearly stretches the boundaries of traditional collective-action research, William A. Christian Jr. reminds us that the hierarchy of the Catholic church in Spain always regarded religious visionaries as potential challengers to their role as intermediary to the divine. The regular clergy insisted that although it was possible for angels to appear to the laity, it was also possible for devils to disguise themselves as angels. By asserting its right to validate visions, the church retained for itself a powerful role in defining the authentic visionary experience. Christian's careful attention to the changing character of visions and visionaries presents an interesting example of the ways in which a complex set of actors who were potential rivals—religious authorities, visionaries, interpreters, and their audiences—combined to produce a varied but mutually validated set of visionary performances. Christian also reminds us of the inherent difficulties in the very sources from which we must try to reconstruct the history of such interactions.

Dutch *Bokkeryders* and Spanish visionaries provide us with especially colorful examples of the repertoires of contention through which challengers and authorities interacted; the Burgundian villagers of 1750 to 1850 studied by Robert M. Schwartz give us a striking example of a repertoire's gradual transformation. First Schwartz demonstrates how the French Old Regime fostered and channeled political contention within agrarian communities. Surveying five Burgundian villages, Schwartz reveals that the patterns of holding elected office were remarkably open, thus spreading both the burdens and the opportunities of public office to a broad social spectrum. Raised in the historically specific political culture of the Old Regime, the politically experienced peasants of Burgundy were then forced to acclimate themselves to the repeatedly changing political culture of France during and after the revolutions of 1789, 1830, and 1848. For the first decades of the nineteenth century, Schwartz focuses on the political experiences of one particularly powerful family and explores the family's ever tighter grasp on local government during the Republic, the Empire, the Restoration, and the July Monarchy. Official reports sent to central authorities as well as complaints and petitions filed by jealous local opponents illustrate how local quarrels were eventually translated into the terms of an increasingly national politics. As a result, longstanding local quarrels took on the language of national politics and were adapted to a national political culture.

A national political culture might be invoked to win support for local feuds, but political language can also be employed to make defeat more endurable. Kim Voss locates her study of the framing of defeat within the contrasting national political cultures of Britain and the United States. She argues that the ways in which social movements view defeat can be crucial to their ultimate survival. In order to explain the ultimate political failure of the American Knights of Labor she compares their experience with that of the British "new unionists." In both countries the 1880s witnessed a major upsurge of trade union organization among unskilled workers, but in both countries stunning initial victories were followed by crushing defeats. By 1895 the Knights of Labor had been reduced to a shell and was on the way to disappearing; yet although the membership of the new unions was also heavily reduced, British trade unions managed to survive, to rebuild their lost membership, and, in time, to play a key role in British politics. Voss argues that a greater cultural creativity allowed the British labor movement to adapt its repertoire of contention to the changed circumstances. She maintains that one reason why

British unions of unskilled workers were able to rise again from the ashes is that, in contrast to the Knights of Labor, they were able to portray their defeats as only temporary setbacks, as partial successes, or even as moral victories. Thus the success or failure of leaders in addressing issues of defeat, Voss believes, conditions a movement's chances for success in the next round of interaction.

The language of politics and its relationship to states and social groups is also the subject of R. Bin Wong's chapter on Chinese tax rebellion over three centuries. Wong's chapter contributes powerfully to the subject of protest repertoires because it places Chinese tax revolts in a larger comparative context. Many historians have tied the rhythm of tax protest to the pressures of war, which forces states to intervene ever more directly in local affairs in order to extract funds for war making. Although war making was an important contributor to Chinese tax resistance, the different relations between state and society yielded a different pattern of protest. Whereas in nineteenth-century Europe tax collection acquired new legitimation as the suffrage expanded, in China the central state (under the same pressures as its Western counterparts) was never strong enough to intervene directly at the local level; it always required powerful local allies. In eighteenth-century China tax revolts often rallied the entire community against inequitable methods of collecting taxes or demanded tax remission because of harvest conditions. As financial pressures mounted, the government increasingly was forced to recognize the role of local organizations in tax collection. As a consequence Chinese tax revolts became contests among coalitions of local groups to determine who would bear the brunt of taxation, and in the process the legitimacy of taxation itself eroded.

The blasphemous rites of Dutch robber bands, the fervent claims of Spanish visionaries, the language of the French Revolution spoken by Burgundian peasants, and accusations of corruption used by Chinese rebels to justify tax rebellion all helped to constitute repertoires of contention or political interaction. But repertoires cannot be understood outside the context of conversations, direct or indirect, between challengers and authorities. Depending on the context, Black Masses, religious visions, charges of official corruption, and militia mobilizations can all be used to convey messages to opponents as well as to allies, messages that are rarely transparent or fixed. Opponents are always free to try to subvert or to distort them, and they can entail commitments that might later prove cumbersome: The language of the devil may result in accusations of witchcraft; the language of citizenship implies duties as well as rights; the language of moral outrage evokes a universal moral code, binding on challengers as well as on established authorities.

Constellations of Political Opportunity

The five chapters in the third part—by Marifeli Pérez-Stable, Sonia De Avelar, Marjolein 't Hart, Carl Strikwerda, and Sidney Tarrow—especially underscore the complex ways in which variable constellations of political opportunity channel the political action of subjects and rulers alike. Whereas Risto Alapuro's chapter on revolution in Finland focuses on the extensive but failed mobilization of artisans, Marifeli Pérez-Stable's study of the Cuban Revolution looks at political opportunity from the other side of the barricades and asks why Cuba's rulers were unable to forestall revolution. To be sure, Pérez-Stable recognizes that Fidel Castro's unswerving commitment to armed struggle and his refusal to accept compromises were an important part of the political process of revolutionary conflict, but she also shows us that Castro's revolutionary determination depended on the political failures and inadequacies of the Cuban dictatorship for his final triumph. Emphasizing the vulnerability of "neopatrimonial regimes" to revolutionary challenges, Pérez-Stable argues that the key factor that led Cuba to revolution was the sequence of events over the preceding twenty-five years in which Fulgencio Batista, the corrupt dictator whom Castro overthrew, had alienated key constituencies. Though many have studied the revolutionary technique of the *fidelistas,* Pérez-Stable reminds us that it is just as important to investigate the mistakes of the established order.

The constellation of political opportunity is also central to Sonia De Avelar's analysis of women's chances for exerting political influence in contemporary Latin American and Caribbean countries. De Avelar begins by describing the enormous gender inequality that persists in these countries, and then she turns to an examination of the major political and social institutions in the region to see if they can provide a political opening for the growth of a feminist movement. She postulates that a powerful feminist movement can only develop within the framework of existing institutions (or at least cannot develop without their patronage) and that previously politicized women are its most likely constituency. De Avelar does not discount the possibilities for the growth of strong currents of feminism within the larger population as a result of culturally creative framing, but she argues that without support and encouragement within the existing order the prospects for real political advancement are small.

In her careful reconstruction of a rural revolt in seventeenth-century Europe, Marjolein 't Hart stresses the dialogic dimensions of contentious politics in terms that recall Marc Steinberg's analysis of social protest in nineteenth-century England. Hart carefully explains the political tension resulting from the city of Groningen's efforts to tax and regulate its economic hinterland in the district of Oldambt during the formative years of the Dutch Republic, 1639–50, but what her account highlights in particular is the constellation of political opportunity that was afforded by two competing claims to political authority within this rapidly developing area: Both the city of Groningen and the States General in The Hague—through a provincial assembly—claimed the authority to adjudicate conflicts and to make legal rulings for the people of Oldambt. After long years of increasingly bitter conflict during which the rebels in Oldambt appealed to the authority of the States General, the States General finally ruled in favor of Groningen while granting amnesty to those in Oldambt who had resisted the city's authority. These actions of the States General left the rebels of Oldambt with little recourse, for they had long acknowledged the States General's authority. Thus the relatively peaceful and bloodless resolution of this potentially violent quarrel was a result of the ways in which both parties channeled their grievances through legal processes; having adopted a legalistic rhetoric, the Oldambters were condemned to follow its logic when it turned against them. The choice of rhetoric, however, flowed from the peculiar political opportunity presented by the ambiguities of sovereign authority within the emergent Dutch Union.

The shifting nature of political opportunity often favors the mobilization of some contentious groups over others. This point is made convincingly in Carl Strikwerda's chapter on the conflict between the forces of nationalism and internationalism in Europe on the eve of World War I. Though Strikwerda argues that, contrary to traditional historical wisdom, the forces of internationalism were stronger than is generally realized, he emphasizes the particular advantages that their nationalist opponents in the press and the diplomatic world could call on to hinder the internationalist peace and labor movements from mobilizing their full strength: The closed aristocratic world of diplomacy made it difficult for internationalists to keep abreast of the latest diplomatic developments; more seriously, a free press that was informed and able to discuss foreign policy hardly existed. At the beginning of the twentieth century, then, the world of foreign policy remained largely closed to public debate, and nationalist diplomats were able to engineer a war because they operated in a world apart from international economics, peace movements, and genuine press debate.

From Strikwerda's analysis of both the strength and the weaknesses of internationalist forces in individual nation states in pre-1914 Europe, we turn finally to Sidney Tarrow's discussion of the prospects for international social movements today from the specific perspective of the so-called tuna wars in the summer of 1994. Some social analysts predict that our era will be seen as the beginning of the era of "transnational" collective action; cheap transportation and the Internet, the globalization of the economy, increased international immigration, and the growth of international organizations, they claim, have led to the rise of transnational movements and a transnational civil society. Tarrow is skeptical that transnational collective action will so effortlessly dominate the future of protest.[2] For example, he points out that the proponents of a transnational future have not been altogether clear in identifying the distinctive features of this new phenomenon. After all, the diffusion of social movements from one nation to the other, political support of groups in developed nations for those in the less developed ones, and the growth of international ties among activists have been characteristic features of modern contentious politics since at least the French Revolution. The weakness of international collective action sketched out in Carl Strikwerda's chapter reinforces Tarrow's point on this score. Like the internationalists in Strikwerda's study, the fate of Spain's tuna fishermen was bound up with their ability to influence national policies and to exploit the political opportunities afforded them within a single state. More than anything else, Tarrow asks us to recall the enormous, if variously structured, power accumulated by national states over centuries of development. Genuinely transnational movements such as Greenpeace and Islamic fundamentalism do exist today, but so far their major successes and failures have been confined to the arena of the individual state.

Sidney Tarrow, and indeed, all the authors in this section, emphasize the importance of varied and shifting political opportunities within consolidated modern states. New political opportunities arise especially when serious policy differences emerge within ruling elites, though typically consensus continues in other areas. Initially, at least, those challengers who are able either to precipitate such divisions or to adapt themselves creatively to the opportunities opened up by them enjoy the greatest likelihood of recasting their relations with authorities; they are the generators of what Doug McAdam (1995) calls "initiator movements." And it is the agenda set by these movements that produces those "derivative" movements that follow and seek to imitate their success.

Conclusion

In contrast to the resource mobilization theories of the 1960s and 1970s, our reconstructions of a variety of episodes in the history of contentious politics stress both the structural and the rhetorical dimensions of the drama of political interaction. Instead of viewing identities and interests as fixed features of political and social systems, we recognize that identities and interests are constituted in relationship to other groups and that they change as these relationships change. Dramatic shifts in political opportunity, then, insofar as they open up new possibilities for changing the political order, are necessarily moments of identity crisis and collective redefinition. Nonetheless, the chameleon character of identity in moments of political crisis, though highly contingent, is neither arbitrary nor random. The historically specific character of the political crisis creates new opportunities only for those who can mobilize effectively for contentious action. The ever transient outcome of the political process, meanwhile, validates new relationships, consolidates new identities, and reinforces new repertoires of contentious politics, which serve, in turn, to channel the next round of political interaction.

Notes

1. We have been influenced by Shepley Orr's integration of Bakhtin's dialogism in a structural context; see Orr 1995. For Mikhail Bakhtin, see Bakhtin 1986 and 1992. On linguistic analysis, see Silverman and Torode 1980.

2. Following this line of argument, Doug Imig and Sidney Tarrow have recently emphasized that transnational institutions provide leverage for nation-states as intermediaries; see Imig and Tarrow 1995.

Part I

Networks, Identities, and Claim Making

Chapter 1

Political Identities

Charles Tilly

Though William Cobbett acted the proper British patriot during his Canadian military service of 1784–91 and played Tory loyalist during his Philadelphia exile of 1792–1800, he soon thereafter turned toward a radical critique of Britain's ruling class. During the surge of working-class action and mobilization for political reform that followed the Napoleonic Wars' ending in 1815, his *Political Register* and other writings transmitted radical messages across Britain. In a vivid dramatization of his claimed political genealogy, Cobbett carried Thomas Paine's bones from America to England on his return from another American exile in 1819. He advised popular Princess Caroline in her futile bid for coronation with her estranged husband George IV in 1820–21, then continued to write eloquently for parliamentary reform and for justice in the countryside through the next decade. During the tumultuous British election campaign of May–June 1826, Cobbett plunged even more deeply into national politics: He stood for parliament in the borough of Preston, Lancashire.

After having been a hotbed of working-class mobilization between 1815 and 1820, in 1826 Lancashire entered its fifth straight year of intensifying strikes, accelerating attacks on industrial machinery, and swelling workers' demands for political reform. Handloom weavers were trying desperately to maintain their slipping position by means of attacks on power looms in cotton mills. In this time of mounting class conflict, Cobbett's radical temper appealed to industrial workers as well as to the agricultural laborers who formed the particular object of his sympathy and a substantial body of his supporters (Dyck 1992, 1993).

Preston, a major cotton-textile town, maintained one of England's most generous suffrage provisions. In addition to the usual landlords, rentiers, professionals, merchants, and manufacturers, a number of workers actually voted there. As a center of Irish immigration, Preston also housed many Catholic electors—a significant fact when a massive new mobilization on behalf of Catholic political rights had begun in Ireland and British reformers were lining up in favor of those rights, which Tories generally opposed. Cobbett arrived in Preston committed to both radical reform and Catholic Emancipation: not only manhood suffrage and frequent parliamentary sessions but also full eligibility of Catholics for nonreligious public office.

Far more than legal electors, however, thronged the hustings in Cobbett's support; he attracted a large following of disfranchised workers, both male and female. They sported Cobbett's colors: light green and white in this election, since green was the independent color, and his independent opponent had already preempted plain green. His supporters met him outside of town, paraded with a band in his honor, carried flags nobly depicting their hero as well as a series of political motifs, displayed hefty green-leaved branches, and cheered his long speeches. (Those green branches may have shown partisan colors, but they also recalled a tradition of liberty trees that ran back to the American and French Revolutions.) During the house-to-house canvass of early June, Cobbett and his four sons became the toast of working-class Preston.

Once the polling began on June 10, nevertheless, Cobbett's life grew more difficult. Cobbett had entered the Preston race against Whig E. G. Stanley and independent John Wood. They had agreed not to require of Preston's Catholic voters the oath of supremacy, which involved a public repudiation of papal authority. Then Robert Barrie (navy captain and resident commissioner in Kingston, Ontario) entered for the Tories, with the apparent intent of scaring off Cobbett's supporters by demanding the oath.

Preston's mayor Nicholas Grimshaw and his election officials collaborated with Barrie and against Cobbett, not only by insisting on the Anglican oath but also by physically blocking Cobbett's electors from the polls (Spater 1982, 2: 458–63). Preston's electors customarily voted in tallies, standard-sized groups of voters who proceeded to poll for their candidate, then gave way to an equal-sized group of supporters for another candidate until the inability of one side to supply its next tally signaled the election's outcome. Tallies enormously slowed down an election's progress, but they reduced violent jostling for places in the electoral queue and provided opportunities for the demonstration of a candidate's mass support, complete with banners, ribbons, and colors. By means of challenges, harassment, and delays that discouraged faint-hearted voters, authorities could use the tally system against threatening candidates.

That happened at Preston in 1826. Mayor Grimshaw's forces not only instituted the tally system and deliberately slowed it down—the entire poll finally consumed fifteen days—but they also built segregated channels to the hustings for each candidate's electors. "One of the worst examples of slow voting," reports Frank O'Gorman,

> came at Preston in 1826, when William Cobbett was a candidate. Day after day he justifiably complained that the slow progress of the poll threatened to disfranchise half of the Preston electorate and to damage his own prospects . . . Only when mob violence threatened to get out of hand did the mayor agree to speed up the poll, in this case by abandoning the use of tallies. (1989, 135–36)

Mob violence? In response to complaints from Mayor Grimshaw about intimidation of electors, troops from the King's Dragoon Guards and Foot Guards occupied the city on June 16. Cobbett accused the mayor of calling in troops for the express purpose "of terrifying my voters, and preventing them from exercising their rights" (Spater 1982, 2:462). Obliquely, the military concurred: On orders from regional Commanding General Sir John Byng, who "disapproves very much of the Troops being allowed to remain, without the existence of an actual riot," Captain Charles Hall soon moved his forces out of town (Public Record Office, Kew, Home Office Papers, series 40, box 20 [hereafter HO 40/20]).

They did not, however, go far or long. After billeting a short distance away, they came back a few days later. Major Eckersley, Manchester commander of dragoons, wrote undersecretary Henry Hobhouse at the Home Office on June 22 about the return of troops to Preston:

> The Mayor of Preston reports, under date of last evening, that in consequence of the most serious outrages which had been committed by a Mob, armed with Bludgeons, at one of the Entrances of the Poll Booth for the Election now holding in that Borough, preventing the access of Voters to the Hustings, Captain Barrie, one of the Candidates had protested against the admission of any more Voters, until free access was allowed to every Voter; and that being in vain tried to force a free access by means of the Civil Power, except to such persons as the Mob chose to admit, he had been under the necessity of calling upon the Troop of Cavalry, stationed at Kirkham, to place itself at Broughton, four miles from Preston, on the road to Garstang, this morning by eight o'clock, to remain there until the close of the Election on Monday next, unless circumstances should arise which might justify him or the Magistrates in bringing it into Preston. (HO 40/20)

Cobbett's people had fought to reach the polls despite the mayor's interposition, and the many special constables that Grimshaw had recruited (the "Civil Power" of Eckersley's dispatch) could not contain them. The "Bludgeons" Eckersley mentioned consisted of Cobbett's supporters' electoral staves cut into fours; until dragoons drove them away, Cobbett's forces used their cudgels to keep supporters of Barrie and Stanley out of the channel that Grimshaw had assigned to Cobbett's electors. Eventually Cobbett himself, despairing of election as the authorities turned back his voters by the dozen, opened his channel to Wood's electors (Cobbett 1829, Letter 1). Both sides used force to influence the outcome. Cobbett's side lost.

Despite his electoral defeat, Cobbett later exulted in recollections of the Preston campaign. In his *Political Register,* he boasted:

> I went to the North a total stranger as to person. I had no friends. Yet, on my first entrance into Preston, I was met and accompanied by, at least, ten thousand people, and was received with marks of attention and respect surpassing those ever shown to any other man . . . calumniators of mine began to comfort themselves with the thought that I was a "Poor Old Man"; and that I could not possibly last long. It was an "old man", recollect, who could travel five hundred miles, make speeches of half an hour long twice a day for a month; put down the saucy, the rich, the tyrannical; that could be jostled out of his majority at an election; and that could return towards his home through forty miles of huzzas from the lips of a hundred and fifty thousand people. (Cobbett 1933, 202)

At sixty-three, Cobbett found such a reception a vigorous vindication of his long radical career.

Government spies among the region's workers, to be sure, reported the situation differently. The worker-spy who signed his frequent reports George Bradbury, George Bradley, and G___ B___ portrayed northern radicalism as a conspiracy abetted at a distance by Cobbett. In a letter from Walsall dated June 19 he reported that

> I was invited to Preston to assist in the return of W. Cobbet to Parliament and to Consider of any Measures along with others of the Party alluded to in my Communication of the 27th of May to further the ultimate ends of these Men whose work is to get a Voice in Parliament for the purpose of spreading principles subversive of the national faith, There principle object was it not for the Six Acts [repressive legislation passed in 1819] to call Meetings at all places at one time where they can spread their principles under the specious pretex of Equal Representation in the House of Commons . . . the secret idea is to carry by force of arms those [wild?] measures which have devastated every Country where they have gaind the Ascendency—and in 1819 secret instructions were given to prepare every Man his own Picke head and to stick it in the ground below the Reach of the Plough—and Nearly all were in Lancashire and Yorkshire of that party prepared for any Chance which might offer. I began a Reformer and soon became a principle leader when I found on being admitted to Confidence their object was Republican Government to be effected by force or otherwise as Circumstances offer. (HO 40/20)

As summer wore on, Bradbury/Bradley warned increasingly of the possibility of armed insurrection—a threat that no doubt justified his government pay but that also represented the current talk of some determined radicals and recalled a series of regional working-class rebellions between 1816 and 1820.

British politics of the 1820s deserves attention not only for the exploits of such heroic radicals as William Cobbett but also for the great transformations of popular political life that were occurring. In the course of struggles over parliamentary reform, workers' rights, and Catholic Emancipation, the British people were fashioning forms of political participation that marked public life for another century. They were installing public meetings, demonstrations, mass associations, petition campaigns, firm-by-firm strikes, and related forms of claim making as the standard repertoire in Great Britain.

That momentous transition strongly affected Britain's popular politics, including the identities people assumed as they made collective claims. It therefore permits some general observations concerning political identities wherever and whenever they appear. Political identities vary enormously in form and content; nevertheless, there are principles that hold for all of them:

- Political identities are always, everywhere relational and collective.

- They therefore alter as political networks, opportunities, and strategies shift.

- The validation of political identities depends on contingent performances to which other parties' acceptance or rejection of the asserted relation is crucial.

- That validation both constrains and facilitates collective action by those who share the identity.

- Deep differences separate political identities embedded in routine social life from those that appear chiefly in public life.

These propositions break with two very different but common ways of understanding political identities: (1) as straightforward activation of durable personal traits, whether individual or collective, and (2) as malleable features of individual consciousness. The first view appears incessantly in interest-based accounts of political participation, which generally depend on some version of methodological individualism. The second view recurs in analyses of political commitment as a process of self-realization and correlates closely with an assumption of phenomenological individualism, the doctrine that personal consciousness is the primary—or, at a sollipsistic extreme, the only—social reality. As will soon become obvious, my view denies neither personal traits nor individual psyches, but places relations among actors at the center of social processes.

What does "relational and collective" mean? A *political identity* is an actor's experience of a shared social relation in which at least one of the parties— including third parties—is an individual or organization controlling concentrated means of coercion. (If the coercion-controlling organization in question enjoys some routine jurisdiction over all persons within a delimited territory, we call it a *government;* to the extent that it lacks rivals and superiors within its territory, we call it a *state.*) Political identities usually double with shared public *representations* of both relation and experience. Thus in Preston of May–June 1826 Cobbett's supporters as such shared relations not only to their hero but also to competing candidates, Mayor Grimshaw, the borough of Preston, the British state, and its ever ready dragoons. They represented that shared identity by wearing colors, bearing staves, marching, attending meetings, drinking toasts, and jeering Cobbett's opponents. They proudly bore a political identity.

Well before 1826 British elections provided occasions for the assertion of political identities by electors and nonelectors alike. In parallel with civic festivals and public executions, elections permitted ordinary people to fill the streets, voice their preferences, criticize authorities, and identify themselves collectively by means of symbols, shouts, songs, or dress (Epstein 1990; Laqueur 1989; Linebaugh 1992; O'Gorman 1992). That candidates often spent lavishly on food, drink, cockades, and other gifts for nonelectors (including families of electors) does not gainsay the political interest of ordinary people in British parliamentary elections. Ordinary people and local leaders had complementary interests: In addition to treats, plebeian participants in elections gained affirmations of solidarity, claims to patronage, and protected opportunities to voice their preferences. On the other side, as often happens in public rituals, the capacity of a candidate to bring out orderly, committed crowds in his support confirmed or denied his standing within the community and thereby affected his subsequent credibility as patron or broker even when it had little influence over an election's outcome (cf. Benford and Hunt 1992; Marston 1989; Paige and Paige 1981; Schneider 1995; Trexler 1981).

British election activities, then, asserted, displayed, or confirmed political identities: candidate, official, elector, partisan, keeper of the peace. Most of these identities, furthermore, correlated weakly or not at all with the identities of routine social life: wife, son, neighbor, debtor, parishioner, butcher, baker, candlestick maker. Such routine identities did often figure in local conflicts: Parents and children fought, neighbors massed to tear down houses of ill repute, debtors attacked creditors, parishioners demanded changes in church government, silk weavers collectively resisted wage cuts imposed by their masters, and so on. As a generation of feminists have insisted, available public political identities rested on strong implicit assumptions about gender differences in political capacity. But only contingently did these routine identities play significant, direct, acknowledged parts in electoral proceedings, as when Catholics lined up against Anglicans in disputes over suffrage, or weavers, who saw their legal standing threatened, gathered en masse to assert their rights. Instead, elections then primarily confined relevant identities to officials, constables, troops, candidates, supporters, electors, and spectators. Such identities were relational and collective: Individuals possessed them only as a function of their relations to others and in company with others.

We must therefore distinguish carefully between identities that appear chiefly or exclusively in public life (*disjoined* identities) and those that operate in routine social existence (*embedded* identities). The first category typically includes candidate, supporter, party member, and election official; the second covers identities found in the range of kinship, friendship, work, and neighborhood. Of course the distinction is relative in three senses: First, some identities pivot explicitly and importantly between the spheres; Mayor Grimshaw of Preston remained mayor before, during, and after the 1826 election, just as Captain Hall's dragoons had chosen careers that moved them incessantly into and out of the public political sphere. Second, ties of kinship, friendship, gender, work, and neighborhood clearly underlie public political identities; Cobbett chose to stand for parliament from Preston rather than some town with highly restricted suffrage precisely in the hope of inducing bloc voting from the city's less wealthy electors. Third, over the longer run disjoined identities sometimes embed themselves, and embedded identities spread from their bases to become disjoined in other settings; with mobilization around Catholic Emancipation, for example, the identity "Catholic" was coming to have a salience and scope it did not ordinarily enjoy in the routine lives of many people who nominally belonged to the Roman Catholic church. Nevertheless, in Britain of the 1820s relations between public and routinely embedded identities were becoming increasingly distant and contingent. Electoral positions as special constable, political supporter, election official, or even candidate spilled over little or not at all into relations among workers, masters, kinfolk, neighbors, or fellow members of the local market.

As the Preston election illustrates, relevant political identities were undergoing a momentous transition during the 1820s. Although organizers of political associations (both clandestine and public) had been working for a decade to weave national coalitions of reformers and radicals, neither candidates nor local supporters presented themselves in their guise as associational activists. Even though some continued to insist on local connections in good eighteenth-century style, by the 1820s candidates increasingly aligned themselves with nationally available categories: Whig, Tory, reformer, other. Despite recurrent displays of colors and symbols, however, their supporters (electors or not) still declared themselves publicly not as party members but as local candidates' supporters. In two-seat elections, the standard distinctions among plumpers (those who cast just one vote, for their favorite), splitters (those who divided between two candidates of different tendencies), and straights (those who followed a party line) reveal the weak state of partisanship as a political identity (O'Gorman 1982, 1984, 1989; Phillips 1982, 1990, 1992).

Yet in Preston and over the country as a whole available political identities were changing emphatically. National parties were consolidating, political unions and similar reform (or, for that matter, antireform) organizations had been proliferating since 1817, workers' associations had enjoyed a precarious legal existence since 1824 after decades of underground ebb and flow, a Catholic Association was beginning to mobilize masses in Ireland and to gain a substantial following in Great Britain, public meetings to promote political causes (often organized, secretly or otherwise, by special-purpose associations) were multiplying, drives to prepare mass petitions for Parliament were becoming more common, and the combination of meetings, marches, pamphleteering, symbol mongering, and lobbying that we now recognize as the apparatus of social movements was acquiring uneasy legality.

For more than a century British authorities had generally repressed ordinary people who undertook such activities on the ground that they were usurping parliamentary privileges, that they were establishing subversive organizations, or that they were directly disturbing public order. But now, through just such struggles as we have seen unfolding in Preston, authorities were reluctantly conceding the rights of ordinary people who refrained from overt violence, openly seditious talk, or explicitly illegal programs (for example, the republicanism of which Bradbury/Bradley accused Cobbett and his cohorts) to assemble, to associate, to identify themselves collectively, to exhort each other, and to state their views autonomously and publicly. Thus Parliament and the courts simultaneously validated new political identities and claimed their own prior right to do such validating.

Much was at stake in the validation of political identities, for once accepted they both constrained and facilitated collective action. Identities as candidates, electors, supporters, or officials imposed significant constraints on their holders, who found themselves bound by the laws and customs of electoral campaigns. Thus candidates had no choice but to endure celebratory entries into town, to give repeated speeches on the same theme, to flatter local constituencies, to treat supporters lavishly, and in the event of victory, to submit to being *chaired:* paraded in a brilliantly decorated chair, a sort of throne. But the same identities facilitated collective action by justifying assemblies, marches, cheers, epithets, and other expressions of opinion that outside of elections would have run the risk of severe repression. Indeed, postelectoral speeches generally signaled the end of license by explicitly calling for members of the community to forget their recently expressed differences and work together.

The increasing differentiation of a public political sphere with its distinctive identities correlated with significant changes in the forms of collective claim making. For intermittent years from 1758 to 1834, my research group has prepared a large catalog of British "contentious gatherings": occasions on which people outside the government gathered in publicly accessible places and made collective claims on others, claims that if realized would affect the others' interests (Tilly 1993a, 1995b). We may group the bulk of such British events during the eighteenth century as follows:

Claim making within authorized public assemblies (such as on Lord Mayor's Day): taking of positions by means of cheers, jeers, attacks, and displays of symbols; attacks on supporters of electoral candidates; parading and chairing of candidates; taking of sides at public executions; attacks or professions of support for pilloried prisoners; salutation or deprecation of public figures (such as royalty) at the theater; collective response to lines and characters in plays or other entertainments; breaking up of theaters at unsatisfactory performances

Celebrations and other popularly initiated gatherings: collective cheering, jeering, or stoning of public figures or their conveyances; popularly initiated public celebrations of major events (for example, John Wilkes' elections of the 1760s), with cheering, drinking, display of partisan symbols, fireworks, and so on and sometimes with the forced participation of reluctant persons; forced illuminations, including attacks on windows of householders who fail to illuminate; faction fights (such as the Irish versus the English or between rival military groups)

Attacks on popularly designated offenses and offenders: mocking routines such as Rough Music; ridicule or destruction of symbols, effigies, or property of public figures and moral offenders; verbal and physical attacks on malefactors seen in public places; pulling down or sacking of dangerous or offensive houses, including workhouses and brothels; smashing of shops and bars whose proprietors were accused of unfair dealing or of violating public morality; collective seizures of food, often coupled with sacking the merchant's premises or public sale of the food below the current market price; blockage or diversion of food shipments; destruction of tollgates; collective invasions of enclosed land, often including destruction of fences or hedges

Workers' sanctions over members of their trades: turnouts by workers in multiple shops of a local trade; workers' marches to public authorities in trade disputes; donkeying, or otherwise humiliating, workers who violated collective agreements; destroying goods (for example, the silk in looms or the looms themselves) of workers or masters who violated collective agreements

Attacks on coercive authorities: liberation of prisoners; resistance to police intervention in gatherings and entertainments; resistance to press gangs; fights between hunters and gamekeepers; battles between smugglers and royal officers; forcible opposition to evictions; military mutinies

In summary, we might call such claim-making events parochial, particular, and bifurcated: parochial because they were chiefly limited in scope to a single locality; particular because the precise routines, participants, and symbols varied significantly from group to group, place to place, and issue to issue; and bifurcated because they were split between events in which local people (1) took direct action on local objects as the occasion required and (2) appealed to patrons or intermediaries for intercession with powerful outsiders. Parochial, particular, bifurcated claim-making events generally emerged from routine local gatherings for work, marketing, recreation, or authorized rituals rather than from deliberately convened and preplanned assemblies of interested parties.

Such events contrasted with the emerging nineteenth-century forms of claim making, which we can characterize as cosmopolitan, modular, and autonomous: cosmopolitan because their scope so regularly exceeded a single locality and indeed, often extended to a national or even international scale; modular because standard forms served for a wide variety of claims, claimants, and localities; and autonomous because the claimants took major initiatives in determining the time and place of their action. Public meetings, petition drives, firm-by-firm strikes, demonstrations, street marches, and other still-familiar forms of collective action constituted this emerging repertoire.

These newer forms of action not only frequently made claims on extralocal authorities and entailed coordination with claim-making groups in other localities but also offered strong assertions about the actors and the constituencies they represented—assertions that they were worthy, unified, numerous, and committed and therefore deserving of serious political attention. By the 1820s these cosmopolitan, modular, and autonomous means of claim making were rapidly displacing authorized celebrations, attacks on stigmatized offenders, and mass destruction of barriers. Here is one sign of the shift that was going on: During the 1750s and 1760s, 3 percent of the events in our catalog consist of preplanned public meetings outside of government auspices; by the 1830s the figure has risen to 24 percent.

The numbers matter less here than a salient contrast: the predominant eighteenth-century forms of claim making flowed directly from routine local activities such as markets or work and drew on the everyday identities embedded in those activities. The predominant nineteenth-century forms broke with routine activities and identities, calling people away to meetings, demonstrations, and other concerted actions in which they appeared not as spinners, neighbors, or tenants of particular landlords but as citizens, partisans, association members, or workers in general. Participants frequently shared those identities with many people outside their own localities. Even where these identities were relevant differed, on balance, from the geography of everyday life: seats of authority, meeting halls, and major thoroughfares drew disproportionate shares of the action.

No need to exaggerate the novelty or the extent of the change from the eighteenth to the nineteenth centuries. During Britain's seventeenth-century revolutions and no doubt before, local people had reached out in coordinated claim making across the country. During the 1830s agricultural laborers still smashed threshing machines, and workers who caught an informer in their local pub often drubbed him and drove him out of town. Nevertheless, between the 1750s and the 1830s the net shift in forms of claim making went much farther and changed local politics much more definitively than any previous transition of the sort. Britain's ordinary people entered and re-created the national political sphere as never before.

As familiar and inevitable as the transformation seems in retrospect, it has a puzzling side. People abandoned forms of direct action that had long brought results within their own fields for other forms that depended on extensive organization, that only worked cumulatively and indirectly, and that hardly ever achieved their stated ends in a single outing. Social-movement tactics of meeting, marching, demonstrating, and self-identifying seem ineffectual compared with the destruction of threshing machines and the forceful expulsion of pariahs. Why should anyone exchange direct for indirect action?

The change occurred in part because authorities acquired increasingly effective means of repression, such as organized police forces; and in part because the organizational bases of the older performances disintegrated; and in part because national affairs (where the older forms of direct action had rarely made much difference) became increasingly crucial to ordinary people's interests. But something else was happening as well: Indirect, cumulative, cosmopolitan, modular, and autonomous forms of action not only made specific claims on extralocal authorities but also asserted political identities on a larger-than-local scale. They asserted the existence of valid, weighty political claimants to participation in the national polity. They declared: "We exist and have a right to exist. We have strength, coherence, and determination. National politics must take us into account."

Britain's creation of mass national politics had distinct historical properties that set off nineteenth-century Britain as a peculiar combination of aristocratic power and popular democracy. Yet the transformation of political identities that occurred in Britain deserves close attention for its general implications. For not only in Great Britain but in general (1) political identities are relational and collective, (2) they therefore alter as political networks, opportunities, and strategies shift, (3) the validation of political identities depends on contingent performances to which other parties' acceptance or rejection of the asserted relation is crucial, (4) their validation both constrains and facilitates collective action by those who share the identity, and (5) deep differences separate political identities embedded in routine social life from those that appear chiefly in public life.

These principles have enormously wide application. Because authorities and analysts alike have drawn stark lines between institutionalized and exceptional politics—between collective action and collective behavior, between elections and social movements, between moments of calm and moments of madness, between routine and revolutionary action—neither has seen the incessant interplay among standard political means, challenges, and innovations. Let us retrieve the old metaphor of the polity for a set of political identities that afford their holders routine access to some government. Then we can think of identity validation as an entry into such a polity, as the constitution of a valid member. Each polity has a history; its existing membership and the processes by which they gained entry strongly constrain succeeding challenges and entries.

Each new challenge and entry entails innovation in two senses. First, promoters of a new identity constitute themselves and call attention to their worthiness, unity, numbers, and commitment by performances that are recognizable to existing members of the polity but sufficiently novel to dramatize the new candidate's distinctive qualities to potential adherents and allies. Second, the success of an actor in gaining recognition, hence entry into the polity, alters the rules for the next round of challenges. Thus the radicals and the Catholics who were challenging in Britain during the 1820s established the mass-membership association as a legitimate basis for political claim making after centuries during which only churches had enjoyed a semblance of such rights, and those only within much more stringent limits than came to prevail in the 1830s.

Students of what they called "new social movements" of the 1960s and thereafter—especially movements for peace, women's rights, gay rights, and environmental protection—have often stressed the identity-affirming activities of those movements, in supposed contrast to the narrower interest orientations of preceding movements for suffrage or workers' rights. Their analysis combines a proper critique of narrow interest group interpretations with a misunderstanding of earlier social movements (Calhoun 1993b). Identity affirmation has always played a crucial part in social movements; indeed, it has provided one of their major rationales. Once we understand that the identities in question were relational and collective, that they constituted claims for recognition by public authorities, the contradiction between "interest" and "identity" interpretations disappears.

The establishment of identities results from political mobilization and struggle as well as action by authorities, but it also affects subsequent political processes. Anthony Marx (1995) offers an important comparison of racial categories in South Africa, the United States, and Brazil. After the Boer War, the white South African regime established a set of racial categories that corresponded only grossly to the much more differentiated populations in the country but that became facts of life strongly affecting the fates of putative members of different categories. In the United States during Reconstruction and its Jim Crow aftermath, both individual states and the federal government built legal systems that redefined racial categories and attached differential advantage to them. Brazil, arguably sustaining as much social and economic inequality by race as the United States, avoided legalizing racial distinctions to anything like the degree found in South Africa and the United

States. In the short and medium runs, the difference surely worked to the advantage of Brazil's black populations. But over the long run stringent racial categories provided bases for political mobilization and legal claims for redress in South Africa and the United States, whereas in Brazil the very absence of legalized racial categories, statistics, and agencies inhibited black collective action. Clearly the legal validation of political identities works both to facilitate and to constrain.

National processes of identity assertion have direct counterparts on an international scale. Nationalism provides the most obvious case in point (see Brubaker 1993). Nationalism in general asserts two main ideas: (1) The world's population divides, and ought to divide, into historically formed, connected, coherent, and relatively homogeneous nations. (2) Nations should correspond to states, and vice versa. As it has prevailed over the last two centuries, nationalism therefore takes two related forms: state-led and state-seeking. State-led nationalism involves the attempt by those who control a given state to homogenize its population culturally, to enforce a preferred understanding of its population's history, and to give obligations to the state priority over all other obligations. State-seeking nationalism consists of efforts by ostensible representatives of populations that currently lack states of their own to establish the historical distinctness, coherence, connectedness, and determination of their followers, thereby claiming the right to political autonomy. The parallels with identity-affirming activities of social movements are dramatic.

Other fascinating parallels suggest themselves. We could follow the analogy into industrial relations, where the legalization of strikes simultaneously facilitated some workers' claim making vis-à-vis their employers, confirmed "strikers" and "union members" as political identities, and separated the strike from a whole series of sometimes effective tactics—for example window breaking, community-wide marches, and attacks on nonstriking workers—that workers had previously employed. We could examine how relevant identities change in the course of what Sidney Tarrow calls "protest cycles" (Tarrow 1994). We could ask how international institutions form and acquire recognition (Wendt 1994). We could explore further the widespread nineteenth-century creation of political identities on a national scale, a process that played a crucial part in the development of strong citizenship and extensive democracy both in Britain and elsewhere. The point would remain the same: For all their apparent hardness and durability, political identities undergo incessant challenge and alteration as a consequence and constituent element of political struggle.

Chapter 2

The Riding of the Black Lad and Other Working-Class Ritualistic Actions: Toward a Spatialized and Gendered Analysis of Nineteenth-Century Repertoires

Marc W. Steinberg

In almost countless publications Charles Tilly demonstrates how repertoires of contention were slowly transformed from largely parochial, informal, and patronized action to a claim making focused in mass action that was more consciously public, formal, national, and autonomous (1982, 25; see also 1986a, 1995b). Tilly shows how the rising concentration of power in the modern nation-state, rapidly expanding urbanization, and the ever widening grip of industrial capitalism effected massive changes in the opportunities for and ways in which ordinary people gave voice to grievances. Focusing on only one small parcel of territory—the industrial towns in the area of Ashton-under-Lyne in Lancashire, England—in the later 1820s, I will show what this transition in collective action meant for the production of social space and how these changes in turn combined with capitalist transformations of public space and the gendering of public and private spheres, altering the landscapes of lived experience and the possibilities for future contention.

Tilly details the transition in the articulation of discontent from popular festivities to strikes, assemblies, and demonstrations: "In 1830 and, especially, in 1848," he remarks, "carnival and revolution linked arms and danced in the streets" (1983a, 73). This shading, that is, the uneven and incremental transition in which carnival and other rituals give way to other forms of assembly, is where I begin my questioning. We need to further our understanding of how the capitalist transformation of social space influenced both repertoire changes and the transmutation of women's actions in public places. As ordinary people gained increased access to the polity through collective action, the security of the capitalist construction of space increased. Additionally, the new repertoire marked a change in the gendering of public space and contentious action. The place of what I will term the "disorderly woman" was increasingly marginalized.

I provide a case analysis that highlights key issues for further research. I start with a general description of the region and then move on to two events to illustrate my thesis, the annual festival of the Riding of the Black Lad as it was held in the late 1820s and the explosive regionwide strike of the cotton spinners in the winter of 1829–30, and I conclude with reflections on how these case studies might help us think through larger issues.

King Cotton Country

Cotton spinning began to transform the southeast corner of Lancashire County in the 1790s, and during the cotton boom of the 1820s factories sprouted throughout the district. By 1831 one of the largest mill towns, Ashton-under-Lyne, contained a cramped 15,000 people, and its parish as a whole held almost 36,000 people. By the start of the 1830s the *Manchester Times* characterized Ashton as "a place of great business, containing seventy large establishments for spinning cotton, besides many manufacturers of cotton and silk, employing many thousands of weavers in the surrounding area." An admirer gushed that the modest market town had become "the most important commercial area in the world" (*Manchester Times* [*MT*], August 27, 1831, November 18, 1829, January 1, 1830; *Manchester Guardian* [*MG*], April 4, 1827; Baines 1824, 490; Bowman 1960, 365; Butterworth 1842, 95, 98).[1] Neighboring Stalybridge and the surrounding industrial villages experienced even more dramatic spurts of growth. During the 1820s Stalybridge's population grew by 158 percent and pulled even with Ashton (Kirk 1985, 43). Growing at a dizzying pace, factory villages were products of the mill owners' vision, capital, and unfettered power. Hyde, a village of about 800 at the turn of the century, boasted fifteen mills and almost 7,000 people by 1830 (Baines [1835] 1966, 387), and it alone, anchored by the mammoth complex lorded over by magnate Thomas Ashton, produced one-eighth of all exported cotton yarn (House of Commons Select Committee Report PP 1824, 5:301, 303). By the late 1820s many of the region's firms were noted for their high proportion of integrated mills with both spinning and mechanized weaving. Although most mills employed between 100 and 400 workers, a half-dozen of the integrated technological titans sustained a thousand or more operatives (Butterworth 1842, 144; Kirk 1985, 43, 50; Kirby and Musson 1975, 10; Sykes 1982, 1:18–19).

King Cotton's reign was visible in the starkly divided social structure. "There seems to my eye's judgment" observed the astute union leader John Joseph Betts of Ashton, "hardly any proportion of the middle class of society in this community. The grinders and the ground make up the bulk of its inhabitants" (*United Trades' Co-operative Journal* [*UTC*], May 8, 1830, 78). A survey in the middle 1830s found Ashton to be 81.5 percent, Stalybridge 90 percent, and Dukinfield 94.7 percent working class, respectively (Kirk 1985, 49; Sykes 1982, v. 1:17). Sharp class cleavages demonstrably etched into class-segregated social areas were encoded with profoundly different trappings of life. Nouveau bourgeoisie erected "elegant mansions" with "tastefully disposed pleasure grounds" (Butterworth 1842, 93; Cotton 1977, 33). At a distance and below their employers in the valley, factory workers lived in cottages and boarding houses. These dwellings were themselves stratified, from the sturdy stone cottages of the working elite to closely packed and hastily constructed courtyards and a few dank cellars for lowly operatives (particularly the Irish) (Coulthart 1844, 14, 27, 32–34, 36–37). Workers in the surrounding villages depended on paternalism for their quarters.

The Capitalist Transformation of Social Space

Mill owners not only set about fashioning the built landscape to their desires, but they also sought to fundamentally transform the construction of social space. As Henri Lefebvre suggested, a critical process of capitalism is the development of "abstract" space, which is voided of historical custom and is thus homogeneous (Lefebvre 1991, 50). Yet abstract space is also fragmentable in its homogeneity and subject to the divisiveness of commodification for the grand logic of exchange and accumulation (Lefebvre 1991, 282, 285–87; Gottdiener 1985, 162, 164, 401; Harvey 1986, 13, 205).

This appropriation and transformation of space is basic to both class formation and class struggle. Social space is not just a terrain upon which class formation occurs but the very "domain within which—and in part through which—class relations are constituted" (Derek Gregory, quoted in Soja 1985, 115). The embeddedness of ruling-class power desocializes it, creating space as an abstract disciplinary container for public behavior. As Lefebvre argued, this kind of strategic space becomes "a space that classifies in the service of a class" by marginalizing the subordinated and at the same time centripetally organizing wealth, political power, and information in a hegeomic center (1991, 375). The production of power in and through space is thus a set of social and political practices and a cultural formation that the subordinated both actively reproduce and contest (Pred 1990, 9–10, 12; Ross 1988, 9; Shields 1991, 52–53, 63; Soja 1985, 97). Group power and struggle thus establish the boundaries for the activities of daily life, and class struggle often involves this conflicting cartography of power (Harvey 1989, 232, 234; Ross 1988, 9).

At the same time space and place are gendered and ethnicized in dynamic and contestable ways. The rise of separate spheres of ideologies and working-class respectability was saturated with gendered spatial notions of propriety and appropriate action (Ryan 1990, 59; Hall 1992; Rose 1992, 1993).

By the 1820s the regions' capitalists were busily pursuing their worldview by opening and parceling the landscape. Manufacturers confronted the complex problem of facilitating the great flows of materials and labor necessary for production, somehow keeping order and control, even when they shared space with working people. Capitalists keen to the task set about constructing fields of power across the terrain of social life starting with the mill and hearth. This control and the production of social space were accomplished most easily at the point of production (Catling 1970; Lazonick 1979). Outside, housing and recreational spaces that were provided for workers created clear opportunities for control. "In small places, such as that degraded hole in England, Hyde, the masters could do as they pleased, and no one there dare blame them," observed the union activist Thomas Foster (Doherty 1829, 31). A Hyde manufacturer boasted: "We have them more under control than is possible in any large town; most of them are tenants and are bound by ties unnecessary for me to name" (*Stockport Advertiser* [*SA*], February 20, 1829).

The manufacturers transformed the spatial order of sociability far beyond the mill gates. Thomas Ashton erected only one pub for his entire community and pointedly prohibited all other publicans (Felkin 1844, 463). Dissenting minds defined public space with sobriety and reserved behavior (Cotton 1977, 205). The elite of Dukinfield organized a posse to suppress all amusements on the Sabbath within a seven-mile radius of the town, but to their dismay, when they attempted their first prosecution they found that their efforts had no basis in law (*Wheeler's Manchester Chronicle* [*WMC*], August 7, 1830).

Mill owners ultimately effectively used the law to organize public space. With the cooperation of the earl of Stamford, police and improvement acts were enacted by Parliament for Ashton in 1827 and 1828 and for Stalybridge in 1828 (*MG*, June 23, 1827; October 27, 1827). These acts also gave the commissioners de jure control over all public space, empowering them to demolish and modernize areas, to supervise markets, and to coordinate all law enforcement to preserve town order. In Ashton all commissioners automatically assumed the powers of justice of the peace, while in Stalybridge three mill owners initially ran the local constabulary (Bowman 1960, 634; Cotton 1977, 198). Most empowering of all were the acts' clauses providing for public order.

The 1827 act provided Ashton's commissioners with the authority to prose-
cute any individual "standing, loitering, . . . or in any other Manner obstruct[ing] or incommod[ing], hinder[ing] or prevent[ing], the free Passage
of any such Footway or Causeway, or prejudic[ing], insult[ing], jostl[ing], or
annoy[ing] any Person or Persons travelling, passing, or going thereon" (Acts
of Parliament: An Act for lighting, cleansing, . . . 1827, p. 1731). Similar provisions prohibited demonstrations and parades.

These acts legally opened all town space for commodity exchange while
allowing the prohibition of any collective action. Ashton and Stalybridge became large swaths of space administered by manufacturers qua police commissioners. Lieutenant Colonel Shaw, in command of part of the Northern
Army responsible for repressing contention, marveled: "Their police acts are
such that there are no places in the Kingdom where the struggle against
the Union would be more favorable to the Masters as at Ashton under Line
and Staley Bridge" (Home Office [HO] 40/26, folios 46–50, Shaw to Bouverie,
August 29, 1830).

Throughout the 1820s mill owners constructed a new cartography of
power, but working people were not wholly quiescent. If we pause to scruti-
nize the twilight forms of collective action and festivity in which working
people engaged—those undergoing transmutation between old and new
repertoires—we find that these annual festivals (or "wakes," as they were
termed) sometimes revealed concerted symbolic contestations. These actions, unlike many of those in the new repertoire, more actively contested the
bourgeois construction of space. They also gendered space, albeit temporal-
ly, in ways that allowed for greater participation of women and more valoriza-
tion of the feminine than did subsequent repertoires that emphasized mass
meetings and strikes.

Carnival and Parade

A wealth of literature on popular gatherings such as charivari, rites of symbolic violence, carnival, mock politics and political protest, popular calendar
customs, and religious observances reveals such festivities to be central to
the construction of social divisions and hierarchies. Social scientists and historians suggest two divergent (though not mutually exclusive) functions of
these gatherings. Many indebted to functionalist reasoning argue that symbolic inversion operates as a safety valve reaffirming the status quo (Kertzer
1988, 131; see also Belmont 1981). Emmanuel Le Roy Ladurie, for instance, in
his analysis of the carnival in Romans, observes that "if men exchanged roles

during Carnival it was only to reaffirm the strength and performance of the social hierarchy" (Le Roy Ladurie 1979, 192). These analysts, however, also recognize the potential danger of temporarily suspending rules of authority and hierarchy, thus creating liminal moments of *communitas* and antistructure (Darnton 1984, 99; Kertzer 1988, 145–49, Turner 1969, 109; 1977, 281).

Despite the last proviso, the liminal/safety-valve perspective has been rightly criticized for being overly static and preoccupied with the maintenance of order to the neglect of subversion and struggle (Bristol 1985, 27; Cresswell 1994, 40–41; LaCapra 1983, 305; Scott 1990, 178).[2] The alternative perspective employed in this study is to analyze the carnivalesque as a process of transgression rather than suspension, as a "catalyst and site of actual and symbolic struggle" (Stallybrass and White 1986, 14; cf. Scott 1990, 174, 181; also cf. Cresswell 1994, 43; Stallybrass and White 1986, passim; Thompson 1991, 524). Carnivalesque festivities, through their inversions, parodies, and mimicking, portray willful misrule and often pose explicit challenges to existing hierarchies. The carnivalesque does not present alternatives as much as it serves as a vehicle of collective critique that creates possibilities for more open and violent power struggles (Bristol 1985, 52; Cresswell 1994, 57; Stallybrass and White 1986, 18, 43).

Two features of the carnivalesque highlighted by Mikhail Bakhtin (1984) are particularly important. First, as Stallybrass and White suggest, the marketplace was the cross section and hybridization of the communal and the commercial, of work and play, of the civil and the pleasurable: Bourgeois culture sought to disassociate and isolate these features (1986, 30–31). Carnivalesque democratizing and leveling subverted capitalist cannibalization of such areas in the production of abstract space, and as a form of collective action it concretely challenged this capitalist transformation (Bakhtin 1984, 10, 154, 255; LaCapra 1983, 301; Stallybrass and White 1986, 27). For Bakhtin this transgressive possession is also realized by the debasing forms of speech and interaction with which its participants engage all who find themselves within this realm. Through billingsgate and laughter, plebs could highlight the dualities of class power, exposing the supposed neutrality of the capitalist-controlled space (Bakhtin 1984, 10–12, 16, 151–53, 432–33). This appropriation of space, however temporal, can thus be viewed as an act of both ideological *and* spatial counterhegemony

Second, women and the feminine are strikingly integral to the carnivalesque in comparison to the other forms in the repertoire that gradually succeed it. In particular, the disorderly woman, rather than the feminine symbol of virtue, saintliness, or domestic order, is a valorized emblem of the people.

As Natalie Zemon Davis, Mary Russo, and others maintain, the disorderly female was central in symbolically validating the subversive and riotous behavior of men and women alike (Davis 1975, 131, 147; Russo 1986, 214–15).[3] Bakhtin argued that carnivalesque symbolism of degradation and dirt was ambivalently connected with the image of the woman, conjuring up a potentially inferior status but also a link to life-giving and renewal (1984, 240; see also Stallybrass 1985, 122–25).

In many carnival festivities gender inversion figured centrally, either involving crossed-dressed men or allowing women more extensive license for sexual expression (Davis 1975, 136; Gilmore 1987, 105–6; Hunt 1984, 66). Indeed, in Ashton's home county, Lancashire, "lifting" or "hocking," the practice in which women collectively accosted and raised genteel men in the air until they were promised payment, was common on Easter Monday or Tuesday (Bushaway 1982, 172–74). The equality proffered to women or the feminine or the plasticity of gendering should not be romanticized. However, women and feminine symbolization were important to the collective construction of social space and to the protest that was frequently coupled with carnival, especially when compared to succeeding collective action repertoires.

These new forms of contention could also be important vehicles for contesting concepts of territoriality and public space. The transgression or occupation of public spaces by demonstrators both announced the parading group's civic and social worthiness and contested powerholders' exercise of control over place. English parades and ceremonial processions historically provided rituals for the transfer of political power, as in the pageantry for new lord mayors of London, in which trades featured prominently. With the increasing separation of capitalists and journeymen in the Anglo-American case, the procession was slowly transformed into part of the new repertoire of demonstration, used alternatively to dramatize the claims of labor, as in strike parades, or the claims of unempowered and unenfranchised working people and women to democratic privileges (in the U.S. and English cases respectively) (Davis 1986, esp. 115–58; Tilly 1995b; Ryan 1989, 1990).

Prior to the Combination Laws (passed in 1799), processions publicly articulating grievances to manufacturers, sometimes combined with Rough Music to intimidate strikebreakers, were part of the trade dispute repertoire (Dobson 1980, 90). By the later eighteenth century, trade groups added the petition processions to Parliament (Dobson 1980, 81–85). In the nineteenth century, workers' parades increasingly articulated journeymen's and factory workers' often contentious interests and were incorporated into the emergent strike repertoire. Their growing importance in part served to heighten a social construction of masculine presence and authority. As John Bohstedt suggests, women's independent moral voice was seeded in the community politics of a moral economy of the food riot, and though "women continued to lead them, they were marooned in a 'traditional' form of protest, while their brothers and fathers formed more modern political and labour associations to take up the cudgels on the frontier of the capitalist labour market" (1988, 113). Women and the feminine were by no means removed from collective action, but theirs was a limited kind of politics, representing or represented alternatively as angels of the state or bearers of civic virtue (Clark 1992, 77; Colley 1992, ch. 6; McCalman 1989, 162–77; Ryan 1990, 25–31, 52).

Increasing Tensions

The late 1820s in the Ashton region offer a window on both how workers contested capitalist constructions of social space through carnivals and parades and how such contests were increasingly masculinized. The region simmered with labor tension and sometimes reached an open boil. The cotton spinners were among the most skilled and privileged of all mill workers, and the trade was largely male, particularly outside of Manchester (Catling 1970; Freifeld 1986; Kirby and Musson 1975; Lazonick 1979; Morgan 1992; Sykes 1982, vol. 1; Valverde 1988). They were among the best organized of all workers, having a history of regional unionization from 1810 and establishing a Grand National Union in 1829. In the large regional strikes of 1810 and 1818 spinners refined several features of their repertoire, including using regularized pickets, parading, and using alien and anonymous watches to pass information and to report on blacklegs (strikebreakers) (Cotton 1977, 112; Doherty 1829, passim; Kirby and Musson 1975, 14, 25; Tufnell 1834, 2, 13, 118–19).

In late 1824 and early 1825, with the repeal of the Combination Laws, the spinners of Hyde, a few miles south of Stalybridge, unsuccessfully turned out (struck) for a piece-rate increase. The Ashton spinners followed with a bitter and frustrating strike. Three hundred of their ranks were permanently replaced by blacklegs, while the remaining vanquished were forced to denounce the union. A few fearless spinners turned out again the following year, but the mill owners sat firmly in control (Cotton 1977, 150–51; Kirby and Musson 1975, 31, 43; Tufnell 1834, 18–19).

After suffering through the severe depression of 1826–27, the trade was again buoyant in 1828, and spinners began to press for lost piece rates. In December of that year the spinners in the Stockport area (south of Ashton) engaged in a fractious strike, idling over 10,000 mill workers and garnering support from local unions throughout the Ashton region. Led by the magnate Thomas Ashton, twenty-four manufacturers in Stalybridge, Hyde, and Dukinfield mandated that their operatives sign a declaration repudiating the union or face a 10 percent reduction of piece rates every fortnight. At least three Hyde mills struck in defiance, but by July the district manufacturers once again exerted complete authority (*MT,* April 4, 11, 1829; *MG,* April 25, 1829; Kirby and Musson 1975, 57–59).

We should view the rituals and parading of the late 1820s within this fractious context. The Ashton region was increasingly saturated by an accumulation of divisive interests, all of which spilled forth in the winter of 1830–31. Before turning to the great strike of that period, I examine one of the area's premier festivities, the Riding of the Black Lad.

The Riding of the Black Lad as a Ritual of Struggle

Lancashire was a region known for its saturnalian wakes and fairs, and the Ashton wake was an integral part of the calendar. Despite the consternation of the manufacturers, factory workers would bypass the mill gates during the week for this high moment of frivolity. The union paper *Voice of the People* advertised the event in bacchanalian terms:

> Those who derive amusement from hurdy girdy grinders, cat-gut scrapers, drums and ginger bread, noise and dirt, gin and penny-whistles, beef and pudding, ale and spice-cake, broken heads and bloody noses, terminating in empty pockets, blood-shot eyes, and comfortable lodgings in the lock-ups, to have ample means of gratification at the exhibition y'cleped [called] the wakes. (*Voice of the People* [*VP*], July 23, 1831, no. 4:2)

As the traditional market town, Ashton also hosted a series of fairs that diminished in importance over the course of the century, while several surrounding mill villages also sustained annual wakes inaugurated by factory workers in the 1830s and 1840s (Bowman 1960, 299–307; Butterworth 1842, 152–53; Harland and Wilkinson 1882, 85–87, 286–88).

While wakes and fairs were a carnivalesque contrapuntal to the solemnity of mill town life, they could also serve as proletarian countertheater, mocking established power and contesting the bourgeois construction of public space. In Ashton the Riding of the Black Lad was such an event.

The origins of the celebration are obscure, but folklore attributes its nascence to the ignominious reign in the fifteenth century of Sir Ralph Assheton, lord of the neighboring manor of Middleton.[4] Henry VI had awarded Sir Ralph the life privilege of guld riding (the yearly practice of policing the tenantry's fields for their weeding of the wild flowers that hampered cultivation) in Ashton parish. Recalcitrant peasants were liable for stiff fines, and lore had it that Sir Ralph relished his function as he rode through the fields in a suit of black armor every year around Easter exacting his toll. Upon his death, relatives, who scorned the knight's memory, were said to have abolished the practice and to have reserved a small amount of estate money to memorialize the dreaded visits in an annual ceremony.

By the nineteenth century the rituals' classic carnivalesque color had developed a distinctly proletarian hue. Prior to the Easter Monday on which it was held a pit was dug on a lane above the marketplace and filled with water, and an effigy of the Black Lad was constructed for the riding ritual. A correspondent provided this eyewitness account in 1826:

> Every year on that day a rude figure of a man made of an old suit of clothes stuffed with rags, hay, &c., is carried through all the streets. The people who attend it call at every public-house, for the purpose of begging liquor for its thirsty attendants, who are always numerous. During its progress the figure is shot at from all parts. When the journey is finished, it is tied to the market cross, and the shooting is continued till it is set on fire, and falls to the ground. The populace then commence tearing the effigy to pieces, trampling it in mud and water, and throwing it in every direction. This riot and confusion are increased by help of a reservoir of water being let off, which runs down the streets, and not unfrequently persons obtain large quantities of hay, rags, &c. independent of that which falls from the effigy. The greatest heroes at this time are of the coarsest nature. (Hone 1827, 2:468).

As businessmen traversed the space that they had constructed as an area of modern commerce, thousands of working people appropriated it as an arena for degradation. People in fine attire and proper manners mingled helplessly among disorderly men and women and encountered the egalitarian effects of dirt. Ashton's elite fell prey to the practice of "dowsing," those on the street pelting them with mud and refuse-soaked wads of straw and rags. An 1829 *Manchester Times* account unhappily observed that this practice had never been so widespread. Both men and women were assaulted by dowsers, who engaged in "the most unjustifiable assaults; several highly respectable individuals are abused and one has obtained warrants" (*MT,* April 25, 1829). The man who obtained the warrants, the owner of a local hat manufactory, was dissuaded from prosecuting only when a magistrate promised more thorough policing at subsequent rituals (*MT,* May 5, 1829).

The riding exhibited all of the billingsgate and degradation that Bakhtin argued are the hallmarks of carnival. The working people who clogged Ashton's streets and freely dowsed their superiors actively and rudely transformed bourgeois space. Through their overwhelming numbers, and much to the consternation of the local bourgeoisie, working people usurped authority, and the wheels of commerce ground to a halt. Just as significant, both genders were active participants. The market square and the town streets became a space of the people, as disorderly women played their part in the process of usurpation. At a time when male mill workers, often led by the spinners, were beginning to define women of the factory as weak and vulnerable, the riding provided an opportunity for a different gender construction.

The ritual riding continued to mark Easter Monday throughout the course of the century, but dowsing was soon suppressed, and by the 1860s the riding was no longer a symbolic and spatial struggle. In part, this can be accounted for by the new repertoire created by working people to press their grievances, one significantly represented by the spinners' strike of the winter of 1830–31.

The Strike Parades and the New Repertoire

The Ashton branch of the Grand National Union was headed by John Joseph Betts, an ex-spinner who was both a skillful organizer and among the area's chief purveyors of radical literature (Bowring to Lamb, December 12, 1830, Lancashire County Record Office [LCRO], DDX/880/2). In yet one more attempt to narrow the region's piece-rate disparities, Betts (in consultation with the union committee in Manchester) initiated a campaign in April 1830. The spinners commenced with a turnout against William Hegginbottom, a mill owner who refused to raise piece rates and belligerently hired blacklegs. The striking spinners responded by surrounding the mill; pelting their replacements with mud, sticks, and stones; and individually attacking blacklegs about town. Alarmed local authorities had troops dispatched to the area. Tensions continued to build into June, when the Hegginbottoms received a bomb in the post that, fortunately for the family, had an inadequate triggering device. A week later Hegginbottom capitulated to the union's piece-rate demands, but he refused to rehire any of the turnouts (*MG,* June 12, 26, 1830; *SA,* April 30, May 25, June 11, 1830; *UTCJ* May 29, 1830; HO 40/27, folios 268–73).

Rancor deepened in July when local mill owners announced piece-rate reductions on the most commonly spun yarns (Cotton 1977, 213). In response 4,000 spinners and mill workers met outside of Ashton, and several weeks later, after a shaky truce, 7,000 again convened in Stalybridge to firm their turnout plans. Soon after, they commenced a rolling strike in Stalybridge (*UTJC*, July 24, August 14, September 11, 1830; *MT*, July 31, August 14, 21, 1830).

The union set up an elaborate strike operation, monitoring traffic on all major roads to examine unknown foot travelers, as well as posting pickets in front of the mills. Fearing violence and lacking effective force, the local military commander, Lieutenant Colonel Shaw, quickly dissuaded the firms from introducing blacklegs, and within several weeks the mills acquiesced to a modified settlement offered by the union (*UTCJ*, September 11, 1830; Bouverie to Peel, August 29, 1830, HO 40/26, folios 46–50; Shaw to Clerk September 2, 1830, HO 40/27, folio 20; Shaw to Bouverie September 4, 1830, HO 40/26, folios 65–66).

Local and national authorities expressed worry about the spinners' triumph and, more particularly, their capacity to essentially usurp control of town space (Cotton 1977, 213, note 84; Shaw to Peel, September 4, 1830, HO 40/27, folios 522–23). The picketing and surveillance tactics of the spinners thoroughly transgressed local spatialized authority and denied the very essence of abstract space: the free flow of commodities and labor. A concerned Robert Peel wrote to the Northern Army commander that "it would be very desirable, if there should be an opportunity, of rigidly enforcing the Law against the Parties who are employed in what is called the Picquetting System" (September 6, 1830, HO 40/26, folios 69–70). Selected work stoppages continued, and in November fifty-two mill owners entered into a bond to set piece rates at a uniformly low level. The spinners responded with a standard action in their repertoire: large rallies around the district to mobilize workers for impending strikes. At the beginning of December the fifty-two sent out public notice that the drop in piece rates was effective in two weeks and set off one of the largest strikes England had ever seen (Nightingale to Home Office, November 11, 1830, HO 40/27, folios 338–39; Bouverie to Peel, November 14, 1830, HO 40/26, folios 131–32; *MG*, October 23, November 6, 13, 1830; Bouverie to Melbourne, December 2, 1830, HO 40/26, folio 146; *VP*, January 8, 1831).

On December 4 workers streamed out of the mills with considerable fanfare in the first of many strike processions. Starting in Stalybridge the procession was ordered in a military formation with ten to twelve abreast in lines and contained "some hundreds of decently dressed women" (*MG*, December 11, 1830). Led by a band, several hundred boys, and a tricolor flag, it concluded with another tricolor banner. Many of the men wore tricolored cockades or ribbons in their hats, and several reports noted with some alarm that from 800 to perhaps as many as 4,000 carried firearms.[5] Betts and others had drawn analogies to the July revolution in France, and the military authorities worried about the radical fervor that they saw as spreading infectiously through the town (Shaw to Bouverie, August 24, 1830, HO 40/27, folio 305; Nightingale to Home Office, November 11, 1830, HO 40/27, folios 338–39). The procession stopped at each factory, appealing for mill workers to join them, subduing the managers, and evicting unresponsive workers. Passing each mill or owner's estate they raised a loud chorus of "Four and twopence or swing!" The former was the desired piece rate; the latter was a threatening reference to the recent agricultural laborers' actions in the south. The procession moved through Ashton's main thoroughfare to a meadow near Dukinfield. Accounts put its numbers as high as 20,000, and it stretched a mile. The procession symbolically unified workers across the region, and their forceful incursions into mills demonstrated that they were not the exclusive space of capital. The parade can also be seen as a means of demarcating control over social space (*WMC,* December 11, 1830; Foster to Melbourne, December 6, 1830, HO 40/26, folios 160–63; Astley to Melbourne, December 9, 1830, HO 40/26, folios 178–80).

To announce proletarian discontent, commercial space was transgressed symbolically. On walls the slogans "Liberty or death" and "Four and twopence or swing" signaled the determination of the spinners. Processions of workers, armed and with tricolors, sometimes in small groups and sometimes in formations of up to several thousand, daily paraded through Ashton and Stalybridge. Several mills in Stalybridge had their windows smashed by these members of processions. The local magistrates, who could not raise a large special constabulary, grew alarmed. A few days before the strike Lord Lieutenant Henry Bouverie in Manchester reluctantly authorized the services of two regiments (Foster to Melborne, December 9, 1830, HO 40/26, folios 160–63; Bouverie to Phillips, December 7, 1830, HO 40/26, folios 170–73; Astley to Melbourne, December 9, 1830, HO 40/26, folios 179–80; Bouverie to Phillips, December 11, 1830, HO 40/26, folios 190–91).

In the early weeks of the strike parading became a routine feature of the spinners' repertoire. During the first week a bugle called from 1,500 to 2,000 workers to Ashton's marketplace, many with weapons in hand; they assembled behind a band and a tricolor and carried many hostile banners. In military fashion the strikers paraded to outlying regions to turn out working mills, assembled on main streets to harangue mill owners on their way to Manchester, or rallied to win support from fellow workers.

In the second week of the strike the fearful magistrates banned all further demonstrations and called in a large contingent of soldiers. On the morning of December 18 several thousand spinners marched off in their regular fashion to extend the strike in nearby Glossup. In their absence an impressive force headed by four pieces of artillery and both General Bouverie and Lieutenant Colonel Shaw ceremoniously marched into Ashton to reclaim the district. Soon afterward the spinners returned to town and faced off against the army, finishing a rousing chorus of "Rule Britannia" with shouts of "Liberty or death" before dispersing. The entrance of the military was the visible signal of the procession's demise (*MG,* December 12, 1830; *MT,* December 18, 1830; Cotton 1977, 222; Astley to Melbourne, December 21, 1830, HO 40/27, folios 356–59; Bouverie to Phillips, December 21, 1830, HO 40/26, folios 225–27).

Striking spinners turned to more violent tactics (including one assassination and several other attempts as well as violent raids) and repression increased. "Alienation and hatred between the two interests are getting intense," Bowring warned the Home Office, "and terror is becoming the weapon among both operatives and their employers" (Bowring to Lamb, December 30, 1830, LCRO DDX/880/2). Some pallid efforts were made to fashion a compromise in late January, but the mill owners, sensing that they had the upper hand, rejected the spinners' proposals. By the first week in February mills in Glossup, Stalybridge, and Ashton began to reopen on their owners' terms, and by the following week the strike had collapsed (*MG,* January 8, 15, 22, 29, February 5, 12, 19, 1831; *MT,* January 8, 22, February 19, 26, 1831; *VP,* January 8, February 5, 19, 1831).

The spinners' parades were well-orchestrated efforts to mobilize solidarity and to publicize their grievances, but we can also see them as attempts to appropriate social space. With a combination of carnival cheer and military rigor the spinners marched through the main streets of the region's mill towns proclaiming that the manufacturers were imperious tyrants in workers' territory. Each procession was a palpable effort to redraw the lines of authority and legitimacy, a signal of spatial prerogatives and therefore of effective physical *and* moral control. As their banners and tricolors passed through the streets of each mill town, abstract space was provisionally transformed with their fluttering. "Rule Britannia" it certainly was, and precisely whose Britain and which rules were being contested by every step.

Redefining such space was even more topsy-turvy than the upside-down world of the carnival, for ultimately it spoke to issues of fundamental power over people and property. Creating effective barriers to blacklegs devalued both the mill owners' authority and their capital, for without ready command over labor power they became disempowered players in their world of production. The strike processions realized this process on a grander scale. The mill owners, local authorities, and military commanders thus perceived that there were larger issues of territorial control at stake. The state ultimately secured this space for capitalist hegemony. After calm had been restored the magistrates and mill owners requested a permanent military presence for the town (Shaw to Bouverie, August 8, 1831, HO 40/27, folio 305; Petition of the Magistrates, Constables, and Inhabitants of Ashton . . . to Melborne, HO 54/4, Civil A).

The parades perhaps signaled the gendered transformation of social space. In their display of weaponry, martial formations, and occasional violence to property, male workers demarcated strike space as a distinctly dangerous masculine zone of participation. With the exception of the grand procession of early December women seemingly played little part in these actions, even though many were themselves factory workers as well as spouses and kin to factory workers. In comparison to the Riding of the Black Lad there appears to have been less room in this space for disorderly women in either their corporeal or symbolic forms.

Tilly consistently reminds us that collective action is *inter*action, a relational process in which all actors seek to impose their competing claims and definitions of the world on their adversaries. In complementary fashion new social movement theory underscores that through participation actors interactively construct identities. Logically, then, those who are not in the fray lose some capacity to define their adversaries, their compatriots, and themselves. As the male strikers' actions increasingly redefined the region as a zone of masculine contention and participation as a marker of class solidarity and identity, we must wonder what impact it had on the definitions of the women as members of the community of workers.

Conclusion: Musings on the Interactions of Spatialization, Gendering, and Repertoires of Collective Action

This analysis offers only gleanings of much larger transformations in the spatial and gendered dimensions of the working people's collective actions that occurred throughout subsequent decades. Both the Riding of the Black Lad and the strike parades provide us with some significant variations in the contested class process of constructing social space. Both demonstrate how forms of collective action simultaneously gender this space. These analyses of working people's actions also throw into question the analysis of popular ritual as a primarily liminal process, suggesting instead that such ceremonies and festivities are bounded opportunities for dissension and counterhegemony. Finally, in a modest way, both illustrate that the capitalist construction of social space was still only beginning.

What the examples do not provide is a clear sense of the lineaments of the complex dynamic among repertoires, the development of capitalism, and the concentration and extension of state power, spatiality, and gendering over the course of the century. But taking this small skein of history and placing it in the contexts of others' much larger yarns we can begin to consider these complexities. Tilly's account of changing repertoires signals that there might have been a mutually reinforcing dynamic among the construction of abstract space, the concentration of state power, and popular repertoires of contention as the century progressed (1986a, 387–98; 1995b, 106–49). Tilly provides us with two linked processes by which changing interactions among these main actors might have secured the expansion of abstract space even as they opened up increased opportunities for working people's claim making. First, as he suggests, the wedding of capitalists' interests and expanding state power changed the opportunity structure to "contain and channel popular collective action; in so doing they first extended state structure into direct rule at the level of the individual community and then built a centralized apparatus of surveillance and control" (1986a, 389). Not only did that apparatus of control more effectively limit the capacity of ordinary people to physically seize or symbolically cordon a territory, but it could also radically transform the very structure of particular places themselves.

Second, the implosion of capital might also have transformed the spatiality of contention between workers and capitalists. The turnout, as Tilly argues, was a matter more of community and occurred throughout a locality. In its marches and demonstrations, much as I have detailed for Ashton, it placed pressure on employers and authorities in an entire area, and I would argue that it did so partly by endangering the stability of social space. The firm-by-firm strike, however, had a different spatiality, and we need to ask whether its tighter focus on the point of production shifts collective action away from active contention over larger definitions of space (Tilly 1986a, 394).

Repertoires crystallize over time, and as they do they provide a learned set of expectations and historical lessons. We need to consider a perverse effect of these lessons, that abstract space—the space that a growing industrial capitalism was etching across many surfaces—was left increasingly presumed and unquestioned *because* of this transformation of repertoires. In the 1820s Ashton's working people saw the occupation of space as a viable and necessary part of their repertoire, and their actions suggest that they contested the mill owners' hegemony. Local authorities and military officers fretted over just such possibilities, and neither they nor the capitalists took the definitions of space and place for granted. But we have to question how often working people generally imagined such definitional contests as a possibility by the turn of the century. If they did not, we should further investigate how their presumptions concerning social space might have affected the ways in which they maintained and developed their repertoires in this complex dynamic of spatial definition and patterns of contention.

The contrast in the Ashton case between the participation of women in the riding festival and in the strike is only a hint at a process that took many decades. In the 1830s and 1840s disorderly women could be still very much a part of mill workers' strikes and Chartist campaigns (Clark 1992, 84; see also 1995; Thomis and Grimmett 1982, 79; Thompson 1984, 133). Yet the participation of women in these riots may, as Anna Clark argues, have paradoxically linked the disorderly female with the very degradation of the factory that the Chartist rhetoric of militant domesticity championed (Clark 1992, 72–73, 78, 84–85; Hall n.d., 8–9). This militant domesticity presaged further change, for by the 1860s many of the large mill owners in the area had come to an accord with their male workers over the virtues of the male breadwinner model, as paternalism in the factory and home meshed (Joyce 1980, 188; Hall n.d., 13). We thus need to investigate how the rising importance of respectability and the heightened emphasis on the masculinity of public order in the Victorian years transformed the gendering of the couplet order/disorder and in so doing changed possibilities for women's participation.

As recent work by Blewett (1992, 1993), and Rose (1992, 1993), among others, demonstrates, the gendering of orderliness was a central ideological component of strike actions in the late nineteenth century. By the mid-Victorian period the feminine and order were linked in at least two ways to male working-class respectability and virility. First, women were mobilized by male leaders in their roles as bearers of family and civic virtue, emphasizing working-class respectability and distancing collective action from the disorderly. Second, the disorderly woman could be present but was marginalized within the public spaces of contention (Rose 1992, 166–77, 1993; Blewett 1992, 2). In either case women had ancillary positions in the public places in which they appeared, and their opportunities for action were more bounded than were males'. The gendering of social space was thus reconfigured by this growing masculinization of contention and by the ways in which employers responded to and validated these conceptions of masculinity through their own growing paternalistic practices. We need to further investigate how gendered and ethnic conceptions of social spaces interacted with their parallel dynamics in union politics and working-class life to reshape the boundaries of participation.

Throughout his analyses of the great transformations of the nineteenth century, Charles Tilly illuminates how ordinary people struggled to make their place in a world in which the concentration of people, capital, and political power fundamentally altered the terrain of common life. An essential part of their collective response was the development of repertoires of contention, the shared stock of collective actions by which they sought to influence this sometimes fitful process. I have argued that we in effect should elaborate upon Tilly's metaphor and pay more attention to the stage. We must focus more carefully on how its construction bounded the repertoires of action of the mere players—the many roles they played and their entrances and exits. We need to understand more fully the ways in which ordinary people did or did not contest the dictates it imposed on them, and when in the former case they did not find the stage as they liked it, we must analyze more carefully how their repertoires were acts of demolition and reconstruction.

Notes

Thanks to Michael Hanagan, Leslie Page Moch, Wayne te Brake, and Mary Jo Maynes for their comments.

1. For the sake of brevity all newspapers will be listed by their initials after their first citation in this section.

2. Turner himself has reacted to some of this overapplication by distinguishing between the liminal and the liminoid, with the latter referring to secular activities, often associated with named groups in nontribal societies, that "are not merely reversive, but subversive, representing radical critiques of the central structures and proposing utopian alternative models" (1977, 45).

3. Russo is also quick to emphasize that the marginal status of women in the normative world, coupled with the suspension of order during these periods, could make the carnival a danger space for women (1986, 216). This validating function parallels the role of women in various forms of riot in the old repertoire (Bohstedt 1988; 1983, 93; Thomis and Gimmett 1982, 138–46; Thompson 1971, 115).

4. Numerous accounts and explanations exist for the Black Lad ritual. Among these are Axon 1870; Bamford [1841] 1967, 1:141–43; Baines 1824, 1:493–94; Harland and Wilkinson 1882, 285–94; Hone 1827, 2: cols. 467–69.

5. *Wheeler's Manchester Chronicle,* December 14, 1830, specifically mentioned that a number of the women appeared to be carrying both knives and firearms, though this is one of the last references to disorderly women.

Archival Sources

British Public Record Office (Kew Gardens), Home Office (HO) Papers

HO 40/26–27. Correspondence, Civil Disturbances
HO 52/14. Correspondence, Counties
HO 54/4. Petitions and Addresses

Lancashire Country Record Office (LCRO), Preston

Letters of Dr. John Bowring, to the Right Honourable George Lamb, M.P., Under-Secretary of State for the Home Office, about Attempts of the Masters to Reduce the Wages of the Spinners in the Ashton Area and the Organization of the Spinners into a Trades Association (DDX/880/1–2)

Tameside Library (Stalybridge), Local History Collection

Stalybridge Improvement Commissioners Records, Minute Books June 1828–April 1833 (IC/STA/1)

House of Commons Select Committee Reports

PP 1824 (51) V. Reports from the Select Committee on Artizans, Machinery, and Combinations, First Report

Acts of Parliament

An Act for lighting with Gas the Town of Ashton-under-Lyne and the Neighborhood thereof, in the County Palatine of Lancaster, and the Township of Duckinfield, in the County Palatine of Chester; and for supplying with Water the said Town of Ashton-under-Lyne and the Neighborhood thereof (6 Geo. IV, c. 67), 1825

An Act for lighting, cleansing, watching, and otherwise improving the Town of Ashton-under-Lyne in the County Palatine of Lancaster, and for regulating the Police thereof (7 & 8 Geo. IV, c. 76), 1827

Chapter 3

Political Networks and the Local/National Boundary in the Whiskey Rebellion

Roger V. Gould

Having understood that networks of social relations and shared collective identities are instrumental in mobilizing people for collective action, a few scholars are beginning to explore the third edge of this triad: the link between collective identities and networks. Rather than seeing network ties as stockpiles of a fungible resource that movement entrepreneurs can use in recruitment much as they would leaflets or loudspeakers, we are starting to see that *patterns* of ties inform individuals' judgments about the collectivities or political groupings to which they and others belong (see especially, Padgett and Ansell 1993; Bearman 1994; Gould 1993, 1995a, 1996). The basic idea underlying this work is that the abstractly defined groups benefiting (or not) from collective action do not come from nowhere or from detached ideologies but are built endogenously from concrete systems of social relations.

It is one thing to state this proposition and another to demonstrate its validity concretely. It is yet another thing to give a detailed account of just *how* collective identities depend on patterns of social relations, and another still to link various accounts of disparate empirical settings into something like a theory of how collective identities emerge. We are a very long way from the last of these achievements, and a bit further along than the first. For the moment, I hope to make some additional progress by examining a specific historical case of elite-led political contention from the postrevolutionary United States, the Whiskey Rebellion. In a separate study (Gould 1996), I have demonstrated that the principal factor differentiating the set of elites who eventually became insurgents from those who did not was the difference in their respective positions in the regional network of political patronage. Insurgent leaders were disproportionally likely to be (1) local elites without connections to the patron client network that included federal officeholders or (2) elites whose clienteles overlapped substantially with those of federal officials and whose influence was thus threatened by the increased authority that centralization afforded the latter. Though the literature on state formation has shed a great deal of light on the role played by resource extraction (taxation, labor and military conscription, and so forth) in provoking mass mobilization against state builders, it has paid less attention to the role of patronage ties in shaping such contention (Tilly 1985, 1990a; Barkey 1994). Co-optation through patronage is a powerful tool that centralizing agents use to win over potential elite adversaries (and by extension through patronage ties, their clients), but it simultaneously threatens the local influence of elites who lack secure patron–client connections. The point is that preexisting patronage networks determine who opposes and who supports state-building efforts through a mechanism that operates independently of the differential impact of resource extraction.

In this chapter I address an issue not considered in that earlier study, nor indeed in much of the literature on elite challenges to state-building efforts: Why on earth would wealthy political elites respond to a threat to their influence with a violent insurgent effort if the effort stood little chance of success? Elite insurgent challenges to would-be centralizers are more spectacular than their absence, a fact that leads us to overestimate the ease with which people resort to such actions and to forget how often they don't. As the sociological literature on protest continues to remind us, the fact that considerable numbers of people have an interest in challenging authority does not guarantee that they will do so. Similarly, even powerful notables with the capacity to mobilize an armed following may choose to capitulate to state builders rather than resist if the risks are sufficiently great. The puzzle is that resistance occurs anyway, despite often overwhelming odds and catastrophic costs. Discussions of state making and collective action would benefit from an account of why this is—of why elites might choose to lead popular revolts against state builders even when the latter are very likely to win.

In this chapter I will provide evidence that members of the southwestern Pennsylvania elite placed themselves at the head of the Whiskey Rebellion because they saw the insurgent effort as a way of protecting their position as "brokers" between their region and the more cosmopolitan east—even if the insurgency were to fail, as it undeniably did. The passage of a federal excise tax and the appointment of a politically prominent local landowner to the post of excise inspector undermined the political influence of elite members who had no patronage connections to the new federal officer or to any of the other federal officeholders in the region. Enhanced coercive power in the hands of one set of elite members—those with federal authority or their clients—spelled probable political doom for the rest, who could not intercede on behalf of their supporters when the latter fell foul of the tax collector. For this second group, taking the lead in the insurgent response to the excise would thus have the double effect of enhancing their local popularity with small-scale distillers (an oft-noted theme in the historiography of the event) and of warding off the threat to their influence if the insurrection were to succeed in forcing the tax's repeal. On the other hand—and this is my main point in what follows—even failure could have beneficial consequences, provided that a notable's actions could be suitably recast in retrospect: Elite insurgent leaders could (and did) claim that they had participated in the mobilization to rein in the angry mob of distillers who were terrorizing tax collectors and promising to sack Pittsburgh. This version of events simultaneously shielded insurgent elites from accusations of treason and portrayed them as important arbiters of the conflict between the rural western region and the urbane political class in Philadelphia. What local elites lost by virtue of their lack of patronage ties to federal officers they could regain with this claim to mediate the social boundary between east and west. The implication is that political identifications are not merely constrained by networks of social ties, in the sense that network position helps to determine which of a variety of exogenously available self-understandings an individual might embrace; in this instance, at least, the relevant identification was defined *in terms of* the network.

A Frontier Uprising

The Whiskey Rebellion is the name commonly given to the uprising that ended three years of resistance to the federal excise tax on the domestic manufacture of distilled spirits. In southwestern Pennsylvania (principally the counties of Washington, Westmoreland, Fayette, and Allegheny), farmers typically converted most of their grain into whiskey either for local use or to reduce the cost of transportation across the Appalachian Mountains. Under the 1791 excise law, a cornerstone of Treasury Secretary Alexander Hamilton's plan to solidify the federal government and pay off the Revolutionary War debt, anyone operating a still had to register it with the tax collector and make payments proportional to production volume. In western Pennsylvania, where whiskey was produced as much for private consumption as for the market, distillers naturally viewed the tax as a major intrusion. Pennsylvania's own excise had been unenforceable, largely as the result of noncompliance combined with regular tarring and feathering of collectors. When Congress enacted the federal excise, the independent-minded farmers in the trans-Appalachian corner of the state denounced it both as a discriminatory measure (because per capita consumption of whiskey was greater in their area than in the east) and as a harbinger of future despotism on the part of the central government.

Between 1791 and 1794 distillers in southwestern Pennsylvania mounted determined resistance to the whiskey excise. Opponents of the tax effectively discouraged compliance through public denunciations of distillers who registered. In some instances Pennsylvanians who complied with the law saw their stills destroyed. Such attacks were usually followed by the appearance of notices, signed "Tom the Tinker," threatening similar sanctions against others who paid the tax. Several tax collectors were tarred and feathered, and landlords who rented office space to collectors were threatened with destruction of their buildings; at least two such threats were actually carried out. Protest also took a more sober form: In 1791 and 1792 a number of prominent westerners held public meetings to voice their grievances, and in Washington County they formed democratic societies modeled after the Jacobin clubs of the French Revolution.

The resistance escalated in July 1794 when a federal marshal, accompanied by General John Neville (a prominent landowner and former Supreme Executive Council member who had accepted the post of excise inspector for the western counties), attempted to serve sixty delinquent distillers with summonses to appear in a Philadelphia court. One farmer, upon seeing the approaching officials, fired his rifle at them, obliging them to retreat. When word of the confrontation spread, several hundred men surrounded Neville's mansion, to which the general and the marshal had fled, and demanded that the summonses be destroyed. Shots were fired from the house, killing two protesters and wounding several others. On the second day the leader of the siege, another prominent landholder and veteran of the Revolution, was shot and killed while attempting to establish negotiations with the house's occupants. In response the rebels set fire to the building, but the defenders of the Neville mansion escaped unharmed. Neville himself had managed to flee on the first day, leaving his nephew, Major Abraham Kirkpatrick, to defend the property.

Several Washington County men, including Deputy Attorney General David Bradford, arranged at this point to intercept the mail from Pittsburgh to discover whether any of its citizens were communicating with the federal authorities about the recent event. Discovering that certain individuals (some of them connected personally with Neville) were actively organizing against the incipient uprising, the small group of self-appointed rebel leaders issued a circular letter to militia officers, calling for a muster on August 1 in preparation for a march on Pittsburgh. On the appointed day 5,000 men assembled at the appointed place, but a group of citizens from Pittsburgh, in negotiation with the rebel army's leaders, persuaded them to march through the city in a demonstration of discipline rather than sacking it, as some had threatened to do. In return the Pittsburgh delegates promised to banish the individuals accused of conspiring against the insurrection—among them Colonel Presley Neville, son of John Neville and a prominent officeholder in Allegheny County. The rebels agreed, but some nonetheless saw fit to demonstrate their capacity for destruction along with their discipline by setting fire to a barn belonging to Major Kirkpatrick.

On word of this mobilization, President Washington ordered the mobilization of 15,000 federal troops to march west and quell the disturbances. As the army approached, resistance quickly melted. Following a series of public meetings attended both by rebel leaders and by several dozen other prominent individuals, delegates from all four counties arranged with commissioners from the U.S. and state governments to circulate an "oath of submission to the laws of the Unites States," to be signed as a condition of amnesty for anyone in the region who had taken part in the resistance. By mid-September most of the rebels had signed the oath, although a number, including David Bradford, fled to Ohio. Thirty-two men were arrested and tried in Philadelphia for treason. Only two were convicted, however, and even these were pardoned soon after by President Washington.

Historiography

I have offered a brief account of Whiskey Rebellion historiography elsewhere (Gould 1996); here I shall give an even shorter sketch. Early histories explained the insurrection with reference to frontier spirit and Scots Irish traditions of hatred for tax collectors; revisionist scholarship paid greater attention to elite political intrigue (for an example of the former, see Baldwin 1939; for the latter, see James 1950 and Cooke 1963; Slaughter 1986 is a recent synthesis). There are three main lessons to draw from this debate: First, little is gained by appealing to cultural traditions of resistance to excise taxes, as these varied little across regions of the early United States; western Pennsylvania's Scots-Irish contingent was not especially large, and the War of Independence itself had begun with a dispute over taxation that involved all thirteen American colonies. Though hatred of "internal taxes" may well have been a precondition for armed resistance, the former was quite general whereas the latter occurred only in the southwestern corner of Pennsylvania (Slaughter 1986).

Second, the excise did not affect all distillers in the same way. The demand for whiskey was inelastic, making it relatively easy for producers to pass much of the tax burden on to consumers. This fact was irrelevant to farmers producing for their own consumption, but it diminished the impact of the tax on large-scale producers and could actually benefit them by forcing some farmers to buy liquor rather than making their own (see Whitten 1975).

Large-scale producers of whiskey also tended to be the wealthiest land-owners and were well represented in the region's political elite. But despite their relative immunity from the effects of the tax, many of these men were central actors in organizing resistance to it. The leaders of both the initial, petition-oriented protest movement and the final, mass mobilization were prosperous men who occupied key political and administrative posts in the region.

The central role of these notables in a frontier uprising underlies the third axis of Whiskey Rebellion historiography: the explanation of elite insurgent participation as the product of political ambition rather than economic griev-ance. By joining in the public clamor against the tax, according to this view, political leaders in the region hoped to enhance their popularity with those voters who actually were threatened economically. One historian has argued that the leaders "were self-seeking politicians who hoped to ride the waves of popular discontent to the secure shores of political office" (Cooke 1963, 345). Similar assertions occur in the firsthand accounts published by Hugh Henry Brackenridge and William Findley, two western leaders who had attended a number of the public meetings following the attack on Neville's mansion. Brackenridge, an attorney and writer (though not an officeholder until later) who appears to have urged moderation at the meetings he attended, wrote that to denounce the excise "was the shibboleth of safety, and the ladder of ambition" ([1796] 1972, 17).

Networks and Boundaries

In my earlier analysis (Gould 1996), I argued that the political ambition expla-nation successfully accounts for the general fact that most local leaders spoke out against the excise law immediately after its passage. Publicly, at least, western Pennsylvania notables who depended on voting clienteles for their continued political influence needed to convey the impression that they opposed the federal tax. But for the same reason the general popularity of the anti-excise stance cannot explain differential behavior when resistance reached the point of armed insurgency. Almost all of the political elite in the western counties denounced the tax as a tyrannical infringement of democratic liberty, but only a few went so far as to openly support armed resistance and to assume command of armed rebel forces.

As I noted at the beginning of this chapter, the chief difference between those local notables who became insurgents and those who did not was that the former occupied disadvantaged positions in the system of patronage tying westerners to the eastern political establishment. The expansion of federal power that the excise augured benefited federal officeholders and elites with patronage ties to them at the expense of elites who did not have such connections (and also at the expense of elites whose clienteles overlapped with those of federal officers). Contrary to the anti-Federalist interpretation of the insurrection, the crucial matter was not that the excise appeared to be the first of a series of federal encroachments on local autonomy. Rather, the central issue was that the elites whose political connections permitted them to mediate between the western counties and the state government in Philadelphia rightly saw the arrival of federal officials as rendering their position irrelevant by shifting the locus of brokerage from the state to the federal level.[1] Local elites with links (either direct or indirect) to the federal bureaucracy would increasingly be the key mediators of patronage, whereas those with ties only to the state would have comparatively little to offer.

The position of broker between the western counties and Philadelphia had been valuable in at least three ways. The most mundane (and least significant for this study) was monetary: Members of the state-level Council of Censors, the Supreme Executive Council, and later (after the 1790 Pennsylvania Constitution eliminated these bodies) the state assembly and state senate were entitled to a nontrivial daily fee of approximately £1 (plus travel expenses) for their public service, which took up several months of each year.

Second and more important, state-level bodies confirmed the elections of county judges and justices of the peace and appointed prothonotaries, coroners, and sheriffs (although the constitution of 1790 gave the right to appoint judgeships to the governor alone). Representatives of the western counties could thus easily build up local clienteles by appointing potential supporters to such positions. It is quite clear, moreover, that this sort of patronage was the norm long before it became notorious in the Jacksonian period: For example, upon his election to the U.S. Congress Thomas Scott of Washington County ensured that the Supreme Executive Council would appoint his son Alexander to replace him as prothonotary.[2] Conversely, upon his appointment to the state supreme court in 1799 Hugh Brackenridge (hitherto an unsuccessful politician, a Princeton-educated satirist, and a chronicler of the Whiskey Rebellion) had one of his long-time rivals on the court summarily removed.

Third, participation in eastern politics facilitated the procurement for one's western associates of material resources, most notably cash, munitions, and equipment for the military attacks on Indian villages that western settlers occasionally mounted (partly out of well-founded fear, partly out of sheer racial hatred). The importance of having friends in the state legislature was enhanced by the fact that militia officers usually undertook such missions on private initiative and could not expect ready support from urban easterners, who had only a distant and hazy image of the rigors of frontier life. Indeed, the indifference of eastern elites to the conflicts with Indian communities, which westerners perceived as a fundamental threat to their existence, was a perennial source of resentment (for extensive documentation of this controversy, see *Pennsylvania Archives* n.d., series 2, 4:527–652). Influential westerners with ties to the east mediated this conflict in two ways that ensured their continued preeminence: On the one hand they routinely petitioned the governor (and through him the secretary of war) for authorization of militia expeditions and attendant guarantees of reimbursement; on the other hand, through their control over western judgeships, they made sure that the outright murders of Indians that white settlers periodically perpetrated were dismissed from court as acts of war.[3]

An incident that occurred toward the end of the War of Independence illustrates the way an ordinary citizen might seek a political favor through the sometimes fragile chains of patronage relations linking western farmers indirectly to Philadelphia powerholders. In 1782 a Washington County man named Robert Wallace discovered that his entire family had been abducted by a group of Indians, who subsequently killed his wife. According to one account:

> Wallace, thinking that his wife was held in captivity among the Indians, came to Cross Creek, to Marshall's Fort, to get Colonel James Marshall to intercede with General William Irvine at Fort Pitt, and have him intercede with General Washington, so that his wife might be exchanged or ransomed. This General Irvine did not do, as he said General Cornwallis had now surrendered and we would soon have peace, and giving other reasons, he did not make the request to Washington as Wallace wished him. (McFarland 1910, 89–90)[4]

Evidently the chain of intercessions failed to produce the petitioner's aim in this case; but the experience only underscores the importance of pursuing the right social contacts at the right time. With resources and authority predominantly located east of the Appalachians, westerners with eastern contacts played a crucial role in mediating the flow of patronage. This was just as true in peaceful moments as it was during times of strife. For example, the Supreme Executive Council, and after 1790 the governor, frequently had to make decisions regarding accusations of electoral "irregularities" in the contests for legislative and administrative offices of outlying counties. (Not surprisingly, such accusations typically came from the losing candidate or his associates.) Whether the Philadelphia authorities commissioned justices of the peace to investigate the accusations or made a determination immediately on the recommendation of westerners who were present in the capital, they relied on boundary-spanning political elites to settle such disputes.

By shifting some of the power to fill offices from legislators to the governor, the new state constitution of 1790 began to erode the basis on which mediators between western Pennsylvania and eastern elites built their influence. At the same time, active federal intervention in the struggle with Indians (in the form of federal Army expeditions in 1791, 1792, and 1794) diminished the importance of local leaders in securing militia funds from the governor. Finally, the relocation of the U.S. capital from New York to Philadelphia and the creation of a small but significant federal excise bureaucracy threatened to destroy the clientelistic resources available to elites without federal ties. The excise law gave tax inspectors the right to enter and search homes and to seize property (including the all-important still) if they determined that a violation of the tax law had occurred. In part, of course, public outcry over the law grew out of the standard political discourse available at the time: The threat of arbitrary search and seizure lay at the heart of anti-Federalist language, and denunciations of the excise couched in these terms were made all the more convincing by the recent experience with British officialdom. More significant, though, was the fact that it was completely beyond the (formal) authority of state-level officials to prevent federal tax inspectors from inflicting such indignities on their western constituents. The state excise tax had remained unenforceable in the west precisely because local elites with trans-Appalachian connections had used their control over the court system to protect delinquent distillers and those who attacked collectors. To the extent that the influence of these prominent men depended on their ability to shield constituents from the menace of the eastern legal establishment, the federal tax put their future as political brokers in doubt—unless they were linked through patronage connections to federal officers. For certain members of the western Pennsylvania elite, then, the danger of a federal bureaucracy with coercive authority was not that it would infringe on local liberties but that it would supplant those elites as arbiters of those liberties.

A specific empirical implication flows from this focus on the issue of control over the east–west boundary. Unlike the general political view summarized earlier (that is, the argument that rebel leaders were "office seekers"), the brokerage argument singles out a specific subgroup of the western elite as the most likely to pursue extralegal means of resisting the excise law: officeholders with ties to state-level politics in Philadelphia but no links to the federal government. Elite members with exclusively local roles had less to lose from the fact that federal authorities now had more power than state leaders, whereas those with positions in the federal government could only benefit. It was those in between—those whose influence had derived precisely from the fact that they *were* in between—whose structural position as political patrons faced the most severe threat and who consequently had the strongest reasons to become insurgents. In the next section I shall present systematic empirical evidence in support of this claim.

Determinants of Elite Insurgency

Extensive details concerning the data sources and coding procedures employed here are furnished in Gould 1996; I note here merely that the southwestern Pennsylvania political elite, which overlapped substantially with the economic elite (Harper 1991), was identified through archival records of officeholders in the region between 1783 and 1793. In my earlier study, I related insurgent participation to measures of wealth and political officeholding, along with position in the political patronage network as measured in terms of surety bonds posted by elite members on behalf of other officeholders. Here I restrict attention to wealth and position as defined by the locus of political authority: local, state, and federal.

Of thirty-nine elite members, seven played an active role as leaders of the Whiskey Rebellion: James Allison, David Bradford, John Cannon, Edward Cook, John McDowell, James Marshall, and Craig Ritchie. "Active role" means taking at least one of the following actions: commanding the armed groups that laid siege to the Neville mansion, chairing one or more of the meetings that immediately followed the burning of the Neville house, signing the illegal circular letter assembling the militia at Braddock's Field, or arranging the interception of the U.S. mail. The analyses reported here model insurgent leadership defined in this way as a function of economic resources (still ownership and number of slaves owned), overall political activity (total number of offices ever held), and state-level political activity (a dummy variable coded 1 if the elite member had ever served in the state legislature, 0 otherwise).[5]

The reasons for using these variables are as follows: First, to the extent that insurgency had anything to do with the whiskey excise, it is necessary to control for ownership of a still—even if, as I argued earlier, large property owners (who owned larger stills on average) stood to benefit from the burden the tax placed on small-scale producers. Second, total number of slaves owned is the best available proxy for overall wealth, a factor that should be controlled given that wealthier elite members might have had more to lose from insurgent activity. Third, the revisionist account, which focuses on the political ambitions of local leaders, implies that the most likely insurgents would be those members of the political elite with the fewest posts—in particular, men who possessed sufficient standing to consider themselves contenders for greater political power but who had not yet acquired offices east of the Appalachians. My account, in contrast, focuses on those whose eastern connections made them influential as mediators between the west and state-level elites in Philadelphia but who had no ties to federal elites and institutions. These elite members were the most vulnerable to a decline in influence as connections to federal authorities increased in importance relative to state-level ties. According to this view, the most important comparison is that between western elites with state-level offices and purely local elites. The five federal officers from the region can be assumed a priori to have had strong reasons to oppose the insurrection (which indeed they did), and they are accordingly not included in these analyses.

The logistic regression results, shown in Table 3.1, furnish strong support for the broker hypothesis and weak support at best for the economic and "office seeker" accounts of insurgent behavior. Across all the models in which it appears, the sign for the still-ownership term is positive, which would suggest increased odds of taking a leading role in the rebellion contingent on owning a still but for the fact that the point estimate for the coefficient is not significantly different from 0 at conventional significance levels. Slave ownership likewise exhibits an insignificant association with insurgent participation. There is no persuasive evidence, then, that economic position measured in either of these two ways was related to participation in the insurrection.

The analysis further shows that, controlling for still ownership and membership in the state legislature, each additional political office held by an elite member decreased odds of insurgent participation by 64 percent. (Logit coefficients describe the change in the log of the odds of the outcome variable as-

Table 3.1 Logistic Regression Models of Insurgent Participation (standard errors in parentheses)

Variable	Model 1	Model 2	Model 3	Model 4	Model 5
Still ownership	1.15 (1.03)		.98 (1.03)		.69 (1.08)
Number of slaves	−.02 .17	.10 (.15)		.24 (.19)	.17 (.20)
Total offices held		−.27 (.51)	−1.02 (.73)	−1.18 (.73)	−1.12 (.75)
State legislature			2.77** (1.36)	3.66** (1.54)	3.32** (1.65)
Constant	−1.59	−.91	−.41	−.85	−.82
−2*log-likelihood	32.20	35.90	26.26	26.27	25.53
Improvement chi-square	1.42 (d.f. = 2)	.81 (d.f. = 2)	7.36* (d.f. = 3)	10.43** (d.f. = 3)	8.09* (d.f. = 4)
N	32	39	32	39	32

Note: The number of observations is smaller for models in which a coefficient for still ownership is estimated because this information is unavailable for elite members in Westmoreland County.

*$p < .10$

**$p < .05$

sociated with a unit change in an independent variable x_i. Thus for any value of x_i, say a, exponentiating the coefficient b_i thus yields the ratio of the odds given by $a + 1$ to the odds associated with a. In this case, $e^{-1.02} = .36$). Here again, however, the coefficient estimate is not significant even at the .10 level. Elimination of measurement error—hardly a simple matter for data of this kind—might increase our confidence about the importance of this factor.[6]

The evidence concerning elite members with state-level but not federal offices is much more unambiguous. In all five estimated models, past or present occupancy of a seat in the state legislature dramatically increased the odds of taking a leading role in the insurrection. For instance, the coefficient estimate of 2.77 in Model 3 means that, all else equal, elite members with state but not federal connections were well over ten times more likely than other elites to take part in the uprising ($e^{2.77} = 15.9$).

Brokerage, Ambiguity, and Insurgency

The evidence presented in the previous section shows with considerable clarity that western Pennsylvania elite members were particularly likely to become actively involved in the Whiskey Rebellion if they had held political offices primarily at the state level. Owning a still does not appear to have mattered much for elite members (though it probably did make a difference for insurgent participation among small-scale farmers), and those who had occupied numerous offices—controlling for the level of those offices—may have been somewhat less likely to join the insurgent effort.

My interpretation has thus succeeded in identifying a key dimension along which insurgents and noninsurgents differed prior to the events of July and August 1794. Western elites who had already held federal offices were securely tied to the individuals and organizations that would increasingly determine how resources and patronage would be distributed both in eastern and western Pennsylvania. Though these connections might have been an important source of prestige prior to the 1791 excise law, they had not made much of a difference when it came to supplying local clienteles with what mattered most to them: a reliable flow of resources to battle (and sometimes steal from) the Indians populating the frontier area and legal protection against penalties for tax resistance and other forms of transgression. The most valuable positions to occupy in this regard had been state offices, whose holders were able to channel resources westward and offer particularistic sponsorship to clients aspiring to local judgeships and other offices. Until 1791, then, anyone with a durable tie to state officials in Philadelphia was assured a significant role as broker between the west and the east. With the arrival of excise officers, the vanguard of what we can retrospectively see as a major national state-building enterprise, the situation changed drastically. If the process were to continue (as it of course did), elites with exclusively state-oriented social contacts would be thoroughly eclipsed as brokers by those with access to federal circles; even their local clients would see little advantage in remaining loyal if they could more fruitfully attach themselves to patrons with federal ties (Gould 1996). It is this shift in the locus of authority, together with its impact on patron–client relations—specifically, the devaluation of contacts at the state level in favor of federal ties—that accounts for the participation in heterodox collective action of a particular segment of the western elite.

But why insurrection? Just as it fails to furnish an independent basis for distinguishing rebel leaders from mere petition signers, the "political" interpretation of the Whiskey Rebellion glosses all too easily over the puzzle I raised at the beginning of this chapter. For someone seeking election to political office, it would surely not be wise to engage in overtly illegal (in fact treasonous) military actions, no matter how much local popularity might accrue to a person who did so. Indeed, the elections of the autumn of 1794, which sent two prominent insurgents to the state legislature, were voided by the federal government—an outcome that could hardly have come as a surprise to westerners, who knew that they were participating in a quasi revolution. Observing that anti-excise talk and activity made local leaders popular with western farmers is clearly insufficient as an explanation for elite involvement in insurgent collective action. Given that, before the fact, failure must have appeared to be about as likely as success, western leaders must have seen something potentially useful even in presiding over a defeat.[7]

Here again, the brokerage account sheds valuable light. If elite members with eastern ties could use these connections to enhance their positions in the west, they could equally well take advantage of their local influence to convince an uneasy eastern establishment that they were indispensable to the integrity of the federal system. With few channels of communication between Philadelphia and the trans-Appalachian section of Pennsylvania, it was at least reasonable for western leaders to imagine that they could simultaneously appear to be friends of order to the former audience and champions of tax resistance to the latter. The fact of assuming the leadership of a band of angry farmers could, depending on the circumstance, be construed as a bold act of insurrection or as a brave and altruistic bid to stave off civil war. If resistance was successful in forcing Congress to repeal the tax, these leaders could claim credit; but if the rebels capitulated, the same individuals could claim to have been instrumental in persuading them to do so. In the latter instance, federal officials might have to recognize the importance of such leaders in ensuring the governability of western farmers.

There is some evidence that this two-sided game was very much on the minds of the principals. For example, the following message was posted publicly a few days after the militia march through Pittsburgh and the destruction of Abraham Kirkpatrick's barn:

> We, the undersigned, on behalf of ourselves and the great body of the column that marched from Braddock's Field on the 3rd of Aug. 1794, think it necessary to express our disapprobation of the disorderly proceeding of those of the troops who were concerned in setting fire to the house of Abraham Kirkpatrick, on the hill opposite the town of Pittsburgh, also of the attempt made by others of burning his house in the town, as these acts was not within the sentence of the committee of volunteers in Braddock's Field, and therefore, there could be no authority for carrying them into effect. We consider it as a blemish on the good order of the march of the column through the town of Pittsburgh, and their cantonment in the neighborhood of it. It has been endeavored to be removed as much as possible by repaying the tenant of Kirkpatrick his damages. (Quoted in Creigh 1870, appendix, 72)

Fifteen men signed the message, most of them well-known officeholders and landowners. Several (notably Absalom Baird and John Hamilton) held key militia posts in one or another of the western counties and were thus implictly accountable for the actions of militia companies. The group also included James Marshall and Edward Cook, two of the most active leaders of the insurrection: Not only had both chaired meetings leading up to and following the march through Pittsburgh, but Marshall had signed the militia circular letter calling for the march, and Cook had been named marshal of the Braddock's Field assemblage. The point of the disclaimer should be clear: Elite participants in the event were dissociating themselves from overt violence and simultaneously arguing that the majority of the insurgents were following their sober lead. Attacks on property were to be attributed to the actions of a small band of hotheads, not to the insurgent rank and file as a whole. Elite insurgents hoped to convince the public and the eastern authorities that but for their involvement, things might have turned out far worse for Pittsburgh.

Similarly, after the insurrection's collapse nearly every western leader claimed to have been publicly opposed to the excise while working privately and subtly toward conciliation and compromise. Most, in fact, had appeared at public meetings urging tax resisters to sign the oath of submission, arguing that this was the only way to prevent a deadly civil war. (Note that the weight that this argument would carry with local farmers was probably enhanced by an elite member's past actions in opposition to the tax—thereby reinforcing the image of such leaders as influential figures who ought to be taken seriously by federal officers in the east.) Only one prominent officeholder, David Bradford, had publicly, unambiguously, and repeatedly advocated armed struggle against the federal government, and he was one of the rebels who fled westward with a price on his head. In a few cases, it appears that elite claims of having encouraged moderation were accurate; this was most notably true of the federal legislators William Findley and Albert Gallatin. In most of the other cases, however, the historical record remains fundamentally ambiguous. Historians of the event have generally endeavored to give an answer one way or the other with respect to specific leaders (see, most recently, Slaughter 1986, 183–84). My point, of course, is that the ambiguity is itself the answer, along with the boundary that made it possible.

Conclusion

My purpose in this article has been twofold: to make sense of a key moment in the history of political contention in the United States and to illustrate the merits of a general argument about the role of network structure in constituting the interests and identities that shape individual decisions about whether to engage in protest.[8] I have addressed the first of these goals in the preceding pages and consequently devote these last paragraphs to the second goal.

Students of social conflict tend to work with only a handful of heuristics for describing the ways in which groups of people coalesce into collective actors. These include above all the familiar triumvirate of class, gender, and race, with occasional nods to ethnicity, nation, and religion. Recognizing that these dimensions do not exhaust the possibilities for loyalty or hostility and that even within this narrow set there are multiple ways for conflict to be understood, some scholars have embraced a radically constructivist view of identity by arguing that our attention ought to focus on the cultural and discursive practices through which forms of difference are produced. In concentrating on the network context of collective action, I have implicitly accepted the premise on which this argument is based while challenging the pure culturalism for which it calls. That is, I acknowledge that people may understand their positions in social settings in ways that are not uniformly determined by relations of production, racial distinctions, anatomical differences, and so forth, either jointly or singly. But at the same time, I have offered evidence here and elsewhere (Gould 1995a) that people do not freely assemble their collective identities through unconstrained ideational bricolage; instead, they are powerfully influenced by the patterns of social relationships in which they are implicated, in the sense that these patterns govern the plausibility of various identifications.[9]

Attending to the role of social networks in the formation of collective identities is thus critical on two levels. On the first level, as I have just noted, detailed knowledge about patterns of social relations yields essential insight into the reasons why class, gender, racial, regional, religious, or ethnic differences translate into open conflict in some contexts but not others. In the case studied here, the existence of a profound network barrier between east and west allowed a political dispute to escalate to such a point that the U.S. Army was deployed within the nation's borders, setting a precedent for the Civil War. But the significance of network structure for culturally meaningful identities makes possible a second-order form of collective identity—that is, one that derives directly from the network itself rather than from a preexisting cultural framework for establishing difference. As far as it is possible to ascertain from the historical record, the brokers I have identified as the leaders of the Whiskey Rebellion were culturally and economically indistinguishable from other members of the political elite who opted for order. Their reasons for becoming insurgents are instead traceable to their network position—a position whose importance derived principally from (1) the relational boundary between their western clients and eastern patrons and (2) their threatened exclusion from the set of social relations through which federal patronage would henceforth flow.

Notes

The author wishes to thank Doug McAdam, Bill Roy, members of the Organizations and Statebuilding Workshop at the University of Chicago, and the editors of this volume for their helpful comments on an earlier draft of this paper.

1. Likewise, complete autonomy, an option at which a few of the bolder insurgents hinted, would have eliminated the advantages accruing to brokers and made them indistinguishable from those with purely local influence.

2. The scandal surrounding political patronage during Jackson's presidency presumably came not from the growth of the practice in this period but from the emergence of the idea that it was a form of corruption.

3. Some natives engaged in unprovoked and murderous attacks on whites as well. These were redressed not in court, however, but through mob justice.

4. Wallace is said to have later discovered his wife's dress at Gnadenhutten, a Moravian Christian Indian community, and participated in the infamous massacre of nearly a hundred of the settlement's residents.

5. Even though occupancy of any given office was temporary, the social contacts such positions facilitated were cumulative in the sense that social ties forged while holding office survived after the term had expired. It is thus more sensible to view variables such as total offices held as measures of social capital—network ties—rather than of formal authority. This reasoning also justifies counting a currently occupied state office in the same way as a formerly held state office: What we are observing, albeit indirectly, is not formal authority but access to influential others.

6. Note that I am paying attention to tests of statistical significance for reasons that are rather different from those typically invoked in social science research. The data do not reflect a sample drawn at random from a large population of individuals but, rather, the universe of political leaders in the four western counties of Pennsylvania in the 1780s and early 1790s. Statistical significance of a coefficient estimate is therefore not taken to imply that under a null model of no relationship, samples of the same size could be expected to yield coefficients of at least the observed magnitude with probability less than $\propto$. The logic for interpreting these findings rests instead on a probabilistic interpretation of the behavior of the actual set of individuals represented in the data. In other words, the null model for any particular variable is that the a priori odds of becoming an insurgent leader were no different for those with one value of the variable than for those with another value. The observed values of the dependent variable are then realizations of the underlying stochastic process. If these observations differ for enough individuals who, say, owned stills, we can conclude that the underlying odds for still owners were *not* the same as the underlying odds for non still owners. What makes the analysis probabilistic, in other words, is not that the data might have come from another sample but that the actual behavior of the very same people might have differed if a few substantively insignificant (that is, "chance") circumstances had been different.

7. There is always the possibility, of course, that these men were simply unbalanced—an

accusation that many have leveled at least at David Bradford. But most of them were considered "respectable," even by Alexander Hamilton. It is difficult to reconcile this characterization with an account of insurgent activity predicated on confusion or mental instability.

8. In one sense, this goal is not twofold at all: It seems to me to be incumbent upon historical sociologists to relate any explanations they offer for the specific events they study to a more abstract conceptual framework.

9. One simple example is that of a worker who resists class identification either because of a close tie to his or her employer or because of relational barriers—along gender, ethnic, or craft lines—within the category of laborers.

Chapter 4

Collective Protest and the Waning of the Communist State in China

Andrew G. Walder

The spectacular collapse of European communist regimes in the fall of 1989 immediately brings to mind images of large street demonstrations in Leipzig and Prague and the storming of Communist Party headquarters in Bucharest. These instances of defiance are linked in our historical memory with Poland's earlier Solidarity movement—which mounted a remarkable nationwide challenge to the party-state in 1980–81 and which eventually triumphed after a decade of repression—and we have already woven a historical narrative in which collective protest and popular resistance take center stage. In this narrative the story line is the triumph of "society" over the "state"—not just any state, but one of history's most thoroughly organized and effectively repressive dictatorships. The master plot is one in which ordinary citizens, initially through small individual acts of resistance and then through the creation of informal networks and overtly "nonpolitical" forms of activity, are able to create for themselves an enlarging public sphere of action and thought, alternative identities and political languages, which eventually are enlarged to the point of effective collective action in the final challenge to the state (Arato 1981; Brovkin 1990; Brødsgaard 1992; Hável et al. 1985; Mastnak 1990). A number of arresting epigrams now champion this image of Lilliputian activity in the downfall of Leviathan: "the advantages of being atomized" (Rev 1987), "the weapons of the weak" (Scott 1985, 1990), "the society with a strategy—antipolitics" (Konrád 1984), the "triumph of civil society" (Arato 1981), and "the quiet revolution from below" (Szelényi 1988).

This resolutely bottom-up view has inspired excellent studies of the organization and strategy of Solidarity and of the role of social networks in less formally organized instances of collective action (Ost 1990). One of the more intriguing innovations of some of this work has been an emphasis on what might be called the "cultural" dimensions of political mobilizations: the "framing" of mass appeals; the use of traditional symbolism; the borrowing of historically legitimate repertoires of protest. These are interesting variations on themes long familiar to students of Charles Tilly: collective organizational capacity, the role of network ties in group mobilization, custom and tradition, and historical repertoires of collective action and contention.

Whereas these studies of collective protest emphasize familiar themes, a broader Tillyan perspective suggests that we view this inspiring bottom-up perspective on the demise of communist states with some skepticism. Doesn't the emergence of collective action also depend crucially upon opportunities provided by existing political arrangements or by the temporary suspension or immobilization of the state's repressive capacity? Doesn't the success of challenging groups depend crucially upon the availability of coalition partners elsewhere in the polity, especially within the regime itself (Tilly 1978c)? Isn't the historical rise and fall of states also a story about the rise and decline of organizations designed to extract revenue, administer territory, and compete with other nation-states, both economically and militarily—organizations that have their own internal dynamic that operates independently of popular pressures (Tilly 1990a)? Though it is true that collective protest contributes to regime change, it is also true that collective action itself is a "tracer" of historical change—a political expression of underlying shifts in the structures of the state, in the control of economic and political resources, or in patterns of political opportunity (Tilly, Tilly, and Tilly 1975; Tilly 1986a). We may legitimately ask whether the collective protests of 1989 were not as much a symptom as a cause of the deterioration of communist states.

Let us not forget that 1989's largest and longest wave of collective protest was in China. Demonstrations by university students in Beijing in the last half of April drew increasing public support from the working population of the capital. By the week of the student hunger strike the second week of May, Tiananmen, the city's central square, was continuously occupied by hundreds of thousands of students and citizens. Delegations of students from other provinces swarmed into Beijing to join those from the capital already encamped in the square. Workers and staff from large state factories, research academies, newspapers, and radio stations formed large delegations that marched in long street processions in support of the striking students' demands. Students and wage earners in at least eighty other cities in China followed suit, staging their own smaller sit-ins and similar processions of supporters. In the large inland cities of Xi'an, Changsha, and Chengdu the processions degenerated into riots after confrontations with police forces. In the capital and throughout the country students and ordinary citizens began to form themselves into a bewilderingly large array of new political organizations in order to carry forward the protests against Beijing hard-liners' refusal to negotiate. For weeks the central government was divided and paralyzed, unable to control the streets of the capital. Harsh rhetoric and the declaration of martial law accompanied the dispatch of armed troops into the city on May 19, but the effort failed as tens of thousands of ordinary citizens blocked army columns in the streets of the city's outer neighborhoods, and the local press reported widespread fraternization among the citizens and soldiers, with several officers pledging to the crowds that the People's Army would not fire on the people (Walder 1989a). If ever there was a massive popular awakening in which "society" rose up to confront a corrupt and recalcitrant regime, this was it—and several observers of these events described them in precisely these terms (Strand 1990; Sullivan 1990). Yet as we know, this massive political awakening did not lead to the scripted triumph of "society." A ruthless military operation in the capital on June 3–4 crushed the demonstrations, and hard-line communists regained political ascendancy.

From the perspective of Beijing, the emphasis on the irresistible causal force of a politically mobilized population seems badly misplaced. Viewed from the east, what is remarkable about the collapse of communism in Europe in 1989 is how *little* collective organization and mass mobilization was required to bring once fearsome regimes to their knees and how easily the leaders of these regimes capitulated, for the street demonstrations in East Germany, Czechoslovakia, and Romania were by Chinese standards relatively small (even controlling for population differences!), isolated geographically, not highly organized, and short in duration. And let us not forget that by the fall of 1989 a negotiated transfer of power through free elections was already under way in two key countries in the region. In Poland this was the delayed aftermath of a massive and sustained political mobilization under Solidarity. In Hungary popular political mobilization played a relatively small role in that nation's political evolution toward multiparty rule (Bruszt 1991; Bartlett 1995). Clearly, other important forces were at work that served to bring down the regimes of eastern Europe—forces that affected the cohesion of these regimes independently of the popular organization and protests that they faced at the end.

Closer examination of the Chinese upheaval reveals that these "other important forces" can in fact be seen as *causes* of the massive popular mobilization. Preexisting divisions within the leadership of the party and a prior weakening of discipline and control within the party-state apparatus served to create opportunities for collective protest by immobilizing the state's forces of repression. More important, however, members of the state apparatus itself—especially editors and reporters in the nation's newspapers and television stations, and also the managers and party secretaries of large state enterprises—either actively used their resources to mobilize citizens against hard-liners within the party leadership or permitted protest delegations to use state resources in their protest activities. The popular political mobilization of April reached massive proportions in May because key members of the party-state apparatus, whose loyalty and discipline were among the distinctive features of communist regimes in a past era, defected from the regime and used their considerable resources in highly effective and visible ways. In a very real sense, the long-term evolution away from strict discipline and control within the party apparatus in the post-Mao years, combined with short-term divisions among the leadership, emerged as a crucial cause of popular political mobilization. In place of a "bottom-up" process in which "society" organizes itself to push back "the state," we observe an "inside-out" process in which divisions, conflicts, and organizational decline within the regime itself interact with nascent popular mobilization to greatly magnify both the scale and effects of that mobilization.

The result is a Tillyan perspective on 1989 in which collective protest is placed firmly within a broader historical framework and in which the networks and organizations of "challengers" to a polity are part of a seamless web of causal forces that includes both the organizational capacities (or incapacities) of the state itself and the political conflicts within it. Within this framework, our appreciation of the impact of protest upon the regime is tempered by an awareness of the impact that the regime itself has upon the pattern and scale of protest. In this chapter I will offer a historical narrative that emphasizes the ways in which China's 1989 upheaval was an expression of a prior decline in the cohesion of the state's organizations and of short-term divisions among its top leaders. First, I will show how the regime's own mass media publicized the split in the party's leadership and mobilized citizens to action. Second, I will describe the ways that the leaders of important state organizations and enterprises acquiesced in the use of state resources in protest delegations, helping to turn a once formidable mechanism of political control into a setting that facilitated collective organization and group identity. And third, to counter the common impression that the protests of ordinary citizens were not as well organized as those of students, I will describe the profusion of popular organizations that rapidly emerged in response to the opportunities and media rhetoric of May.

Leadership Division and the Defection of the Mass Media

The evident disintegration of party unity after the first week of May is perhaps the most important cause of the size and tenacity of the protest movement, especially its paradoxical growth after the May 19 declaration of martial law. The student demonstrators' invocation of the memory and progressive political legacy of former party general secretary Hu Yaobang drove wedges into an already divided party. Significant portions of the party-state apparatus openly supported the student campaign. Especially important was the defection of key organizations in the mass media, which on the eve of Mikhail Gorbachev's visit began to report openly and sympathetically on the growing demonstrations. This reportage helped to magnify public sympathy and involvement and, during a pivotal period, made it appear that the demonstrations might succeed in toppling the hard-line leadership.

It is apparent that the regime, beginning in the weeks leading up to martial law, was grappling with divided sovereignty in two respects. First, the Politburo Standing Committee itself found its powers usurped by Deng Xiaoping and members of the senior advisory group. This usurpation lasted a period of weeks, during which time there was no clear political center. Second, once these party elders, whose power rested not on formal position but on personal influence, forged an alliance with Premier Li Peng, President Yang Shangkun, and others, many of the personal followers of Zhao Ziyang and Hu Qili, who headed leading central and provincial institutions, including part of the armed forces, contested the rule of Premier Li Peng and the Politburo majority manufactured by Deng. In essence, key governmental institutions—such as the Foreign Ministry and leading newspapers—resisted the directives of the Li Peng government. The true magnitude and shape of this divided sovereignty is still not entirely clear, but a divided party and state apparatus played a central role in feeding the popular rebellion.

Beijing's mass media—local and national newspapers, the New China News Agency, and national radio and television—also played a major role in mobilizing popular protest, initially through accurate and sympathetic reporting on the student demonstrations and the popular response and later by openly challenging the party leaders who ordered martial law. As early as April 24, such newspapers as Shanghai's *World Economic Herald* and Beijing's *Science and Technology Daily* ventured sympathetic reports on the student protests, drawing the ire of officials (*New York Times,* April 25, 1989). However, the official media remained hostile or silent on the student movement and followed the line enunciated in the *People's Daily* editorial of April 26, which attacked the students for engaging in a "planned conspiracy" aimed at overthrowing the party, until May 4, when Zhao Ziyang, speaking at the reception for members of the Asian Development Bank, declared that "the just demands of the students must be met" and that "we should solve the problem in a democratic and legal way" (Walder 1989a).

During this time, the student demonstrations were massive and enjoyed clear popular support. In the demonstration of April 27, tens of thousands of students and their supporters marched through the streets for hours, repeatedly breaking through police barricades to fill Tiananmen Square. On May 4, hundreds of thousands of students and supporters again marched, and this time they were joined by organized intellectuals and journalists under banners of their own and by young workers who "easily outnumbered" the students *(Washington Post,* May 5, 1989; *New York Times,* May 5, 1989).

Despite the enormous size of the demonstrations, they did not yet constitute a popular rebellion. They would become one only after the protesters came to see themselves as having the clear sympathy of one wing of the party and government apparatus and as helping this faction in its fight against the conservatives. This process began after Zhao's May 4 speech, which was followed by a series of conciliatory statements about "patriotic" students that continued up to May 17. Beginning on May 5 the official media began to run brief but objective reports on student activities and demands; by May 9 the reports had become longer and more detailed, leading quickly to actively sympathetic media coverage for a period of about two weeks, ending on May 25 *(Washington Post,* May 5, 10, 1989; *New York Times,* May 10, 1989).

At two distinct points, the suddenly independent and assertive mass media played a pivotal role in the development of the popular rebellion. First, from around May 13 through May 19, the media's detailed and sympathetic reporting riveted the city's attention on the drama of the hunger strikers, building a huge groundswell of popular support and openly seeking to pressure top leaders to reverse their intransigent stand against negotiations. During this period, for the first time, protest marches swelled to 1 million or more (on May 15, 17, and 18). White- and blue-collar workers, professionals, and cadres began to march under banners naming their workplaces (including at least eight agencies of the central government), and a force of several hundred thousand began to occupy the square continuously *(New York Times,* May 16, 18, and 19, 1989; *Washington Post,* May 17, 1989). During this period the people of Beijing were told by their press and television that "hundreds of thousands" or "more than a million people" "from all walks of life" were going to the main square "to show their support for the students."

Having so effectively mobilized public opinion for the cause of the students (and by extension for the cause of liberalization and reform), in mid-May Beijing's mass media also laid the foundation for massive popular resistance to the martial law that began in the early-morning hours of May 20. This second stage marked the start of an open popular rebellion against the Li Peng–Deng Xiaoping faction. Until troops moved into the compounds of broadcasting stations and newspapers on May 25 (*Washington Post,* May 25, 1989), the mass media openly encouraged resistance to martial law, making it appear that practically the entire capital was united in opposition against it.

During this week hundreds of thousands of students and ordinary citizens continued to demonstrate in the square, while massive numbers of other demonstrators rushed to countless barricades throughout the city to block troop movements. People could read and hear in the official media that the masses were opposed to martial law and that military officers were pledged not to attack the demonstrators. Photographs in newspapers showed citizens and soldiers fraternizing at the barricades. New China News Agency reports claimed that more than 1 million people marched in the streets to oppose martial law on May 23, when foreign observers put the number at 100,000, and the agency's interviews with citizens on the street directly refuted the rationale for martial law (*Washington Post,* May 23, 1989).

Mobilization in Government Agencies and Workplaces

The response of China's urban workers to the students' demonstrations, and especially to the hunger strike and the publicity surrounding it, must be understood against the background of the prior deterioration of the party hierarchy and the open divisions publicized in the mass media. During the 1980s enterprise managers were released from the tight grid of restrictions created by the past system of central planning and party supervision and were made increasingly responsible for the performance of their firms and the welfare of their employees. The Communist Party's formerly central role in the enterprise had eroded, especially the politicized reward system that characterized Chinese enterprises in the 1960s and 1970s. Managers' former role as disciplined agents of party and state organs was exchanged for a new role as representatives of the interests of their enterprise, including, to a considerable extent, as representatives of the interests of their employees (Walder 1989b, 1991).

The Impact of the Student Movement in Factories

Throngs of workers lined the streets, cheered on the student marchers, and helped clear police barriers in the pivotal and defiant demonstration of April 27. Workers performed the same roles, while also donating money and food to students and joining in behind the student ranks, in the huge march of May 4. But factories were not greatly affected by the movement until after May 4, the day that Zhao Ziyang declared the student demands "patriotic," permitting national newspapers and television stations to broadcast objective (and later openly sympathetic) accounts of the student movement. At this point workers began to receive abundant information about the student protests and their aims.

The first response among many workers was sympathy, a feeling that was intensifed by the nature of the media coverage. A second response, common especially after the beginning of the hunger strike on May 13, was surprise and wonder at the spectacle unfolding on the square. As May progressed, work slowed as workers talked excitedly in groups about what was going on. As many of the former pillars of party rule—such as newspapers and television stations, retired generals, and members of the National People's Congress—expressed public sympathy for the student demands for negotiation, groups of workers in hundreds of workplaces throughout the city began to form "sympathy brigades" (*shengyuan tuan*), make up banners, collect donations, and request that their factory directors lend them trucks to drive to the square in a show of support (Walder 1991).

The Response of Managers to the Movement

Some managers publicly supported the student demand for negotiation and urged moderation on the part of both the government and the protesters. Ten directors of large enterprises in Beijing published an appeal to this effect in *Guangming ribao* (Wu et al. 1989, 251). Managers of at least one Beijing factory—the Beijing Coking Plant—personally led the entire workforce out to march on the square. And the Beijing workers I have interviewed all relate that many of their managers, from shop director up, expressed sympathy for the students in unmistakable ways, although they cautiously refrained from taking any open public stance or organizing any activities themselves.

Here is the point at which the gradual relaxation of bureaucratic controls over factories and the weakening of factory party organizations played an important role. Once it was clear that a major popular challenge was under way and that the government was divided, many managers prudently stepped aside to await the outcome. They did so despite a prior series of Beijing municipal government regulations strictly forbidding any factory personnel to participate in demonstrations or show any other expressions of sympathy and despite Li Peng's personal visit of May 13 to Capital Steel to ensure that workers remain at their posts (Wu et al. 1989, 267; *Jingji ribao* 1989, 131–33).

State Factories as Organizing Centers for Protest

By mid-May the support for students evident in the news media and among other government institutions, combined with factory cadres' general hesitance to enforce standing orders not to permit workers to demonstrate, allowed workers in Beijing and many other cities to stage a massive outpouring of support. Long the linchpin of social and political control in urban China, in mid-May 1989 work units suddenly became centers of political organizing and protest. The characteristic form of protest in the week preceding the declaration of martial law was the organized work unit delegation. As hundreds of such delegations from factories and other work units filled the streets in the huge demonstrations of May 14 through 18, the student protests were transformed into a broad popular movement.

According to official accounts published after June 4, over 700 work units sent delegations into the streets that week, at least 160 of which were from industrial plants or other enterprises (*Guojia jiaowei* 1989, 137). In the demonstrations of May 17 and 18, both of which were estimated to number more than a million people, Beijing Jeep Corporation sent over 3,000 workers in identical uniforms, all marching and shouting slogans in unison. Among the factories that sent large delegations were some of the city's largest heavy industrial concerns: Beijing Crane, Beijing Construction Machinery, Beijing Internal Combustion Engine, and (on several occasions) the Capital Steel Corporation. As heavy rain began to fall during one of the demonstrations, employees of the Beijing City Bus Company drove ninety vehicles to the square for the students to use as shelter, and the Beijing Oxygen Bottling Plant sent tanks of oxygen with which to revive hunger strikers (Wu et al. 1989, 264).

The Beijing scenes of mid-May were repeated, albeit on a smaller scale, in other large cities throughout the nation. On May 18 alone, over 50,000 people marched in Shanghai and Xi'an, with delegations of factory workers prominently represented. Marches of some 10,000 were reported in at least fourteen other cities (*Guojia jiaowei* 1989, 135–37). These work unit delegations were expressly political. They marched to the square in support of students, not as workers with separate grievances of their own. They demanded that the government negotiate student demands and expressed their heartfelt support of the "elder brothers." They repeated student slogans that called for an end to official corruption and speculation and called for greater democracy and freedom. In light of the evident sympathy expressed by the mass media, these workers must have felt that their actions were supported from above and therefore had a real chance of success.

The Rapid Rise of Popular Political Organization

Few observers of the political upheaval of 1989 have failed to remark on the massive popular response to student protests throughout the country. Some have argued that the primary novelty and political significance of 1989 lie in the scope of this popular response and not in the student movement itself. Yet even those who have emphasized popular participation in 1989 have portrayed ordinary citizens primarily as players in a national media drama centered on the student movement, especially the hunger strike of mid-May.

The idea that popular protest played a key supporting role in student demonstrations is not without foundation, but it neglects a very important phenomenon: Ordinary urban citizens were not simply mobilized by students into public demonstrations; they were also active in organizing themselves into a wide variety of associations with a broad array of purposes. Within a mere seven weeks, between the death of Hu Yaobang on April 15 and the military operation of June 4, thousands of citizen associations were formed by workers and other "city people" (*shimin*). Some of these organizations were self-defense groups, designed to keep order at demonstrations, to protect students and other protesters from police suppression, and, if necessary, to confront the military and police. Others were protest brigades formed to take part in public demonstrations in support of student demands. Others were political associations and proto-parties, organizations designed to further political ends beyond the mere acceptance of student demands. And still others organized themselves into embryonic labor unions with explicit political and economic demands.

This phenomenon is important not simply because the propensity of ordinary citizens to form political associations has been obscured in the glare of publicity focused upon the students. It is important for another reason: These organized citizens did not merely support student demands; they forwarded distinct demands of their own. Past portrayals of city residents as a strong supporting cast in a national political drama neglect the fact that these actors often were working from a different script. City people refused to limit themselves to the subservient roles of disciplined cheering section, human shields, and generous donors that student leaders had assigned them from the outset. These popular tendencies created some tension with the student movement and led some citizen groups explicitly to reject the elite-dominated game that they felt the students were playing.

Types of Popular Organization

It appears plausible that in the hothouse atmosphere of the spring of 1989 perhaps as many as a thousand groups of workers or other city people may have formed for political action. More than ten such organizations achieved some publicity in both Beijing and Shanghai. A survey of all province-level newspapers for the month of June 1989 alone yielded a list of eighty-eight separate political organizations of workers or city people in public arrest reports. Autonomous labor unions were reported in nineteen provinces, with two or more reported in several cities. These reports make clear that this list is only a minority of the organizations active in 1989, primarily those in provincial capitals targeted by local bureaus of public security. In Hebei it was reported that "various organizations" in the province had called themselves "autonomous workers' federations"(*Hebei ribao,* June 11, 1989); "various autonomous workers' federations" formed in the factories of Wuhan (*Hubei ribao,* June 16, 1989) and were prominent among the thirty-four "illegal organizations" broken up by the Liaoning Bureau of Public Security by mid-June (*Liaoning ribao,* June 21, 1989). A more extensive survey of the provincial press and of prefectural and county-level newspapers would no doubt increase this number by severalfold, and the majority of protest groups that formed during the period probably dispersed without leaving a trace on the historical record.

It is nonetheless evident from the sample of organizations that we have identified that these groups varied widely in their size, longevity, activities, and aims. There are four types (see Walder 1992, tables 1–4). I shall offer a description of the social base, purposes, and political activities of each type of group, to the extent that this can be determined.

Picket Corps and Dare-to-Die Corps: Organizing for Self-Defense

The first type of citizens' group might be termed a "self-defense organization." The distinguishing feature of such a group is that it came together for the explicit purpose of protecting demonstrators or keeping public order around demonstration sites. The self-defense groups appear overwhelmingly to be composed of single males under the age of thirty, but they varied considerably in size, duration of existence, formality of organization, and activities. Those established before martial law was declared in Beijing were generally called "picket corps" (*jiucha dui*) and were formally organized with recognized leaders, and the larger ones, which in Beijing claimed hundreds of members, formally divided into named subunits. Those established after the declaration of martial law on May 20 were usually called "dare-to-die corps" (*gansi dui*) and were smaller and more informally organized. These groups established a continuing presence in the central squares of cities where student protesters were camped or engaged in hunger strikes, and they sought to keep order in the crowds and to protect protesters from arrest. In some cases where protesters were arrested, they confronted public security forces. After the declaration of martial law in Beijing, these groups became more numerous (especially *gansi dui* variety) and mobile, shuttling around the city to confront advancing troops or to reinforce barricades at intersections. In Beijing, in addition, the resistance to martial law troops was enforced throughout the city by unnamed neighborhood-level organizations that sprang up throughout the city immediately after the declaration of martial law. These organizations set up barricades at intersections and maintained twenty-four-hour watches (*Zongzheng wenhua bu* 1989). After the final advance of troops into Beijing on June 3, the mobile dare-to-die corps helped take the lead in violent resistance to the troops' advance, and in Shanghai, Xi'an, and elsewhere new dare-to-die corps sprang up to paralyze public transportation and otherwise protest news of the massacre in Beijing (Warner 1990; Esherick 1990).

Protest Brigades: Demonstrating for the Students

A second kind of citizens' organization is the one I shall label "protest brigades." The distinguishing feature of such groups is that they came together for purposes of public demonstration in support of student demands or in sympathy with student hunger strikers. The vast majority of such organizations were protest groups that coalesced within work units in mid-May to march under banners naming their places of work. Others, however, were not expressions of work unit solidarity but were creatures of the free space created in public squares throughout China by the presence of student protesters and large crowds of onlookers and supporters. Some of these organizations maintained an organized presence in public squares throughout the period of public protest and took part in many marches and demonstrations. As they did so, they would take on additional aims and activities and come to resemble other types of organizations. Some protest groups, such as those in Shanghai and Xi'an, for example, turned into de facto self-defense organizations after June 4 and took to street barricades to resist the impositions of the "fascist regime."

Public demonstrations throughout the country were in large measure processions of informally constituted sympathy brigades formed in places of work. The delegations typically marched under banners naming their places of work, often using vehicles and materials from the work unit. Workers and staff who sympathized with the student movement would typically collect donations from coworkers, draw up banners, and request factory vehicles and permission to go to the square. In Beijing over 100 garbage trucks joined one of the street processions, and the first two trucks carried a banner reading "Fellow classmates, we sanitation workers have come out too late." Ten large cement mixers from one of the city's construction companies joined the procession, sounding their air horns, revving their engines, and drawing a lot of attention (Li et al. 1989, 114–29). Such sympathy brigades made a huge public impression, but they do not appear to have lasted beyond the one or two marches in which they took part, and this variety of sympathy brigade disappeared shortly after the declaration of martial law.

Political Associations and Proto-Parties: Organizing for Political Change

The third kind of popular political organization is the political association, or "proto-party." The distinguishing features of this type are that it is formally organized and that it has political aims that go beyond the mere expression of sympathy for student demands. Some of these organizations grew out of the activities stimulated in public squares by the student demonstrations. Others were in fact established earlier in the spring, or in some cases before, and experienced a spurt of growth during the period of street protests. Some of these groups were in fact little more than loose-knit alliances of protest brigades that declared themselves to be in favor of democratic reform. Others were formally constituted political parties that had formal programs and a hierarchy of offices, that met in secret, and that even made plans for armed resistance to Communist Party rule.

Various "city people's" political associations established themselves in public squares throughout China in the midst of the student demonstrations.

A fairly representative example is the "Kunming City People's Patriotic De-mocratic Sympathy Brigade," which had an organized presence on East Wind Square from May 19 until early June. It had a formal organizational structure with a chairman and vice chairmen. During its twenty-day career, the organization established a broadcasting station on the square, organized protest marches and sit-ins in front of government offices, and later took the lead in setting up street barricades, paralyzing traffic throughout the city for days. Its resistance to martial law reportedly reached a high tide on June 9 when, with the student protesters in East Wind Square down to a very few, they attacked the Communist Party in a number of radical speeches, called for a general strike and the burning of military and police vehicles, chanted "Long live the Guomindang" (the Nationalist Party on Taiwan), organized two protest marches, and got into nasty arguments with students, who now counseled everyone to clear the square (*Yunnan ribao,* June 13, 1989).

In addition to the political associations that formed in the public squares during May and that confined their activities primarily to the streets, there also emerged a significant number of militant proto-parties. These organiza-tions are noteworthy for the surprising directness with which they expressed their anti–Communist Party mentalities and aims and for a militant rhetoric whose style, if not content, hearkened back to the Cultural Revolution. Many of the political entrepreneurs who started such proto-parties in fact were middle-aged veterans of the struggles of the late 1960s. In Lanzhou there was the "City People's Sympathy Brigade," led by a fifty-six-year-old "Jin XX," an assistant engineer in a factory and former leader of a rebel organization dur-ing the Cultural Revolution. He set up a "Chinese Human Rights Alliance Central Committee," reportedly organized a 100-person "urban guerrilla unit," sent out emissaries to make contact with like-minded organizations through-out the country, and sought to purchase arms, saying that this was the best opportunity there would be for decades to overthrow the communists (*Gansu ribao,* June 20, 1989).

Some of these proto-parties, however, had been established even before the emergence of the student movement and had sought to remove the Com-munist Party from power well before the martial law and killings that radical-ized so many others against a government increasingly termed "fascist." The "Chinese League for Democratic Supervision" was established in Shanghai in March 1989 by Li Zhiguo, an employee of the engineering department of the Shanghai Railway Bureau. Originally known as the "Freedom Society" [*Ziyou she*], this party declared that it was open to any non–party member under the age of fifty. The group pasted up handbills and distributed party membership applications at universities and railway stations. In May the group became more active, acquiring their own printing presses, sending out delegations to many major cities, including Beijing, and passing out handbills announcing the formation of their league (*Jiefang ribao,* June 12, 1989; *Qunzhong ribao,* June 12, 1989).

Workers' Organizations: Union Organizing and Political Protest

A final variety of popular political organization was the "workers' autonomous federation." Many of these appear to have grown out of protest brigades that coalesced in public squares early in the student movement. Their distinguishing feature is that they declared themselves to be workers' organizations interested in furthering the interests of that constituency, and this usually meant at the same time democratic reform that would permit collective representation of workers' interests. These organizations distributed handbills, published manifestos and charters, and participated in street demonstrations, but they do not appear to have had branch organizations extending into factories. Most of them appear to have called for political strikes in late May and early June, but with little apparent success.

The best-documented case of an independent labor union is the Beijing Workers' Autonomous Federation. At least three people involved in some way with its leadership have escaped abroad to publish their accounts and submit to interviews, and over thirty of the federation's handbills, including its charter, are available in U.S. archives. The union's leaders came together on Tiananmen Square in late April and did not know one another before the movement began. The leading group of around twelve people was made up primarily of young workers from medium or large-scale state enterprises and between twenty-five and thirty years of age (Walder and Gong 1993). At its highest point of development after mid-May, the federation had between 100 and 200 activists at its location in front of the western reviewing stand at Tiananmen, organized into departments for logistics, organization, and propaganda. It also established a liaison department to maintain communication with various large factories (notably Capital Steel) and university campuses, a workers' picket corps and four dare-to-die corps. It set up a broadcasting station on the square that operated continuously, and it had at least one printing press at a separate location. Its broadcasting station became a "democratic forum" every evening, a forum in which listeners could write down statements or turn over purloined classified documents to be read out to large and appreciative audiences. The federation issued a continuous stream of handbills and pronouncements from April 21 through early June. It participated in all of the major demonstrations after May 11 and took an increasingly active and visible role after the declaration of martial law on May 20. It confronted the security forces on two separate occasions before June 4 (Walder and Gong 1993). Like many other city people's organizations, it became progressively radicalized by martial law and resisted the military operations of June 3 and after.

From its very first handbills, the federation directly challenged the party leadership, especially the reformers, who were seen as responsible for inflation and falling living standards. While it supported the student movement wholeheartedly, it also insisted that the movement did not belong to the students—a position that created tensions with student leaders from the outset and would in the end lead to open antagonism. The federation's consistent demand, stated repeatedly in its handbills and laid out carefully in the organization's charter, was simple and clear: It wanted both national and plant-level representation of worker interests by an independent union. In other handbills, however, the federation maintained a consistently militant rhetoric that sometimes appeared to draw on the iconoclasm of the Cultural Revolution. The group repeatedly denounced the "corrupt oligarchy" and poured scorn on the special privileges of officials and their families. It stated repeatedly its desire to "sweep away this last remnant of Stalinist dictatorship into the dustbin of history." Inevitably, as martial law continued into late May, the adjective "fascist" began to be attached to the party and government with greater frequency, and the group settled on the theme of "sacrificing" themselves "for the sake of the freedom of a future generation."

We know very little about the activities of the more than two dozen such workers' organizations that we have identified in the provinces, and it is possible that none of them developed as far as did the Beijing organization. But brief official accounts from the provinces do make clear that many of these groups appeared to fit the same pattern of activities as their Beijing counterpart. Similarly named workers' organizations in Changsha, Nanchang, Shanghai, Tianjin, and Hangzhou also established themselves in the main square and protested alongside the students, passing out handbills and broadcasting speeches. The workers' groups in Changsha, Yueyang, Nanchang, Huhehaote, Shanghai, Xi'an, Taiyuan, and Tianjin also played a pivotal role after the declaration of martial law, coordinating street barricades and calling for general strikes (Walder 1992). This is the single most common type of organization among those we have been able to identify—there are twenty-eight of them on our list, from nineteen different provinces. The rapid emergence of such militant and independent organizations throughout the country was probably very influential in pushing China's leaders toward martial law and a military solution.

Conclusions

It is hard not to be impressed with the organizational capacity and commitment displayed by Chinese students and other urban citizens during the political opening provided them for a few short weeks in the spring of 1989. The protests grew to massive proportions in a relatively short period and spread across the nation. Protesters successfully employed a variety of repertoires of collective action, borrowing from earlier Chinese protest movements and from movements abroad. Street protests that appeared spontaneous and unorganized on the surface in fact employed existing organizational structures provided by the regime itself, while at the same time thousands of small independent political organizations were formed throughout the country. This proliferation of political activism served to immobilize a repressive state and to precipitate a crisis of leadership at the top. It is tempting to fit the entire episode into the Polish-inspired historical narrative of the "rise of civil society" in which ordinary citizens gradually achieve greater autonomy and self-organization to combat domination by the state.

But we have seen that these protests were more an "inside-out" than a "bottom-up" affair. The initial student protests were magnified into large-scale popular rebellion by a public split in the party leadership and by the consequent rebellion of pro-reform organizations and individuals within the party-state apparatus. Most important, perhaps, were the mass media: the central newspapers, the New China News Agency, and the central television station, which covered the student hunger strike intensively and favorably and which, as the political stalemate at the top dragged on, turned toward an openly oppositional and exhortative role. The mass media sent clear signals to the population that the legitimate general secretary was being undermined by retired elder leaders and hard-liners and that large numbers of official organizations—such as trade unions and research academies—were firmly on the side of the legitimate pro-reform government in its struggle with the elderly hard-liners.

This argument—about the role of opportunity and levels of repression in modulating rates of collective action—may sound like an old and familiar one to students of Charles Tilly; it may also sound like more-recent adumbrations of this idea in more "state-centered" discussions about political opportunity structures. In part, it is. Indeed, it is tempting to enlist this case as yet another example of an argument about historical conjunctures, à la Barrington Moore and Theda Skocpol, in which the historical combination of conditions or events leads to certain kinds of outcomes. The case does, in fact, illustrate these well-known arguments about historical contingencies.

However, I am arguing not simply that elite divisions and the loss of discipline within the party-state apparatus combined to create an opening for protest; I am arguing that defecting members of the regime acted themselves to mobilize the general population into the streets, signaling to the populace that staged shows of support for hunger strikers were reasonable, even encouraged. Instead of the "additive" effect usually implied in studies inspired by resource mobilization theory or by reasoning about historical conjunctures, I am arguing that the *interaction* of regime defectors with street protesters had a "multiplicative" effect that vastly expanded both the scale of the street protests and the paralysis of the government in a very short period of time.

Consider as an example the argument that the student protest repertoire employed to great effect the traditional symbolism to shame the government and sway public sympathy (Esherick and Wasserstrom 1990) and that this cultural element provides the crucial explanation for the spread of the protests. This is an insightful argument, but consider also the fact that this symbolic positioning would have gone completely unnoticed by the population at large if it had not been for the lavish and sympathetic national media coverage—both print and electronic—of the entire event! The students' symbolic strategy was powerful, to be sure, but it certainly would have come to naught had only small audiences in the streets been able to observe it. The defection of the media massively multiplied the impact of an effective cultural repertoire. As Charles Tilly circa 1978 might have put it, the equation is not

$$\text{strategy} + \text{opportunity} = \text{collective action}$$

it is

$$(\text{strategy} + \text{opportunity}) \times \text{regime defection} = \text{collective action.}$$

In closing, I would like to call for a broader organizational and historical—or should we just say Tillyan?—perspective on collective action in the waning years of communism. The social movement–centered accounts inspired by Solidarity and the uplifting European protests of 1989 communicate a bottom-up vision of a "society" rising up to pull down "the state," a vision that, except for the innovative new emphasis on the cognitive and cultural dimensions of social movements, is a one-sided and somewhat old-fashioned version of resource mobilization theory. A broader and more historical version of resource mobilization analysis is called for—one that is also capable of seeing the bottom-up mobilizations as themselves *symptoms* of the long-term evolution and short-term crisis of this kind of party-state. We are already sensitive to the ways that collective protest has contributed to the waning of the communist state; we should now consider the ways in which these collective protests are "tracers" of historical change, in this case of the decline of a once formidably centralized type of state organization so central to twentieth-century history.

Chapter 5

Artisans and Revolution in a Finnish Country Town

Risto Alapuro

On Networks, Opportunity, and Political Contention

The criticism leveled at the purposive image of revolution maintains that, rather than focusing on deliberately revolutionary efforts, one should mainly analyze conjunctures that bring together separately determined processes and actions. In this view the context is nearly all, and it definitely includes the international environment of the state in crisis. From this perspective it is no wonder that revolutionary intentions have commonly developed only in the course of the challenge itself (see, e.g., Skocpol 1979; Aya 1990).

The abortive Finnish revolution in 1917–18 seems to constitute an extreme case supporting the conjunctural view of revolution. For the challengers in Finland, an autonomous grand duchy in the Russian Empire up to 1917, the context was provided by World War I. The war dissolved the multinational empires of the epoch and agitated minority regions under their control. In Finland it launched a revolution, even though a liberal-democratic political system had been established there (with limitations dictated by Russian supremacy), and the workers' movement had an active role in the system (Alapuro 1988, ch. 9). What counted most were networks making up an organized movement, coupled with the opportunity created by the two revolutions in Russia in February and October 1917.

This chapter examines the character of the Finnish revolution by looking at networks and contention in a small but expanding country town prior to and during the revolutionary period. A microhistorical analysis of the Finnish upheaval can show us how the forms of organization and mobilization are embedded in the structures of everyday life. It enables us to explore the relationship between long-term preconditions for collective action and the situational crisis in 1917. It also allows a look at the relationship between local and national processes. This dimension, linked to the previous one, is highly relevant in a dependent polity like the Grand Duchy of Finland.

The Commune of Huittinen

At the beginning of this century the large and relatively prosperous commune of Huittinen, characteristic of the south, the most densely populated and politically active part of Finland, was a community of 7,500 inhabitants, with a wealthy freeholding peasant upper class, a numerous tenant farmer population, and a very large group of agrarian workers.[1] Dairy production dominated, and grain cultivation was a second major industry. In the center of the commune, where four rivers met near an impressive fifteenth-century stone church, was the main village, called Lauttakylä (literally, a "raft village"). With a nucleus of 125 dwellings in a square kilometer, and more than 2,200 people in all, Lauttakylä actually constituted a small country town. In 1901 more than forty different small entrepreneurs or tradesmen carried on business there. As a prospering commune, Huittinen, and Lauttakylä as its expanding consumption center, provided opportunities for artisanal workers.

Artisans as Leaders of the Labor Movement

Basic units in the popular challenge in early-twentieth-century Finland were the workers' associations (*työväenyhdistykset*), whose political, economic, and cultural aspects were largely undifferentiated. In Huittinen the first workers' association was founded in 1896 in Lauttakylä. At the turn of the century, after a few years under the tutelage of the local educated class, the association became closely linked to Lauttakylä's volunteer fire brigade. The volunteer fire brigades had evolved in Finland during the late nineteenth century, at the time of the dissolution of the legal bonds of the guild system and other elements of the regime of corporate regulation. Their ideology of gathering people from different social strata on equal terms to further the common good and their propagation of the ideal of a socially responsible and respectable working man attracted craft workers (Stenius 1987, 234–67). In Huittinen at the turn of the century, artisans, many of whom owned small enterprises, provided the majority of the leadership for the volunteer fire brigade.

The artisan-dominated fire brigade provided the workers' association with its new leaders. In 1900 the association had a mason, Kusti Lindqvist, as its chairman and a local policeman as its secretary. Both were leaders of the fire brigade. The change in the leadership coincided with a political reorientation. In 1901 or 1902 the association joined the Workers' Party of Finland, founded in 1899; in 1903 the party adopted the Social Democratic label and a socialist program. However, the change did not lead the association to any determined opposition to the local upper strata, that is, to the wealthy freeholders and the civil servants. Kusti Lindqvist, for example, was active in the local youth association, an organization of the local teachers and the offspring of the freeholders. He also accepted a seat in the communal council (the municipal organ of representation founded in 1904), which was dominated by the upper classes.

Finally, the local consumer cooperative gathered enthusiastic supporters among the leaders of *all* local organizations, from the workers' association to the freeholders' economic and professional organizations. Founded in 1905, the cooperative soon became the dominant retail store in Huittinen.

In October 1905 the rebellion in Russia extended into Finland and led to a general strike and an unprecedented mobilization in towns and countryside. It began in a national and patriotic spirit, but in the long run it particularly swelled the Social Democrats' ranks. Soon, because of the critical situation in Russia, the emperor was forced to reverse the Russification policy of preceding years and to authorize the transformation of Finland's political system. The mainly Social Democratic demand for universal suffrage was pushed through, and Finland experienced Europe's most radical parliamentary reform. A very restrictive estate-based Diet was replaced by a unicameral assembly based on universal and equal suffrage for both men and women. In the first general elections, in 1907, the Social Democrats gained a stunning victory, more than one-third of the vote.

An enormous wave of organization radically enlarged the basis of the local working-class movement. In the course of one year eight new workers' associations were founded, and membership momentarily rose to 550, about 15 percent of the workforce in the commune. In the first general elections the Social Democrats received 57 percent of the vote (typical in the region as a whole), and in subsequent elections they consolidated their position.

New associations were formed in the agrarian milieu, associations whose leaders and members were mainly agriculturalists—agrarian workers, farmhands, cottagers, and tenant farmers and their offspring (Table 5.1). Significantly, the Russian crisis launched in Huittinen, as elsewhere in Finland, a large-scale *organization,* thus consolidating the highly organized character of the Finnish labor movement; in contrast, in Russia's Baltic provinces the same crisis provoked widespread jacqueries (Raun 1984).

Table 5.1 Leaders of the Worker's Associations in Huittinen, 1906–1916, by Occupation

Occupation	Lauttakylä Association	Other Associations
Artisan	17	12
Worker, farmhand	0	68
Tenant farmer	0	15
Tenant farmers' offspring[a]	0	49
Cottager	0	18
Shopkeeper, shop assistant	2	4
Other	1	7
Unknown	0	62
Total	20	235

Note: Leaders are those persons who are identified as members of the board, as auditors, or as members of the entertainment committee (who were often important in the day-to-day activities of the associations).

[a]Those expressly given as tenant farmers' sons or daughters. Among "workers" there undoubtedly were more tenant farmers' offspring.

Also, the artisans maintained their hold on the local working-class movement. They continued to provide leadership for the Lauttakylä association (see Table 5.1), which maintained its dominant position after the organization in the purely agrarian villages.

The character and the timing of the political reform in 1905–7 is of crucial importance to an understanding of why a common network came to unite both artisans and agrarian workers and cottagers in the same movement. In localities like Huittinen, the sudden opportunity—which resulted from a crisis of the Russian autocracy and not from the strength of domestic collective action—fell on a community where socioeconomic relations in agriculture largely remained encased within a traditional framework. The structure of authority was based on interpersonal relationships between employers and employees, and grievances against people of quality and freeholders were shared by various groups of common folk (*rahvas*). The artisan-led local Social Democracy was able to fuse this discontent, which had pronounced moral overtones, when a large-scale opportunity unexpectedly opened itself (cf. Kettunen 1986, 59–61, 68, 81–82). As a result a "common folk's movement for equality" (Haapala and Hyrkkänen 1988, 3) emerged in which political, economic, and cultural aspects constituted a rather undifferentiated whole.

The Political Activists' Craft and Position in the Craft

Who were the artisanal activists in the early period, and did the same activists continue into the period after the turbulent year of 1905?

Fifteen of the seventeen known leading members of the Lauttakylä workers' association in 1900–1916 were artisans in various crafts: There were four carpenters, three masons (one of them worked mainly as a builder), two potters, a stonemason, a coppersmith, a tinsmith, a harness maker, a tanner, and a mechanic (who originally was a tailor). Most of them lived close to each other near the center of Lauttakylä, and some were related to each other.

Kusti Lindqvist, a self-styled "master builder," built and fixed houses. He was responsible for the construction of the salt and cheese cellars for the local dairy, and he designed a three-story building for a merchant (who was the chief of the fire brigade) in Lauttakylä. In 1909 he bought a small farm. Emil Falén, the harness maker and upholsterer, usually employed two or three workers. In 1912 his harness shop had been "expanding from one year to the next." A few years later he purchased a tannery with two or three employees. At the turn of the century in A. V. Sevón's workshop he and one to four coworkers made coffee pots and kettles. A little later he started to make fire engines and roofs. Kalle Kaneva had a furniture workshop in which two to four employees and his son Kosti made furniture; they also built houses. At the beginning of the century Albert Myllykangas and two other people in his small workshop made Dutch tiles and dishes. The potter Kustaa Vahala specialized in crocks; in 1913 he had three workers. Fredrik Tuomi, the founder and first conductor of the brass band of the fire brigade, made "both elegant and simple furniture." In 1899 he employed two workers. Erland Reunanen made tombstones, and his craftsmanship was locally famous. Alvar Tammineva, originally a tailor, passed a course to become a mechanic and had a repair shop in the 1910s. Finally, from 1899 to 1907 the carpenter K. E. Laaksonen managed the local telephone exchange.

It is striking that many of the leaders were small artisanal entrepreneurs engaged in the construction or maintenance of the small but expanding town. To give an idea of the representation of various crafts in the leadership, their distribution is compared to the distribution of the artisanal households both in the commune as a whole and in Lauttakylä in 1901 (Table 5.2). The comparison is rough because the time periods are not the same and the division between employers and employees is difficult to establish for 1901, but it gives an approximate idea of the differences and lends additional support to the foregoing impression of the "typical" occupations in the workers' association;

Table 5.2 Percentage Distribution of the Artisanal Households in Huittinen and
Lauttakylä, 1901, and of Artisanal Leaders in the Lauttakylä Workers' Association, 1900–1916, by Occupation

Occupation	Huittinen as a Whole, 1901[a]	Lauttakylä, 1901	Lauttakylä Worker Association, 1900–1916
Shoemaker	19	10	—
Tailor	13	12	—
Tanner[b]	5	4	12
Smith	10	10	18[c]
Carpenter	14	12	29
Mason	6	4	18
Stonemason	6	9	6
Potter	0	1	18
Painter	3	3	—
Turner	6	13	—
Baker	5	9	—
Watchmaker	2	4	—
Miller	6	4	—
Other	5	4	—
Total	100	100	100
N	224	69	17

Note: Seamstresses and weavers are omitted.
[a] Including Keikyä; based on chapters 3 and 4 of Risto Alapuro, Suomen Synty paikallisena
ilmiönä 1890–1933 (Helsinki: Hanki ja Jää, 1994). This study deals with Huittinen proper
and excludes the organizationally and socially dinstinct northern part of the commune,
called Keikyä.
[b] Includes a harness maker.
[c] Includes a mechanic who originally was a tailor.

indeed, masons, carpenters, tanners, and potters are relatively well represented, whereas shoemakers, tailors, bakers, watchmakers, and millers, who
were easy to find in Lauttakylä, did not figure among the activists.

Another striking feature of the activists is the considerable mobility of the
artisanal leaders: Half of them had moved to Huittinen from elsewhere, though
mostly from the same county. In material terms the Social Democratic leaders'
situation was apparently similar to that of the other artisans in Lauttakylä—
and consequently they were better off than the artisans in the commune as a

whole. The minimum yearly income of 200 marks required for a person to be included in the tax rolls was earned by practically every activist. Not only did women not figure in the leadership (unlike in many agrarian workers' associations in the commune), but in the 1910s they were not even members.

All in all, the Lauttakylä workers' association had, in its upper echelons, almost a touch of respectability. It was an organization of middle-aged males who had more or less well-defined places in the local division of labor; were tied together through work, leisure, and dwelling; did a little better than the majority of local people; had experience in organizing their affairs; and necessarily had well-regulated contacts with various people in the commune.

The Activists' Links to Other Organizations

This characterization may be amplified by an analysis of the artisanal leaders' involvement in other organizational activities. Despite the enormous expansion of the workers' movement and the forceful entrance of distinctly socialist politics into the local life in 1905–7, the artisanal leaders' relations with other cultural and political organizations did not greatly alter. As before, the volunteer fire brigade and the consumer cooperative continued to serve as links to other organized groups. The fire brigade remained in the hands of the artisans, nearly all of whom were leaders or members of the workers' association, but it also had ties with other groups, notably with shopkeepers, as well as a common brass band with some other voluntary associations.

In the consumer cooperative the activists of the workers' movement worked alongside the landowner and civil servant elite. Nearly half of the members of the administrative board between 1906 and 1916 were at one time or another leaders of the Lauttakylä workers' association; most ordinary members of the cooperative were workers, tenant farmers, and artisans. At the same time a considerable number of the board members were freeholders who held high positions in the dairy (the landowners' principal economic enterprise), in the savings bank, or in the professional farmer society. At least one-quarter of the board members were engaged in the Finnish Party, which provided the main local opposition for the Social Democrats.

Moreover, the Social Democrats, represented above all by Lauttakylä artisans, accepted a role in the communal council, although their participation still depended on the benevolence of the landowners: At the municipal level the system of representation remained as restricted as it had been prior to 1905. And in 1913, when the local newspaper was launched mainly as a bourgeois initiative, leading Social Democratic artisans joined the project.

The Workers' Movement and Class Integration

What do the artisans' roles in the local labor movement and their links to other organizations tell us? One thing is clear: They do not support the view, found in some national-level studies, of the pre-Civil War Workers' Party as a militant movement that increasingly cut society into two hostile camps.[2] Rather, they tell of a process in which working people—with artisans as their foremost representatives—assumed a new place superseding the corporate-based society of the nineteenth century. Actually the political organization *complements* the popular groups' entrance into the local society. Above all, class-based politics appears as only one more field of activity emerging alongside the economic and cultural fields. At least for the artisanal activists, politics was not, as it was in some other revolutionary situations, an all-encompassing sphere that permeated all other spheres and offered a total explanation for the artisans' situation.

In Huittinen political opposition did not exclude cooperation in other fields. Politics constituted only one dimension, though a central dimension, in the shaping of other relations. By deciding to accept labor activists into the communal council, its upper-class members, while not appearing under political banners themselves, acknowledged that running local affairs included a political dimension and that the Social Democrats were legitimate representatives of the common folk. Just as noteworthy is the fact that the Social Democrats, on their part, were willing to accept the deliberate concessions of the local elite as a basis for cooperation. Still, the establishment of local democracy constituted one of the central objectives of the workers' movement.

In the administration of the consumer cooperative the Social Democratic leaders were, in a peculiar manner, on the border of politics and nonpolitics. They were elected in the council as representatives of the labor movement, but in the words of a local Social Democrat in 1908: "As members of the consumer cooperative we have joined only and exclusively as purchasers of what we need, and as such we are not the least concerned by our mutual party preferences" (*Sosialidemokraatti,* January 9, 1908). In the volunteer fire brigade the Social Democratic leaders were not even representatives of the worker movement: "The existence of the fire brigade is no factitious enterprise built on distinctions between political parties; its activities are in the same way beneficial to all individuals" (*Lauttakylä,* August 21, 1915).

The artisan-led movement was engaged in collective action marked by formal organization. Craig Calhoun has claimed that formal organization and rational plans tend to obscure any view of alternatives. Moreover, because of "their investment in formal organizations and their awareness of numerous possible courses of action, the members of such groups are not often likely to be very radical in their actions. This is a central reason for the characteristic reformism of the modern working class" (Calhoun 1983, 487–88). Indeed, the artisanal activists in Huittinen were men of organization.

What seems to characterize these artisanal activists are their capacity for collective action and a search for reformist solutions. As leaders of the workers' movement migrated to Huittinen, they were looking for a place "respectable" in their own eyes as well as in those of their alleged betters (cf. Calhoun 1983, 490). Besides, they were looking for a place for their children. At least Falén, Lindqvist, and Sevón put their children into the local secondary school.

This view of the craftsmen's role in the community may be put in a larger perspective. Rural artisans' economic and social position in late-nineteenth- and early-twentieth-century Finland was generally improving. Handworkers in many trades did reasonably well, especially in expanding rural centers when artisanal occupations were increasingly legalized in the nineteenth century (Hjerppe 1981, 232).

From this angle, the emergence and consolidation of the working-class movement in Huittinen was an element in the social integration of a modestly successful group. It may not be purely accidental that two of those traditional crafts that were definitely losing in economic terms—shoemakers and tailors—were absent from the leadership.

It might be objected that the focus on the activists dismisses the grievances and a possible lack of integration of the agrarian poor, whom the leaders represented. But it seems significant that before 1917 no overt sign of collective action disrupting the frame of peaceful party activity can be found in Huittinen. Perhaps J. K. Paasikivi, a leading Old Finnish politician, was not so wrong when he thought in 1913 that with time the Social Democrats would develop into a "radical progressive party" (Paasikivi 1957, 180).

The Revolutionary Situation in 1917

As in 1905, in March 1917 the outbreak of revolution in Russia was also a great relief for all groups in Huittinen.[3] Two days after the Provisional Government had been formed in St. Petersburg, all the local organized groups, including the workers' movement, joined forces to reorganize the police force. The "Russified" police were forced to resign—a common occurrence in Finland in 1917. They were replaced by a militia that was led jointly by the

bourgeois elite and workers' movement activists. Thus the distinction between public and private maintenance of order became unclear immediately
after the February revolution. The resulting ambiguity (which was never really eliminated during the year 1917) was aggravated by the lack of Finnish
troops; the Finnish armed forces had been dissolved at the beginning of the
century. Now the maintenance of order was in the last analysis in the hands of
those groups that themselves were contenders in the political struggle.

Two other, and in the short run more obvious, developments gave the
local workers' movement a favorable opportunity to act collectively. The political system was reactivated and many restrictions on political rights were
revoked. The Social Democrats, who in 1916 had gained the majority—103
seats out of 200—in Parliament, formed a government in coalition with bourgeois parties. In Huittinen the labor movement could now pursue its main
objectives, especially the eight-hour workday and the democratization of local
government. A wave of organization and mobilization multiplied the ranks of
the workers' associations and created two local trade unions, making total
membership figures comparable to those of 1905.

In mid-July the agrarian laborers went on strike for the eight-hour day;
this was an unprecedented challenge to labor conditions. On the second day
of the strike an armed encounter occurred at the cooperative dairy. Eight
people, who refused to accept the dairy's closing, shot at strikers, six of
whom were wounded. Only one of the assailants was a landowning member
of the cooperative; among the other assailants were three veterinarians, a sea
captain, a master builder, a businessman, and a police official; none of them
belonged to the organizational core of the commune. Two days later the landowners and workers' movement leaders concluded an agreement, and the
laborers resumed work.

Thus, in the absence of established means of coercion, the tension in labor
relations resulted in an armed incident. A small number of upper-class
people, accompanied (and not led, as one could assume) by a newly appointed
police official, decided to take control of the situation. A few weeks later the
same people engaged in setting up an armed organization to protect "respectable citizens" against "hooligans." Toward the fall the organization progressively consolidated into a civil guard attracting freeholders and particularly their sons.

The working people's challenge increasingly crystallized around the issue
of communal democracy, fueled by unemployment and fears about food
scarcity. By mid-July 1917 the reform had advanced rapidly, and reform measures were passed by Parliament.

At this moment, however, the Social Democrats were expelled from political power, and in a manner whose legality they always questioned: Parliament was dissolved through a conflict between the Finnish government and the Russian Provisional Government, with the cooperation of Finnish bourgeois groups. As a result the local governmental acts were left unconfirmed, and in the subsequent national elections the Social Democrats lost their majority. In Huittinen, however, the struggle for communal democracy continued. The retreat at the national level seems to have reinforced local determination. Under the pressure of workers' mass meetings and petitions, local power-holders consented to an increased access by workers to the communal council and other communal organs, but the contention continued during the last months of the year.

In November, following the prompting of the national Social Democratic trade union organization, the leadership of the Huittinen workers' movement began to form a security guard to protect working people against the bourgeois guard. At the turn of the year, the guard activists attempted to acquire arms, but until the end of January 1918 all attempts were fruitless.

At the end of January 1918 the bourgeois government, after a declaration of independence and its recognition by the Bolsheviks in December, declared that the civil guards were the troops of the government and ordered the disarming of the workers' guards, now generally called "Red guards." The Social Democrats launched a revolution, and in a couple of weeks the southern core regions of Finland, including Huittinen, were established as a revolutionary stronghold. In three months, however, the war ended in a total defeat of the revolutionaries.

The Labor Leaders in the Revolutionary Situation

Was the composition and the role of the labor leaders different in the earlier period from that in 1917 and 1918? Despite a certain amount of individual turnover and although more contentious forms of collective action were adopted, the established organizational framework was maintained.

In the four or five months following the February revolution previously elected officials continued to dominate. But subsequently, established veterans were accompanied by many who were apparently new to the board, elected only at the beginning of 1917: The pressures of the war in 1915 and 1916 may have effected this change in tone. Food prices were rising, and modest measures of rationing were initiated at the end of 1916. In any case, those who were the major speakers at mass meetings, who drafted petitions and represented farm strikers, were mainly the same men who ran the established organizations.

A more marked change took place at the end of 1917, when the officials of the associations were elected for the following year. Then a number of people, mostly artisans from the same milieu as the more experienced leaders, emerged or reemerged to consolidate their positions.

A few examples give an idea of the degree of the change. The first big mass meeting following the February revolution and gathering participants from all strata was presided over by Kusti Lindqvist. He was a veteran activist, but he had spent the preceding years elsewhere and was now making a successful comeback. New people in active roles were the baker Heikki Mikkola, a recently returned migrant, and the coppersmith J. O. Nordlund, an employee of A. V. Sevón. The latter had the reputation of being quarrelsome. He returned to the fore after a hiatus of half a decade. The potter Oskar Reunanen was a new leader but a relative of Erland Reunanen, the stonemason. At the turn of 1918 the board of the Lauttakylä association was considerably reformed. Emil Falén was replaced by Kusti Lindqvist as the chairman, and Oskar Reunanen and Heikki Mikkola, respectively, continued as vice chairman and secretary; they had assumed these posts in 1917. Those apparently elected for the first time were: A. E. Kallio, a shoemaker and the proprietor of a shoe store, and J. O. Nordlund. A. V. Sevón now returned to the board. If it is kept in mind that Lindqvist and Mikkola had been away from Huittinen for some years and that Oskar Reunanen and A. E. Kallio had not assumed functions in the fire brigade, it becomes clear that the new leadership was somewhat less rooted in the organizational life of the community than the earlier one had been.

Moreover, these men constituted the core activists of the workers' security guard set up in November. The tailor and mechanic Alvar Tammineva was elected commander in chief of the guard. Apparently he had not been active in the Lauttakylä association since 1906, but as a young man he had served in the Russian army.

The changes in the consumer cooperative and the fire brigade provide another indication of the way the former arrangements were eroded. The workers' movement seized both in the fall of 1917. In the former case a completely Social Democratic board was elected in December, preceded by a large-scale entrance of new members from popular groups. Emil Falén, who stepped aside from the leadership of the worker association, now assumed the post of chairman in the cooperative. Politics now prevailed in a sphere that earlier had been kept separate from it, and the consumer cooperative became a front in the political struggle. Yet more striking still was the rearrangement in the volunteer fire brigade, in whose hall the nascent worker guard had held military exercises from late November. Emil Falén and the non–Social Democratic leaders were put aside, and Kusti Lindqvist was elevated to leadership.

Thus the associational life was politicized as a part of a progressive polarization. Mass action did not disrupt the associational form but extended the majority principle to a new sphere. Now it concerned not only communal politics but also fields that the workers' movement had earlier kept separate from politics.

When the revolution was declared at the end of January 1918, the Social Democrats began to run the communal affairs. The local takeover, however, was only decided on February 18, and it was considered a temporary necessity made inevitable by the war. Even after the takeover the new powerholders tried to persuade the bourgeois chairman of the communal board to keep his post.

Understandably, the main roles fell to persons already in charge of the workers' movement. Kusti Lindqvist, Emil Falén, and Heikki Mikkola ran the new administrative organ, the communal delegation; the revolutionary tribunal was led by Kusti Lindqvist, Heikki Mikkola, and A. V. Sevón; the Red guard was under the command of the same men as the worker guard in the fall, including one more time Lindqvist and Mikkola.

Almost all of the inhabitants consented to live under a local regime that controlled free movement, inventoried and confiscated food, and subjected some suspect individuals to interrogations. Externally organized life continued its course much as before. Religious services were held, banks and shops were open. The cooperative dairy was running, and its board held meetings. Still, the bourgeois population lived under a fear and uncertainty enormously reinforced by five murders. Three people were killed in the first days of the war by nonlocal troops passing through Huittinen on their way to the front. Two more were shot later, at least one of them by a local worker, who was not involved in the worker movement. The revolutionary tribunal sent him to be convicted by a superior court.

All in all the revolution in Huittinen was an administrative revolution. Even the experiences of 1917 failed to provoke the discontent to dynamite the old order and raise a new type of revolutionary leadership. The artisanal leaders never envisaged a radically new order; instead, they continued to act in the old organizational framework. Even Lindqvist, Mikkola, Nordlund, and others who had emerged or reemerged in 1917 shared a conception of politics that implied full-scale membership of the community for everyone as its main objective. Consolidation of the new rule was attempted without a powerful police force or effective censorship (cf. Moore 1978, 291–99).

The White Terror

The victorious White troops arrived in Huittinen April 20, 1918. During the next four or five weeks at least thirty-seven local people were executed. The majority of those missing, twenty-three in all, apparently belonged to the same group. Kusti Lindqvist, J. O. Nordlund, and A. E. Kallio were shot in Huittinen; A. V. Sevón and Alvar Tammineva were shot while fleeing from there. Heikki Mikkola was executed in September, the only leader who was convicted by a special tribunal instituted to deal with high treason. His wife had been killed in early May in flight with their three children. Of those who had kept aloof from the revolutionary administration Fredrik Tuomi was also murdered.

The majority of the killed were workers, agrarian laborers, and farmhands. Relatively speaking the craftsmen were hit very hard: They constituted one-fifth of those shot. Artisans supplied a disproportionate number of victims, just as they had supplied more than their share of political leaders and activists in the prerevolutionary movement.

Consistently, those victims who died in the prison camps of hunger and diseases in the summer and early fall of 1918 were almost exclusively workers. Their number amounted to about 90, raising the total toll to 140 or 150 people.

A Dependent Revolution

In the early years of this century the workers' movement in Huittinen was integrating into the local life, but in 1918 it participated in the revolution. Its progress conforms to the general pattern of developments in the southern countryside and its population centers.[4] The similarity lies not in the particular local events but in the ways that people formed unifying networks as well as interconnections and oppositions between them and in the importance of the association-based regulation. The artisans' role captures a significant aspect of the challenge prior to 1917, even though it was unusually pronounced in Huittinen: Lauttakylä provided a very good ground for artisanal activity.

The case of Huittinen shows how problematic it would be to consider the occurrence of revolutions as the last stage in a long-term polarization. Rather, it supports the view that "contingent events with no particular connection to the ideal-typical developmental path have powerfully shaped the outbreak and course of revolutions" (Goodwin 1994, 756). Here the control of the means of coercion appears to be a key aspect. In Barrington Moore's words:

> There is a tendency . . . to underestimate the importance of control over the instruments of violence—the army and the police—and the significance of decisions taken by political leaders [behind revolutionary outbreaks]. The long-run trends merely provide temptations and opportunities for political leaders and set outer limits on what is possible in terms of thought and action. (1978, 82–83)

The experience of Huittinen captures some elements instrumental in the *interplay* between the national and the local level in the Finnish revolution. Clearly the disintegration of the apparatus of coercion was linked to both levels. The entrance of the Social Democrats, the majority party in Parliament, into the government thanks to the February revolution altered the power balance at the highest level of the polity. The large-scale dismissal of the police, instead, was a local-level reaction to the same event; Huittinen is a good example.

What then happened is that the ambiguity in the local maintenance of order prolonged itself because of the Social Democrats' grip on state power. The bourgeois parties soon called for a return to "normalcy," but the Social Democrats did not agree. For them the shared control of the provisional arrangements for maintaining order was an asset, and in the spring and the summer they were reluctant to restore the pre-March situation. In these circumstances occurred the dairy incident in Huittinen.

Unsurprisingly, the absence of a regular police force—which coincided with large-scale worker organization and mobilization—soon inspired bourgeois attempts to restore order. Emerging from the grass roots, they led to private organization. The paramilitary organization in Huittinen, which began as a reaction to the dairy encounter and the farm strike behind it, is an example of this.

Also in the fall the national and local developments were interconnected, but in a different sense. The Social Democrats were forced out, illegitimately in their view, from the top of the polity. An alternative power bloc consolidated itself, based on the party, the trade union organization, and the worker guards that existed mainly in the biggest centers. At the same time the local challenge concentrated itself in the question of communal power, intensified by unemployment and a deteriorating food situation. Among the popular groups the growth of bourgeois civil guards raised fears and indignation.

When the national Worker Security Guard was established, it found a fertile ground in a multitude of communes. In Huittinen, for example, the foremost Social Democratic leaders apparently had no difficulty in accepting the setting up of a local guard. In this phase the national and local processes were parallel or even linked to each other: Actually, the decision to form a national Worker Security Guard was made mainly because the party found that a central organization was the only way of controlling the swelling movement, notably in southern Finland.

The Finnish revolution was, then, a dependent revolution. It was Finnish because it occurred in the Finnish polity and the main contenders were Finnish groups. And it was dependent because the Russian crisis unleashed the whole process. Finally, it was also an abortive or a failed revolution.[5] It broke out as a by-product of an epochal crisis whose main arena was elsewhere. Hence its contingent character. But however contingent may have been the upheavals that World War I provoked in small polities, the impact of the upheavals was profound and lasted long. One significant fact was to be the presence or absence of a substantial Communist Party: Whatever the result was, it was "largely attributable to situational factors associated with World War I" (Zolberg 1986, 408).

In Finland the communists emerged from the underground only at the end of World War II. Then, in the first postwar elections, they became the biggest party in Huittinen.

Notes

1. The presentation is based on Alapuro 1994, chs. 3 and 4, if not otherwise indicated. Full references are given there. See also Raimo Viikki's excellent work (1989). This study deals with Huittinen proper and excludes the organizationally and socially distinct northern part of the commune, called Keikyä.

2. For somewhat different formulations see, e.g., Soikkanen 1967, 183–99; Rasila, Jutikkala, and Kulha 1976, 76–78. The question of the degree of political polarization prior to 1917 is far from settled even today.

3. The references to the Finnish polity as a whole in this paragraph are based on Alapuro 1988, ch. 9.

4. Unfortunately there are few systematic studies of this development. The most important among them is Pertti Haapala's (1986) inquiry into Tampere, an industrial center. See also Rentola 1992, 456–691.

5. It depends on the definition of the revolution, of course, whether the Finnish revolution counts or not. If Charles Tilly's definition is accepted, it certainly counts (Tilly 1993b, 8–9).

Part II

Repertoires of Political Contention

Chapter 6

Bandits and Boundaries: Robber Bands and Secret Societies on the Dutch Frontier (1730–1778)

Anton Blok

The strength of collective biography is not in supplying alternative explanations, but in specifying what is to be explained. Historians who have specified what is to be explained via collective biography often find themselves turning to explanations stressing the immediate setting and organization of everyday life, or relying on something vaguely called "culture". That moves them back to anthropology.

Charles Tilly

Banditry has been defined as the easiest form of rebellion because it is the most difficult for states to counteract, especially in mountainous frontier zones where central authority is weak (Wallerstein 1974, 141–42; Braudel 1973, 745–46). A case in point is the so-called *Bokkeryders*, who in three successive episodes between 1730 and 1774 operated in the hinterland of Maastricht—the border area between the Dutch Republic, the Duchy of Gulik, and the Austrian Netherlands. It took the local authorities in these fragmented territories well over forty years to come to terms with a form of banditry that easily survived the first two efforts in the 1740s to repress it.[1]

The raids of the bands fell into three distinct periods, each of which came to an end with mass arrests, trials, and executions in the hometowns of the convicts. The first period (1730–42) saw more than sixty outings, most of which were directed against churches, though ten raids involved massive attacks on farms, inns, and rectories. The second phase (1749–50) included just two operations and was for the most part a short-lived revival of what had remained of the earlier bands. In the third phase (1751–74) the ranks of the robbers swelled considerably. Assorted local bands participated in several large-scale attacks against a dozen farms, two rectories, one hermitage, one monastery, and one church. As had happened in the early 1740s, a haphazard outing not authorized by the leaders and carried out toward the end of 1770 led to the discovery and subsequent demise of the robber bands in the Lower Meuse.

In the early stages of Lower Meuse banditry, most of the robbers came from the easternmost enclaves of the Austrian Netherlands and the adjoining reaches of the Duchy of Gulik. The Dutch territories were only modestly represented at that time, by the towns of Nieuwstadt and Heerlen. Later, large groups of people from neighboring Dutch districts joined in the raids, while some Austrian territories and the Duchy of Gulik stopped being important areas of recruitment. All attacks took place late in the evening or in the early morning. During these nocturnal ventures the robbers looked for money, jewelry, clothing, food, and other valuable goods. Victims were often maltreated (to make them talk first and to keep them quiet after), and some of them lost their lives. But not all operations involved the same amount of violence, nor were they all equally successful. Several important outings failed— some because the victims or their neighbors managed to give the alarm; others because the robbers found only items of little value. It is significant that on a number of occasions, most notably during the large-scale operations in 1770, the victims were conspicuously spared, if they woke up at all.

How many people actually participated in the operations of the bands we cannot possibly know. What we do know is that about 600 people were tried for being members of the "notorious band" and that many others fled and successfully avoided prosecution. In the early 1740s, about 170 people appeared before local courts. The defendants included well over twenty women; most of them were linked to band members through kinship, marriage, or concubinage. About ten years later, some thirty people were tried, including five men who had also been active in the first period. During the trials of the 1770s, close to 400 people, including six women, were convicted. In all, I could trace more than 500 verdicts, all of which were carried out. Most of these convictions involved sentences of death by hanging, burning, or the rack.

This chapter seeks to trace the development of two forms of collective violence: banditry and its repression. It has been argued that no simple distinction between instrumental and symbolic practice makes sense anywhere: Instrumental action is always simultaneously semantic (Comaroff 1985, 125; Leach 1966, 403–4; 1976, 9). Directed against property and people (expropriation and elimination), both forms of violence include a powerful cultural import affecting the reputation and social status of all dramatis personae.

We notice, first, that the occupational backgrounds of the robbers, their kinship structure, and their place of origin strongly favored the development of banditry in the Lower Meuse and, of course, also militated against stopping or controlling it. Second, we will see that the military and political history of the area is crucial for understanding the rise and fall of the *Bokkeryders*. The bands emerged sometime after 1730 in a peripheral area characterized by a high degree of territorial fragmentation, which had resulted from a long period of wars. This raises a third issue: the means the local authorities could deploy to control the bands. Fourth, in studies of popular collective violence, the issue of "claims" usually looms large. Claims may be obvious when we deal with tax revolts, conscription riots, and similar examples of popular politics. But in cases of organized banditry claims are less clear, or at least difficult to pinpoint, since motives, goals, and agendas vary among participants and also change over time. This may be one reason why banditry, often itself elusive, diffuse, and intermittent, does not take up a prominent place in studies of collective action. Writing about banditry in sixteenth-century Mediterranean countries, Braudel characterized it as a "cruel, everyday war hardly noticed by traditional historians, who have left what they consider a secondary topic to essaysists and novelists" (1973, 745). Before returning to the issue of claims, we look at the context in which the bands took shape.

The Area

The *Bokkeryders* operated in the Lower Meuse, in the rural area enclosed by the towns of Maastricht, Aix-la-Chapelle, Gulik, and Roermond. From the sixteenth to the early nineteenth centuries this area was part of a larger military frontier zone, with Maastricht as a strong fortress and garrison town and Liège as an important center of the arms industry. It was in the Lower Meuse, at the crossroads of major east–west and north–south thoroughfares, that the spheres of influence of the great European powers touched and often collided. France, Spain, the Dutch Republic, Austria, and later Prussia disputed sovereignty over this part of Europe. Up to the early eighteenth century, the area had suffered from frequent military operations and subsequent territorial fragmentation, most notably the division of the so-called *Landen van Overmaas* between the Dutch Republic and Spain in 1662. Including Dutch and Spanish (after 1713, Austrian) territories, together with sections of the Duchy of Gulik and various semi-autonomous seigneuries, it was, in several respects, a border area par excellence.[2]

Apart from the political frontiers there were many different legal jurisdictions, and the boundary dividing Protestants from Roman Catholics—the result of the Protestantization that the Dutch (largely unsuccessfully) tried to impose on their territories—ran right across the area. The transitional character of the entire region was reinforced by its location on commercial and military crossroads. Situated in a major European interaction zone, the Lower Meuse connected Flanders with the Rhineland and the Dutch Republic with the Southern Netherlands and France. Finally, we should note the extremely peripheral location of the Dutch and Austrian territories of the Lower Meuse with respect to their political centers, The Hague and Brussels. Disconnected from the other parts of the Dutch Republic and the Austrian Netherlands, respectively, these fragmented territories constituted true exclaves.

At a time when there were no barracks, this part of the Lower Meuse—a fertile region of mixed farming where large, often fortified tenant farms prevailed among patches of veld, wood, and heather—was much sought after as winter quarters for armies. As a deep hinterland of Maastricht, part of the area also functioned as a granary for the city and its garrison. But these resources also invited the scourge of disbanded soldiers, of which any number of villages in the area had received their share. There were several industries in the area, not only in the towns but also in the villages, which produced textiles, metal, and leatherwork. The entire region formed an offshoot of the important industrial concentration around Liège (Thurlings and Van Drunen 1960). Apart from agriculture, therefore, people lived off several rural domestic manufactures and commerce.

These arrangements reflected a highly stratified, "seigneurial" social formation, which included a landed gentry and clergy who lived comfortably in splendid country houses, including the famous monastery Rolduc, and controlled most of the land; a group of landowning farmers who also managed the tenant farms; and a larger, more diversified group of artisans, laborers, and retail merchants with little or no property. The local courts and other public offices were staffed by gentry and farmers. The power of landlords, clerics, and farmers was also vested in the images of authority and subordination—in the architecture of the courtroom and the gallows, the country houses and castles, the monastery, and the scattered, walled-in tenant farms—and should therefore be understood in terms of cultural hegemony as well. Together with the lifestyle, dress, and gestures of the gentry, these houses and spaces were part of the orchestration of aristocratic power.[3]

The Bands

From about 1730 through 1774 numerous Roman Catholic churches and farms in this part of the eastern Meuse valley were plundered in nocturnal outings by the *Bokkeryders*. The collective biography of the *Bokkeryders*, which I composed on the basis of court records, reveals that these people were not bandits, that is, "outlaws," in the strict sense of the term. On the contrary, virtually all of them led ordinary lives in their home towns. Most of them were married with children and had a fixed residence. In fact, many were born and had grown up in the same area in which they carried out their raids—the politically fragmented territories north of Maastricht and Aix-la-Chapelle. Some of them lived in the same village as their victims, and a few were even their close neighbors.

Familiarity with the victims may explain the various forms of disguise that the robbers adopted. They operated by night; hence their nickname, *nacht-dieven* (night thieves). We know that female participants dressed as men, while the men often wore military attire and used military idiom. Others blackened their faces and put on visors, wigs, false beards, caps, and other outlandish headgear "in order not to be recognized," as one of the accused explained in court. It should not surprise us, then, that the robbers fled when the victims succeeded in raising the alarm and mobilizing their neighbors, as happened on various occasions. As local people, the *Bokkeryders* had good reason to fear recognition; they were part-time robbers, organized in secret societies of sorts, with dual identities, whose secret part they concealed behind their public face as ordinary villagers and workmen.[4]

Looking at the occupational background of the robbers (which I could trace for two-thirds of them), one finds artisans (skinners, saddlers, shoemakers, ironworkers, spinners, weavers) and retail merchants (peddlers, carters, cattle dealers) strongly represented. Together they made up about 60 percent of the participants in all three stages of band operations, while farmers and day laborers accounted for scarcely 20 percent. In a distinctly rural area, people of agrarian background remained notably underrepresented in the bands (see Table 6.1).

Rural artisans, most notably skinners, played pivotal roles in the bands. In fact, the first bands coalesced around a widely extended network of skinners from no less than ten different places. It was the skinners' job to kill sick animals, to dispose of dead cattle, to flay horses, and to remove other organic remains from public domains. Skinners also assisted the executioner in the sessions of judicial torture and helped with his work on the scaffold; they were charged with the transport of dead bodies of convicts from the prison to the gallows (invariably located at the periphery of the jurisdiction), where they had to hang them in chains or bury their remains. Their ritual uncleanliness resulted from their handling "matter out of place" and forced them to settle at the outskirts of the villages and towns, prevented them from marrying outside their occupational group, and made it difficult for them to find other work. As a consequence, the skinners constituted a widespread, regional, and endogamous network.[5] The women who participated in the outings of the bands dressed as men, and some of them showed a capacity for great cruelty. Among them we find wives, sisters, and daughters of skinners, which reflects

Table 6.1 Occupational Background of *Bokkeryders*

	Phase I	Phase II	Phase III	Total
Artisans	62	15	142	219
Skinners	17	—	5	
Ironworkers	17	5	18	
Saddlers	1	—	6	
Shoemakers	5	7	20	
Spinners & weavers	14	2	49	
Other	8	1	44	
Commerce and transport	21	5	33	59
Agriculture	10	5	73	88
Authorities	3	3	11	17
Miscellaneous	27	2	29	58
Total	123	30	288	441

the close-knit character of the first bands (Blok 1995, 57–88, 435–36). When in the later bands the number of skinners decreased, the participation of women also dwindled.

Faced with economic hardship in the postwar years and virtually barred from other work because of their "pollution," the skinners could draw on their far-flung occupational network and the cultural capital entailed by their profession to organize themselves in bands across the borders of the Lower Meuse. Thus the skinners not only dominated the first bands in terms of numbers, they also had an important part in the preparation and organization of the raids, and the division of the booty and the sale of stolen goods (through Jewish receivers in the bigger towns) were mostly in their hands. To understand their prominence (which they maintained in the later bands even though their numerical dominance had drastically decreased), the implications of their profession deserve close scrutiny.

The skinners shared their low social status, their peripheral location, and their mobility with other occupational groups that were strongly represented in the bands. We hear of peddlers, part-time beggars, musicians, jugglers, carters, retail merchants, innkeepers, and ex-soldiers. Although all these people had a fixed residence (and thus certainly did not belong to the *fahrende Leute*), they moved a lot between the villages and towns, while some of them, most notably the innkeepers and shoemakers, formed main junctions of social networks.[6] Apart from these more or less itinerant folk (including the spinners and weavers, who were strongly represented in the later bands), the skinners also maintained relations with other professional killers, like butchers and other craftsmen involved in leatherwork—saddlers, shoemakers, and cobblers.

The bands were thus tied together by occupational links, kinship, and marriage. But local bonds were also important. It is striking that the vast majority of the *Bokkeryders* were settled in smaller neighborhoods and hamlets near the bigger villages and on the outskirts of these places. Some of these settlements were built on poor soils (heath), like Heerlerheide and Chèvremont, and developed a distinct subculture (Wichers 1965, 94–97). Given their mobility and peripheral location, the *Bokkeryders* could not be easily subjected to tight forms of social control. These conditions held particularly true for the skinners, who could organize themselves over considerable distances. For a long time, they did so much more successfully than did the judicial authorities, who were bound to small jurisdictions. In a way, therefore, the regional, endogamous network of the skinners provided the infrastructure of the first bands. Many outings in those years had, indeed, the character of family affairs.

No less important for understanding the organization of the *Bokkeryders* bands and the collective violence they deployed were other implications of the skinning trade. Visiting farms at unusual times enabled the skinners to acquire an intimate knowledge of the area in which they worked. Their sense of place must have been formidable, for they could find their way in the middle of the night around a large area, going to the rendezvous and target and returning home before dawn, every step of which required precise timing. Even more than the peddlers, carters, entertainers, and other itinerant people, the skinners had an excuse to hang around at unlikely times and places. As they were the emergency butchers, their presence at uncommon times and places did not raise suspicion, nor did their transport of heavy packs and bundles. The cultural capital entailed by the skinning trade also included skills in the use of violence and inflicting pain as well as familiarity with death. From descriptions of the raids on farms and rectories given by both victims and offenders, we learn that the skinners did not hesitate to use the same means on their victims that they employed in their work with animals and in their role as the executioner's assistant.

The circumstances bearing on the social and spatial organization of the skinners and their allies cannot, of course, explain why these people organized themselves in robber bands and secret societies, breaking into churches and farmhouses, maiming and sometimes killing the habitants. These circumstances only tell us how the skinners and their accomplices could operate. They throw light on their power chances vis-à-vis the authorities, who were tied to jurisdictions of limited size. At this point, we have to consider the cultural aspects of collective violence and the way in which notions of identity, pride, and meaning were implied in banditry and its repression. We take our clues from the more "expressive" aspects of the raids, from what these outings had to "say."

Violation from Below

It is obvious that the skinners and various of their associates provided the community with indispensable services. Yet the established rural population of farmers (from whom the local authorities were largely recruited) excluded them from its ranks. It should not surprise us, therefore, that the *Bokkeryders*—from their first outings in the early 1730s to their very last one at the end of 1774—directed their operations against the principal symbols of the rural community: churches and farms. Even if the stigmatization to which the skinners and their associates were subjected may have provided them with a cause, we are still left with the question of why the bands took shape around 1730 and not before.

It is very likely that the skinners in the Lower Meuse enjoyed a certain measure of prosperity in the decades around 1700. Both the military operations that afflicted the area until the early eighteenth century and the cattle plagues that struck various regions of western Europe between 1713 and 1719 may have favored the skinning trade as much as they must have taken a toll on the farmers. By about 1720 these afflictions came to a temporary halt, but this meant that prosperous times for the skinners had gone. As mentioned before, wars and other military operations, including military presence, provided work not only for those taking part in them but also for people whose services were required to sustain military activities. Among these we find skinners, butchers, tanners, saddlers, shoemakers, locksmiths, blacksmiths, and other ironworkers—occupations that were all strongly represented in the bands.[7] There are various indications of a marked decrease in employment for skinners, in particular, in the 1720s and 1730s. Some of them had to insist on their local monopoly; others were continually on the move in search of work; still others removed their business to other locations. As skinners they had few chances of finding employment outside their trade.

Although artisans remained prominent, the later bands also included people from different backgrounds and with different aims. In the 1750s and 1760s the bands came under the control of a local *chirurgijn* (surgeon) who had been an officer in the Austrian army and who could rely on preexisting networks of the robbers as well as on the services of a string of innkeepers and various shoemakers—professions that had also been salient in the first bands.[8] In this way the bands, which had been and continued to be a segmented assortment of secret societies, were cast in a military mold. Recruitment became a serious business, more important than the raids themselves, which, apart from five large-scale outings in the Duchy of Gulik in a single year (1770), took place less frequently and were hardly profitable. The operations of the *Bokkeryders* in this stage looked very much like those of a *Freikorps* or militia in the making.[9] Whatever the ulterior political aims the leaders may have had in mind (and one cannot exclude the possibility of a secessionist movement), their project proved abortive when the authorities started the massive roundups of *Bokkeryders* in early 1771 after an outing, not authorized by the leaders, led to the discovery of the bands.

The raids on churches, especially frequent in the early years when the bands were dominated by the skinners, involved more than the theft of goods and money—not only because the goods included sacred objects. By itself, breaking into a church was already an act with strong symbolic overtones. Since the church, as a center of sociability, formed the core of the community and was the "House of God," such intrusions were defined as major violations and, if followed by theft, were considered sacrilege and were punished "with fire," a sanction that evokes images of pollution and purification of both the church and the community of believers.[10] As Raymond Firth reminds us, this community of believers forms a body—the Body of Christ, its members being in mystical union with him: The elect are knit together "in one communion and fellowship, in the mystical body of thy Son Christ our Lord," as the Book of Common Prayer phrases it.[11] The attacks on churches assumed the features of what E. P. Thompson called the "countertheater" of the poor.[12] On several occasions the operations included parodies of the Mass, during which one of the leaders acted as a "priest" and distributed the Host among his followers. These performances involved the violation of another body: the eucharistic Body of Christ, the consecrated bread (and wine) that is received in Holy Communion.

"Every religious ceremony creates the possibility of a black mass," wrote Goffman (1967, 86). Through parody and contrast, the skinners imitated and at the same time distorted and violated the Holy Communion. The profanations with the *Corpus Christi* in an inverted mass foreshadowed initiation rituals, the first of which may have taken place as early as 1737. With the expansion of the bands the countertheater of the *Bokkeryders* received further elaboration in secret ceremonies that marked incorporation into the bands. These ceremonies served as an offensive and subversive frame to recruit new members. On these occasions the initiates were encouraged to affront holy bodies: images, icons, and effigies of the Virgin, the saints, and Christ. New members had to swear an oath of allegiance in wayside chapels and other liminal locations. The ceremonies took the form of an inverted Roman Catholic liturgy and were performed in front of an improvised altar with burning candles, holy statuettes, and images of saints. The neophytes had to spit on a crucifix, throw it on the floor, and step on it while renouncing God and the Holy Mother and swearing allegiance to the Devil, promising secrecy and commitment to theft. On some occasions the initiation ceremonies took place around a burning candle put into a dead man's hand cut off from the corpse of an executed criminal, to which the skinners, because of their profession, had easy access. Credited with magical power, the so-called *Diebshand* or *Diebslicht* was believed to facilitate burglaries: It would open locks, put the victims to sleep, prevent them from waking up, or, if they were awake, keep them from speaking, moving, and so on.[13]

The simple symbolic act of stepping and spitting on a crucifix also included references to that other Body of Christ—the community of believers. In this way the sacrileges helped the initiates to separate themselves from "society" and become members of a countersociety of sorts. For the skinners and several of their associates, this separation also involved an "imitation"—the working of the mimetic faculty—since they had already been excluded from ordinary social life because of their occupation, their social exclusion being symbolized by their spatial segregation.

As in rites of passage elsewhere, the secret meetings of the *Bokkeryders* must have enhanced the social cohesion of the robbers' network and underscored the difference between them and ordinary people (La Fontaine 1985, 58, 72–73). The initiation rituals may also have reinforced the *Bokkeryders'* daring. They made their appearance at the time when the bands started to grow rapidly and could not be tied together solely by links of kinship, marriage, friendship, occupation, and other local bonds. But these ties continued to play a significant role—both in terms of structure and in terms of sentiment. The robbers emphasized "equality" and, during the third and last phase, the imminent foundation—by violent means—of a "New Kingdom" and a "Brotherhood of Happiness" (Blok 1995, 113–52).

It must have been the news about the intitiation ceremonies as well as the remarkable mobility of the bands that earned the robbers the epithet of "*Bokkeryders*" (in German, *Bockreiter*), that is, "Goat Riders," a popular name bestowed on them only in the early 1770s when the last trials were in full swing and by which they have been known ever since. One does not find this denomination in the court records, which speak of "bandits," "night thieves," "extortioners," "members of the famous band," and the like, although the judges acknowledged the existence of a sworn confederacy. Rooted in an ancient and widespread folk belief that associates the billy goat with evil and with the Devil and his work, the use of the name "*Bokkeryders*" suggests that the speaker regarded the robbers as antisocial and attributed to them supernatural power—the ability to make magical, nocturnal flights on animals to far-off places to steal and make their rendezvous.[14] But we do not know, of course, for whom—and for how many contemporaries—the name may have had ironic connotations.[15]

After having sketched the main features of the context in which collective violence from below took shape, it is tempting to reflect briefly on the subversive bent of the swearing of the formulaic oath, the "sacrilegious oath," as the judicial authorities phrased it, because it shows how closely popular and elite traditions and both forms of collective violence were related. Always the focal point of initiation rituals of secret societies, among the *Bokkeryders* the oath taking took up most of the ceremony. It included references to (and suggested similarities with) proofs of allegiance and incorporation into four major social institutions: first Holy Communion, enrollment in the army, recruitment for the local *schutten* (civil guard), and installation of new members of the local court. These inaugurations were imitated and at the same time, together with the institutions, parodied and subverted. It is significant that the main locations for the oath-taking ceremonies during the 1750s and 1760s, when membership was soaring, were wayside chapels. One of them, the Saint Leonardus chapel, was situated on a hill of the same name, not far from the Rolduc monastery. During the repression of the bands in the early 1770s, the authorities required an additional place for the gallows; they demolished this profaned chapel and raised the new gallows on the place of the former sanctuary. These displacements and substitutions involved a twofold mimesis of attacks on bodies and illustrate the idea that there is a dialogue or "circulation" between popular culture and elite culture.[16] This brings us to the second form of collective violence: the means the authorities had at their disposal to repress banditry in the fragmented territories of the Lower Meuse.

The Repression

For a long time the local courts charged with the prosecution of criminals in their relatively small jurisdictions were ignorant of the real authors of the plundering of churches and farms. The magistrates believed that groups of vagrants were responsible for these crimes. All they could do in the absence of a regional police force was to enforce the *plakkaten* (decrees) against these people and insist on the vigilance of the local civic guard. In each of the three great operations against the *Bokkeryders,* local courts started their coopera- tion (exchanging information, handing over prisoners) only after the first members of the bands had been arrested. It is also telling that local prosecu- tors depended on the "mistakes" made by those members of the band who went on haphazard and unauthorized outings or who were recognized by their victims, as happened in 1741, 1750, 1770, 1773, and 1774.

As noted before, magistrates of several local courts were related by ties of kinship and marriage, which facilitated their cooperation. Yet in the absence of a regular police force and houses of correction, the courts did not have means to repress the bands other than by theatrical violence, terror, and defamation—as explicitly specified in the motive for capital sentences, "*tot afschrik en exempel* [to inspire fear and set an example]" and in the additional stipulation that the body of the convict should be denied a Christian burial. For these reasons alone, it would be wrong to consider the hangings— between 1741 and 1778 in these territories there were more than 300 of them—in only instrumental or pragmatic terms, that is, as simple elimina- tions. Such an approach to collective violence from above would indeed miss the main point of criminal law under the ancien régime: The refusal of burial added infamy to death (Linebaugh 1975; Spierenburg 1984; Rupp 1992).

In all recorded cases of hangings, the body of the condemned was to hang in chains for birds to feed on until its total decomposition and decay. In their denial of a burial in consecrated earth and their spectacular displacement of the convict from center (church) to periphery (veld, heather, moors), these punishments represented major cultural inversions. As extreme, public as- saults on the body, they brought ultimate outrages to a person's honor and status and to the reputation of his family and decendants as well. Thus the im- agery of the violated body of convicts assumed great importance during the repression of the bands. Leaving aside the phases of arrest, detention, and the rituals of judicial torture—which constituted serious infringements on a person's honor and status mediated by his physical body—we will examine briefly the ritual and symbolic aspects of the sentences and their execution.

The magical realism of the repression was most noticeable when the ac- cused was a fugitive and was tried in absentia. In most cases these persons were banished, *voor eeuwig* (forever), from the Dutch or Austrian territories, with the specification that they would be subjected to capital punishment if they returned. This written sentence was read in public and then nailed to the gallows. But we know of at least fourteen such cases (in which the accused had ignored the court's citations and remained at large) in which the absent convict was hanged in effigy. An ordinary banishment did not suffice, and the convicted person—by means of an effigy, a dummy, an imitation of his body—had to be magically removed from the community. Like produces like, and like acts upon like (cf. Mauss 1972, 64ff.; Tambiah 1985, 64–72).

Attacks on the social identity of the convicts were also evident in three recorded cases in which the court ordered that the convicts' houses be destroyed, with the stipulation that their locations were not to be built on for a period of 100 years "because of the horrible crimes committed by the owner and because it has served as shelter and rendezvous for thieves and *schelmen* [rogues]." The attack on one's house or home—a quintessential *lieu de mémoire*—making the convict posthumously homeless, provides us with another instance of ritual cleansing, of an attempt to remove a polluted person magically from the community and from social memory as well.

The punishment directed against the house of the convict perhaps illustrates the interplay between elite culture and popular culture, the dialogue between authority and subversion. Some of the operations of the bands, most notably some of the attacks on farms that were also inns, involved willful destruction of furniture, doors, windows, closets, barrels, and the like. This violence against property looks like acts of revenge and bears some resemblance to the more violent forms of charivari or Rough Music, forms of popular justice that in the German areas were called *Wüstung* (destruction) and were intended to drive the residents out of the community as undesirable persons (Meuli 1975, 457–75).

An important aspect of the collective violence inflicted on the *Bokkeryders* concerns its topography: the space of violence and death. Situated at the limits of the jurisdictions, the place of execution was a clearly demarcated location, usually an elevation or hill. The condemned had to be escorted from that other space of violence, the place of detention, usually located in the basement of one of the castles or country houses, all the way down to the outskirts of his hometown. These processions were very much part of the choreography of punishment since they reinforced humiliation and disgrace. Each punishment also conveyed something of the crime that had been committed. Ordinary thieves were whipped and banished; those who had committed qualified thefts were hanged; murderers and bandit leaders were broken on the wheel; and arson and sacrilege (for example, church robberies) were punished by various forms of burning (cf. Foucault 1977, 43). In some cases elements of the crime were literally reproduced in the punishment. Such reenactments happened at the execution of some of the condemned who had blackened their faces when breaking into farms and had sworn allegiance to the Devil. As Gustav Radbruch notes in his commentary on the *Carolina* (1532): "Wer mit dem Feuer gesündet hat, der Brandstifter, der Münzfälscher, soll durch das *Feuer* sterben [Who has sinned with fire, the arsonist, the counterfeiter, should die by *fire*]" (1960, 10; see also Langbein 1974, 167). In short, the collective violence the authorities deployed to repress banditry revolved around terror and infamy. Hence the major elements of the punishments included the disintegration of the corpse and the denial of funeral rites.

The popular sensibilities regarding the integrity of the body and post mortem care are obvious from attempts to intervene in the judicial process. We know of attempts to remove the bodily remains of kinsmen from the gallows at night and to provide for a decent burial. If discovered, such ventures were defined as theft and punished. For those who had died in detention, the authorities had, in most cases, no less dishonorable punishments in store. A sentence was passed on the corpse, which the skinner had to drag on a sledge to the gallows to be buried there or to be hanged to rot, depending on the condition of the remains. We know of a widow whose husband had died in detention without a confession and been buried under the gallows. She wrote a request to the States General in The Hague in which she asked for a revision of the dishonorable sentence, explicitly referring to the role of the skinner, and for a Christian burial for her husband. Her request was denied. Before it had passed sentence on the corpse the court had (according to a standard procedure) asked advice from a lawyer in Maastricht. This impartial legal expert had suggested that the body should be returned to the next of kin and be "buried *de noctu,* without homage, but also without any offense against it from the department of executioner and skinner" (Blok 1995, 168–71, 417).

The image of the decaying body is of considerable interest, and not only in the context of the repression of robber bands accused of theft and sacrilege. The decomposed, corrupt body enshrines a powerful metaphor. As Bruce Lincoln has pointed out in another but very similar context—the notorious exhumation and public display of the long-buried corpses of priests, nuns, and saints in several towns and cities in Spain during the Civil War—the image of bodily decomposition provides a metaphor of moral corruption: "Like its near-synonyms *rottenness* and *decadence,* corruption is most concretely and emphatically manifest in the state of bodily decomposition" (1985, 257). From a theological point of view, bodily corruption

> is a moral process as much as a natural one, for decay is the final physical result of a sinful—that is to say, corrupt—life. And what is more, the bodies of those who are purified of sin through the sacraments of the Church and the practice

of a saintly life do not decay, but partake of eternity, freedom from decomposition being one of the foremost proofs of sanctity. (Lincoln 1985, 257)

Conclusion

Considering the extent to which elite culture and popular culture in the Lower
Meuse formed models of and for one another, it would certainly not be an ex-
aggeration to say that they developed in a mutually constitutive relationship.
There was indeed a great deal of "reflection"—imitation, mimicry, parody—
on the part of subaltern groups, while the violence of the punishments reflected something of the scale, volume, form, and meaning of the crimes, real
and imagined. The massive violence that both groups inflicted upon the other
(unprecedented in the history of the Dutch Republic and strangely neglected
in offical Dutch historiography) and its explicit magical realism cannot be
understood without reference to the main features of these territories: their
political fragmentation, their peripheral location, and their seigneurial structure, which juxtaposed aristocratic splendor with plebeian misery. It is obvious that these conditions provided considerable space for dissident groups.

But these conditions also prompted and shaped the repression. Confronted
with massive and sustained forms of subversion, members of the ruling class,
loosely tied together in a regional network of kinship and marriage, restored
their domination through the theater of law, drowning the voices of insubordination in the process. In this assertion of cultural hegemony, the courtroom, the place of detention, the street, and the place of execution provided
the setting for the emphasis on and dramatization of the distinction between
the integral body, on the one hand, and the violated, dishonored, and decaying body, on the other—a distinction that served the restoration magically as
a *pars pro toto*.

Notes

I owe special thanks to Rod Aya, Wayne te Brake, Anthony Robbin, and James C. Scott for
their helpful suggestions and comments on earlier versions of this paper.

1. Most of the surviving court records are preserved in the State Archives at Maastricht (RA LvO). For a detailed account of the sources, see Blok 1995, 235–445.

2. On the military and political history of the Lower Meuse (the *Overmaas*), see
Wouters 1970; Haas 1978; Gutmann 1980.

3. For the importance of the gentry in the Lower Meuse, see Wouters 1970, 325–28;
Haas 1978, 202–6, 234–36; Janssen de Limpens 1982. E. P. Thompson writes that ruling-class
control in eighteenth-century England "was located primarily in a cultural hegemony, and
only secondarily in an expression of economic or military power" (1978, 254).

4. The quintessential role of secrecy in social life was long ago recognized by Georg

Simmel, who regarded the secret, the hiding of realities by negative or positive means, as one of man's greatest achievements (1950, 330, 345–36).

5. In some European areas the skinner remained a social outcast until the end of the nineteenth century (Weiss 1946, 113).

6. On the subversive role of taverns and inns, see the work of James Scott, who writes: "Here subordinate classes met offstage and off-duty in an atmosphere of freedom encouraged by alcohol" (1990, 121–22). See also Burke 1978, 109–11). On the pivotal role of *cabaretiers* in the *Bande d'Orgères,* see Cobb 1972, 191. For the influence of innkeepers in Dutch village life, see Wichers 1965, 37–38. On the leading role of shoemakers in popular movements in early modern Europe, see Hobsbawm and Scott 1980.

7. The vicissitudes of the Eta in Japan, a despised occupational group that specialized in butchering, tanning, and leatherwork (which in a Buddhist society are considered defiling pursuits), were, in this respect, very similar to those of the skinners in the Lower Meuse. They were prosperous during the period of civil wars when their services were in much demand. But the Eta suffered during the relative peace of the Tokugawa period (1603–1868), when their trades lost the importance they had held during the time of civil war and discrimination against them intensified (Price 1972).

8. In eighteenth-century France (and elsewhere), surgeons were the primary medical practitioners and have been called "the physicians of the poor." The development of their profession was stimulated by the rise of the standing army in the seventeenth century; see Wellman 1992, 16–17, 29.

9. On the genesis of the *Freikorps* in the German territories in the mid-eighteenth century, see Childs 1982, 119.

10. The *Carolina* (1532) (see Radbruch 1960, 172ff.) specifies punishments for these forms of sacrilege. For similar cases of theft from churches in eighteenth-century France—and similar punishments—see Ferrand 1989, 65, 71–73, on which I have drawn in some detail.

11. In his remarks on the symbolism of the body, Firth (1973, 227) distinguishes between three bodies of Christ: the physical body, the mystical body, and the eucharistic body.

12. There is little doubt about the presence of elements of protest and parody in the way a successful theft from a church was celebrated (Thompson 1978, 254; 1974, 387). For a massive documentation of more covert forms of protest and resistance, see Scott 1990, 136ff.

13. This belief seems to have been common in early modern Europe: "Die vom Galgen abgeschnittene Diebshand sichert, beim Stehlen angezündet, das Gelingen des Raubs" (The thief's hand, cut from a corpse on the gallows, when lit during the robbery, assures success) (Danckert 1963, 42); see also Bächtold-Stäubli 1929–30). On the luck-bringing power of the *Diebsdaum* (thief's thumb), see Angstmann 1928, 93–94. For a general account of the magical power of liminal material, see Leach 1964; 1976, 33–36, 61–62, and passim).

14. Courts in western Europe had long since lost interest in demonology (Levack 1987, 170ff.). This was particularly the case in the Low Countries, which saw few witch trials anyway and dropped the subject long before its heyday in Germany and France. The sentences in the Lower Meuse that contained explicit references to the oath taking phrased this profanity invariably in terms of blasphemy or sacrilege, that is, "*de godslasterlijke eed.*"

15. Two contemporary reports refer to the denomination "*Bokkeryders,*" but they merely record the use of the term and the associated folk belief, while expressing personal reservations; see Mengels [1773] 1887, 269; Sleinada [1779] 1972, 61–62. One cannot, of course, exclude the possibility that for some people the initiation rituals of the robbers and the term "*Bokkeryders*" included references to representations current during the witch trials in the sixteenth and seventeenth centuries.

16. Carlo Ginzburg, quoted in Luria and Gandolfo 1986, 108.

Chapter 7

Six Hundred Years of Visionaries in Spain: Those Believed and Those Ignored

William A. Christian Jr.

Visions at Lourdes, Fatima, and Medjugorje are part of a long series in Europe that began before the existence of Christianity and continues to the present day. For Spain we can document the existence over the past 600 years of lay visionaries claiming to have messages for the public. The kinds of seers, what they say they saw, and the messages that they say they heard vary systematically in different periods. A clear lesson of this variation is that what we know about visionaries and visions is severely controlled by prevailing notions about who can be believed and what can be seen and heard.

The variations over time in seers, visions, and messages may usefully be seen as the outcome of a complex historical interaction involving several different actors: the authorities, the visionaries, their interpreters, and their audience. Depending on the situation, these interactions may involve fundamental challenges to the religious authorities who claim the right to authenticate religious visions. Because of the complexity of the process, however, the historical record from which we must try to reconstruct these developments is often skewed to privilege those who chose what to record, who did the recording, and who controlled the records. The purpose of this chapter is to sort out the main lines of development over 600 years of Spanish history and where possible to analyze the dynamics of the interaction.

Principal Phases of Spanish Apparitions, 1399–1990

1399–1520

In the lay visions that we know about for the fifteenth century, men and children see Mary or saints who offer ways to avoid the plague. Towns usually require the seers to provide some kind of physical proof of visions. Men and especially children play a prominent role as intermediaries—some of the seers are children, and sometimes Mary or the saints appear in the form of children. Adult women are almost entirely missing. The divine figures point the human community toward the cross. Rather than establishing new devotions, the visions tend to revitalize older, dormant devotions or to reemphasize abandoned sacred places. They generally orient devotion away from towns to salient places in the landscape. Two hundred years earlier theologians had condemned some of the same motifs as pagan: Mary clothed in white light on a tree; a nocturnal procession of a woman accompanied by the dead. The format of the late medieval visions harkens back to stereotyped accounts of miraculous discoveries of buried relics and to legends of the finding of images.

This series of visions was cut off in Castile by the Inquisition in the second decade of the sixteenth century, not because the visions were a threat to church authority (their scope was local and devotional) but because of a more general need to curb freelance prophets like Savonarola and doctrinal innovation like that of the Protestants and the Alumbrados (Christian 1990a, 199–236). The old-style visions were tolerated longer in Catalonia, where the Inquisition had other priorities, and in Italy as well (Monter 1990; Niccoli 1990).

1590–1765

Subsequently lay Spaniards found safer ways to provide new sources of grace. In the early modern period an ancient tradition of images that sweated or bled became the dominant mode. In these apparitions without messages everyone is a seer, and what the divinity means to convey can safely be interpreted by the clergy, who generally take control of the image in question. Most of the three dozen or so cases I could document were of images of Christ associated with the Passion—the Crucifixion, the meeting with Veronica, Ecce Homo, or Christ bound to the column. A secondary way to find new grace in this period involved the miraculous discovery of images or paintings, most of them of Christ.

These devotions, appropriate to the Catholic Reformation, created holy places in towns, not in the countryside. In Spain they occurred particularly in years of political, military, or economic crisis, such as 1627, 1640, 1646–48, and during the 1706–13 war (Christian 1989, 1991, 234–41). Neo-Jansenist and liberal clergy at the end of the eighteenth and the beginning of the nineteenth centuries discouraged the image-centered religiosity of which, in a sense, this kind of miracle was a paradigm.[1]

1900–1926

Many Spaniards were enthusiastic about the 1846 apparition at La Salette in France. Later the Sisters of Charity brought to Spain the story of the apparitions in Paris of the Miraculous Mary to Catherine Labouré. And toward the end of the nineteenth century, a number of Spanish bishops, followed by clergy in general, adopted the shrine of Lourdes as a place for spiritual refreshment and help. French religious and Spanish religious trained in France encouraged the Lourdes devotion in the border dioceses. By the end of the first decade of the twentieth century there were regular annual pilgrimages to Lourdes from the eastern half of Spain (Christian 1992, 6–16, 149–51; Kselman 1983).

To the Spanish pilgrims the role of Lourdes in the revival and revitalization of French Catholicism was obvious; they began to wonder when there would be a Lourdes in Spain. Finally reports of Spanish visions began to reach the press. Most involved images of Christ in the zone of devotion to Lourdes, images that people saw moving, weeping, bleeding, sweating, or in agony (such events occurred in the towns of Manzaneda [province of Orense] in 1903; Arganda del Rey [Madrid] 1917; Gandía [Valencia] 1918; Limpias [Santander] 1919; Piedramillera [Navarra] 1920; Mañeru [Navarra] 1920; Melilla 1922). They were thus a revival of the early-modern style of visions, deeply influenced by the passion-oriented piety preached in parish missions. But unlike in the early-modern events, in those of the 1920s there was rarely liquid on the images, and not all present saw them move. This trend came to full fruition at Limpias, a small town in Cantabria near the north coast, precisely when, during World War I, it was not possible to visit Lourdes. The Christ of Limpias attracted over a quarter of a million pilgrims in the period 1919–26, including many from other countries. About one in ten of the pilgrims in these years saw the image move. The diocese modeled the pilgrimages on those of Lourdes.

The visions occurred in the context of serious labor unrest due to inflation at the close of the war. Many Catholics understood them as divine help for Spain in a time of trouble and related them to the cult of the Sacred Heart of Jesus. The visionary promises in 1672–75 by the Sacred Heart of Jesus to a French nun, Marguerite Marie Alacoque, that he would reign on earth had been followed by a similar promise in 1733 to a Spanish Jesuit, Bernardo de Hoyos, that Christ would reign in Spain with more devotion than elsewhere. This cult gained considerable publicity in the nineteenth century, spread above all by the Jesuits and through eucharistic congresses. Spaniards enthroned images of the Sacred Heart in houses, factories, and town halls, and in May 1919 the Spanish king Alfonso XIII dedicated the nation to the Sacred Heart at a massive shrine outside Madrid. The general idea of the reign of the Sacred Heart, whether in the here and now or in some apocalyptic period at the end of time, was common among Catholic Spaniards in the early twentieth century (Caballero 1972; Christian 1992).

1931–1936

Rarely did seers claim to hear the moving Christs of the 1920s speak. In very few places after 1500 had Spaniards believed laypersons who reported apparitions of divine figures with verbal messages. But in 1931 Spaniards voted in the Second Republic, and mobs burned convents in a dozen cities from May 11 to May 13. These circumstances were sufficient to make old-style apparitions containing explicit divine messages for the general public credible for Catholics and plausible for at least part of the clergy.

After a series of false starts a new sequence of apparitions began in June with two child seers in the Spanish Basque country at Ezkioga (in the province of Gipuzkoa). By the end of 1931 newspapers had named more than a hundred seers, especially children and adult men, and the nightly pageant of visions had attracted around 1 million spectators. There were similar, smaller, events in much of the Basque country and in other parts of Spain.

The seers of Ezkioga at first addressed the plight of Spain; they described a sorrowful Virgin who called for prayer and penance and promised a great miracle. But as the diocese of Vitoria gradually turned against the visions, the messages became darker, like those of La Salette before them, and the Virgin spoke of an apocalyptic chastisement in which only a faithful few would be spared. Starting at the end of 1932 a parallel set of apparitions in Belgium seemed to address a similar acute social and political division. In Spain the opposition of the republic, the bishops, the Vatican, and later Franco eventually converted the 1930s cycle of apparitions into a kind of embarrassing historical taboo (Burguera y Serrano 1934; Christian 1996; Joset 1981a, 1981b, 1982).

1945–1959

The next round of visions to gain public attention in Spain were part of a wider phenomenon associated with the Cold War and the Iron Curtain. They clustered especially in the period from 1947 to 1954, as Spanish dioceses sent the image of the Virgin of Fatima from town to town (as did other dioceses in Catholic Europe) on a missionlike crusade. The visionaries we read about in the newspapers of this period are almost exclusively children. In several cases the seers came from poor families of the Republican or socialist left, and the visions of Mary comprised a kind of charismatic rural resistance to the dominant society and were typically opposed by the urban upper class. Censorship of the Spanish press limited the scope of the seers' messages and appeal, but even so some of them, as at Cuevas de Vinroma (in the province of Castellón de la Plana), attracted enormous crowds.

After a period of sympathy, the sheer number and variety of visions throughout Europe so overwhelmed church leaders that Cardinal Alfredo Ottaviani issued a warning against them as an outbreak of "natural religion," and in Spain the Jesuit Carlos María Staehlin published a critical and skeptical explanation of the phenomenon that convinced much of the Spanish clergy (Staehlin 1954; Christian 1984).

1960 to the present

After the Second Vatican Council new visions in Spain, beginning in 1961 with those at San Sebastián de Garabandal, included messages against changes in the church. Gradually from the 1970s on there have come to be places on the outskirts of most major cities—Seville, Bilbao, Barcelona, Madrid, Valencia, Granada, and Córdoba, where on given days of the month seers have public visions and provide ways for believers to be blessed by the Virgin. Visionaries from different sites are in touch with one another and hold national meetings. This series largely predates but has been given a boost by the visions of Medjugorje in the former Yugoslavia. As have those from the United States, Ireland, and Italy, Spanish believers returning from Medjugorje have begun to have their own visions.

With the support of some members of religious orders, these visions have become a long-term, ongoing counterpoint to the established church. Finally, adult married women have gained a place as key visionaries (Roma 1991). The seers' followers include disgruntled urban traditionalists as well as the kind of exurban poor, migrants without kin networks, and disoriented villagers who are attracted to the Jehovah's Witnesses. The poor, understaffed, and divided dioceses of Spain have been unable to cope with massive migration to the cities.[2]

Apparitions as Social Products

The periods and the trends outlined above are based on the study of original documents, firsthand reports in the press, and, from the 1920s on, interviews with protagonists. But the more one finds out about any particular set of visions, the more one comes to realize how selective the documentation is about visions in general. The patterns described above seem to be scenarios that the society of the time picked out and adjusted.

For the whole matter—the temporary intersection of heaven and earth—is so fraught with mythic importance and cultural protocol that virtually all the recording, whether by a parish priest, diocesan investigators, town councils, the Inquisition, newspaper reporters, television crews, or anthropologists, is highly mediated by those who decide who is heard and who is silenced, what should be written down and what should be omitted. We must continually ask what our sources do not reveal (Apolito 1990, 1992).

Who Are Seers? Gender and Age

In any given period people will consider some seers, whether because of age, gender, wealth, or poverty, intrinsically less credible. Some of these less-credible seers never tell anyone of their visions because they know they will not be believed. Others tell family members or close friends, and the matter goes no further. Others tell local authorities, who instruct them to keep their visions to themselves. Others have their visions only for an intimate circle of believers. Those whose visions never make the newspapers (or the fifteenth-century word-of-mouth or manuscript equivalent) are more likely to be persons who because of cultural bias are to be held unlikely recipients of visions or unbelievable: in Spain up to the 1960s adult married women; in the United States children; in modern Europe adult men.

One occasionally hears of the kind of vision that would normally go unreported. At many Spanish apparition sites after a vision gains some level of credibility persons come forward who tell of visions that they have had at the place previously but that they did not make public or were not believed when they did. There were "previsions," for instance, at Griñón (in the province of Madrid) in the 1550s, at El Bonillo (Albacete) around 1640, at Limpias about 1915, at Ezkioga a few months before the main visions, and at La Codosera (Badajoz) in the 1940s.

In other words, when a vision event becomes credible it casts a light backward in time that reveals similar local events that had hitherto remained private and in the dark. Such public credibility also projects light forward and outward, eliciting reports of similar contemporary events elsewhere that would not otherwise have been recorded. There is an internal shut-off mechanism as the glut of reports jades the appetite of the public or those who control the media, banalizes what purports to be exceptional, and temporarily discredits the phenomenon as a whole. The unwary observer gains what is sometimes a false impression that there has been an unusual rash of similar events when in fact some of the events have been going on for a long time.[3]

The many visions that go unreported should make us careful about generalizing from the few that we know about. When historians baldly state that there were few female visionaries from the sixth to the twelfth centuries, they surely reflect the biases of their sources.[4] Discrimination against the visions of adult lay women is explicit in the warnings of theologians against false or demonic visions. Female prophets who were nuns attracted clerical followers throughout Europe in the late medieval and early modern periods, and there were lay equivalents (Prosperi 1986; Vauchez 1987; Bilinkoff 1992; Ahlgren 1995). Lay women seers are a constant in the records of the Spanish Inquisition. There was no lack of married female visionaries in seventeenth-century England (Mack 1992).

Yet in the legends of the origins of Catalan shrines recorded in the 1650s, probably dating back at least to the fourteenth century, adult women are almost entirely absent; three out of four protagonists are adult men, and almost all the rest are children. Among the prime visionaries people believed in the fifteenth century, women are again virtually absent; boys and girls are in the majority, and almost all the rest are adult men. In the case of the events in the seventeenth and eighteenth centuries in which images bled or sweated, either there are no visionaries or everyone was a visionary, for there actually was liquid on the images, so the gender of seers was not a factor. But in twentieth-century visions once more there was a general effort to suppress the news of a high incidence of women seers and to emphasize instead men and children.

Authors favorable to the events at Limpias and Ezkioga substantially underreported women in order to make the visions as a whole more credible. Books about Limpias would lead one to suppose that most seers were men, while the vision register in the sacristy showed the opposite, that a majority were women. At Ezkioga by my reckoning there were almost three times as many adult women seers as adult men, yet just the opposite, three times as many men as women, were named as seers in newspapers, and five adult male seers but no adult females had their pictures in the press.[5]

Given the models of Mélanie and Mathurin of La Salette and Bernadette of Lourdes, people were far more inclined to believe children in the apparitions in the 1930s. In the Cold War period, when Fatima was added to the model, people tended to frame adult men as well as adult women out of the picture.

Table 7.1 Gender and Age of Known Spanish Lay Visionaries

	Men	Boys	Girls	Women	N
Camós legends[a]	.78	.09	.11	.02	93
1399–1592[b]	.40	.33	.20	.07	15
Limpias 1919–20, seers named in books	.86			.15	486
Limpias 1919, seers signing registers	**.38**			**.62**	330
Ezkioga seers pictured in press	.38	.14	.48	.00	21
Ezkioga seers named only once in press	.43	.22	.22	.13	69
Ezkioga, habitual seers, my compilation	**.08**	**.22**	**.50**	**.21**	116
1945–1959	.07	.33	.60	.00	30

Note: Note the contrast between figures for "official" sources and those, in bold, which I could control more carefully.
[a] Protagonists in apparitions and discoveries of images
[b] Prime seers believed by authorities

Such systematic biases limit the usefulness of generalizations about seers based on secondary accounts (see Table 7.1).

Adult lay women, even married lay women, have only gained respectability as public, serial, lay visionaries in Catholic Europe in the 1960s and 1970s. Their recognition is the culmination of a slow, cumulative process, dating back at least to the nineteenth century, related to the emergence of women in other public spheres and the massive involvement of female religious in social work, teaching, and mission activity (Langlois 1984).

Lay women as Catholic visionaries lagged behind other, less orthodox female charismatics like somnabulists and spirit mediums (Gallini 1983; Braude 1989; Owen 1989; Edelman 1995). But one kind of charismatic lay Catholic woman early "acceptable" to the general public was the stigmatic, whose wounds, like those of cloistered nuns, were often accompanied by ecstasies. Louise Lateau, Marie-Louise Jehanney, Thérèse Neumann, and Marthe Robin all acheived fame throughout Europe in their lifetimes, and their bodies comprised a kind of permanent challenge to rationalism (Imbert-Gourbeyre 1873; Thurston 1952; Guitton 1985; Christian 1996, 262–301).

Some lay women gained a similar kind of fame when they were cured at Lourdes. Their stories were publicized in the *Annales* of the shrine and were reprinted in the Catholic press, often with photographs. The age-old category of "a person miraculously cured" was revived and enhanced by scientific certification at the medical bureau. And as a result Catholics attentive to sanctity and charisms became more alert to persons suddenly and inexplicably healed, whether or not at Lourdes, and such persons (Thérèse Neumann and the Catalan mystic Magdalena Aulina are examples) themselves became more attentive to the idea that they might have a divine mission.

Political factors also came into play. As men fell away from Catholicism, the church turned to women as a central constituency and as its representatives in family units (Scaraffia 1994). In the first decades of the twentieth century the canonization of Jeanne d'Arc and the beatification of Gemma Galgani spoke to a female constitituency that was increasingly militant. Catholic labor organizers like María de Echarri and Catholic political activists like Rosa Urraca de Pastor and Haydée de Aguirre were publicly prominent in Spain before women gained the right to vote in 1934. Catholic parties supported female suffrage, though many Republicans were unsure whether it would be politically expedient.

The clergy, nevertheless, retained a deep-seated suspicion of women as seers. Spanish dioceses were able to control the news of visions that reached the press, and through their vetting of religious literature they were able to avoid the publication of books or pamphlets about unorthodox visions. Not until the late 1960s, when church censorship of Catholic literature became ineffective (it was finally abolished in 1969 by Paul VI [Jelly 1993]), did full-fledged series of visions to adult lay women receive publicity in Spain's media. By 1995 publicly acknowledged seers were predominantly women. Pepita Pugés, for example, had public visions in Cerdanyola, near Barcelona, and Amparo Cuevas (a married woman), had visions at San Lorenzo del Escorial, near Madrid. Both claimed to have been cured at Lourdes. Since 1965 there have been other adult women serial seers at El Palmar de Troya, Monte Umbe near Bilbao (a married woman), Girona, and Granada.

Elsewhere in Europe a few lay women seers had gained prominence earlier in the century—in France Claire Ferchaud at Loublande (in the province of Vendée) during World War I and, starting in the 1940s, a woman in Kerizinen in Brittany. In Amsterdam from 1945 to 1959 Ida Peedeman promoted with her visions the cult of Our Lady of All Peoples. In Italy the visions of Caterina Richero at Balestrino from 1949 to 1971 overlapped with those of Rosa Quattrini of San Damiano, near Piacenza, from 1964 to 1981 (Zimdars-Swartz 1991). But almost all of the women seers before the 1970s gained a following only gradually and at great cost, in some cases after years of private, unpublicized visions, for church regulations impeded the spread of their messages. We can have no doubt that in Europe for each of these lay women who became known there was a myriad who never reached the public eye, in the twentieth century and in earlier centuries.

Content of Visions: Who or What Appears and What Do They Say?

Just as conventional sources filter seers, so they filter vision content. When there are several divine figures this process determines which are accorded the most attention, what spirits are demonic, and which ones are simply the family dead and therefore are not of public interest. Before the fifteenth century there was the problem of which lady in white was the Virgin and which a pagan spirit, or in Catholic terms, a devil in disguise. Seers know that if they tell some things they see or hear they will be ridiculed. Incongruous or unusual messages may not be understood by believers or authorities. Successive scribes substantially changed the vision message received at Cubas in 1449, for instance (Christian 1990a, 115).

In the twentieth century the press weeded out, summarized, and adjusted messages until they resembled what people expected or wanted to hear. At Ezkioga at first seers described the dead alongside the Virgin, but the press made fun of these visions. So a kind of two-tier system evolved: less orthodox private messages, including sightings of the dead, for specific followers and more orthodox public messages for the world at large.

Vision messages are also bent when interested observers put questions to the divine figure through the seer, often while the vision is in progress. These questions set the terms and pose the issues for the visionary response. In this way, in particular, groups with a special supernatural agenda find messages to suit their needs.[6]

The possibility of an unusual or innovative vision message having a major impact on Catholicism is further reduced by the basic rule of all systems of discernment: that any message not in consonance with church doctrine is not divine in origin. Hence Mary Ann Van Hoof, the seer at the visions that began in Necedah, Wisconsin, in 1945, was suspect, first, because she had previously been a spiritualist and, second, because the Virgin told her that Catholics and Protestants should ignore their differences and pray together (Kselman and Avella 1986).

Similarly, just where the new holy place is supposed to be and how it is to be configured—whether with trees, a rock, a spring, a cave, or the Stations of the Cross; whether on a hillside or in a previous holy place—is the product of a complex collective negotiation between what the seer or seers report, what they are asked, and what believers expect or want. In the modern visions journalists, believers, priests, and photographers home in on holy trees, set up paraliturgical emblems, build grottos, and strain to approximate established configurations such as that of Lourdes, although the seers may in fact see the divine figures in a number of places or moving across the landscape.

This process, as it occurred at Ezkioga, was somewhat experimental. Seers, priests, reporters, and designers of souvenir postcards tried out various features of the apparition landscape that did not "take" or that were gradually superseded by others. Apple trees and blackberry bushes quickly were abandoned (as "the" vision site) for oak trees. In a kind of wishful remembering, the seers and the media adjusted the story of the first apparition to fit the changing sacred landscape. One of the sacred oak trees was converted into a cross, and within a year all four of them had died after pilgrims took their leaves and bark as talismans. Thereafter seers and believers shifted their attention to a newly built chapel with a fountain of holy water (Christian 1990b).

The Role of Informed Enthusiasts

When watching for the way observers structure visions, one does well to pay attention to ongoing groups that cultivate divine transcendence and the marvelous. The Catholic Church as a whole must maintain a systematic skepticism toward independent revelation, if only to to protect its own carefully accredited and well-organized stock of truths. But the institution's impulse toward consistency and control inevitably provokes a reaction in those seeking more spontaneity and a closer involvement with the divine in their daily lives.

Such groups, like the Beguines, the Alumbrados, young religious orders, or the charismatic Catholics that began to meet in the 1960s, create closed circles to protect their experiences from more profane outsiders and dwell in a heightened state of immanence in which revelation and vision can almost be banal. Within such groups the kind of persons whose visions would be denied credibility by outside society have a space in which they are believed.

These circles at times have a symbiotic relation with more traditional, less "prepared" lay visionaries. Their members attend the public visions and find in them confirmation of their own particular charisma and mission, and then in turn confirm the public seers in their own divine mission. In some of the recent Irish and American visions connected to Medjugorje, and apparently in the Medjugorje visions themselves, it appears that the visionaries were trained in prayer groups to expect the supernatural before their visions began, following the inspired procedures of Catholic Pentecostals (Bax 1995; Bearak 1989; Zimdars-Swartz 1989a, 1989b, 1991). The more public visions, then, feed on the heightened sensitivity of these groups trained in mysticism, cross over to them, confirm them, and take nourishment from them (Apolito 1992, 216; Christian 1996, 43–48, 217–42).

Paradoxically, what appear to be most spontaneous in Catholic culture, the visions of lay seers, including those of children and the unlettered, come to us in highly formulaic and controlled reports. These are serious, touchy, sacred matters, and what we have to work with is a complex social product that first and foremost reflects what certain groups of people *wanted* to be seen and heard.

By uncovering how communities selected some seers for gender, age, and personality (Bernadette and not the other child seers of Lourdes) and rewarded them for seeing some things and not others, we glimpse a multi-layered, anonymous process by which societies and their institutions construct their reality and formulate their hopes. The seers not listened to and the messages unheard, voices calling in the desert, join the other lost matter, matter seen but not socially perceived, that surrounds us every day and in every aspect of our lives.

Western societies have often fixed on members whose lack of authority, supposed ignorance, and quasi-sacred purity enables them to deliver the messages the societies require (Scott 1990). Their apparent social defenselessness and lack of power enhance their credibility. Such persons—honorable poor rural men, children, boys, girls, cloistered nuns—are not in a position to control the interpretation or even the content of their visions once the messages enter public channels, which makes the messages even more malleable and responsive to public needs.

At any given time certain categories of seers are less likely to enter the historical record. Historians and other fashioners of social products have a natural difficulty in imagining what it is like not to have a voice. And since our job, especially lately, has been to point out things normally imperceptible, it is hard to stop and think about the kinds of matter and events that even we cannot find but that by all logic surely occurred.[7]

Notes

The author wishes to acknowledge the suggestions of Paolo Apolito, Gábor Klániczay, Michelle Perrot, Lucetta Scaraffia, James Scott, and the editors of this volume. Salvador Palomar and Josefina Roma provided the first opportunity to develop this paper at a conference in Reus, Tarragona.

1. For the persistence of child visionaries in this period in Protestant Europe, see Cosmos 1992 and Frijhoff 1995.

2. Personal observations at San Sebastián de Garabandal, El Palmar de Troya, Monte Umbe, C'an Sardà, Sant Vicenç dels Horts, El Escorial; unpublished papers of J. Roma on apparitions around Barcelona; and Cadoret-Abeles 1981.

3. For instance, in a three-page treatment of the weeping Madonna of Civitavecchia, *La Repubblica* of Rome (April 8, 1995, 2) included accounts of thirteen other Italian images that had wept in the past four months, few if any of which, I venture, it had reported previously.

4. Gurevich 1988, reviewing Dinzelbacher 1981.

5. There is no way to know how many of the seers at Limpias were children, for children do not appear to have been encouraged to sign the vision register.

6. For studies of this process in the case of a dreamer-prophetess in Madrid see Kagan 1990 and Blázquez Miguel 1987.

7. Charles Tilly discusses systematic bias in the reporting of contentious gatherings (1995b). One wonders whether any of the changes he finds over the eighty years of the study might have been affected by changes in what journalists defined as "news" and whether there were kinds of contention that journalists omitted altogether.

Chapter 8

Beyond the Parish Pump: The Politicization of the Peasantry in Burgundy, 1750–1850

Robert M. Schwartz

If scholars continue to investigate when and how peasants in France came to share a common interest in national politics, it is partly because they embrace a key article of the Gallic faith: France is a country of wondrous regional diversity. It follows, then, that rural politicization was bound to vary by region. In keeping with that faith, this chapter examines the evolution of village politics in Burgundy during the eighteenth and nineteenth centuries. It provides further support for the view that the politicization of the peasantry, at least in certain regions, had advanced significantly by the 1840s (cf. Weber 1976; Jones 1985). As a piece of microhistory, it also offers something new by looking closely into rural political developments, not from the standpoint of Paris and the central state but from the perspective of specific rural communities themselves. This point of view helps restore complexity to the thinking and actions of villagers. It shows how they came to understand the interplay of local and national politics and were able to frame their immediate concerns about communal affairs in terms of national ideological issues. Though they remained chiefly concerned about the repair of the parish pump, they were nonetheless able to see beyond this parochial issue to grasp the relevance of national politics for local affairs.

This chapter offers an addendum to the "Burgundy Battles" that Charles Tilly depicted in *The Contentious French* (1986a). To that history of collective challenges to urban authorities and the state from the seventeenth to the twentieth centuries it adds an exploration of the origins, nature, and timing of another form of popular contention. In this form subordinate villagers sought, sometimes successfully, to use state power to promote their own interests, not through highly visible public demonstrations but through shrewd, behind-the-scenes lobbying of state administrators. To understand this kind of contention, it will be useful to look first at communal life in rural Burgundy during the Old Regime. There we can examine the *formal* means of participation in local governance and see how that participation, together with increased contact with the royal administration, helped shape an evolving political consciousness that was favorable to democratic and republican ideas and sensitive to national political issues as well.

Village Politics under Seigneurial Domination

The political culture of the peasantry under the Old Regime is a topic of considerable interest about which comparatively little is known. In Burgundy, rural political culture evolved under the dominating structures of the church, the state, and the seigneurial system, which was particularly formidable there. Thanks to the rich documentation for Burgundian lordships, much can be learned about the functioning of village governance, the distribution of power in rural communities, and the use by villagers of prevailing structures of power for their own purposes. To see this, let us consider developments in five villages, which ranged in size from 150 to 400 people each, rather typical in this respect for late-eighteenth-century Burgundy as a whole. The first four (Tart-le-Bas, Tart-le-Haut, Tart l'Abbaye, and Longecourt-en-Plaine) formed a cluster of communities located in the rich agricultural plain to the southeast of the provincial capital of Dijon. A fifth village (Thenissey), provides a case of some contrast. Situated in a relatively remote and isolated area of hilly woodlands northwest of Dijon, it was a village where as much as 40 percent of the arable land was given over to vineyards of mediocre quality (Archives Départementales de la Côte d'Or [ADCO] E 623).

Every year in these villages, a special session of the lord's court, or *grands jours,* was held, usually in August or September following the harvest. From one perspective, the *grands jours* served as a ritual affirmation of lordship, a ceremonial session intended to affirm communal unity and respect for the seigneur's right to administer justice in his seigneury. It was this right on which the power, honor, and profit of lordship rested. Accordingly, all heads of household, including women so designated, were required to attend, and those who failed to attend were to be heavily fined. At the beginning of the proceedings the court solemnly proclaimed anew the regulations concerning seigneurial rights and monopolies. Restated, therefore, were prohibitions against taking wood from the lord's forest, against fishing in the lord's streams and ponds, against selling wine without seigneurial license, and so forth. And to ensure that the desired effects of exemplary punishment took hold, those charged with poaching and other infractions against seigneurial law were brought before the court for a summary hearing and sentencing in the presence of all household heads.

But that was not all. In addition to enforcing rights of lordship, the *grands jours* also served the collective and individual interests of villagers themselves. In 1757, for example, at the proceedings for the Tart villages, much of the session was devoted, as usual, to the management of village agrarian life. For peasants, the scarcity of land made the smallest holding a sacrosanct possession. The court thus declared the inviolability of a household's garden and the produce it contained: Anyone caught entering another's garden by day or night was subject to a fine of 300 livres—an enormous sum for an ordinary household, somewhat more than a male wage worker would earn in a year. After the seigneurial prosecutor read out these and other admonitions, the court turned next to deal summarily with the large number of minor offenses. The vast majority were trespass cases, the inevitable misdemeanors of an agrarian system based on small plots scattered among open fields. Typically the guilty party received a small fine for the unauthorized passage of animals or carts across another's field; when damages to crops or fields had resulted, the judge ordered that fair compensation be paid in addition to a fine (ADCO, BII 896/16). Thus despite the written and spoken threat of ruinous penalties, justice in these cases was not only swift, it was reasonable, readily accepted, and effective in administering the civil law as well as seigneurial law and custom. Indeed, when faced with its disappearance in the early days of the Revolution, some Burgundian peasants asked the National Assembly to restore their seigneurial judges so that their trespass disputes could be settled as effectively as before (Archives Nationales, D^XIV3).

The *grand jours* served community members in another important way, for it provided the occasion for the formal incorporation of village representation in local governance. Each year at this special session, the provost (*procureur syndic*) and other communal officers were formally installed. This followed their election by the village assembly, which was the community's organ of self-government, to which all household heads belonged, and the recognized source of authority for all decisions made by the village and its chosen representatives. Because the annual election of officers reflected the political choices of community members, patterns of officeholding offer a rare view of village politics.

In each of the villages, seven officers, always men, were chosen each year: a provost, who served as the village chief executive; two collectors (*asséeurs*), who shared the weighty responsibility of keeping the tax rolls and collecting

Table 8.1 Economic Position and Officeholding in Tart-le-Haut, 1752–1789

| State Tax Category[a] (in sous) | Number of Village Offices Held | | | | |
	None	One	Two or Three	Four or More	Total
<200	28	6	3	0	37
	76%	16%	8%	0%	100%
200–600	26	21	21	16	84
	31%	25%	25%	19%	100%
>600	6	2	5	7	20
	30%	10%	25%	35%	100%
Totals	60	29	29	23	141
	43%	21%	21%	16%	100%

Sources: ADCO, 6091 rolls of the *taille, capitation,* and *vingtième,* 1757, 1758, 1769, 1778, 1789; B II 896, registers of the justice and *grands jours* of Tart-le-Haut; Archives de Longecourt 121, Justice of Tart-le-Haut, 1761–66.
[a]Based on the mean of all annual tax assessments recorded for the years 1757, 1769, 1778, and 1789. Widows and women, who were ineligible to serve, were excluded from the analysis.

taxes; two *prudhommes* (councillors), who inventoried the possessions of deceased residents, inspected chimneys, and generally helped to adjudicate minor disputes and police the village; and two field wardens (*messiers*), who, charged with the security of fields and crops, investigated incidents of trespass and damage and cited the offending party in the seigneurial court (Saint Jacob 1960, 79, 126; Colombet 1936, 198–99; Vignier 1962, 281–83). Using information from the land tax records and the *grands jours,* I have examined the possible relationship between officeholding and estimated wealth from the 1750s to the eve of the Revolution. The results show, somewhat unexpectedly, that village government was, in fact, rather "democratic," as Table 8.1 illustrates.

In these communities officeholding was not monopolized by an oligarchy of wealthy residents or rich tenant farmers (*fermiers*) but was instead widely shared. Inhabitants routinely rotated through different offices, and rarely did a man hold the *same* position for two years in succession or more than two or three times in the thirty-seven years studied (1752–89). Annual elections with the high degree of rotation in and out of village offices meant that 40 to 80 percent of the male heads of household held office at least once during the period. The principle of rotation also meant that the proportion of men called to office was greater in smaller communities than in larger ones. Not surprisingly, the poorest men were very rarely called to office, and the likelihood of holding office one or more times typically increased as one moved up the social ladder. Nonetheless, the men who were chosen as village officers were drawn, more or less proportionately, from the middle as well as the upper economic ranks of the community. Moreover, in all five villages the frequency of holding office was more strongly related to length of residency in the community than to estimated wealth.

This pattern of officeholding is suggestive in several ways. Apart from the practice of excluding the poorest taxpayers, the selection of village officials was evidently based less on wealth than on other considerations. Among them, no doubt, was a person's family connections and the influence he could mobilize through informal networks based on kinship and patron-client relations, a question I am still exploring.[1] Trustworthy character and proven abilities, including literacy, were probably chief considerations: These were the traits of a good reputation that were apt to be tested time and again the longer one resided in the village.

"Competent," "literate," and "honorable" were suitable terms to describe Jean Baptiste Moreau, a blacksmith of middling economic standing who was repeatedly called to office in Tart-le-Haut. Chosen as provost for three years in succession (1776–79)—an exceptional record in itself—he then served as tax collector in 1782 and 1786. His second term as collector led to a severe test of character in a prolonged dispute with Simon Renaudot over the latter's alleged overcharging for the feeding of communal livestock. To confront Renaudot was no small matter because the accused was the head of the wealthiest family in Tart-le-Haut. After lodging a complaint with the intendant, who was the head of the royal administration in Burgundy, Moreau pressed his claim for two years more, undeterred by Renaudot's counteroffensive. Although the cause was lost in the end, the blacksmith's persistence in challenging a dominant family reconfirmed for his supporters a trust already earned (ADCO C 604).

The term "trustworthy" was unlikely to come to mind when residents thought of Nicolas Martin. A farmer turned merchant who enjoyed one of the highest incomes in Tart-le-Haut, he was a wheeler-dealer who speculated in leasehold land and profited from the contract he held from the seigneur to collect the *dime* (tithe). To a certain degree he fit the description of a *fermier,* a rural producer cum entrepreneur who leased large farms and the rights to collect seigneurial levies and to exploit seigneurial monopolies. As a large farmer producing for the market, as the exploiter of seigneurial rights, and as an intermediary landlord and the chief employer in his community, a *fermier* belonged to the dominant class of many eighteenth-century villages. Within this broad class, Martin was a small-timer with large ambitions. The influence he acquired on his own was fortified by family connections that linked him to kinsmen of wealth and influence in the village of Rouves and the market town of Genlis. His uncle in Genlis—a royal notary—was apt to be especially helpful. By virtue of his numerous clients in the vicinity, the uncle had privileged access to information and personal contacts that could assist the nephew in his dealings. With these various advantages and with a formal education to his credit as well, Martin was well equipped to enhance his economic standing through the political power vested in the office of tax collector or provost. In 1759 and again in 1760, he served as one of two village tax collectors. Years later, after a term as a lowly field warden in 1767, he reached the top of the village government, being named provost in 1771. This achievement would not be repeated. As provost Martin secretly leased to a friend village lands at a price well below the market rate, violating both his neighbors' trust and the rule requiring that the village assembly approve any lease of community land. Once discovered, this offense strengthened suspicions about Martin's mishandling of communal funds, which were all but confirmed when he refused to present his accounts to the village assembly. The resulting complaints, which were passed from the assembly up to the office of the royal intendant, attested to the popular resentment and distrust that Martin provoked. After that the authority connected with the management of communal resources and the assessment and collection of taxes was never again entrusted to the arrogant Martin (ADCO, C 5820/20; C 604).

Stepping back to view things more broadly, village officeholding reflects key elements of the subordinate political culture in these communities. Among these elements were two rather different political tendencies, one of which was arguably "democratic." From the 1750s to the 1780s the choice of village officers shows a marked preference in communal affairs for broad participation, for rotation through positions of authority and responsibility, for the sharing of the unwelcome burdens of communal life, for democratic governance in the sense that Montesquieu thought admirable but impractical and that Rousseau envisioned and defended. These preferences were probably reinforced by the shared desire to prevent the wealthiest residents, particularly the *fermiers,* from dominating the village's own domain of political authority. Since offices carried power as well as responsibilities, they were circulated so as not to be monopolized by a few influential men.

Viewed from another angle, however, officeholding was not so much a privilege as a chore. Onerous and imposed from above, the duties of office amounted to a corvée—obligatory service for the lord and the king. Among the most onerous duties were the unpopular job of citing fellow residents for fineable offenses and the contentious tasks of tax assessment and tax collection. Held accountable by the village assembly, the seigneurial court, and the royal administration, officers were fined for derelict or abusive performance of duties, while those responsible for tax payments—the *procureur syndic* and the *asséeurs*—faced the further financial risk of having to cover any shortfall in tax collections with their own funds. From this perspective, then, office-holding attests to the subservient status of French peasants under the Old Regime. And yet even in this light, the pattern of practice possessed a democratic element that was repeatedly underscored by Rousseau: the practice of sharing the unwelcome burdens of local administration.

However different, the democratic and subservient aspects of village government were complementary and interconnected. They were conspicuous threads in the fabric of *village communalism*—patterns of social cooperation based on collective obligations, broad participation, rotation through positions of authority, and accountability. Situated beneath the dominant political structures of lordship and the state, communalism and its tradition of broad participation in the community's own sphere of political authority was a well-established part of subordinate political culture.

Another conspicuous part was the growing role of the state in village affairs. Animated by the desire to augment the king's share of peasant resources, the royal administration expanded and tightened its supervision of communal resources and of local governance generally. For villagers this process created additional burdens as well as new opportunities to enlist royal support to protect or promote their own interests. In the course of affirming the community's collective obligation to meet royal tax payments, the intendants of Burgundy reconfirmed the authority and responsibilities of the village assembly and its designated officers. This policy gave community members a more effective means of holding their own officials to account and of checking abuses by the more powerful among them (ADCO, C 1207; C 604; 4 E 2–2688). As communities grew accustomed to dealing with a more intrusive royal administration, they looked increasingly to the intendant or his subordinate, the subdelegate, for help in settling many kinds of disputes and problems to their advantage (see, for example, ADCO, C 1207). In sum, although royal intervention rarely prevented defeat at the hands of a seigneur or other powerful antagonist, occasional victories proved for villagers that the intendant was a potential ally and source of beneficial power.

Political Change in the Village, 1789–1848

With the Revolution of 1789 and under the regimes that followed, the politics of rural life changed considerably. To see this it will be useful to begin with a few points regarding the Revolution's effect and legacy for ordinary country folk. In the short term the suppression of seigneurial rights and the *dime* was bound to have a positive effect on peasant budgets. The value of these rights was considerable, particularly where the lord held title to the *dime* in whole or in part. In Longecourt, where the seigneur, Nicolas Berbis, held the right by himself, 45 to 55 percent of the revenue from his estate came from the *dime* and seigneurial rights, and about half of that came from the *dime* alone. The income from seigneurial dues and the tithe for Tart-le-Haut and Tart-le-Bas was 25 percent of total income (Archives de Longecourt [AL], 52); it was somewhat less for the lordship of Thenissey, where in the 1760s it amounted to 17 percent of a total income of 11,000 livres (ADCO 35 F 221).

As seems to have been true for France generally, for the bulk of the rural inhabitants of Burgundy other material benefits of the Revolution were limited (Bart 1996, 318–23). Lands confiscated by the state from the church and émigrés were mainly acquired by urban bourgeois, though some significant acquisitions were made by the wealthier rural inhabitants, sometimes acting together in open or covert association. The division of community lands, as authorized by the National Assembly and the Convention, also often led to disappointed hopes (Woloch 1994, 151–53). Of the divisions made in Longecourt and each of the Tart communities, only those in Tart l'Abbaye provided a secure benefit. In the other three communes the divisions were overturned during the Empire (ADCO, E. Dépôt 623/32 TLH; L 774). Then in 1819, in a bid for the political loyalties of smallholders, the restored Bourbon government adopted a policy that gave so-called usurpers the opportunity to secure their disputed parcels through purchase from the community in question at favorable rates. In this way the vast majority of those affected opted to buy their parcels by means of a perpetual mortgage. This reprieve did not last. In the decade that followed even the small annual payments apparently became burdensome; consequently, circumstances forced many to sell their plots, often to notaries who were well positioned to turn the hardship of clients to their own advantage (ADCO, E. Dépôt 622/27 TLB N3/8). In sum, the limited material gains of smallholders during the Revolution were often reduced or eliminated during the Empire and the Restoration.[2]

For a number of families, the inflation of the revolutionary period offered a welcome opportunity to reduce or eliminate debts. According to an account of 1811, of twenty-two households in Longecourt with prerevolutionary debts ranging from 52 to 1,100 livres, eleven had by then succeeded in paying them off entirely, and most of the others had managed to pay down their arrears (AL, 22). A similar pattern of debt reduction occurred in Tart-le-Bas. In addition, revolutionary legislation enabled Tart l'Abbaye and Longecourt to recover communal lands previously appropriated by seigneurs.

Although the material benefits for the bulk of villagers were limited, the Revolution provided critical exposure to the idea and practice of popular sovereignty. Some men who were previously excluded from the higher village offices of provost and *prudhomme* were elected to serve in the communal administration, especially during the period 1792–95. This expanded political participation, together with the greater degree of self-government, constituted an enduring political legacy of the Revolution. Further, the experience of acquiring new political rights and some limited material gains during the Revolution and of seeing both the rights and material gains taken away or reduced under Napoleon and the Restoration fostered a positive memory of the Revolution as *a time of favorable opportunity.*

Other aspects of political change during and after the Revolution might well have fostered less-positive memories. Beginning in 1789 the abolition of seigneurialism and the reorganization of municipal government meant that communal authority was unequivocally subordinate to the central government and state administration. Newly autonomous in limited respects, communal governments were presented with a broadening range of state fiscal and administrative responsibilities. The reorganization endowed each rural commune with a small executive group, headed by a mayor, and a larger council. In Burgundy at least, this restructuring brought an end to the village assembly (Fortunet et al. 1981, 20–44, 98–105). Consequently participation and local accountability were both reduced.[3] This reduction was carried further during the Napoleonic regime by the complete elimination of elections for communal offices, which were transformed into state-appointed positions, a practice that continued up to 1831 (Woloch 1994, 127–33).

Under the July Monarchy (1830–48) the municipal electoral law of 1831 reestablished elections for municipal councils and extended the eligibility to vote in these elections to about 45 percent of the adult males of rural France (McPhee 1992, 163). Mayors of rural communes, though they continued to be appointed by state administrators, were now to be selected from among the elected councillors. Ending three decades of dormancy, the law restored formal and legal political life in the village. Under the short-lived Second Republic (1848–51) universal male suffrage was revived, and the positions of mayor and municipal councillor were both made elected offices. In sum, from 1790 to 1848 changes in communal government tightened the links between the state and the village and challenged the tradition of village communalism, as broadly based participation was replaced by narrower representation and the formal practice of holding officers accountable to the community was undermined.

In the villages that I am studying the narrowing of popular political participation and its virtual elimination between 1800 and 1830 were accompanied by the rise of dominant local cliques and family clans. Here the example of the Prudent family is worth describing for the light it sheds on a new political consciousness that grew out of the competition between dominant and subordinate groups over the *local use of state power*.

Challenging the Prudents in Tart-le-Haut

Having prospered from the positions of seigneurial steward and *fermier* under the Old Regime, the Prudents benefited handsomely from the Revolution. Beginning in 1792 they joined the ranks of substantial proprietors by purchasing a number of national lands. Through his acquisitions in 1792 and 1793 Claude Prudent, the second son of the late steward, soon became the preeminent resident of Tart-le-Haut, with more land than any other household head. Claude and his brothers benefited further by acquiring large leaseholds of émigré lands that the government offered at bargain prices, parcels of which they then sublet at a substantial profit. As owners and renters of enlarged holdings, their growing economic clout readily translated into increasing political power as more village families became dependent on the Prudents for land and work. And in the face of continually shifting political winds during the Revolution, they managed to preserve their substantial gains by keeping to a pragmatic course.

During the Restoration (1815–30), Claude proceeded to carry the family fortunes to new heights. Appointed mayor under Napoleon, he retained the influential post for two decades (AL, 96). Using his connections with the state administration and his own considerable sources of patronage, he secured municipal councillorships for his sons and nephews and put together a considerable group of subservient supporters. Prudent's administration of the village was not, however, universally popular; indeed, some considered him downright autocratic. According to some opponents, Prudent was a patriarchal "despot" who "ran the commune as if it were his own family" (ADCO, 6 M 57).

Twice during his life, first in 1831 and then in 1848, opponents in Tart-le-Haut succeeded, though only briefly, in turning the Prudent faction out of power. Though both challenges occurred within the favorable contexts of national revolutionary situations, the success of the anti-Prudent forces largely resulted from *their own effective actions* in an opportune moment. Brief accounts of the actions taken in 1831 and in 1848–51 must suffice to make the point.

As noted above, one reform of the July Monarchy transformed municipal councils from appointed to elective bodies. In this way the new national government reintroduced a degree of political participation and choice that had been closed to ordinary rural people since the turn of the century. Even before the elections, though, Prudent's opponents in Tart-le-Haut recognized that the change in the national government offered a propitious moment to get the ear and the support of the new regime. It was the new departmental prefect to whom they turned, for in his hands rested the authority to appoint and dismiss rural mayors and to oversee the forthcoming elections. Thus was launched the effective campaign to replace Prudent and his coterie with a new mayor and council, with men who would better represent the popular will of the commune.

In 1831 four petitions, signed by twenty of ninety-seven male household heads, were sent to the prefect in Dijon. In these documents disgruntled residents attacked Prudent in ways that were intended to capture both the prefect's attention and his support (ADCO, 6 M 57, petitions of January 27, February 9, February 15, and March 10, 1831). Scarcely as politically naive as some accounts would have us believe, the peasants who framed the petitions shrewdly presented local grievances in terms of the political and ideological concerns of the new national regime. Prudent, the petitioners explained, was not just negligent, he was also corrupt, having improperly filled the communal council with subservient sons and nephews. Even worse, he was an obstacle to the new order of "liberty," an opponent of the new constitutional monarchy who exhibited little enthusiasm for its success. Invoking the symbols of national regeneration, another petition stressed the mayor's indifference and hostility to the new regime: Having blocked the popular decision to supply uniforms to the National Guard, he had taken the further unpatriotic step of refusing to allow the guard to carry the commune's treasured flag of 1790, the most magnificent of its kind in the entire canton.[4] A final petition went further, skillfully playing on the government's concerns about the threat of a Bourbon counterrevolution. Although popular will, the petitioners noted, was overcoming his "former despotic influence," the mayor remained "outspoken in his anticonstitutional opinions" and betrayed his allegiance to the partisans of Charles X, the deposed Bourbon king.

These petitions, which stretched the truth to enlist desired political support, achieved their intended aim. At the end of February 1831 the prefect suspended Prudent from his functions as mayor, appointing in his place Pierre Louvrier, the candidate repeatedly recommended in the petitions. Six months later in September, in the first election of its kind in a generation, the anti-Prudent forces consolidated their victory by winning a majority of the ten seats on the municipal council.

Although the reforming regime of Pierre Louvrier and his supporters came to an end in 1834 when the Prudent clan recaptured the mayorship and four seats on the council, the struggles between the Prudents and their opponents persisted. In these struggles the opponents did not forget their victory in 1831 and the means of achieving it. In June 1843 they organized themselves again to petition the prefect in their effort to reverse the clan's return to power. "A large and influential family of our commune," their petition began, had successfully conspired to manipulate the elections for their exclusive advantage "in order to dominate all communal affairs for their own pleasure." The result was "pernicious" since the commune was now under the rule of the current mayor and a Council composed of his two brothers, a brother-in-law, a nephew, and two cousins—all members of the same family, which, it was emphasized, was a clear violation of the national laws governing municipal government (ADCO 6 M 315).

Although this complaint went unanswered, the changed circumstances of 1848 created the opportunity for another round of open contention. When the Prudents captured the municipal government in a rigged election in March— only one month after the revolution of 1848 and the proclamation of the Second Republic—disgruntled villagers appealed to the new prefect to order a new election. The members recently elected to the Municipal Council, they wrote, were scarcely republicans: It was thus their "duty as good citizens" to tell the prefect of "the Jesuitical maneuvers" that the unpatriotic village priest and his allies had used to capture the communal administration. Worse, at an assembly to elect delegates for the canton's electoral board, the priest placed at the top of the list the former Marquis de Saint Seine. Fortunately, a worker who was a "loyal citizen and one of our number" intervened to remind the assembly that they had "made many revolutions to put an end to the domination of the aristocracy" and that this nomination should not stand (ADCO 6 M 315).

In response to the complaint the prefect ordered that a special election be held in April. At the polls the Prudents were turned out of office. In their place were elected some of the petitioners and their leader, Pierre Martin, whom the new Council elected as mayor. This victory was replayed in more dramatic fashion several months later when municipal elections for the whole country were held on July 30 and Martin's supporters were victorious. With universal male suffrage now in force, this election saw 109 men go to the polls in Tart-le-Haut—more than four times the usual participation under the restrictive franchise of the July Monarchy and a good measure of the enthusiasm that greeted the return of democratic suffrage in the community.

Amid this enthusiasm, the struggle for local power continued. As the months wore on, each faction escalated its rhetoric in petitioning campaigns aimed at discrediting their opponents in the eyes of local voters and in the minds of state administrators especially. To counter an anonymous letter charging Martin with grave misdeeds and to keep pace with the national government's growing concerns about popular radicalism, the mayor's supporters went so far as to accuse their local antagonists, who were in fact all conservatives, of being radical revolutionaries who were bent on capturing the two open seats on the council for "the party called *les rouges*" (ADCO 6 M 315).

In the end, the Prudent faction won the day by getting the ear of the increasingly conservative regime. Casting themselves as the Party of Order, their letters both to the prefect and to no less than the minister of the interior himself convinced the national government that Martin, his assistant, and the majority of the Council were the real rebels in the commune. And so it was that Martin and his fellow officials were officially identified in the government's records as partisans of *les rouges,* men to keep under watch and to consider purging. On December 6, 1851, a few days after the coup by Louis Napoleon, a prefectoral decree relieved Martin and his assistant, Jean Baptiste Charbonnet, of their duties, and returned Claude Prudent, *fils,* to the post of mayor. Two weeks later, a second decree completed the counterrevolution by removing Martin and his allies from the Council and appointing men loyal to the new regime and to Prudent (ADCO 6 M 315).

These episodes marked important stages in the political education of Tart-le-Haut's residents. In the continuing contest for power within the community, the petition as well as the ballot became the weapons of the day. They were the means of securing not only the needed local support but the critical help from the state. In seeking such help, the contending factions learned to be politically astute: to get the ear and the support of state authorities, they gave local community issues the ringing significance of national political concerns and prevailing ideology,[5]

Conclusion

The picture emerging from these Burgundian villages thus yields further evidence that the politicization of rural inhabitants was well underway by 1848 and had begun as early as the 1830s. In addition, the origins and nature of this change become clearer when we consider the functioning of village communalism during the Old Regime, the political experiences of the Revolution, as well as the language and intended audience of political protest during the 1830s. By moving across the usual chronological boundaries of French history and closely examining specific communities in the eighteenth *and* nineteenth centuries, we are able to see the broader patterns of political change that might otherwise be missed. They can be summarized as follows.

Within the dominant structures of Burgundian seigneurialism, the subordinate political culture of village communalism contained democratic tendencies associated with broad participation in decision making and the sharing of collective obligations. Moreover, in certain respects, Burgundian seigneurialism itself promoted change in popular culture. Although chiefly designed to promote the lord's interests, the functioning of seigneurial justice furnished subordinate villagers with a practical education in law and schooled them in the use of the courts, both seigneurial and royal, to resolve disputes and to press for their own political advantage.

The central state's supervision of Burgundian communities furthered this education. Largely for fiscal reasons, the state took a direct interest in the management of village affairs. The royal intendant and subdelegates sought to promote prudent management of communal resources through their verification of village accounts and their use of the authority to approve or prohibit all manner of community-sponsored projects, from the repair of a steeple to the prosecution of a lawsuit against a seigneur (see also Root, 1987). After 1750, as the royal administration became more professionalized and more effective, this traditional tutelage grew more vigilant and more routine. In rural communities the increased contact with the royal administration, and its paternalistic side in particular, fostered a strategic conception of the state. It accustomed peasants to view the state not solely in terms of oppressive taxes and intrusive regulation but also as a useful source of external authority to be called upon to resolve problems to their advantage and to defend their interests against seigneurs and other antagonists. In eighteenth-century Burgundy, then, lawsuits and lobbying the state administration had replaced collective violence as the chief form of overt political action by peasants.

With the displacement of the seigneur and the state subordination of the materially weakened French Catholic church, the revamped central state of postrevolutionary France became the unrivaled source of external authority and control in rural society. The adjustments by various groups in the country-side to this new configuration of power and to the advance of rural capitalism constitute the main developments of rural politics in the nineteenth century. With a revived tradition of village communalism and the revolution's legacy of popular political participation serving as inspiration, ordinary rural inhabitants sought to enlist state power to improve local self-government, using the language of prevailing ideology to secure a favorable hearing from state authorities. Well before the Third Republic's campaign to turn peasants into Frenchmen, villagers in Burgundy recognized the relevance of national politics for their promotion of their own concerns.

Notes

I wish to thank Françoise Vignier and her staff at the Archives Départementales de la Côte d'Or in Dijon for much cheerful assistance with my research there and Madame Bertrand de Saint Seine for allowing me full access to the private archives of the Longecourt chateau. I am grateful also for the encouragement and help from Jean Bart and François Fortunet at the University of Burgundy. For their readings, comments, and suggestions for revision, thanks go to John Merriman and the editors of this volume, Michael Hanagan, Leslie Page Moch, and Wayne te Brake. Since the editors also organized the Amsterdam conference in honor of Charles Tilly, they deserve a double portion of gratitude for providing such a marvelous and stimulating occasion to thank our mentor and to sharpen our ideas. A fellowship from the National Endowment for the Humanities, a research grant from the Harry Guggenheim Foundation, and a faculty fellowship from Mount Holyoke College supported the research for this paper. Readers familiar with the work of Charles Tilly will see signs of his influence in my paper but not the extent of my debt to Chuck and to Louise Tilly or my fond memories of the Sunday evening gatherings in their Ann Arbor living room, where they gave their students the enduring gift of intellectual fellowship.

1. The organization of family networks among individual households would seem to have such obvious political and economic importance in small communities that is surprising to find that virtually no research on them is available on French history of this period. My own impressions have been supported by conversations with Roderick Philipps of Carelton University (Canada), a specialist in the history of the family, and Maurizio Gribaudi at the Laboratoire de Démographie Historique of the Ecole Pratiques des Hautes Etudes in Paris. A pioneering work that demonstrates the importance of family alliances is Giovanni Levi's *Inheriting Power* (1989) on a Piedmontese village in the seventeenth century. Harriet Rosenberg's study of a French Alpine village, *A Negotiated World* (1988), offers a rare example of family network analysis in French history.

2. In this respect, Thenissey was unaffected because no church or common lands existed there.

3. The brief restoration of universal male franchise in 1793 was followed first by the reimposition of voting restrictions in 1795 and then by the complete elimination of elections for communal offices during the Napoleonic regime, when the offices were transformed into state-appointed positions, a practice that continued up to 1831.

4. The flag bore the names of Tart-le-Haut, Tart-le-Bas, Tart l'Abbaye, and Essigey. It was taken to Paris in 1790 by delegates who went to the capital to represent the four villages at the first *fête de la fédération,* commemorating the first year of the Revolution. It was now kept at the mayor's office in Tart-le-Haut.

5. As early as 1830 this kind of contention also became a prominent feature of political life in Longecourt, Tart-le-Bas, and Thenissey. In Longecourt, however, political dissension was muffled, in part because of the influence of a resident notable, the Marquis Legouz de Saint Seine, who held a seat on the municipal council there from 1831 to 1848 (ADCO 6 M 211). Saint Seine's influence also worked indirectly through the numerous Bresson family. A syndicate of seven family members farmed the Saint Seine domain, and the patriarch, Claude, held the post of mayor for two decades. These arrangements help explain the muted public enthusiasm for the liberal regime of the July Monarchy (1830–48) and for the more radical changes introduced by the revolution of 1848.

Archival Sources

The Archives Départmentales de la Côte d'Or, Dijon, France

The Archives de Longecourt, private archives held at the Château of Longecourt-en-Plaine, in the village of Longecourt-en-Plaine

The Archives Nationales, Paris

Chapter 9

Claim Making and the Framing of Defeats: The Interpretation of Losses by American and British Labor Activists, 1886–1895

Kim Voss

Culture and Social Movements

Recently more and more scholars have called for a cultural analysis of social movements (Mueller 1992; Johnston and Klandermans 1995; Buechler 1993; Emirbayer and Goodwin 1995). Dissatisfied with the structural tilt of the resource mobilization and political process perspectives, students of social movements have increasingly begun to ask questions about how movements are affected both by the culture of the larger society in which they exist and by the internal cultures of movements themselves.

To date this cultural turn has been long on exhortation and critique and short on research and theory construction. Yet in the end, only research and theory construction will produce a persuasive new perspective. As Johnston and Klandermans remark: "Ultimately, for cultural analysis to be convincing to others it must take as its primary datum some cultural artifact or set of cultural products, either ideational or material, and relate it to changes in collective action" (1995, 17).

Charles Tilly's (1995b) recent work on popular contention in Great Britain provides one model for how social movement scholars might proceed.[1] Tilly treats the cultural repertoire of claim-making groups primarily as a dependent variable and documents a historical shift in the typical symbols and actions used to wage social protest. In mid-eighteenth-century Britain, protest actions generally were limited to a local area, employed symbols and forms peculiar to local everyday life (such as hanging in effigy and food seizures), and were aimed either at specific local authorities or used local patrons to convey claims to faraway rulers. By the 1830s, in contrast, protest was usually large scale; utilized nonlocal, all-purpose means (such as demonstrations and petitions), and was commonly carried out by special-purpose associations acting in the name of a disadvantaged population. In short, the repertoire of contention had shifted to include most of the actions that we now associate with the term "social movement."[2]

Most scholars who have called for greater attention to culture will applaud Tilly for his rich description of a changing repertoire of contention. Since they themselves, however, tend to focus on culture as an independent variable, they are likely to be disappointed at his relative inattention to culture as a shaping force. Generally they are interested either in how the larger culture of a society stimulates or frustrates particular types of social movements or in how the cultures of movements themselves foster or inhibit mobilizations.

The question of movement culture is particularly important once the repertoire of contention shifts toward a social movement logic. Once it does, collective claim making involves *sustained* challenges and *ongoing* displays of support, commitment, and worthiness. Here it becomes critical to ask how actors manage to sustain challenges to powerholders over time.

In this chapter I take up just this question. In particular I examine one aspect of movement culture, the "frame" that movement actors use to interpret setbacks and defeat (Snow et al. 1986; Snow and Benford 1988; Zald 1996). I ask whether the explanations and interpretations that make up this frame help to preserve a social movement's unity and commitment.

It might seem odd to research setbacks and defeats. After all, setbacks and their aftermath are not especially fashionable topics in the social movements field. Yet most social movements experience reverses or losses, and though some survive these setbacks and eventually flourish, others wither and die.[3] Why do some movements overcome setbacks and others not? Most obviously, since social movements involve powerholders as well as challengers, the actions of authorities go a long way toward explaining social movements' success or failure. Other factors, too, are clearly important, including the actions of countermovements and the numbers, commitment, and unity of challengers when setbacks occur (Tilly 1994b; Voss 1996; Meyer and Staggenborg 1996).

But is this the whole story? I suspect that the lessons that activists draw from defeats also matter for the longevity, solidarity, and fate of social movements. This suspicion grew out of research I did on the Knights of Labor (the first mass-based organization of the American working class) (Voss 1993). In what follows I will summarize this study, and I will then describe my current research on a group of British labor movement organizations known as the "new unions." I ask whether the British new unionists, unlike the American Knights, dealt with setbacks by framing their defeats, and if so, how?

In the interest of full disclosure, let me make a disclaimer. The research I will describe is in its early stages, and although I offer some documentation for my claims, what follows contains more speculation than evidence.

Why Interpretations of Defeat Might Matter

The late nineteenth century was a critical period in the development of the British and American labor movements. It was a moment of fundamental restructuring, when large factories came to dominate the industrial landscape and less-skilled workers began to outnumber artisans in many of these factories. These changes meant that the labor movement had to be remade if it was to represent the new working class and not simply the minority of workers who were skilled craftsmen (Hobsbawm 1984b; Katznelson and Zolberg 1986).

Acting on this fact, labor activists in England and the United States began to construct more inclusive ideologies and union structures. Union membership increased, and labor's organizational reach expanded to include the growing army of less-skilled wage earners. In England in 1889, "new unions" were founded, so called because they actively recruited unskilled workers, charged low dues, and were more militant and political than the entrenched craft unions (Hunt 1981, ch. 9; Clegg, Fox, and Thompson 1964; Hobsbawm 1964a, 1984a). Within two years, union membership had expanded by 80 percent (Hobsbawm 1984a, 157). In the United States, the explosion came in the early 1880s after the Knights of Labor was slowly transformed from its craft origins into what Friedrich Engels enthusiastically called "the first national organization created by the American working class as a whole" (1968, 357).

Initially the Knights of Labor was the more successful organization. Founded in 1869 as a secret society, its goal was to unionize all workers. Eventually shedding its shield of secrecy, Knights' membership expanded rapidly in the early 1880s, following its participation in highly publicized railroad strikes. By 1886 over three-quarters of a million workers—skilled, unskilled, native-born, immigrant, black, white, male, and female—had joined (Garlock 1974; Ware 1929, 66).

The ideology that drew this diverse membership was a diffuse but powerful vision of labor solidarity and cooperative social relations. It drew heavily on republican political ideas, especially the conviction that both workers and the American republic were threatened by a growing concentration of wealth and power.[4] Only by extending democracy to the workplace and ensuring all citizens equality at work as well as equality before the law would it be possible to maintain the republican form of government. To do this Knights' members

pursued a variety of tactics, but above all they endorsed organization, education, and cooperation.

The Knights' initial success led activists in England to suggest that the
American labor movement pointed the way to a more inclusive labor movement. In the mid-1880s the American labor movement in no way seemed des-
tined to become the weaker and more politically conservative of the two
movements.

Eventually, however, this is exactly what happened. The new, more inclusive unions in England became established fixtures. The Knights of Labor,
their opposite number in the United States, collapsed, and the American labor
movement reverted once again to a movement of a small group of skilled
workers, organized primarily along craft lines.

Why did the Knights fail? Elsewhere, I explore this question through statistical analysis of the collapse of the Knights' local assemblies in New Jersey
and through a detailed case study of one city, Newark (Voss 1993, ch. 7). The
most important factors were the actions of employers and of the state. Specifically, the Knights' rapid growth and early successes resulted in the counter-
mobilization of powerful employers' associations. Unlike those in England,
these associations had the benefits of rapid economic concentration at their
disposal and no interventionist state to constrain them. As a result they were
able to prevail in their battle to defeat the Knights.

In this chapter, however, the aim is not to explain the Knights' defeat but to
explore the actions of the Knights once they began to experience significant
reverses. As I first noticed in my research on Newark, Knights' activists offered little in the way of analysis and interpretation of their reverses. I soon
discovered that this was also true of big, nationally publicized setbacks as
well: For the most part, silence followed in the wake of defeat. Aside from a
smattering of speeches and articles in which a few national officers leveled
personal attacks at other officers, there were virtually no commentaries or
published speeches that assessed the Knights' experiences and drew lessons
from their collapse. There were no martyrs, no brave projections of how, next
time, the U.S. working class would triumph over its enemies. Indeed, there
was no sense at all of a next time. In short, the Knights did not construct what
I call a "fortifying myth," an explanation of defeat that linked current failure to
future triumphs, keeping hope alive so that activists could mobilize support
when new political opportunities arose (Voss 1996).

Without this fortifying myth, Knights' activists were disheartened, their organizational structures were scorned, and their working-class republicanism
was rejected. This made it difficult, I suggest, for radical labor activists to

recognize and act on subsequent political opportunities when they occurred. In the 1890s, for example, a large populist movement provided the opportunity for farmer–labor cooperation. At the same time the American electoral system underwent a critical realignment, offering an even more opportune moment for mass insurgency than had existed in the 1880s when the Knights were in their heyday. But chronic despair clouded the vision of those who might earlier have attempted to mobilize a movement, and those who had earlier spoken out in favor of a broad-based labor movement were silent.

Unlike the Knights, other movements have been able to construct fortifying myths. Labor movements influenced by socialist ideologies, for example, use socialism's doctrine of the historical inevitability of working-class triumph to attempt to explain how today's reverses can lead to tomorrow's victories. Another example is provided by Poland's Solidarity movement, whose activists invoked the Catholic belief in the successive stations of the "*via dolorosa*" to explain failures, the implication being that though early uprisings resulted in Crucifixion, eventually insurgency would bring Resurrection and Life (Weschler 1982). These myths, I suggest, can help social movement organizations survive setbacks by maintaining the commitment of activists and their followers.

The British new unionism provides a good case to assess this line of speculation.

Studying Interpretations of Defeat by New Unionists

The British new unions resembled the Knights of Labor in many ways. They originated at approximately the same time, adopted a radical and inclusive creed, and experienced explosive growth.[5] And like the Knights, the new unions suffered dramatic membership losses in the wake of an employer counteroffensive.

The new unions and the Knights, however, also differed in important ways: First, the new unions, unlike the Knights, were not completely destroyed by the employer counteroffensives, and thus some new unions still existed when the next resurgence of labor unrest occurred in Britain in 1910–13. This time, new union activists were able to permanently extend the labor movement's organizational reach and political power. Second, the relationship between the new unions and political parties was different in England from that in the United States. In England new union activists were instrumental in creating the Independent Labor Party, whereas in the United States, Knights' activists were able to establish local, but not national, labor parties. Third, most new unionists endorsed a mild version of socialism, with its tenet that the working class was a historical agent of social transformation, whereas most members of the Knights embraced the ideology of working-class republicanism, which included no such notion of inevitable triumph. This belief that the working class would ultimately prevail provided a possible line of interpretation that activists could use to explain setbacks to workers.

Most scholars have stressed the first two differences in their accounts of the different trajectories of the British new unionists and the U.S. Knights of Labor. Eric Hobsbawm (1984a), James Holt (1977), and Sanford Jacoby (1991), for example, all argue that British employers were less ruthless than American employers in their efforts to rout the inclusive unions and that this is the primary reason inclusive unions were more successful in England. Gary Marks (1989), Ira Katznelson (1985), Victoria Hattam (1993), and Edward Hunt (1981), in contrast, emphasize differences in the political institutions of the two countries. They note that the English electoral system was more accessible than the American party system to working-class political action and that the different political opportunities aided the survival of the new unions because electoral gains helped convince old and new unionists alike to support inclusive union strategies.

Though I believe that both lines of argument have substantial merit, I do not think that these differences alone can fully explain the *survival* of the British new unions, especially in the difficult years in which they began to experience defeat after defeat. After all, it is important not to underestimate the difficulties the British new unions encountered, both from employers and in the political arena. Consider, first, the employers. As J. Saville (1974) documents, throughout the 1890s and into the twentieth century employers and the press waged a fierce campaign against trade unionism in general and new unionism in particular. Police and military forces were employed in industrial disputes with unprecedented frequency, strikebreakers were introduced on an unparalleled scale, and most of the contemporary press was unremitting in its advocacy of free (that is, nonunion) labor. In the political arena, the courts were increasingly hostile in their rulings against labor in the 1890s, culminating in the Taff Vale decision that stripped unions of important legal rights. And both Liberal and Conservative administrations sanctioned the intrusion of extensive police and military force in labor conflicts. In short, though the obstacles the new unions faced were not as overwhelming as those encountered by the Knights of Labor, they were still formidable. The survival of the new unions was an achievement, not a given.

How much of this achievement was due to the efforts of new union activists to interpret and draw lessons from the defeats that their unions suffered? In my current research I am examining whether new union activists interpreted their unions' defeats, and if they did whether these interpretations had any effects on union solidarity, longevity, or militancy. More specifically, I ask: Did new union activists "frame" their defeats? If so, what themes were developed? And, most difficult to assess, what is the relationship between the framing of defeats and sustained collective action?

To answer these questions I selected a sample of failing strikes in three industries where new unionists were active: docking, railway transportation, and gas making. Using the *Reports on Strikes and Lockouts* published by the Board of Trade, I included every fourth failing strike in the sample, a procedure that generated a total of forty-two strikes. All these strikes took place between 1890, the year a counterattack against the new unions began, and the end of 1893, three years into the counterattack. This period was chosen because it represents the most active years of the employers' counterattack against the new unions and therefore it is comparable to the period of the Knights' defeat.

For each failing strike in the sample, several newspapers were read in order to discover whether or not the failure was addressed and debated. Three kinds of newspapers were consulted: local, union, and left/labor. In the case of local newspapers, I looked for framing statements by union activists and strike leaders, usually reported in interviews or in accounts of speeches. When examining union and left/labor newspapers, I looked at editorials as well as interviews and speeches.[6]

Newspapers were chosen as the source for this project because they offer accounts of strike activities in various communities and industries. Moreover, unlike union records, their preservation is not affected by the fame or fate of unions and union leaders.

Newspapers, however, have some limitations that affect their comprehensiveness. Particularly in the case of the left/labor press, extensive accounts of strike speeches are infrequent and rarely provide lengthy quotes.[7] Strike meetings are frequently reported, but all too often, little detail is given. Thus the results reported here probably underestimate the amount of framing actually done by union leaders.

Results

New union activists did sometimes interpret defeat and draw lessons for the future. In twelve of the forty-two sample strikes—31 percent of the time—

framings of the defeat were provided in speeches and editorials.[8] The defeats that were addressed were usually discussed repeatedly, frequently by multiple activists; in all, forty-seven newspaper articles were written about these twelve strike defeats.[9]

Framing statements were usually fairly elaborate and developed a variety of themes that cast defeats as moral victories, setbacks as temporary or partial, and particular strikes as part of a larger, eventually successful struggle (what I earlier termed a fortifying myth). In addition, statements often included an analysis of the causes of defeat and drew tactical lessons from the strike.

Moral Victories

In two-thirds of the defeats (eight of the twelve), activists claimed the moral high ground and challenged the notion that the strike was in any larger sense a failure. For example, the leader of an 1891 Scottish railway strike asserted:

> We are not disgraced [for] such a fierce labour war was never fought in this country, and morally speaking we have won. (*The Labour World*, February 7, 1891)

Similarly, Ben Tillet proclaimed a moral victory in the 1891 Cardiff dockers' strike:

> When the mist and smoke of battle has rolled away, [workers] will find that they have not so many wounded upon the field after all, and they will know that they have captured a strong position. They have taught themselves how to fight, and they have shown other people that they can fight. (*South Wales Daily News,* March 14, 1891)

Even after a catastrophic Hull dockers' defeat in 1893, which finished off the Dockers Union there, a local leader told the dockers that morally they had won:

> They had fought a memorable and splendid battle . . . having been swayed by [only] one motive, which was to make the condition of the toiling masses better, to ensure that life was worth living. (*Eastern Morning News,* May 22, 1893)

One especially creative way of claiming a moral victory was put forward by leaders of an 1890 Irish railway strike. A union activist told a meeting of strikers that the workers had called off the strike because they were willing to "sacrifice . . . for the good of the country":

> While the directors [of the railroad] were callous to the injury which was being done . . . the leaders of the men, as well as the rank and file, were painfully impressed with the hardships, and even absolute ruin, which the strike was causing to hundreds of poor people in the country districts. It is only the truly great who can be generous and we venture to say that the Irish strike will long be

remembered as an instance of self-denial and restraint when such qualities were the most difficult to put into operation. (*Railway Review,* May 9, 1890)

Temporary Setbacks and Partial Successes

Those activists who did not claim a moral victory offered other grounds for avoiding a crushing acknowledgment of failure. Some stressed the impermanence of the defeat. For example, at a large public meeting following the collapse of the Irish railway strike in 1890, one local leader declared that the strikers

> need not be frightened by the result of the strike, for victory always waits on those who persevere. (*Railway Review,* October 17, 1890)

Some searched to find a word less stark than "defeat" to describe the strike's outcome; one railway unionist suggested the term "truce," saying the strike had ended in "neither a surrender nor a victory." But he had to struggle mightily to come up with a reason why, when workers had lost on every issue, the defeat could be considered a truce. His argument:

> It is beyond question that the men were in a far stronger position at the close of the strike than at the commencement. (*Railway Review,* May 9, 1890)

And some, like Ben Tillet, attempted to snatch victory from the jaws of defeat by emphasizing that the defeat had not been a total rout. Speaking of the 1893 Hull strike in which an employers' association won the right to employ nonunion men, Tillet stressed the fact that the employers had not succeeded in completely preventing the employment of union dockers:

> We are quite satisfied in having defeated the efforts of these [employers] to interfere with the right of free institutions. (*Eastern Morning News,* May 27, 1893)

Altogether, partial defeats and temporary setbacks were themes in about a quarter of the strikes in which framing occurred.[10]

Inevitable Triumph

In one-third of the strikes, activists combined moral victory, temporary setback, or partial success frames with the idea that the defeat was part of a larger struggle that the labor movement would inevitably win. Contrary to my expectations, only twice was the idea of inevitability tied to some idea of the working class as an agent of history. Talking about the 1893 Hull strike, an editorial in *The Workman's Times* asserted that the strike proved that there was indeed an ongoing

> class war, so long proclaimed by Socialists, and so long denied by apologists of the established social order . . . It is raging around us every day in every city,

town, and village in the land. It is not a local fight; it is a universal contest in which workers are, mostly unconsciously, engaged against those who live upon their labour. When they awaken to the full knowledge of the hopelessness of their struggle for existence under present conditions, we shall have the Social Revolution. Object lessons like this at Hull have their use. They hasten the inevitable day. (April 29, 1893)

In the 1891 Cardiff dockers' strike, Ben Tillet did not explicitly mention socialism, but he did imply a historical role for the working class. He told workers that

what they had done was to lay a groundwork on which to build a larger, more powerful, more irresistible force than they had dreamt of. (*Labour World,* February 7, 1891)

Victory might be a long time in coming, but that was tolerable because

trades' unionists had entered upon a fight not for one year, nor for one generation, nor for two generations, but for all times, and as long as there were men who had to toil and sweat, this battle had to go on. They were only doing their duty to their day and generation to be worthy of those who had gone before, and to assist in the raising up of those coming after. (*South Wales Daily News* March 14, 1891)

In the two other strike defeats in which activists alluded to inevitable success in the future, they used nonsocialist justifications for their assertion that the working class would eventually win. In one of the Irish railway strikes, for example, it was a principle of "independence" that would eventually guarantee victory:

[Employers] might as well attempt to stop the flow of the tides as endeavor to uproot those principles of independence which are gradually but surely transforming the old order of things. (*Railway Review,* September 12, 1890)

In an 1891 Scottish railway strike, the rightness of the cause (an eight-hour day) and the demonstration of political support ensured future success:

Who can contend that the object for which the Scottish railway workers were contending is not on the eve of attainment? Shorter hours of labor on the railways of the United Kingdom will come as surely as tomorrow's sun, and all the sooner for the splendid stand which has been made in Scotland. (*Labour World,* February 7, 1891)

In short, by claiming a moral victory, arguing that the defeat was only partial or temporary, alluding to the inevitability of eventual triumph, or all three, almost all the framings put a positive slant on the defeat. They gave workers reasons to believe that their sacrifices had not been in vain.

Reasons for Defeat

Efforts to ennoble the strikes went hand in hand with an analysis of why they had not been more successful. Almost all the speeches and editorials gave reasons for the setbacks. In half the strikes for which there were framings, the primary reason given for defeat was inadequate solidarity, especially between organized and unorganized workers. In particular, the availability of workers willing to serve as strikebreakers ("blacklegs") was identified as the cause of defeat. The overwhelming power of employers was specified almost as often, in one-third of the cases. And sometimes, both causes were cited, as in this explanation for the failure of the Cardiff dockers' strike in 1891:

> [S]trike(s) . . . fail because capitalists present a solid front but only about one-sixth of the working classes are organized as yet into trades unions. Unions cannot defeat organized capital, aided by an almost unlimited supply of blacklegs. (*Labour World,* March 21, 1891)

Only once was bad leadership given as the primary reason for a strike defeat. It was mentioned three other times, but not identified as the principle cause of failure.

Lessons for the future

Almost all the articles offered explicit lessons for the future. The most common lesson drawn, in discussions of three-quarters of the strikes, was that strikes were "barbarous," and "no remedy for the wrongs of labour." The strike is a "double edged weapon," intoned *Labour World* in 1891, "which cuts the hand that wields it, even when it succeeds in smiting the foe" (February 7, 1891).

Because of this, workers should use it sparingly:

> The lesson of the strike is a hard one, but invaluable . . . It consists in the necessity of an exhaustive and complete knowledge of the forces at your disposal, and the courage to oppose strikes, if such information does not warrant them. (*Railway Review,* September 12, 1890)

Or not at all, as a member of the Hull Trades Council suggested after the dockers' defeat:

> Were [the strikers] going to rely on old weapons which were defective? Because if they were, then the heroic energy and self-sacrifice displayed during [the recent strike] had all been in vain. (*Eastern Morning News,* May 30, 1893)

Two alternatives to the strike were suggested. In the majority of speeches and editorials, political action was advised. As *The Workman's Times* wrote:

> Behind the present [1893 Hull] dispute looms the larger question of a reform of the economic conditions under which the people live. That reform can never be effected except through legislation. (April 29, 1893)

Here, political action was advised as a way of reforming the economic conditions that gave employers the power to win strikes. It was also proposed as a means of achieving land reform, which would stem the tide of blacklegs:

> The land problem must be attacked in such a way as to make rural existence attractive and to prevent the landlord from robbing the labourer. To this end trades unions should be utilised for political purposes. The land question can only be solved through the action of Parliament, and the working-classes should endeavor to capture Parliament. (*Labour World*, March 21, 1891)

The second alternative suggested to striking was more complete organization of the working class:

> If the [railway] servants were all united, as they should be, there would be no necessity for strikes. (*Railway Review,* October 17, 1890)

> We can only repeat the advice we have already urged: organize, organize, organize! . . . the great "blackleg" army [especially] must . . . be shown the advantages of trades unionism and the oneness of the cause of labour everywhere. (*Labour World,* March 21, 1891)

Conclusion

This research suggests that in a substantial number of cases new union activists attempted to interpret strike defeats. They used a variety of arguments to elevate the struggle so that strikers would feel that they had not sacrificed in vain. They drew explicit lessons for the future in order to give strikers a reason to believe that victory would eventually be achieved. Activists labored mightily to identify something they could call an achievement and to provide lessons for the next time.

This contrasts with the way that Knights of Labor activists reacted to defeats. Knights leaders did not usually offer public analyses of their losses. Nor did they make valiant predictions about how, in the future, the working class would conquer its enemies. In fact, Knights activists gave very little indication that there might be a next time.

Why did new unionists engage in much greater interpretive work than Knights' activists? It does not seem to be socialist ideology in any direct sense that led new unionists to draw lessons from their defeats. What, then, accounts for the difference? I suggest two alternative possibilities. It might be that socialism is not the most significant ideological difference in the two labor movements. As Eric Hobsbawm has suggested, the tradition and ideology of religious dissent might be the more important difference.[11] Another possibility is that my effort to tie the greater interpretive activity of British labor activists to a specific cultural tradition is misguided. Instead, it may be that British new unionists were simply more creative than Knights' activists in their efforts to maintain their organizations.

Finally, did these interpretations of defeat matter? That question will be answered in future research. I plan to assess the extent to which militancy in the second wave of the new unionism was related to framings in the first wave. By comparing communities and industries in which strike defeats were interpreted with those in which strike defeats went unremarked, I hope to evaluate the consequences of activists' efforts to frame defeats.

Notes

I would like to thank Michael Hanagan and Lissa Bell and the editors along with the participants at the Amsterdam Conference for their helpful comments and advice. This research was funded in part by the Institute of Industrial Relations at the University of California at Berkeley.

1. Tilly's work accords well with recent developments in cultural studies, particularly the movement away from the Weberian emphasis on culture as belief carried by committed individuals toward a view of culture as "constitutive, inherently collective, imbedded in symbols and practices, and necessarily infused with power" (Swidler 1995, 38).

2. Though Tilly's explanation for the cultural change is largely structural, he allows a role for cultural practices. In response to changing circumstances people improvise their ways of acting collectively, but this improvisation occurs primarily at the margins and is tightly tied to existing patterns of action.

3. For example, in his study of American social movements, Gamson ([1975] 1990) found that over half the organizations in his sample failed partially or completely.

4. For further discussion of working-class republicanism, see Voss 1993, chs. 1, 3.

5. On the explosive growth pattern of some social movements, see Hobsbawm 1964b.

6. Local newspapers are the most difficult to obtain, and not all strikes have yet been tracked in the local press. Union and left/labor papers are more widely available. These have been searched for every strike in the sample.

7. There are differences between the British and American press in this regard. American newspapers from the late nineteenth century provide more detailed coverage of speeches than do British newspapers.

8. As I expand my study to include more industries, I expect to find more framing. In addition, the reader should keep in mind that I have only sampled failing strikes; presumably, this proportion of framing holds across the larger universe of all failing strikes.

9. Twenty-two newspapers have been searched for framings of defeat.

10. It is important to point out that activists were overtly contesting the dominant interpretation of these defeats. When the sample of strikes was taken, I omitted all defeats defined as "partial" by the Board of Trade.

11. Personal communication, June 2, 1995.

Chapter 10

The Changing Horizons of Tax Resistance in Chinese History

R. Bin Wong

Shops were shut and perfect stillness reigned, as, twenty thousand strong, they wended their way through the streets with banners flying, each at the head of a company and each inscribed with the name of a temple where that company held its meetings. "What is the meaning of this demonstration?" I inquired. "We are going to reduce the taxes" was the laconic answer. Petitions had been tried in vain, and now, driven to desperation, they were staking everything on a last appeal, with its alternative—revenge . . . The conflict was with the mandarins only; the rioters were under strict discipline, and still professed loyalty to the supreme government . . . Their grievance was not taxation, but excessive charges made by local officers to cover the costs of collection. (William Martin, quoted by Hsiao 1960, 434–35)

This abbreviated account by William Martin comes from the 1890s and captures a kind of event, a very large one in this case, enacted numerous times across much of China since the eighteenth century. Collective opposition to the payment of taxes was a modest drama of several acts. A common sequence began with a group of people, sometimes numbering fewer than 100, presenting petitions that protested collection practices to officials. The failure of officials to respond adequately according to the expectations of the people set the stage for violent actions: attacks on the offices and homes of the bureaucrats. The arrests of troublemakers called forth larger crowds in protest. Tax resistance was usually terminated through negotiated settlements, repression by military force, or some combination of the two.

The persistence of tax resistance through the Qing dynasty (1644–1911) and into the Republican era (1912–49) permits us to isolate elements of continuity amid a complex compound of political change. A flash point that exposes the tensions between state demands and social expectations, the kind of tax resistance incident we find and its location in a larger political context

149

identifies the shifting character of state-society relations. On some occasions the resolution of tax resistance issues demonstrates either the state's coercive capacity to repress protest or the social sensitivity of officials who adjudicate the disputes and restore a sense of equity and order on the basis of shared expectations for acceptable official behavior. But at other times, when officials became unable to collect taxes, resistance incidents reveal the state's limited and fragile control over local societies.

In this chapter I will examine the changing horizons of tax resistance in China since the eighteenth century. Taxation has drawn attention as an indicator of postimperial Chinese state-building efforts, seen by some scholars as being parallel to elements of the European state-making experiences of several centuries before. Twentieth-century tax resistance occupies a role analogous to that of tax resistance in seventeenth-century France, where so much of the correspondence to and from Paris centered on tax collection and its problems. More generally, Republican-period China, with its seemingly constant military skirmishes whetting the warlords' appetites for increasing amounts of resources, bears a measure of similarity to war-torn early-modern Europe.

Insofar as European national state making took shape amid the extraction of resources to field armies, it is little wonder that some scholars have seen parallels in twentieth-century China. At both ends of Eurasia protestors opposed state claims that they deemed inappropriate or even illegitimate. Centralizing European states possessed very weak taxation powers compared to those of the late-imperial Chinese central government. Feudal rule provided few useful strategies for increasing central government revenues as modern European state making got under way. Strapped for funds and limited in their capacities to extract additional revenues, European governments turned to a range of other techniques, including taking out loans and developing public credit mechanisms, confiscating properties, and selling offices or royal assets. Tax resistance in general opposed new claims put on people by centralizing governments.

I will argue that in the twentieth century, the Chinese state increased taxation without providing ideological justification. In this respect twentieth-century Chinese tax resistance more closely resembles early-modern European cases than late-imperial Chinese ones. In other important ways, however, twentieth-century Chinese tax resistance diverged from European experiences. The target of European tax resistance was always the central state and its representatives. The protesters were always people seeking to limit the state's penetration. In twentieth-century China the target was usually a local government that was collecting taxes on its own authority, on behalf of a provincial (or warlord) leader, or as an agent of the national state. Protesters could be organized groups seeking to lay hold of the ability to collect taxes and thus to challenge for political power. Twentieth-century tax resistance, therefore, captures the uncertain development of state power in China. Though the expansion of a formal state presence in the countryside is clear, who would control what kind of state power was fuzzy at best.

The Events and Their Ideology

In the eighteenth and nineteenth centuries, people protested tax payments when they believed that officials had violated proper collection procedures and would reform their practices upon hearing popular complaints. Appeal to principles of equity and fairness were commonly made for three reasons: First, people protested when they felt the tax burden was unfairly apportioned among households. Second, they opposed tax payments that failed to reflect harvest conditions. Third, they criticized official use of oversized measures, biased conversion rate from grain to silver, and commutation rates that required more copper for a given amount of silver.

The apportionment of the tax burden among households was a difficult task because the size and quality of individual plots varied considerably, even within a single county, not to mention within a province. Collection rates themselves varied dramatically in late-imperial times across the empire, in very rough relationship to the productivity of the land in different provinces (Wang 1973, 84–109). Since little could be done to equalize the burdens across the empire as a whole, equalization efforts were concentrated at local levels. Officials often expected more from the rich, as is shown by their calls upon the rich to demonstrate virtue through contributions.[1] But the rich were often able to protect themselves and pay less taxes, proportionally, than their poorer neighbors. The fact that tax burdens were unequal is perhaps less surprising than the belief that taxes should be allocated equally, in proportional terms, at the local level. Certainly in Europe, the expectation that the different social orders and corporate groups would have different exemptions and privileges was for a long time a basic feature of old regime state–society relations.

A second general cause for tax resistance was disagreement over the rates of collection appropriate to harvest results. To offer peasants relief from poor harvests, officials reduced tax liabilities and postponed collections (Will 1990, 241–46). In years of poor harvest, peasants anxiously awaited official deliberations on tax liabilities. Failure by officials to adjust adequately collections according to harvest conditions was a recurring theme in Qing-dynasty tax resistance.[2]

A third source of opposition to tax payments was the popular belief that oversized measures or crooked commutation rates were being used to extract additional revenue. This suspicion was reinforced in the mid-nineteenth-century cases I examine later, where different commutation rates were charged for gentry and commoner households. Popular suspicions of official malfeasance were mirrored by official worries that tax payers might use adulterated and inferior grains or silver of insufficient purity.

Each of these forms of opposition is motivated by a belief that appropriate procedures and principles have not been followed by officials. It serves a specific and limited purpose and rests upon beliefs that officials themselves understand and even share. Though officials usually could not tolerate disruptions without assessing penalties, they did accept the rationales of those who protested. These kinds of tax resistance often succeeded in an eighteenth-century environment in which the state had few pressing fiscal problems. After the budget surpluses were spent to suppress the White Lotus Rebellion of the 1790s, officials were forced to meet urgent fiscal needs brought on by the mid-nineteenth-century military challenges; they turned to new commercial taxes and expanded sales of degrees.[3] In this context, officials were, not surprisingly, less likely to respond to requests to reallocate existing tax burdens for equity reasons, to indulge requests for tax remissions and exemptions because of harvest conditions, or to avoid surreptitious methods for increasing collections. Under pressure to respond to a growing crisis, officials found the logic of sustaining social order through positive paternalism and its associated flexibility toward tax collection less appealing than raising revenues by any and all means. Tax resistance actions became for officials a symptom of more serious disorders that were treated with force.

The impact of the state's expanded fiscal needs was exacerbated by the silver deflation associated by contemporaries, as well as by modern scholars, with the import of opium and the export of silver.[4] Households had to sell more crops or goods, for which they received copper cash, in order to pay their commuted land tax payments denominated in silver. Sluggish markets reduced demand, making the economic burden of taxes even greater. Yet the fiscal crisis of the first half of the nineteenth century was usually conceived by contemporaries as a failure of individuals to act morally. Many believed that official corruption was at the root of the state's fiscal difficulties (Suzuki 1958). This perception served to mask the state's basic problems: how to

raise additional revenues to meet the challenges of nineteenth-century rebellion without causing new instances of tax resistance.

Mid-Nineteenth-Century Chinese Tax Resistance

Middle Yangzi

The 1840s and 1850s were unsettled years in the Middle Yangzi region, which
was composed of Hubei and Hunan provinces. Before the Taiping rebel
armies had left the southwestern province of Guangxi for their march up
through Hunan, tax resistance was already a problem, as were rent resistance and struggles over food (Kojima 1978, 117–31; Wong 1982). Major tax
resistance incidents took place in several Middle Yangzi counties. Dear silver
and unstable harvests set the stage for these conflicts. People protested the
excess tax collections made possible by differential exchange rates between
silver and copper that favored gentry households at the expense of common-
ers (Kojima 1978, 96–103; Otsuki 1983, 563–67).

Our view of official responses to these small-scale conflicts is often obscured by the looming presence of the Taiping rebels and the state's response to them. From Philip Kuhn we have learned that officials combined
with local elites to forge local militia that defended communities and regional
armies that pursued and ultimately defeated the rebel forces (Kuhn 1970).
But Kuhn also suggests two ways in which the militarization process and
taxation were organizationally connected: First, he shows that the militia unit
could become the organizational instrument for tax collection, a move he
claims helped to postpone tax resistance because the militia unit was better
able than individual households to resist official demands (Kuhn 1970, 100).
He also gives an example of a group, which he calls a "league," that managed
tax collection without government interference; indeed, it became recognized as a kind of *baojia* unit (a group of households mutually responsible
for each other's behavior) and, like the militia, formed a buffer between local
people and officials demanding taxes (Kuhn 1970, 127–29).

Kojima Shinji, a leading Japanese specialist on the Taiping, finds examples
of tax resistance that cross Kuhn's distinction between tax-collecting militias
and tax resistance leagues (Kuhn 1970, 170–71). It is the very forces of order,
leaders of the militia and militia-like units, that also engage in tax resistance.
Kojima offers examples from Hunan and mentions cases from three additional
provinces studied by other scholars (Kojima 1978, 96–103). In some cases,
such as Anhua in Hunan province, it appears that the tax protest led by a militia

leader protected the local community against outside resource extraction, much as the militia was expected to defend the people against outside threats of physical violence (Kojima 1978, 102). The difference, of course, matters; the threats come from the government and the rebels respectively.

Militia units themselves could become involved as organizational vehicles for protest. In Shandong, as we'll see, tax resistance came to play a serious role in a much larger challenge to replace local governments. Whether militia-based tax collection became an act of tax resistance or not depended less on militia actions than official reactions. The attribution of resistance was often made by officials who were unwilling to accept militia-based tax collection because they lost too much control. In other cases the militia–official relationship was close enough that militia-based tax collection occurred without the friction that would be called tax resistance.

The proper forms of participation in tax collection by resident landlords and lower-degree holders also became an issue in these tax resistance events. Documents show that "rich households" were involved in Leiyang and "rich households known for their good works" in Chongyang; in other places, Kojima suggests, many of the events were led by resident landlords holding lower degrees. These local elites opposed certain official actions, much as their ancestors had before. Unlike the leaders of eighteenth-century tax resistance, however, those spearheading the nineteenth-century episodes were often seeking a larger direct role in the tax-collection process. Nineteenth-century tax resistance therefore reflects the sometimes uneasy expansion of elite participation in local government affairs. To the degree that elites displaced officials in tax collection and did not become integrated into the administrative apparatus, the local government was undermined and compromised. Yet at the same time, elite abilities to collect taxes compensated for the limitations of formal government. The complex role of elites in tax collection would remain contested during the remainder of the Qing dynasty and in the Republican period as well. Tax resistance in the mid-nineteenth century begins to signal fundamental uncertainties about the bases of state authority and control.

Based on the surviving documentation, there certainly appear to be more small-scale protests in the mid-nineteenth century than in the eighteenth century. Certainly the possibilities for tax resistance were augmented by the roaming presence of rebel armies and the state's consequent need for additional revenues. But despite the backdrop of rebel groups marching through the Middle Yangzi region, there is little in the way of direct relationships between those people resisting taxes and those joining in rebellion. In the Lower Yangzi region, however, we'll see that a more direct relationship is possible.

Jiangnan

Jiangnan was a region facing change and crisis in the mid-nineteenth century. Merchants, sailors, and smugglers moved about in response to the trade possibilities created by the foreign presence. They were joined by the Taiping rebels, who swept down the Yangzi and stormed the cities and towns of Jiangnan. Tax resistance was part of the unsettled scene in which these larger events took place. As Kathryn Bernhardt's research has shown, tax resistance occurred in two waves, a long and relatively gentle wave between 1840 and 1846 followed by a shorter, sharper wave in 1853 (Bernhardt 1992, 55–62). These events in the Lower Yangzi shared a number of features with tax resistance elsewhere. Economic hardships spread through the region with the silver deflation and consequent fall of cotton and wheat prices. In this highly commercialized economy, the burdens of taxation were exacerbated by the weak demand for cash crops and handicraft goods. But economic hardship itself was only part of the backdrop. The resistance events were often triggered by perceived injustices. Thus, when Suzhou peasants working government lands paid taxes at a rate above that used in nearby Taicang, they protested.[5]

The maintenance of distinctions among households for tax collection purposes was the cause for tax resistance in a number of Jiangnan cases. In Changshu and Zhaowen counties a distinction between "big" and "little" households meant that normal households had an incentive to have their payments made by "big" households at the more favorable rates. This practice of proxy remittance cut into government revenues, which in turn meant that officials raised the conversion rate between silver and copper to compensate for lost revenues. This in turn reinforced the already strong incentives people felt to avoid taxation at the "little" household rate:

> Once a certain critical level of disparity between privileged and nonprivileged rate-payers was reached, for whatever reason, a self-sustained snowballing effect could be expected to appear before long. The wider the gap between *ta-hu* [big households] and *hsiao-hu* [little households] commutation rates, the more irresistible became the logic of proxy remittance (*pao-lan*) of the tribute rice obligation through indigent junior gentrymen. But the more land that went into the *ta-hu* registry, the greater the share that had to be absorbed by the remaining *hsiao-hu* rate-payers. Thus the process perpetuated itself. (Polachek 1975, 220)

These collection difficulties persuaded some local officials to do away with the distinction between large and small households, since proxy remittance was not in fact sanctioned by officials, who searched for effective alternative means of tax collection. A decision to halt proxy remittance was implemented in Changshu but not in Zhaowen. As a result there was no rioting in Changshu, but there was considerable violence in Zhaowen (Bernhardt 1992, 58–59).

A related distinction among taxpaying households was practiced in the Ningbo region. The so-called red method of direct payment to officials by individual households was followed by wealthier families, who placed their tax payments in red envelopes; the contrasting "white" method of collection by runners sent out to the countryside was used by all other households. The copper–silver exchange rate for the rich using the red method was 2,000 copper cash–silver tael, while the others using the white method paid 3,000 copper cash–silver tael; in other words, their burden was 50 percent higher. This inequity in combination with excess collections stimulated tax resistance (Sasaki 1963, 189–99).

As events, these acts of tax resistance, with their issues of equitable tax burdens, look similar to the incidents of tax resistance recorded in the previous century. But they posed a larger challenge, in part because they were linked to other forms of conflict. In Zhaowen, for instance, tax resistance at the end of 1845 was followed by rent resistance in 1846. The tax resistance was spearheaded by an initial protest by some forty households from an area near one town, whereas rent resistance actions were concentrated around other market towns in the eastern part of the county (Bernhardt 1992, 58). The Zhaowen case points out the danger that a high density of small-scale collective actions posed to authorities. More serious yet, tax resistance in Jiangnan, unlike upstream examples, became tied directly to larger-scale challenges. In Jiading, a certain Zhou Lichun, a tax functionary, led people in a revolt against paying overdue taxes; Zhou represented people who asked for continued tax relief because of poor harvests. After his initial successes Zhou faced arrest and punishment by officials. To avoid capture, he linked up with the Small Swords Society and attacked Jiading with the intention of overthrowing the local authorities. The secret society aspect of the resistance distinguishes the Jiading case from eighteenth-century examples of tax resistance and provides the key to escalation from tax resistance to armed struggle (Perry 1985, 85–100; Bernhardt 1992, 69–73).

The emergence of secret societies was intimately tied to the changing features of Jiangnan society brought on by foreign impact. As Elizabeth Perry has argued:

> In a variety of ways then, we can trace the impact of the treaty port setting on the genesis and character of the Small Swords: cash crop areas affected by the foreign intrusion launched the initial tax resistance, opium smuggling provided

the link between rural and urban protest; merchant guilds spearheaded the formation of rebel militia; and foreign ideas influenced Small Sword ideology and symbolism. (Perry 1985, 98).

Tax resistance became part of the changing social setting of Jiangnan society, even as it remained rooted in older issues.

The solutions proposed by leading reformers, like the problems themselves, followed patterns outlined in earlier centuries. In 1853 Feng Guifen made abolishing the distinction between big and little households a central aspect of his tax reform proposals. The reforms he and others proposed were certainly limited and, as James Polachek has shown, were bounded by factional networks of officials and gentry, but their goals were nevertheless important, for they tied the state to venerable social concerns (Polachek 1975). Statesmen and elites aimed to defuse discontent over tax issues based on a logic of household self-interest, the community's welfare, and the state's desire to sustain a stable relationship with local society.

Shandong

Tax resistance was more widespread in the northern province of Shandong than in the central and eastern provinces along the Yangzi River. Incidents took place in each of Shandong's twelve prefectures in the 1850s and 1860s (Kanbe 1972, 78). Poor harvests, dear silver, and excess tax collections played roles as they did in other parts of the empire. But in contrast to other provinces, in Shandong the militia played a prominent role as instigators of resistance (Perry 1985, 101). Indeed, terms like "militia bandits" and "black militia" in contrast to "white militia" signal the political flexibility of the militia's character and the ambiguity of their actions. The militias' need for funding and inability to work out bases of support with local officials helps to explain the widespread occurrence of tax resistance in Shandong.

The large numbers of relatively poor peasants with small holdings also contributed to the resistance possibilities. From rare nineteenth-century land ownership data Kanbe Teruo has ascertained that places in Shandong where tax resistance occurred had large numbers of individuals who owned all their land or who owned some land and rented additional plots (Kanbe 1972, 77–85). These Shandong peasants with small holdings were especially vulnerable to changes in the tax burden. Even if the burden were in some absolute sense light, the small margin for success could be wiped out by a higher tax rate.

As in the Lower Yangzi, tax resistance in Shandong could become part of a larger direct challenge to local authorities. Perry has presented the case of one Liu Depei, a lower-level degree holder who first organized a protest against grain tribute collections and then organized a militia force with gentry support. Liu took his militia and engaged official authorities in a sequence of skirmishes as he sought to take over the management of taxation and administration of justice in Zichuan County (Perry 1985, 100–108; Yokoyama 1972, 261–64). Liu Depei's first step was a protest against tax collection rates. This act did not challenge the officials' authority to collect taxes; it only argued against then-current collection practices. But the uncertain role of local officials in Shandong and the willingness of gentry to move against the authorities permitted Liu to take further steps. His formation of a militia unit created a military challenge to complement his fiscal challenge to local authorities. When he temporarily took over judicial functions in Zichuan, he had captured the basics of local governance—taxation, military, and justice. This move from mere tax resistance to an explicit assault on local government alerts us to the shift from eighteenth-century to nineteenth-century political possibilities tied to tax resistance.

Nineteenth-Century Tax Resistance in Late-Imperial Perspective

Specific incidents of tax resistance in the nineteenth century were often prompted by the same kinds of motivations that had prompted protests over official collections procedures in the eighteenth century: People came together to oppose inequities of tax apportionment or to protest rates of collection because of harvest shortfalls. But the political meaning of these protests was transformed by important changes in the larger contexts within which resistance took place. The mid-nineteenth-century government faced a broader variety and larger number of small- and large-scale conflicts. Tax resistance could become simply one dimension of a more general challenge to state control and power. The refusal to pay taxes to officials could be coupled with an effort to create alternative bases of authority in local societies.

The linkage between tax resistance and larger scales of conflicts prompted Hamashima Atsutoshi to remark on the "revolutionary" character of nineteenth-century tax resistance compared to the more "traditional" character of late-sixteenth-century and seventeenth-century tax resistance, which, he argues, was aimed at securing more equitable taxation (1982, 527–39). This argument stresses important organizational and contextual changes, the ways people get organized to express commitments to equitable tax assessment and their opportunities to engage in other forms of collective action. But the nomenclature of "traditional" and "revolutionary" obscures the contingent relationships between tax resistance and large-scale collective action. In the examples we have reviewed, three kinds of relationships between tax resistance and rebellions can be seen. In Hunan, the Taiping movement is analytically distinct from the tax resistance events that take place in the province. In Jiangsu, however, the leader of a tax resistance action chose to link up with the Small Swords to embark on a larger challenge to local authorities. In Shandong, protest leaders who first engaged in tax resistance then went on to lead a larger rebellion. From this range of relationships between tax resistance and rebellion, it is clear that some large-scale collective actions grew out of small-scale conflicts. Other large-scale revolts, however, simply supplied the context for small-scale actions. Events like tax resistance matter to our understanding of rebellion because they help us delineate a range of possible relations between small-scale and large-scale protests. There is no single necessary relationship between different kinds of collective action.

Even if tax resistance did not become "revolutionary" in the nineteenth century, it did nevertheless signal significant political changes. Eighteenth-century tax resistance pitted local people against the state with a sense of a community challenging an outside force. In the nineteenth century, the state–community axis of protest was split into a number of new dimensions. At stake in late Qing tax resistance was control over the extraction of resources. This nineteenth-century competition between elites, secret societies, and local officials reflects difficulties more serious than those faced by eighteenth-century officials. The later period's tax resistance reveals the state's twin vulnerabilities to elites and rebels. Limitations on the formal bureaucratic capacities of the late-imperial state had always required some reliance on elites to shoulder political responsibilities, but tax collection by elites was never really sanctioned, let alone encouraged, as was elite participation in welfare (granaries and famine relief) and educational and ideological activities (schools, public moral lectures).

In the nineteenth century, militia and secret societies became involved in tax resistance. Their organizational capacities gave the tax resistance event a more durable presence. These actions often became simply individual acts in larger dramas. Militias often strove to reorganize tax collection, while secret societies rejected local government more generally and attempted to replace the authorities. The relationship of militias to tax resistance was doubly contingent. First, militias in Kanbe's picture of Shandong could engage in tax resistance, whereas those in Kuhn's Hunan examples took over tax collection without any acts of resistance to precede the organizational change. Second, tax resistance could be mounted by secret societies as easily as by the militias, the case both in some of the Hunan examples and in some of the Jiangsu examples. Nineteenth-century officials faced the hard choice between permitting elites a larger de facto role in tax collection and suffering insufficient resources. These difficulties were superceded for a time by the dangers posed by rebels bent upon displacing local governments. But though rebels could be defeated by military force, the problematic relationship with elites would perdure into the twentieth century.

Changes in the organization of tax resistance transformed the political significance of tax resistance. Tax collection and local authority more generally were transformed by the late-Qing and Republican expansion of the elite's paragovernmental activities. Though many of the actors in tax resistance events continued to be the same and the immediate issues remained the rates and methods of tax collection, the relations among actors changed further in the twentieth century.

Tax Resistance: Revolution, State Making, and Political Change

New taxes were a basic component of the reform policies initiated by late-Qing officials. Postimperial governments continued to raise additional revenues with new surtaxes and miscellaneous taxes. Scholars have yet to reach a consensus on the real economic impact of these taxes; some believe increases in productivity absorbed any potential shock of rising real taxes, whereas others remain convinced that peasants must have been seriously harmed by new taxes. Whatever the real economic burden of the taxes, the social response of peasants to additional levies at least is clear-cut: Protests against taxes were the most common form of popular conflict in the Republican period in China. New taxes were often unacceptable because they had no precedent; their implementation often violated old expectations; failures to adjust collections according to harvest conditions and perceived inequalities in the distribution of the tax burden continued to provoke opposition. Distrust of government investigators even meant that people opposed proposals that officials claimed would make tax burdens more equitable (Bianco 1986, 280–85).

Individual instances of twentieth-century tax resistance continued to represent criticisms of collection practices. But much else had clearly changed over the previous 200 years. By the twentieth century, the blurred distinction between local officials and local elites was paralleled by a growing ambiguity

over who could wield the authority to decide basic issues like taxation. The lo-
cale's desire to free itself from extraction by outsiders increased as revenue
needs of expanding government offices became more salient. Twentieth-
century tax resistance captures the tense ambiguities of expanded efforts at
resource mobilization amid growing uncertainties over the bases of political
authority and social order in the Chinese countryside. The Republican period
is hardly one of successful state making by a centralizing government that ex-
pands its bureaucratic capacities at the expense of local and regional authorities. Instead, the period is one in which different levels of government enjoyed unstable levels of autonomy from each other and in which the central
government was by no means a stronger, more effective state than the one
that had ruled the country two centuries earlier. Within a general context of
uncertain relations among levels of government, local government was an expanding force in Republican China doubly vulnerable to failure. From above
came countless proclamations, orders, and plans generally devoid of any logic
for implementation. From below came hostility and opposition to any local efforts to implement new policies. People in rural society pursued two basic
strategies to limit the impact of local government initiatives: First, they strove
to keep the local government out of the villages. Building on nineteenth-
century traditions of organizing a local militia, twentieth-century people mobilized to repel local government advances. Tax resistance was an important
dimension of this larger rejection of local government (Perry 1980, 163, 166,
205). Second, the radical alternative to keeping the government out was taking it over. The expansion of local elite participation in increasingly formal, if
not always bureaucratic, forms of governance transformed government offices into an arena for competition. Thus when people in Changle, south of
Fuzhou in Fujian province, disliked the new opium tax, they replaced local
functionaries with their own representatives (Bianco 1986, 297–99). There is
no question that officials were *attempting* to expand the reach of government
into local society. There is equally little question that popular mobilization
could take place outside official efforts (Perry 1984). Tax resistance exemplifies the relationship of antagonism between community mobilization and official extraction. But there is another dimension to twentieth-century tax resistance that complicates this picture.

Neither the ideology nor the organizational bases of tax resistance appear
to have changed greatly between the nineteenth and twentieth centuries, but
the targets of attack became more numerous. From Roxann Prazniak we
learn that tax resistance in early-twentieth-century Shandong included a

clear antielite component brought on by the expanded role that local elites took on in governmental affairs. Her findings for Shandong offer a hypothesis for other parts of the country (1981). Complementing this theme is an argument made by Kathryn Bernhardt, who suggests that rent resistance struggles in Jiangnan come to include an antistate element because officials had become more intimately involved with rent collection (1992, 165–77). Together these arguments suggest that previously distinct types of small-scale collective action were becoming more similar as their targets became the same. The problems of rule were becoming sharper as officials and elites found themselves the common focus for popular opposition. But some local leaders in some places led popular mobilization against taxes as those elsewhere participated in the expansion of local government. Twentieth-century examples of tax resistance span a range from conventional community-based protests against outsiders to classlike popular antagonisms against elites and officials who form ever tighter alliances. Class and community do not define independent axes of cleavage, since tax resistance examples mark the contingent placement of elites, who can be drawn toward alliance either with the community or with officials. These uncertainties reflect the more general relations among officials, elites, and peasants that twist and turn from late-imperial times to the present.

Conclusions: Narratives of Tax Resistance and Future Prospects

Twenty years ago we could confidently trace the development of Euro-American welfare states. When we reviewed the historical trajectory stretching back into the early-modern era, we spoke of tax resistance as one form of collective protest that marked popular resistance to the expansion of state power. Tax resistance faded from the European scene as states consolidated their powers and in some places incorporated representative power in setting taxes. Our narratives of Euro-American state building did not lead us to expect the most recent chapters of political change, in which the welfare state is being dismantled in numerous Euro-American settings. In the United States this initiative has been spearheaded by a kind of tax resistance that would have been unimaginable in old regime Europe. Political movements persuading voters to favor limits on certain types of taxes is a new form of tax resistance. As the welfare state in the United States is being dismantled, renegotiations of the powers and responsiblities of different levels of government are being considered. No one seeks to defend government as it has been practiced, few seem able to articulate in substantive terms what they believe government can do well and should be doing.

Coming from a very different starting point, the government of the People's Republic of China has also been facing a recent process of contraction and scaling down of its activities. One of the basic issues that has exercised Chinese leaders in the 1980s has been fiscal reform; we discover the central government's real structural weakness as it negotiates to draw resources from provinces and locales whose expansion of political capacities to extract revenues has accompanied the development of the economy. Locales and provinces are pitted against both the center, eager for more revenues, and the enterprises themselves, which are seeking to avoid taxation as much as they can. Structural uncertainties about the roles of different levels of government as well as the overall role of government in society affect China as they do the United States. Issues of taxation matter to both, but tax resistance in China remains very different from what is seen in the United States. While the Chinese economic reforms have reduced the role of state and party in a wide number of social and economic activities, increased participation through representative government has not accompanied these changes. Popular engagement in politics to influence government policies has therefore continued to be expressed in forms of protest. A particularly dramatic example from the mid-1990s involved some 10,000 peasants in Renshou County, Sichuan who, armed with clubs and scythes, protested new grain taxes in a confrontation with officials (Link 1994, 32).

Twenty years ago we set about explaining the operations of the socialist state in China with little, if any, attention to the processes of state formation that had preceded it. We were confident that a rupture of the magnitude of the one that occurred in 1949 made knowledge of earlier history unnecessary, a convenient assumption since much remained unstudied at that time. The persistent possibilities for tax resistance in China today suggest that peasants still oppose the state in ways and for reasons that their ancestors would have understood. But whether this continuity has a future remains to be seen. Institutional structures might further change, and new bases of taxation might come to be accepted by all parties that would make such protests unlikely. But for the moment the changing horizons of tax resistance in Chinese history do not promise future forms of collective action for peasants radically divorced from their past practices. Euro-American welfare states are contracting their span of responsibilities as the Chinese socialist state reduces its range of activities. But wherever these processes are leading, they do not appear, at least yet, to be converging toward a single, common end.

Notes

1. One important use of contributions was to fund granaries, some of which were made in exchange for degrees (Will and Wong 1991, 28–30, 49–53, 63). On contributions for degrees and their more general uses see Xu 1950. Degrees were granted by the state to individuals who passed different officially administered examinations; lower-level degrees could also be purchased. Possession of a degree, even a low one, marked one as a person of some considerable status. Those with higher degrees are often referred to as "gentry"; their degrees afforded them opportunities to receive official appointments in the government bureaucracy.

2. For example, see a 1731 Zhili case, a 1768 Jiangyin case, and an 1815 case from Songjiang (*Kang Yong Quian* 1979, 310–11, 322–23, 323–24).

3. On the White Lotus Rebellion the classic account is Suzuki 1952; for the more general situation of early-nineteenth-century dynastic decline, see Jones and Kuhn 1978. Susan Mann (1987) makes an argument for considering the growing capacities of the nineteenth-century state to extract revenues from commercial sources; on the sale of degrees see Xu 1950.

4. For an assembling of figures on the silver–copper ratios and an analysis of the economic problems caused by the silver deflation, see Peng 1983, 24–71.

5. Two brothers led the resistance when tribute boat sailors came to press for collection of back "rents," which were in essence taxes used to defray the expenses of tribute boat sailors; see Bernhardt 1992, 56–57.

Part III

Constellations of Political Opportunity

Chapter 11

Reflections on Historical Possibility: Cuba, 1956–1961

Marifeli Pérez-Stable

> *Havana has a tempo more like San Francisco or Detroit. Modern Cubans are as much in a hurry as are modern New Yorkers . . . Cubans work hard, and they play hard . . . The average Habanero . . . has an unabashed admiration for Americans who conduct themselves properly . . . the visitor who gets the idea that these eager-to-please people can be pushed around is in for a rude surprise . . . A steady rise in income . . . a significant upward spiral in the standard of living, and the security of sound money indicate that the "Beautiful Island" is doing all right . . . Short of a disastrous revolution at home or a world depression, this economy is destined to rise to new heights year by year.* The Diplomat, November 1958

Two months after *The Diplomat* published this upbeat forecast, "a disastrous revolution" struck the "Beautiful Island." Reading these words in the 1990s one might wonder (as, for that matter, one might well have wondered even in the early 1960s) if the editors of this slick magazine, targeted at a then-nascent upscale international audience, had their heads buried in a deep hole in the ground. In the fall of 1958 few observers could have reasonably doubted that Fulgencio Batista's days were numbered. A revolutionary situation unequivocally gripped the island: The opposition movement claimed exclusive rights to state power; an overwhelming majority of Cubans repudiated the regime; and the government seemed increasingly incapable of wielding the full force of repression against the *fidelistas* and their supporters. Multiple sovereignty rent the Cuban polity.

In January 1959 the anti-Batista coalition seized the reins of state power, strengthened by the presence of moderates opposed to Batista, the support of segments of the capitalist class, and the defection of army personnel to the rebel forces. When Fidel Castro made his triumphant entry into Havana on January 8, Batista's military was in a shambles and the Rebel Army had become the nation's armed force. Just over two years later, after a radicalization that alienated its moderate supporters and a rout of the invasion at the Bay of Pigs that humiliated the United States, the revolutionary government decisively consolidated its hold on power. The revolutionary situation of the late 1950s yielded a revolutionary outcome of a special type: a social revolution that confounded upper- and many middle-class Cubans and the U.S. government. A rude surprise, indeed!

Situations, Outcomes, and Regime-Types: Sociological Perspectives on Revolutions

In *European Revolutions, 1492–1992* (1993b) Charles Tilly definitively dismisses the view of revolutions as unique events that, like solar eclipses, are predictable and occur only under precise, readily identifiable conditions. Instead, he makes a compelling argument that revolutions are like traffic jams. Like traffic jams, revolutions do not occur randomly. Both happen in a variety of circumstances, are prompted by different kinds of conditions, and manifest a broad diversity in type and intensity; both also respond to strong regularities in the operation of routine traffic flows and political processes and, once begun, display regular patterns. Social scientists and historians, however, do not yet have the same level of theoretical understanding of revolutions as traffic controllers do of traffic jams.

The key analytical problem is to identify the "causal mechanisms" underpinning the two crucial moments of revolutions: the revolutionary situation and the revolutionary outcome. The emergence of the first does not necessarily yield the second; even when it does, according to Tilly, the revolutionary outcome is solely a forcible transfer of power to a new governing coalition. The mechanisms that produce a revolutionary situation are

- the emergence of contenders claiming exclusive rights to control the state;
- a commitment to those claims by a significant sector of the population; and
- the incapacity or unwillingness of the rulers to repress the contenders and their supporters.

A revolutionary outcome is more likely when challengers attract some members of the ruling group to their coalition and when that coalition mobilizes substantial military force against the regime. In short, these situations and outcomes are more probable when states are vulnerable and polities divided.

In the Third World, neopatrimonial regimes manifest a constellation of political characteristics that increase the likelihood of their facing and succumbing to revolutionary movements (Dix 1984; Midlarsky and Roberts 1985; Goodwin and Skocpol 1989; Shugart 1989; Snyder 1992; Wickham-Crowley

1992, 1994; Goodwin 1994). The salient characteristics of neopatrimonialism—in essence, a political system built on a network of patronage intimately dependent on loyalty to the chief *pater*—are

- a socially narrow, politically closed authoritarian regime;
- a dictator who bases his power on a loyal, corrupt, inefficient, and unprofessional military as well as on strong ties to a foreign power;
- military, political, and upper-class organizations with little autonomy from the regime;
- the alienation of upper-class and career officers; and
- a broad-based opposition that makes it easier for the foreign power to withdraw its support of the long-backed dictator and to look for alternatives within that opposition.

Identifying the causal mechanisms of the neopatrimonial traffic jams sometimes cleared up by revolutions requires that we answer the following crucial questions:

- What is the nature of the relations between the dictator and the military?
- What is the nature of the dictator's relations with domestic elites and other domestic actors?
- What is the character of the opposition? What is the relative weight of moderate reformers and armed revolutionaries in the coalition?
- What is the role of the dominant foreign power in relation to the regime and to the opposition?[1]

The Batista regime of the 1950s figures prominently in the literature on neopatrimonialism and revolutions; the other two regimes always mentioned are the forty-five-year dynasty of the Somozas in Nicaragua and the twenty-six-year reign of the shah Mohammed Reza Pahlavi in Iran, with the thirty-five-year rule of Porfirio Díaz in Mexico sometimes included. Although neopatrimonialism is a fairly (but not precisely) accurate characterization of the 1950s in Cuba, the *batistato* lasted less than seven years. Tilly's two-moment dissection of revolutions squarely highlights their proximate causes. Although such a focus keeps our feet close to the historical ground and deflects the temptation to craft "grand" explanations, the political dynamics that render states vulnerable and provoke divided polities do not emerge (though they mature and have their decisive impact) in the period proximate to a revolutionary situation; they do so over a longer period.

The regimes of the shah in Iran, the Somozas in Nicaragua, and Díaz in Mexico settled in their respective societies over decades. In what turned out to be their last years, these regimes actively took on new challenges: to take merely some illustrative examples, the shah's attempt to change the political basis of his rule by forming the Resurgence Party in the mid-1970s; Somoza's rapacious corruption and furious repression after Managua's devastating earthquake in 1972; and Díaz's brutal squashing of strikers in U.S.-owned mines and continued preferential treatment of foreign capital in the midst of the economic recession of the early twentieth century. The political dynamics and structural contexts established by neopatrimonialism over decades did not prepare the dictators for new challenges under new circumstances. In fact, their handling of these challenges decisively contributed to the emergence of revolutionary situations in Mexico in 1910–11 and in Iran and Nicaragua in the late 1970s.

In Cuba the crucial period for explaining the revolutionary situation of 1956–58, the contenders' coming to power in 1959, and the conclusive revolutionary outcome of April 19, 1961, is 1933–58. This entire period is often portrayed as Batista-dominated, which it most decidedly was *not,* between 1944 and 1952, and for the years that it was, Batista's domination did not bring uniform consequences for the state and the polity. The twenty-five years preceding the Cuban Revolution included a revolutionary situation that did not produce a commensurate outcome (1933), a Batista–military controlled political system (1934–40), three democratically elected administrations—including Batista's—that promoted civilian control and more-professional conduct by the military (1940–52), and the Batista dictatorship of the 1950s. Although the *batistato* significantly contributed to the revolutionary victory of January 1, 1959, the Cuban state's vulnerability and the polity's divisions cannot be exclusively explained by the regime's neopatrimonial features.

A Vulnerable State and a Divided Polity: The Revolutionary Situation of 1956–1958

The salient attribute of Cuban politics in the two-and-a-half decades before 1959 is discontinuity. Consequently we need bifocal lenses to identify the mechanisms favoring the revolutionary situation of the late 1950s: one part for looking up close at the immediate circumstances of the *batistato,* the other for focusing on the more distant years between 1933 and 1952. The end result, I hope, will be a more-nuanced picture of the Cuban "traffic jam" and the political opportunities that favored the revolutionary victory.[2]

Fulgencio Batista and the Cuban Military (1952–1958)

During the 1950s the Cuban military was undeniably corrupt, inefficient, and led by a coterie of officer-cronies; it was not, however, unquestionably loyal to Batista. Although the regime became almost exclusively reliant on the armed forces, Batista faced opposition from within that institution.[3] Between 1953 and 1957 professional officers (*los puros*), who had in fact supported the coup d'état in 1952 with the hope of bringing order to the increasingly chaotic world of Cuban politics and of subsequently returning to the barracks, organized three aborted revolts; two of these—the conspiracy of army officers and troops (1956) and the mutiny of navy officers and soldiers (1957)—were especially damaging to the image of the regime. Neither did the group of officer-cronies manifest unflinching loyalty to General Batista. In 1958 the chairman of the Cuban Joint Chiefs of Staff made contact with the U.S. embassy, one of several efforts from within the armed forces to replace the general.

Batista did put a brake on nascent professionalization, promoted loyalist officers (some of whom were his relatives), and for too long concentrated elite troops around Havana. There they could best safeguard his person, but they could hardly combat the Rebel Army in Oriente. But the general never quite managed to assemble an institution akin to the *somocista* National Guard. Indeed, diverse crosscurrents flowed within the Cuban military: *los puros,* Batista loyalists, and officer-cronies. The army clearly had little autonomy from the dictator, but neither was it his trusted praetorian guard. In addition, the officer corps lacked a long-standing history.

In 1933 then-Sergeant Batista led a revolt of noncommissioned officers (many subsequently formed the network of officer-cronies) against officialdom. Between 1933 and 1940 now-Colonel Batista presided over the reconstitution of the political system after the frustrated revolution of 1933. He systematically undermined civilian authority and thrust his likewise newly promoted officers to positions in national, provincial, and local administrations. At the same time, after brutally repressing the revolutionary movement, Batista presided over the implementation of a series of social programs. This combination of "sticks and carrots" gained him favor with different sectors of the polity: The upper class celebrated his restoration of order while many ordinary Cubans, particularly those of color and those in rural areas, applauded him for his social programs.

In 1939–1940 Batista directed a textbook case of democratic transition: He called a constitutional convention with representatives from the full spectrum of Cuban politics; the result was the Constitution of 1940. Elections were held, and Batista, at last a general, legitimately became president of Cuba. During his term (1940–44) he assumed the full regalia of a civilian president. Just as systematically as he had enacted them, Batista reversed the measures of the mid-1930s: returning civilians to positions in national, provincial, and local administrations and forcing many of his fellow officers to accept early retirement or transfer to strictly military assignments. The new president pursued his civilian mission with such zeal that some of his former allies plotted to overthrow him in 1941; with the military's support, he defeated the plotters, thereby further enhancing civilian authority. Thus Batista began the military's professionalization, which the Auténtico Party administrations continued between 1944 and 1952. Without his efforts, the *auténticos* would undoubtedly have found the task much more difficult. When his candidate lost the presidential elections of 1944, Batista took a crucial step in democratic consolidation: He turned power over to Ramón Grau, his erstwhile ally in the short-lived nationalist government of 1933–34, whom he had deposed with the encouragement of the U.S. embassy. Without much ado, the opposition became the government.

In 1951 some professional officers contemplating the possibility of a coup against the administration of Carlos Prío approached Batista as much for his civilian political base as for his stature within the now more professional military. Colonel Ramón Barquín, who would lead the aborted conspiracy of 1956, was the natural candidate to head a military movement of national redemption against the chaos, corruption, and violence of the early 1950s; however, though a quintessential professional soldier, he lacked Batista's political skills. Unfortunately, Batista disappointed *los puros:* In contrast to his behavior in the 1930s and 1940s, he never displayed much political talent, and he neglected his civilian base. Batista ruled largely on the basis of repression and corruption—practices in which he had also clearly engaged earlier but that now reappeared unalloyed.

Thus Batista consolidated his grip on power by turning to the officer-cronies whom he had raised from the ranks in the sergeants' revolt of 1933, elevated to positions of authority and privilege during 1934–39, and in part demoted or retired during his civilian presidency. Batista needed them, for *los puros* had a different vision of the coup and intended to call elections as soon as possible. This scenario did not favor Batista, as surveys of public opinion predicted a third-place finish in the elections scheduled for June 1952. The officer-cronies also needed Batista: He was the original mastermind behind their rise, and even if he had curtailed their prerogatives in the 1940s, no one else among them could match his stature. The general spent the 1950s trying to buttress his military base, improving the living conditions of officers and soldiers, weeding out career officers, unmasking conspiracies, and quelling insubordination. His effectiveness in doing so undermined the ability of the military to wage an effective campaign against the Rebel Army and preempted the natural alliance of *los puros* with the moderate opposition.

Batista's Relations with Domestic Elites and Other Domestic Actors

The alienation of upper-class elites and the middle sectors of society provides a strong stimulus to the formation of broad-based movements in opposition to neopatrimonial regimes and increases the chances of overthrowing them. Relations between the Batista regime and the dominant, sugar-based faction of the capitalist class were generally good. The *batistato* did not break the long-standing tradition of state support for the sugar sector's pursuit of optimal conditions for Cuban exports to the U.S. market and preferential treatment in the disbursement of state loans. Other capitalist sectors certainly objected to being sidelined. Rice growers, for example, despaired at the cutback of state funds in the mid-1950s, when the Louisiana rice industry successfully lobbied Congress to make Cuba's sugar quota contingent upon the island's importation of set quantities of U.S. rice. Too often state banks allocated loans on the basis of political loyalty rather than on economic criteria. Likewise, the state's sugar institute, which regulated the industry, linked the size of each mill's cane-grinding quota to the owner's partisanship. Honest capitalists— sugar and nonsugar alike—looked on in disgust.

But with the evidence currently available it is impossible to make a convincing argument that the *batistato* decidedly alienated the nonsugar industrial and agricultural sectors or the honest, more enlightened elements of the sugar sector or that it drove them into an alliance with the more radical elements of the opposition. Although during the 1950s the economy stagnated overall, it also registered hopeful trends. The industrialists, especially, made important strides as nonsugar industry grew at an annual rate of almost 7 percent. The structure of imports was slowly changing, with consumer goods declining and capital and intermediate goods rising. Domestic investments were also mounting, and the prospects for a new influx of U.S. capital—after a lull of nearly two decades—were excellent. This time, moreover, U.S. investments would bolster economic diversification, since the sugar sector no longer harbored the profits of yore. Most important, the capitalist class enjoyed a favorable business climate as the share of wages in the national income fell relative to that of the 1940s.

The case for the alienation of the middle classes is much stronger, but largely on political and ideological grounds. Since the early 1940s the urban middle sectors, especially in Havana, had considerably expanded. In the mid-1950s about one-third of the labor force earned monthly wages of seventy-five pesos or more, at the time a reasonable minimum to secure some of the perquisites of a middle-class lifestyle. The economy of urban Cuba, particularly in the western provinces, registered significant advances in wages and living standards. When looked at through the prism of Havana, as *The Diplomat* did, the future of the "Beautiful Island," indeed, looked buoyant. Batista did not alienate the middle sectors because he excluded them economically; he alienated them because he violated their aspirations for democracy and for a *patria digna* (a homeland of dignity). Thus, restoring the Constitution of 1940 became the rallying cry of the middle-class opposition. Mounting repression after 1957 further convinced these important sectors that Batista would never negotiate in good faith and that armed insurrection was the only way out.

The organized working class also merits attention. After the tumultuous 1930s, the Central Organization of Cuban Trade Unions (CTC) gained a secure place in the reconstituted political system. Under communist control until 1947, the CTC actively and successfully defended the interests of organized labor. A rising share of wages in the national income and a host of measures, including severe limitations on capitalists' right to fire workers, buttressed union members (about 50 percent of the labor force) against the vagaries of an economy with combined levels of unemployment and underemployment of nearly one-third. In 1947 the *auténticos* purged the communists from the CTC and installed their own labor bosses; the change, however, did not significantly alter the confrontational tenor of labor-capital relations.

After the 1952 coup the CTC leadership made meek gestures of opposition but quickly abandoned its *auténtico* loyalties and joined the *batistato*'s bandwagon. The regime rewarded the labor bureaucracy by making the payment of union dues a compulsory paycheck deduction, a practice that rapidly engorged the bank accounts of union leaders. Although labor–capital relations were taking a turn favorable for capital, the regime trod carefully on labor. Capitalists, for example, insisted on the modification of the decree limiting dismissals. Although the CTC leadership agreed to this demand in principle, the regime, recognizing the premium workers placed on job security, never actually worked out a satisfactory modification of the decree.

Neopatrimonial regimes pursue their narrow interests at the expense of those of broader sectors like the upper and middle classes. Though the *batistato* did this to some extent, its social underpinnings were rather complex.

There is little evidence to support the claim that Batista alienated the dominant sectors of the upper class. The story regarding the nonsugar industrial and agricultural sectors is more involved, but there is no reason to expect that, when fully researched, the script will primarily be one of alienation. The case is much stronger for middle-class disaffection from the regime. Finally, the emerging pattern of regime-union-capitalist relations hints at a corporatist-type state. Other than the history of the opposition movement, there is almost nothing on the *batistato* in the Cuban-studies literature. A better grasp of its complex social dynamics would significantly contribute to a more accurate understanding of the political opportunities that the radical opposition so ably exploited.

The Character of the Anti-Batista Opposition: Moderates versus Radicals

Neither President Carlos Prío nor the citizenry at large resisted the military coup of March 10, 1952. The *auténticos,* whose term was due to expire in October, did not defend their constitutional mandate. Elections were to be held in June, and the Ortodoxo Party—founded by dissident *auténticos* in 1947—was expected to win. Although the Constitution of 1940 embodied the highest aspirations of the citizenry, the actual workings of representative democracy in Cuba disillusioned most citizens. Fairly honest elections and the peaceful alternation of power had not corrected, or even curbed, the proclivity of *políticos* to view the public treasury as their private domain—on the contrary. In 1944 the public had enthusiastically greeted the victory of the *auténticos* at the polls. The election of Ramón Grau, who had presided over the nationalist government of 1933–34, raised popular hopes that Cuban politics would at last take a new turn; they did not. Moreover, *grupos de acción* (action groups) proliferated and served the interests of rival politicians. Ganglike violence in the streets of urban Cuba became commonplace. Though aghast at the violation of the Constitution, the citizenry experienced a numbed sense of relief that the *auténtico* farce was over.

Six and a half years later, the *batistato* was nearing its demise. By the fall of 1958 Fidel Castro, the Rebel Army, and the July 26th Movement were indisputably at the helm of the opposition movement; they had won the citizenry's support and had captured the popular imagination. Three factors explain their command of the anti-Batista coalition: (1) the incapacity of moderates to forge and carry out an effective strategy against the regime, (2) Batista's resistance to holding good-faith negotiations with the moderate opposition, and (3) Fidel Castro's dogged insistence on armed insurrection and his un-common sense of purpose, which, with (1) and (2), combined into a winning strategy.

The 1940s, particularly the eight-year *auténtico* administrations, are cru-cial for understanding the disarray of the moderates in the struggle against Batista. The neopatrimonial dictatorship cannot account for the discredit and lack of vision of the moderate leadership. Although not all moderates were *auténticos,* all to one degree or another bore the burden of the 1940s. Un-doubtedly, there were moderates who were individuals of talent, commit-ment, and honesty, but from the start of the *batistato* they were not in a posi-tion of strength as a group. As the decade passed and their strategies for ending the dictatorship came to naught, their position was further weakened. Twice—in late 1955 and early 1958—they failed to convince Batista to negoti-ate and call free elections. On at least two occasions *auténticos* organized armed assaults against the regime; they failed. When in the summer of 1958 most oppositionists signed an agreement of unity, they did so under the aegis of Fidel Castro, the Rebel Army, and the July 26th Movement. Moderates had turned to the guerrillas in the Sierra Maestra, not the other way around.

Batista's intransigence likewise contributed to the ascendance of Fidel Castro over the opposition coalition. Twice the general held rigged elections—in 1954, when he "won," and in 1958, when his candidate did. On the two occasions when he engaged the moderate opposition, Batista apparently had no intention of yielding power. In 1955, for example, he took steps to ease the dictatorial aspects of his regime: He declared an amnesty for political prisoners (freeing Fidel Castro and his associates), allowed the reorganization of politi-cal parties, convened Congress, and relaxed censorship of the media. Negoti-ations with the moderate opposition followed (the then-incipient July 26th Movement refused to participate), and the subsequent convocation of elec-tions appeared to be the next logical step; they did not take place. Had they occurred, the alliance between *los puros* (who were already conspiring against the regime) and the moderates might have jelled; Fidel Castro did not yet have the Rebel Army, and the July 26th Movement would have had to ap-proach the moderates for its place in a post-Batista Cuba. But Batista refused to negotiate, and his refusal rendered credible the *fidelista* insistence on armed insurrection as the only means to end the dictatorship.

Fidel Castro never wavered. Adamant that only the force of arms would prostrate the dictator, he pursued this strategy relentlessly, from the ill-fated assault on the Moncada Barracks on July 26, 1953; through the landing (actu-ally, shipwreck) of the *Granma* on the southern coast of Oriente, the survival of his initial ragtag army in the Sierra Maestra, the organization of the urban underground, and the opening of other guerrilla fronts in Oriente and central Cuba; to the Rebel Army's decisive push against the regular army in November and December. Moreover, when he or his representatives met with other opposition groups, they purposefully upheld two other critical points: no foreign (that is, U.S.) intervention or mediation in Cuba's internal affairs and no merger of the Rebel Army with the regular army. Armed insurrection, no U.S. intervention, and the dissolution of the Cuban military—these three elements constituted the radical essence of the *fidelistas* and were more decisive in configuring the character of their opposition to Batista than their vague and contradictory statements on the changes they would bring about if they succeeded. The strength of Fidel Castro, the Rebel Army, and the July 26th Movement flowed in no small measure from the fact that the course of events—propelled as decisively by the moderates' long-term weakness and Batista's aversion to negotiations as by their own mettle—carried them to power almost exclusively on their own, not someone else's, terms.

Between the Regime and the Opposition: The Role of the United States

The United States backed the Batista regime (Paterson 1994). Though the famous suspension of arms shipments in March 1958 was real enough, it scarcely amounted to an abandonment of the Cuban dictator by the U.S. government. Besides, shortly thereafter the Eisenhower administration resumed the shipment of weapons on a selective basis, even though Batista had not mended his ways in the manner the policy had hoped to effect. Singling out the issue of military assistance as a sign that the powerful foreign patron no longer supported the dictator overlooks the sympathetic ambience between Washington and Havana during the 1950s. A few examples should serve to put the March 1958 suspension in a more nuanced context.

In February 1955 Vice President Richard Nixon lavished warm praise on Batista at the latter's "inauguration"; the vice president made no mention of the fraudulent elections the previous November, which the opposition had boycotted. With the Cold War as background, the Central Intelligence Agency worked closely with Batista, training a special unit of the regime in tactics and techniques to uncover and repress "communists"; the unit saw "communists" everywhere that voices—not to mention arms—were raised against the government. The Federal Bureau of Investigation similarly assisted the *batistato*'s intelligence dragnet against the urban underground. Just as important, U.S. businesses continued to thrive on the island, and U.S. investments expanded. At about the time of the suspension of weapons shipments, the U.S. government indicted Carlos Prío on charges of violating U.S. neutrality laws; the deposed president had been shipping arms to the opposition in Cuba and organizing military operations against Batista from U.S. soil. The sight of the last constitutionally elected president of Cuba handcuffed and jailed in Dade County, Florida, enraged the opponents of the Batista regime.

The policy of March 1958 was intended to pressure Batista to hold elections, ease his dictatorial rule, and generally show more flexibility in handling the mounting crisis of his regime. The United States knew that militarily the suspension would not really be damaging since the Cuban army was purchasing weapons and supplies from other countries. At the same time, however, the Eisenhower administration manifested a surprising indifference to the call for dialogue and negotiations, spearheaded by the Catholic church in February and March. The United States had expressed a similar indifference in December 1955. Now, however, the situation was more critical, and by not actively supporting the moderates' effort the U.S. government probably missed its last chance to buttress that too often elusive "third force" in a revolutionary situation. Ironically, had Washington been more intrusive and truly mediated between the Cuban government and its opposition, as it had successfully done in the 1930s, the revolutionary outcome might well have been derailed (Domínguez 1978). But by the 1950s the United States no longer imposed the same strictures on Cuban sovereignty and thus watched developments on the island with relative detachment.

The U.S. government manifested no ambivalence regarding Fidel Castro, the Rebel Army, and the July 26th Movement: It profoundly mistrusted the rebels. The feeling was mutual. Though the *fidelistas* successfully courted U.S. public opinion, they had no illusions about U.S. intentions in Cuba and never faltered in their insistence that there be no foreign intervention or mediation in the island's crisis. U.S. properties in urban and rural Cuba were often the object of rebel attacks; losses in the first nine months of 1958 alone totaled more than $2 million. Telephone poles and lines belonging to the misnamed Cuban Telephone Company were favorite targets. Several times the rebels cut off the water supply of the Guantánamo Naval Base. No doubt the most daring rebel act against the United States took place in the summer of 1958: Rebels under Raúl Castro's command kidnapped some fifty Americans to protest the air raids the regime was conducting against guerrilla strongholds in the Sierra Maestra and the Sierra del Cristal with U.S.-supplied bombs. Upon seeing the effects of the bombing, the elder Castro wrote to a close associate:

When I saw rockets firing at Mario's house, I swore to myself that the North Americans were going to pay dearly for what they are doing. When this war is over, a much wider and bigger war will commence for me: the war that I am going to wage against them. I am aware that this is my true destiny. (Bonachea and Valdés 1972, 379)

Flamboyant and self-aggrandizing rhetoric, but it reflected an uncommon sense of purpose: Fidel Castro dared to think and act as if there could be a Cuba without the United States. After 1959 the rhetoric would catch on with millions of Cubans, when radical nationalism fired the social revolution. The moderates never broke their psychological dependence on the United States, a crucial element of their weakness in the struggle against Batista and during the early months of the revolution. The *batistato* and U.S. support of the regime clearly contributed to the nationalist uproar, but only an eagle's-eye view over the historical terrain can explain the depth of sentiment behind the cry of *¡Cuba sí! ¡Yanquis no!* that would soon echo throughout the island.

A Revolutionary Outcome in Two Moments: January 1, 1959, and April 19, 1961

Although Tilly defines revolutionary outcomes as entailing only a forcible transfer of power (which in the Cuban case took place on January 1, 1959), the revolutionary situation of 1956–58 did not conclusively come to an end until April 19, 1961. Two days after the U.S.-sponsored Brigade 2506 landed at the Bay of Pigs, the invaders were routed. Their defeat represents the definitive outcome to the crisis of the 1950s: For the first time, the United States failed to impose its will on Cuba. Twentieth-century Cuba had experienced a peculiar form of "multiple sovereignty" whereby the U.S. ambassador was often as powerful as the nation's chief executive in handling Cuban affairs. Consequently, April 19, 1961, marked the de facto expiration of the Platt Amendment; subsequently, the revolutionary leadership charted Cuba's future without the United States.[4] That, however, is another story.

The dictatorship of Fulgencio Batista by itself cannot account for the fast-paced, profound transformation that Cuba experienced between 1959 and 1961. On the surface, the anti-Batista coalition upheld the restoration of the Constitution of 1940 as its platform and thus merely appeared to call for political change. However, the collapse of the *batistato* unleashed a concatenation of popular demands—for jobs, higher wages, lower rents, land reform—that the *fidelistas* encouraged and to which they quickly responded. These demands set the revolutionary government on a collision course with the Cuban upper classes and the United States. The *fidelistas* did little to avoid or to soften the impact; they had the army, a vision of a new Cuba, and the enthusiastic support of *el pueblo cubano* (the Cuban people). The future was theirs, and it was one of a sovereign and just Cuba, a *patria digna*—a promise that touched the deepest chords in millions of Cubans and propelled the social revolution.

Conclusion

The Cuban Revolution was not a solar eclipse; it was a traffic jam. During the 1950s the political opportunities created by the changing relationships among government, opposition, and the citizenry and within each of these actors underscored the two revolutionary moments: the situation of 1956–58 and the outcome of January 1, 1959. Although initially Batista's overthrow of Carlos Prío in March 1952 met with little opposition, the dictatorship of the 1950s confronted an opposition movement that rapidly gathered political will, military power, and broad-based support. Batista, in turn, responded with mounting repression, pervasive corruption, and repeated intransigence, which enhanced the credibility of Fidel Castro, the Rebel Army, and the July 26th Movement. That the United States maintained an attitude of relative detachment from Cuban developments likewise contributed to the revolutionary outcome.

But these compelling interactions and opportunities of the 1950s cannot fully account for the implosion of the Batista regime, let alone the extraordinary events of 1959–61. Like other countries that have experienced revolutions, Cuba had been on a "contradictory developmental path" (McDaniel 1994, 791). Putting the revolution's proximate causes in this context is absolutely essential if we are to do justice to the actual demise of the ancien régime. Though politics-centered, conjunctural analyses of revolutions have notably cleared the analytical terrain and admirably advanced the comparative prospects, we are still left with the challenge of each case's specificity. The devil, after all, is in the details.

Notes

I am grateful to the American Council of Learned Societies for awarding me an international travel grant to attend the conference in honor of Charles Tilly, *Structure, Identity, and Power: The Past and Future of Collective Action,* held in Amsterdam in June 1995. I also thank the following individuals for their critical reading of an earlier version of this chapter: Miguel Angel Centeno, Carlos de la Torre, Jorge I. Domínguez, Jeff Goodwin, Eric Hobsbawm, Jay Kaplan, and Sidney Tarrow. Even in those cases in which we ultimately disagreed, their comments were stimulating and helpful.

1. I have culled these questions from Snyder 1992, 380–385.

2. For a full treatment of the origins of the revolution see Pérez-Stable, 1993.

3. For an overview of the Cuban military, see Pérez 1976; on the various phases of Batista's career between 1933 and 1958 see Thomas 1971, 634–49, 724–36, and 789–802; Domínguez 1978 76–80, 123–33.

4. Between 1902 and 1934 the Platt Amendment sanctioned U.S. intervention in Cuban affairs whenever order and property were threatened. One could argue, however, that the spirit of the amendment cast a shadow over Cuba until April 1961, when the revolutionary government defeated the U.S.-backed invasion at the Bay of Pigs.

Chapter 12

Gender Inequality and Women's Empowerment in Latin America

Sonia De Avelar

Where do rights come from? . . . how have rights of citizenship come into being? . . . Rights exist when one party can effectively insist that another deliver goods, services or protection, and third parties will act to reinforce (or at least not to hinder) their delivery. Such entitlements become citizenship *rights when the object of claims is a state or its agent and the successful claimant qualifies by simple membership in a broad category of persons subject to the state's jurisdiction.* Charles Tilly

Of all the aggrieved populations in the countries of Latin America and the Caribbean (LAC), women have never been accounted for in official historiography. This "hidden history" might very well be described as one of resilience. In it we would find a rich array of both successful and unsuccessful entrepreneurship, a broad spectrum of contentious issues, and a wide variety of conflicts lost to view. Still, we would find that most of the time women's interests are forced to the margins by tight, exclusionary political settings and institutional arrangements and that this political marginality reduces the prospects of changing an unequally defined citizenship.

In this chapter I intend to highlight women's attempts to intervene in national affairs in LAC. I will show how, through both contentious movements and more episodic protests, they have shaped mass national politics, changed the relationship between political authorities and women as political subjects, and promoted the democratization of politics in ways that are not recognized in the current literature. I will conclude with an assessment of the prospects for the future.

Reflecting on women's citizenship, one must acknowledge women's limited success in qualifying as full-fledged members of states. Even though some progress has been achieved in the last fifteen years, the contrasts between the sexes as citizens persist and do not seem to be fading away on the continent (De Avelar 1987).

Despite women's increasing number in the workforce, similar findings across countries in LAC show that, not only do women receive low pay and suffer occupational segregation, the rates of unemployment are higher among women than men, the ratio of nonwage income to wage income is higher for females; women benefit less from social security services provided by the state, especially in countries with a "swollen" informal sector in the economy; there are more women among part-time job holders, in temporary work, and in homework; and women tend to be more vulnerable to job dislocations due to technological change, to slowdowns in economic growth, and to the effects of structural adjustment policies. In addition, women have restricted access to credit in public and private financial institutions and to other aids to entrepreneurship and are in general absent from policy-making bodies that have an impact on the development agenda.

Women, Polity, and Citizenship Rights

In the light of a "distributive" focus of democratic rights, the differential allocation of enforceable claims shapes any group's status in a national community and its access to government and to power resources. Women's prospects, life choices, and relative share in a country's social wealth are bound to a process of enlarging political representation and creating collective capabilities to affect decisions related to distributive mechanisms and to the delivery of goods and services in society.

The argument about citizenship and democracy draws attention to the historical paths of both the inclusion or exclusion of groups in the polity and the range of enforceable claims ("entitlements" or "rights") (Tilly 1990b). If politics is broadly defined as "efforts to affect the distribution of power and resources in a state community," then the redistributive issues are at its center. The political arena can thus be portrayed as a battleground between "contenders," who have routine, low-cost access to resources controlled by the government, and those who do not ("challengers") (Tilly and Gurin 1990, 6).

Despite the quantum leap represented by women's large-scale entry into politics in LAC countries (a spectrum that goes from social movements to other political modes such as partisan politics, pressure groups, voting, officeholding), one must consider the different levels of citizenship, focusing on those groups whose "ability to influence the system through voting or other types of participation is limited, either structurally or because of historical patterns of discrimination" (Tilly and Gurin 1990, 7). In conceptual terms, the gains in citizenship rights are much less a process of gradual and incremental change in "entitlements" than of continuous struggles to narrow the gender gap in the polity as "an ongoing system of institutions, patterns of behavior and mutually accepted understandings" (Verba 1990, 555). As long as that gap remains wide, the less probable it is that the space occupied by

Table 12.1 Average Percentage of Women in Decision Making in Countries (Grouped by scores on women's status index, 1987)

Score on Composite Index of Women's Status	Average Percent of Women in Government Decision Making	Percent of Women in Parliament
Low	1.5	4.4
Low middle	3.7	6.0
High middle	4.6	8.6
High	6.8	20.4

Source: United Nations Centre for Social Development and Humanitarian Affairs, *Women in Politics and Decision-Making in the Late Twentieth Century* (Dordrecht: Martinus Nijhoff, 1992), Table 19.

issues relating to gender on the political agenda will expand and affect public policy. The model of rights "as the product of interest-driven bargaining" (Tilly 1990, 13) is consistent with the view that an increasing role by women in the polity entails an increasing range of enforceable claims and provides the frame for improvements in employment, labor markets, access to capital, legal status, and living conditions.

An illustration is the association between women's standing in parliaments and a well-known composite index of women's status developed by the Population Crisis Committee, as pointed out in a UN study (United Nations 1992). In the composite index, measurement of women's well-being and of the gender gap between men's and women's status are combined to provide a ranking of the differences in women's circumstances between countries (Population Crisis Committee 1988).

As shown in Table 12.1, a positive covariation is found between the scores in the women's status index *and* in women's representation in parliament and in government decision making: Higher scores in the women's status index accompany higher percentages of females in parliament and in government decision making.

This pattern is consistent across the world's regions, including LAC, as shown in Table 12.2. Collapsing the original seven-point scale into a three-point scale for the scores on women's status, we find that higher average rates for women in parliament correspond to higher country rankings in women's status.

A further insight is given by another composite index, the Human Development Index (HDI), developed by the United Nations Development Programme (UNDP), based on measures of "basic human capabilities" (life expectancy, educational attainment, and access to income, taken as proxies of

Table 12.2 Country Rankings of Women's Status and Percentage of Women in Parliaments, LAC Counties

Country Rankings of Women's Status[a]	Number of Countries	Countries	Percent Women in Parliament[b]
High	excellent/ very good	0		
Medium	good/fair	11	Barbados, Costa Rica, Cuba, Jamaica, Mexico, Panama, Trinidad and Tobago, Argentina, Colombia, Ecuador, Uruguay, Venezuela	6.9
Low	poor/ very poor/ extremely poor	12	Dominican Republic, El Salvador, Guatemala, Haiti, Honduras, Nicaragua, Bolivia, Brazil, Chile, Guyana, Paraguay, Peru	5.6

[a] *Source:* Population Crisis Committee, "Country Ranking of the Status of Women: Poor, Powerless, and Pregnant" (Washington, D.C.: Briefing Paper and Chart, 1988).

[b] *Source:* Inter-Parliamentary Union, *Distribution of Seats between Men and Women in National Parliaments: Statistical Data from 1945 to 30 June 1991,* series Reports and Documents, no. 18 (Geneva: IPU, 1991).

access to resources), and whose average scores for the LAC countries also tend to covary with women's representation in parliament (Table 12.3). (United Nations Development Programme, 1993)

These findings, though based on broad cross-national comparisons, offer insights into links between redistributive processes and female representation in politics.

Any assessment of women's relative position in the distribution or redistribution of resources in LAC societies will have to be associated with a discussion of their collective inroads in the political market, grounded on gains and losses in extending "entitlements" or "enforceable claims" on the state and other actors in the polity.

Women, Politics, and Resource Mobilization

Structural constraints, which limit women's pursuit of interests and grievances (that is, constraints in the legal systems, the features of the state, the electoral systems and party politics, capitalist expansion, procedural group representation in the polity, and so on), and women making choices among available courses of action, according to some set of implicit or explicit rules (Tilly 1978c, 6), are two major determinants to be studied if we are to probe

Table 12.3 Human Development Index Scores (1993) and Percentage of Women in Parliaments, LAC Countries

Score on the HDI[a]	High	Medium	Low
Percent Women in Parliament[b]	8.5	7.8	6.8

[a] *Source:* United Nations Development Programme, *Human Development Report 1993* (New York: Oxford University Press, 1993), 135–37

[b] *Source:* Inter-Parliamentary Union, *Women in Parliament as of 30 June 1993* (Geneva: 1993), data taken from poster.

LAC's openness to women's democratic representation. With gender imbalances so deeply rooted in the conscious and unconscious layers of LAC societies, one must ask how and how far women have "broke[n] through and stayed in" (Jennings 1990) to secure their claims to equal citizenship rights. In the long run, women have engaged in pushing forward their interests, and in the process they have formed their collective identities and joined forces in concerted actions: Feminist historians have recorded women's organization and mobilization around legal, political, and work issues at least since the nineteenth century, despite their invisibility in "official" history. This is illustrated by the Brazilian case by the agency of working-class women—who resisted the strains of early industrialization in nineteenth-century cities and played a role in the development of class politics—and by the interclass alliances backing the suffragist movement (Hahner 1976).

The resource mobilization approach provides us with analytic tools for assessing groups' successes and failures in translating collective grievances into political or politically related outcomes. If we see collective action as "all occasions on which sets of people commit pooled resources, including their own efforts, to common ends" and mobilization as the "extent of resources under the collective control of the contender" and as a process through which "an increase in the resources or in the degree of collective control" over pooled resources occurs, then we can include under this conceptual construct any modes of contention as part of groups' efforts to exercise influence (Tilly 1978b, 54; Tilly and Tilly 1981, 17). In this sense, and viewing women's groups' interactions in society and with authorities, we can use Louise Tilly's and Patricia Gurin's three-dimensional framing of women's politics: (1) *forms,* which include political activities as "actions for change in the distribution of power and resources," and proto-political activities, which include "direct collective appeals to authorities . . . often in defense of customary rights and statuses, and membership and actions in organizations that work outside the formal political arena"; (2) *bases,* from locally based organizations to national organizations, depending on group structures, scope, and targets of politics;

and (3) *issues,* from issues that are not specifically female oriented to clearly defined women-centered interests (Tilly and Gurin 1990, 7).

We will briefly survey women's access to power resources in LAC, looking at selected indicators of the political arena's permeability by women. The survey is organized in the following sections: women in "official" politics, including in parliaments, governments, and political parties; women in "nonofficial" politics, that is, in political or proto-political initiatives and actions, including evidence on women's standing in trade unions; and a concluding section on gender and citizenship in democratization. Despite the LAC diversity in patterns of state making, political culture, urbanization, capitalist expansion, party systems, and so on, a broad cross-national comparison will provide an overview of women in contemporary national parliamentary politics and in social movements. We have relied on international databases, which, in spite of their imperfections in terms of coverage and comparability, are what are available at the present time that is, the databases of the Inter-Parliamentary Union [IPU], the United Nations, Parlamento Latino-Americano, and Parlamento Centro-Americano).

Women in Official Politics

Participation in Parliamentary Assemblies

In a survey conducted by the Inter-American Commission of Women, OAS, women in LAC acquired legal rights to vote and eligibility to parliament fairly recently, despite the long-standing (from the nineteenth century) feminist agitation for parity in political rights: Of the thirty countries covered by the survey, only four instituted universal suffrage before the 1940s, twenty-three between 1942 and 1957, and three in the 1960s (United Nations ECLAC 1989). Scanning through recent parliamentary records, we find three basic facts: (1) Women have attained a critical mass in the political systems as voters, in several cases representing more than 50 percent of the national electorates; (2) LAC parliamentary structures are clearly "woman-unfriendly," to the extent that they severely limit women's entry and advancement in its ranks and remain predominantly male in most aspects; and (3) there are few signs of measures and initiatives at the national level for reversing inequality in legislative representation (Brazil 1995; Inter-American Commission of Women, OAS 1992).

The indicators are revealing: Even though there seems to be an upward trend overall, with women's parliamentary representation increasing from 5 percent to 12.7 percent between 1975 and 1995, as of 1995 the rates are still

Table 12.4 Women's Participation in Official Politics, LAC Countries

Country	Year of Women's Suffrage	Year of Women's Right to Stand For Election	Year of First Woman in National Parliament	% Women in Mono-Cameral or Lower Chamber/ 1970–75[a]	% Women in Mono-Cameral or Lower Chamber/ 1987[a]	% Women in Mono-Cameral or Lower Chamber/ 1995[b]
Argentina	1947	1947	1952	7.8	5	21.8
Bahamas	1962–64	1962–64	1977	—	4	8.2
Barbados	1951	1951	1951	4.1	4	10.7
Bolivia	1938–52	1938–52	1966	2.5	3	10.8
Brazil	1934	1934	1934	0.2	5	7.0
Chile	1931–49	1931–49	1951	7.3	—	7.5
Colombia	1957	1957	1958	5.7	—	10.8
Costa Rica	1949	1949	1953	5.2	11	14.0
Cuba	1934	1934	1940	22.2	34	22.8
Dominican Republic	1942	1942	1946 (elected) 1970 (nom.)	4.1	5	11.7
Ecuador	1946	1946	1957	—	1	4.5
El Salvador	1961	1961	—	—	3	10.7
Guatemala	1945	1945	1954	4.0	7	7.5
Guyana	1953	1945–53	1953	11.9	37	20.0
Haiti	1950	1950	—	—	—	—
Honduras	1957	1957	1967	—	5	7.0
Jamaica	1944	1944	—	3.7	12	11.7
Mexico	1947	1953	1952 (nom.)	6.3	11	14.2
Nicaragua	1955	1955	1958	—	15	16.3
Panama	1941–46	1941–46	1946	0	6	8.3
Paraguay	1961	1961	1963	5.0	2	2.5
Peru	1950	1956	1956	—	6	10.0
Suriname	1953	1953	—	5.1	8	5.9
Trinidad/ Tobago	1945	1945	1971	2.7	17	18.9
Uruguay	1932	1932	1942	0	0	7.1
Venezuela	1947	1947	1948	2.7	4	5.9

[a] *Source:* Inter-Parliamentary Union, *Distribution of Seats between Men and Women in National Parliaments: Statistical Data from 1945 to 30 June 1991,* series "Reports and Documents," no. 18 (Geneva: IPU, 1991).

[b] Inter-Parliamentary Union, *Women in Parliament as of 30 June 1995* (Geneva: IPU, 1995).

very low, as shown in Table 12. 4.(United Nations 1991; IPU 1995a). The same gender-based imbalance is found in regional parliamentary assemblies: In the 1991–96 period women have only 10.3 percent of the seats in the Central American Parliament/PARLACEN (IPU 1995a).

Women have also had little success in attaining parliamentary leadership positions, if only in administrative roles, thus reinforcing the exclusionary pattern of the parliamentary structures. As organizations, in more ways than one they marginalize women from communication and power circuits, as shown by the small number of countries (less than one-third) reporting women parliamentarians in leadership roles (generally, as president or deputy speaker of a house of parliament).

With regards to parliamentary committees, women's numerical disadvantage prevents them from being present in all committees, and they are mostly allotted slots in "soft" policy areas, associated with traditional "female skills": social, health, family, and educational matters, instead of economics, security, or foreign affairs, a pattern exemplified by the findings for the cases of Costa Rica, Cuba, and Nicaragua (United Nations Centre for Social Development and Humanitarian Affairs 1991). For Costa Rica, data for the 1978–90 period reveal that only 4 percent and 5 percent of all members in permanent legislative committees on economic affairs and on finance were female, as compared to 18 percent on social affairs. In Cuba they represent 93 percent of members on the education committee, and 84 percent on family-related committees, and are also predominant in commissions on human rights and peace, social communication, sports, and culture. In Nicaragua, women hold 100 percent membership of the family-related committee, 57 percent on the science and education committee, and 72.9 percent in the commission on youth, childhood, and women's rights.

Interesting developments toward changing the parliaments' profiles are given by the emergence of interparty groups of women parliamentarians at the national and supranational levels, aimed at fostering women's interests in the legislatures. At the supranational level, we can cite the Women's Work Group initiative in the PARLATINO of women parliamentarians from all LAC countries around the issue of increasing women's representation in parliament. In a 1995 document, the Women's Work Group, acting as issue entrepreneurs at the supranational level, raised the questions of implementation of gender balance in national parliaments; of appointment of women for leadership positions as cabinet members and for top positions in the civil service, without confining them to traditional "women's" functional areas; of the creation of state machinery for promotion of equal opportunity and affirmative

Table 12.5 Female Ministers and Government Officials, 1987–1994,
LAC Countries (percentage of total positions)

	Female Ministers (percent)		Female Government Officials (percent)	
	All Ministries	Economic Ministries	All Officials	Officials in Economic Ministries
1987	3.1	0.9	7.3	2.7
1994	7.5	5.1	10.4	6.9

Source: United Nations Department for Policy Coordination and Sustainable Development, *Women in a Changing Global Economy: 1994 World Survey on the Role of Women in Development* (New York: United Nations, 1995), data from Tables IV.2 and IV.3, p. 80.

action programs; and of upgrading women's quality of life through improvement of their access to national resources (Parlamento Latino-Americano 1995). Since its inception, the Women's Work Group has invested in regional networking, building their capabilities for claiming egalitarian representation at the national and international levels.

Participation in Government

In recent decades, due to changing demographics and strides in educational achievement, women in LAC have entered the civil service and the ranks of government affairs professionals in significant numbers, in both elective and appointive offices, and have enlarged the pipeline (entry and midlevel) for decision-making positions in government. Yet there is a clear gap between men's and women's patterns of public officeholding, as females tend to plateau at the lower levels and are mostly excluded from the core areas of public decision making, especially from the jobs at the four highest levels of government, as shown by a profile of women in decision-making positions, by level (ministerial and subministerial positions) and by type of ministry (Tables 12.5 and 12.6).

By 1994 only six countries in the region had a woman as head of state or government (United Nations 1995). The pattern for ministerial seats is similar to that for parliamentary committees: Women in ministerial positions in nine countries are often found with responsibility for social affairs, health, women's affairs, and sometimes education and labor, but are rarely found in key ministries like defense, political affairs, or foreign affairs or at the center of budgetary, resources allocation, and policy decision making; in Costa Rica, for example, 8 percent of all ministers and 13 percent of all deputy ministers were female in the period 1978–90, mostly in the portfolios of justice, culture,

Table 12.6 Women in Decision-Making Positions in Governments, by Field, 1994, LAC Countries (percentage of total positions)

	Chief Executive	Economic	Law and Justice	Social	Political
Central America	7.7	9.7	14.6	14.6	6.4
South America	4.9	5.1	5.8	11.5	3.1
Caribbean	7.3	6.7	22.2	22.1	20.5

Source: United Nations, *The World's Women 1995: Trends and Statistics* (New York: United Nations, 1995), data from Chart 6.4, p. 154.

and education (United Nations Centre for Social Development and Humanitarian Affairs 1991).

Official bodies of women's affairs, which vary in scope and organizational form, are found in at least thirteen countries (as of 1988), at the national, state, or local levels or in parliamentary special commissions (United Nations Centre for Social Development and Humanitarian Affairs 1988; Inter-American Commission of Women, OAS 1990; United Nations ECLAC, 1992). Whether these national machineries have a potential for enhancing women's representation in government or whether they instead defer women's interests (as is argued by the critics of "state feminism," who view them as tools for demobilizing women's movements through co-optation) is a matter of controversy in the region, with feminists debating the pros and cons of either side.

Participation in Political Parties

Political parties are another key factor in the analysis of women's participation in politics. How have they responded to women's claims for equality in political representation since the issue of female suffrage was first raised? Despite the large variation in party systems across the continent (multiparty, two-party, one-party dominant, centralized, decentralized, and diverse party ideologies), one finds that women have remained in most cases on the fringes of these political structures. The fortunes and misfortunes of women in political parties are generally bound to the extent to which party programs expand to include women's issues, change selection and recruitment procedures, facilitate women's access to parties' decision making, and so on. Even though data are scanty on these aspects, which bear on the parties' permeability to women's political representation, data, as of 1991, on women candidates and women winning legislative elections held in selected LAC countries with parliaments, show that despite the existence of a large pool of eligible women, when it comes to entry into parliament only a small number of them succeed in being considered for candidacy or are among the pool of candidates contesting elections (IPU 1991). The parties' records on women as members and militants are also faulty and difficult to access, but it seems that the "iron law of gender" prevails in the governing bodies of parties, where women fare poorly (Siim 1994, 23). In a sample of fifty-four parties in fifteen countries, women have gone beyond the 20 percent mark on national boards in only twelve parties, such as the Socialist Party of Chile (25 percent), the Frente Sandinista de Liberacion Nacional (FSLN) in Nicaragua (30 percent), and the National Liberation Party in Costa Rica (30 percent) (IPU 1991; Valdes and Gomariz 1995).

To what extent did gender become an explicit issue for political parties in LAC? Are parties changing to promote women into elected assemblies or into decision-making positions in party organization? At least five LAC countries (Argentina, Colombia, Cuba, Venezuela, and Brazil) reported that parties have taken positive measures to get more women into political office, through the adoption of mandatory quota systems or target quotas in the national legislation and for legislative elections, or through quotas that have been established by parties to bring more women into party decision making, as in the case of the Workers' Party in Brazil, which set a 30 percent quota for women in the party's committees and in the party's executive committees at the municipal, state, and national levels (Workers' Party 1995).

As of 1991 major parties in ten countries reported women's branches in their organizational structure (IPU 1991), but whether these branches are instrumental in including women's issues in the party's policies, in decision making, and in the political agenda or merely a rhetorical strategy to reconcile women's claims is a question of great concern for party women and their allies in the women's movement, who must weigh costs and benefits in designing strategies within party structures.

In political parties, as in labor markets, selection and placement (inclusion in the pool of those eligible for party nominations and appointments to candidacy for political office, for party committees, and for governing bodies) work through two sets of interpersonal networks, demand networks and supply networks. On the one side, individuals search for opportunities to use their skills and motivations in pursuit of a political career and of group representation, and on the other side, recruiters bring in new aspirants, sorting and matching them to jobs, functions, and positions in the political marketplace. In the sorting and matching, most of the inequality occurs through the assignment of "traditional" (male) and "nontraditional" (female) aspirants to different positions in party structures, party activism, political office, and so on

(Granovetter and Tilly 1986, 3, 37, 48–49, 51). Party "gatekeepers" (recruiters, selectors), struck by deeply rooted, subconscious discomfort at seeing females in public, nondomestic roles, screen prospective applicants, male and female, in different ways with respect to acceptability, potential, political returns in career investment for parties, and so on. Decisions are then made according to false assumptions on sex-group differences, built on some type of "mental discriminant function" that permeates parties' policies, practices, and environments and is detrimental to women's claims of increased political representation (Bielby and Baron 1986, 781). As a result, women are frequently seen by selectors as an electoral risk, as low in credibility, and as a negative investment in the long run (especially from the standpoint of balancing career and family commitments), and male candidates resist having women on their tickets for fear that they may jeopardize their election bids. Patriarchalism, as one of the most enduring features of the political cultures across the region, has favored neither women's efforts to reach parity with men in political life nor the spread of an egalitarian ethos carried by feminist ideas. Securing party changes requires both the removal of barriers embedded in political structures *and* insistent women's movements pressing for higher stakes in public affairs.

Women in "NonOfficial" Politics

NGOs and Voluntary and Grassroots Organizations
In historical retrospective, an impressive display of women's organizations are found in LAC: nongovernmental organizations (NGOs) of various types, voluntary and grassroots organizations, centers, networks, leagues, consumer groups, ecology and environment groups, self-help groups, community and neighborhood associations and cooperatives, among others. Much of women's mobilization and actions has taken place within such political modes, although current analysts of democratization in LAC, whose background model of political pluralism mainly emphasizes the politics of conventional groups and organizations (mainstream political parties, lobbies, interest groups), overlook social movement politics, failing to acknowledge women's participation in such groups and to associate gender cleavages with inclusion or exclusion within the institutional framework of participatory democracy (O'Donnel, Schmitter, and Whitehead 1986; Diamond, Linz, and Lipset 1989; Przeworski 1991).

Since the dismantling of authoritarian regimes, a rising number of those groups have engaged in contention (both proto-political and political in form) for civil, political, and economic rights, with a new and fairly crystallized repertoire of demands and collective actions, varying from mainly defensive and reactive to proactive actions, and have expanded their networking capabilities beyond the local level (Tilly 1978b, 1981). We can cite cross-national women's networks such as the Latin American and Caribbean Women's and Health Network, which was formed by linking more than 300 groups working on women's reproductive rights and other health-related issues; the Women's Alternative Communications Unit, associated with women and media (including alternative media); the Grassroots Education Network among Women of the Council for Popular Adult Education in LAC, with sixty-three centers and programs in the region; the Latin and Caribbean section of Development Alternatives for Women in a New Era (DAWN), focused on women in development issues. In the rural sector, several women's organizations were set up in the 1980s, from local to national levels: the Federation of Peasant Women in Honduras, Cuba, and Nicaragua; the Women's Confederation of the National Peasant Confederation of Mexico; the National Federation of Women Peasants of Bolivia; the National Association of Peasants and Indigenous Women in Colombia; the First Congress of Rural Women in Brazil; the First National Congress of Rural Women in Chile (United Nations ECLAC 1992).

Since organizational skills acquired in one setting are transferable across organizations (from proto-political to political or other proto-political organizations), the mobilization of women's groups targeting the authoritarian governments served as training grounds for the building of sustained women's movements,[1] as well as establishing intergroup linkages around broad issues of democratic institutionalization (Leon 1994; Jaquette 1991; Alvarez 1990). From *parochial* (addressing "local actors or the local representatives of national actors") to *national* and international in scope ("lending itself to coordination among many localities"), women's groups' orientation to powerholders has gradually moved away from patronage to assert themselves as more autonomous, professionalized social movement organizations; their statements of grievances and demands are taken through a series of challenges to established authorities (especially national) on behalf of their underrepresented constituency (Tilly 1983b). This is a process emerging and often ignored by political change analysts in LAC.

We have been reminded of the "fluid boundaries between protopolitics and politics, and the continuing pattern of voluntarism in women's politics" and, at the same time, of the "pattern of lesser resources" that goes with voluntaristic and other types of proto-political organizations. In fact, one of the dilemmas for feminists who seek to change political institutions is whether or not they should aim at change from within (making coalitions and complying with the rules of the game) or from outside by "dismissing" established political structures and by framing women's politics within a "sexually differentiated citizenship model" (Squires 1994, 17). Notwithstanding, the "cost of such separatism was [frequently] low effectiveness" (Lovenduski 1993, 6). As "challengers," women in LAC have had limited success in converting claims into policy outcomes, and one of the best indicators for that is the "distributive" issue of women's poverty, as shown by their meager share of national income (approximately one-third, in countries with already highly skewed income distributions) and by the increasing number of female-headed households falling below the poverty line (De Avelar 1993). So as more women enter the political process through "nonofficial" routes, there remains the question of *reshaping* liberal democratic institutions and changing the pluralist order itself by means of *extending* their entitlements, and entering the polity with those "basic prerogatives of members—routine access to decisions that affect them" (Gamson 1975, 140).

Women in Trade Unions

Women in unions in LAC face the same hurdles associated with underrepresentation. Despite their growing presence in the workforce (from 35 percent in 1970 to 62 percent in 1990, the ratio of women to men in the economically active population), they have moved at a much lower pace to membership, leadership roles, and decision-making positions in union governing bodies and in collective bargaining (Gamson 1975, 140). The overall rate of unionization for women in the region is 32 percent, and women make up only 3 percent of union officials and 1 percent of those in national confederations, a pattern that results in underutilization of the industrial relations machinery to press for pay equity and equal opportunity, for enforcement of affirmative action legislation, for inclusion of women's issues in the collective bargaining agenda, and so on (United Nations Department for Policy Coordination and Sustainable Development 1994).

In many ways, women have resented the fact that "women's interests have become subsumed under the universal interests of the worker," with no consideration of their gender-related claims (Siim 1991, 178). But in the last two decades, a number of initiatives have arisen across LAC aimed at promoting women's issues *in* the unions and *in* the working-class movements. The proliferation of women's affairs departments in unions, labor federations, and confederations, pushing for the inclusion of women workers' issues into mainstream policies and for gender balance in running union affairs, can be seen in this light (Valdes and Gomariz 1995).

As women joined forces in the union movement in general, associational ties were created across industrial sectors, regions, and localities. Women workers coalesced with other groups in grassroots organizations, NGOs, women's organizations, and political parties. In the process, loyalties and networks were built, merging with the "catnet" bonds that had grown out of their experiences in the workers' movement. Through the interplay of unionism (Tilly 1978b, 62), feminism, and associativism, new organizational resources have been gained by the women's movements in LAC.

Conclusion

Reflecting on perspectives of democracy and democratization one must go beyond the indicators of narrowly defined institutional politics to the key questions of distribution of power resources in society, *including* gender as a critical dimension of social, economic, and political inequality (Waylen 1994). As long as analyses of transitional politics in LAC downplay the significance of women's groups and movements, to focus only on ideological, class, or regional cleavages or on instrumental maneuvers and bargains among elites, they will (1) altogether overlook the fact that citizenship rights in any given polity are a matter of degree and vary by gender (Tilly 1994a) as an "extrinsic variable" embedded in and interacting with the chances of access to the means of power and influence for women as a group; (2) fail to consider the empowerment of groups that seek to mobilize their constituencies in the efforts to exercise influence; and (3) fail to acknowledge that the lesser access to the means of government of "challenging" groups (see Gamson 1975), like women as would-be competitors in the political arena, exposes the issues of permeability and openness of the political systems in the region.

Notes

1. An illustration is given by the well-known case of the mobilization and concerted actions of the Madres de la Plaza de Mayo, which were the first public demonstrations kicking off the resistance movement against the military regime in Argentina.

Chapter 13

Rules and Repertoires: The Revolt of a Farmers' Republic in the Early-Modern Netherlands

Marjolein 't Hart

Since the publication of Charles Tilly's *From Mobilization to Revolution* (1978c), the terminology of repertoires of collective action has become a familiar feature in social history. Repertoires, the range of actions from which political contenders choose, are an integral part of a "political culture." This political culture is by no means a static entity, as ideas and claims develop in the unfolding of the action. Past experiences and macroeconomic structures are strong determinants of the repertoire, but a choice of action does always exist. The preferences depend upon several factors, among others the opportunity to act together, for which homogeneity of the community matters again (Aya 1990, 63). The easiest choice is always convention, the known part of collective action. But around the skeletons of these major forms, other and less well known tactics may be employed. In fact, one could say that repertoires are caught in between tradition and innovation (Tarrow 1994, 114).

This chapter addresses the question of tradition and innovation in an early-modern repertoire of collective action by examining a revolt in a rural district in the far northeastern part of the Dutch Republic: the Oldambt. The revolt began when the nearby city of Groningen unilaterally declared its sovereignty over the Oldambt in 1639 and the farmers of Oldambt actively resisted that claim. At first their resistance was more reactive than revolutionary, but as the conflict escalated the rebels eventually declared the independence of the Oldambt, established mechanisms for self-rule, and armed themselves for their legitimate self-defense. After one brief armed skirmish in 1648, however, both sides—the city of Groningen as well as the Oldambt rebels—awaited the judgment of the States General, which claimed the authority to resolve this sort of internal dispute, and in so doing they appeared to accept the rules of institutionalized consultation as they had emerged within the Dutch Republic.

In fact, when the States General finally issued its ruling in 1650, the revolt dissolved and domestic peace was restored.

In order to understand the dynamics of this complex political interaction, this chapter starts out by telling the story of the impact of state formation, in particular the attempt by an urban center to impose control over a formerly peripheral territory. But the development of capitalist structures in the area, in the form of the commercial exploitation of peat fields, matters as well. Both invited a reaction by the local populace, with claims that resonated the rights and privileges from the past. Yet in the constellation of political opportunities created by the Dutch Republic, the farmers of Oldambt embraced a forceful ideology that aimed at the creation of a new set of political relations. In doing so, the Oldambters did not stand alone: In several other European regions the rural population rose with new and similar claims. Like so many of their counterparts elsewhere, however, the Oldambters failed. Why their bold actions were unable to transform political relations permanently and why, in particular, other rural representatives in the Republic's institutions refused to support them, will be dealt with in the last section.

The Region and Its History

The Oldambt was part of the province of Stad en Lande (officially the province of Stad Groningen en Ommelanden, today the province of Groningen). Politically the province was characterized by a strong urban–rural dichotomy,[1] with separate administrations for the city Groningen and the countryside (the Ommelanden). For matters pertaining to the Dutch Republic as a whole, representatives of the two constituent parts met together in a provincial diet in which each held one vote. It had been specified in an act of 1594 that the States General (the central body in The Hague where delegates of the sovereign United Provinces met) were to act as a court of appeal in case a dispute could not be settled within the province itself, but an appeal for a special committee from the States General, with the *Stadhouder* as a final judge, was considered a last resort (Waterbolk 1976, 235).

Economically the province, counting about 72,000 inhabitants, was famous for its exports of fat cattle, horses, butter, cheese, and beer (Matthey 1975, 251). In the early sixteenth century the town (which housed about one-fifth of the population) had been able to compete with a major center like Hamburg. From this period Groningen inherited several privileges over the countryside: For example, it held a monopoly on brewing and was the staple for grain, cattle, horses, and dairy products. Being the staple required the farmers to bring these goods to the market in Groningen before they could be shipped elsewhere. This may not have been such a harmful institution for rural folks in the early sixteenth century, but by 1600 the economic orientation of the area had shifted from the northern strip along the coast, the Frisian territories, where Groningen had indeed been one of the major centers, to the western part of the Republic, in particular to Amsterdam. In fact, farmers could obtain higher prices for their agricultural products in Amsterdam than in Groningen (Meihuizen 1976, 298–99, 343).

By 1600, then, the most prosperous period for the city of Groningen had passed. Despite the advantages of being the staple, the city's population hardly grew during the period of the Republic. By contrast, the countryside offered more expansive opportunities, with new lands being reclaimed along the coast and bogs being exploited, mainly for the digging of peat. Added to the economic contraction of the city, the 1594 act had also curbed its political power. All sixteenth-century hopes of building a city-state with a subordinate hinterland were wrecked because the Ommelanden obtained explicitly sovereign rights alongside the city. To Groningen's distress, during a dispute over taxation the States General even sent in troops, disarmed the local militia, and imposed the necessary taxes. Several of the city's privileges, such as those concerning the election of magistrates and the right to levy troops, were eliminated, and a fortress to station republican troops was even constructed just outside the city.[2]

The countryside of the Oldambt was governed by a rather loose construction of village representatives, supervisors of dikes, tax collectors, ministers, church wardens, and participants in the annual meetings of the *eigenerfden,* the landowners (Formsma 1976, 32). Civil servants and representatives (*volmachten*) were chosen for two-year terms at a general meeting in which all landowners (and often the main tenant farmers too) had a vote. There was no nobility, not even a gentry (*jonkers*) as existed in the neighboring Ommelanden. Instead, small farmers predominated: In most villages, 60 to 75 percent had holdings of less than fifteen acres with no more than five cows. In the villages that had a lot of new land because of reclamations, the farms were somewhat larger (Hoppenbrouwers 1991, 77–81). Most farmers were engaged both in dairying and farming the arable lands. The larger holdings produced above all butter and cheese for the market, with the breeding of horses and the fattening of cattle being notable additions. Half of the farmers rented the land they tilled, but their legal right to the land was rather secure. In most of the Oldambt villages the farming families constituted the majority, but artisans' and farm laborers' households might constitute up to half of the population. Yet even those with no agricultural business generally kept one or two cows (Hoppenbrouwers 1991).

From a True Periphery to an Exploitable Asset

The late sixteenth century and the beginning of the seventeenth century was a period of distress for the Oldambt. Because of the Eighty Years' War (1568–1648) against Spain, armies destroyed fields, cattle were stolen, and houses were burnt. With the coming of the Twelve Years' Truce (1609–21) the situation improved, but in 1624 the enemy again invaded the Oldambt (Resolutiën der Staten Generaal [RSG] 1624, 447, 501). The destructions as a result of warfare also depressed interest in new investments in the area, and floods frequently ruined the cultivated area (Knottnerus 1991, 32). Moreover, access to the Oldambt was difficult because of the bogs and morasses. The region's peripheral position nevertheless entailed one considerable advantage: The Oldambt was free from the staple of the city. Farmers were allowed to trade across the Ems and Dollard with Germany without first bringing the goods to the Groningen market (Feith 1856, 15).

As long as the hostilities went on, the city acted as a guardian and represented the Oldambt in the provincial diet, and under the circumstances the inhabitants of the Oldambt were quite pleased to have such a powerful neighbor guarding the interests of the region and providing loans if necessary. In addition, the court system, which was completely dominated by the city, was well regulated. Yet this perspective clearly changed as the impact of the war receded. With the impetus toward territorial consolidation and with the area's growing wealth, the Oldambt became extremely attractive to the city. The Oldambt, whose population numbered between 20,000 and 28,000 (Archief van de Staten Generaal 12548.254; Matthey 1975, 231; Hoppenbrouwers 1988, 10) yielded more in tax revenue than the whole city itself. Moreover, as new dikes were built and the drainage was improved through new canals, the fields proved highly fertile. And as the first bogs were exploited, the sale of peat generated rewarding profits to the pioneer entrepreneurs (Gerding 1994, 263). Even the important brewing industry of the city needed a lot of peat to fuel its production.

No wonder Groningen cast its eye upon the Oldambt, the more so as the city was continuously in financial distress. According to a report of a special committee of the city, commissioned in 1618 to find out how to improve public finances, the city should begin the exploitation of peat fields, renting out parcels of land and levying a new excise on the peat. The bogs, however, were not a no-man's-land. Some belonged the former monastic institutions, some were already in the hands of private entrepreneurs or co-ops, but the majority still belonged to individual parishes. In addition, some inhabitants had the right of *opstrek:* Newly reclaimed land extending in a direct line from an existing property was to become the possession of that property's landowner, up to the border with the next parish (Keuning 1933, 37–38).

Step by step, the magistrates of Groningen sought to extend their authority within the Oldambt. They already controlled legal affairs, but in 1625 they tried to boost their political prestige by demanding that they be addressed as *Edele Mogende* (Honorable Mighty) *Heren* instead of simply *Edele* (Honorable) *Heren* (Waterbolk 1976, 240). They also tried to divert revenues from former monastic properties, which had been specifically designated *ad pios usus* (for charitabe ends), to fund their own expenses and thus threatened to impoverish the local parishes (Huninga, Edsens, and Matthiae 1640). Groningen also extended its peat-digging enterprises by buying up failing commercial enterprises and thereby enjoyed certain economies of scale (Feith 1856; Gerding 1995). In 1612 the city had started digging a canal eastward toward Oldambt, but when the project finally reached the first cultivated fields of Oldambt in the 1620s, Groningen arbitrarily ordered that henceforth the digging was to be done by the local population at no cost to the city. If any parishes refused, the costs would simply be apportioned over all the other parishes (Kooper 1939, 106–7). The new canals, of course, improved transportation to Groningen, but they also had sluices at which new tolls were collected. Meanwhile Groningen also imposed a toll on the traditional overland route that connected Oldambt to the western part of the Republic.

New canal projects were costly undertakings, but they were by no means always to the advantage of the Oldambt farmers. On the contrary, shipping was virtually a city monopoly, in particular for the transportation of peat (Gerding 1995, 195), and even the transportation to the canal was regulated by city wagoners. In 1639 the construction of a barrier in the canal near Finsterwolde was aimed at halting trade over the Ems and Dollard to Germany, which implied that the city was now extending its staple over the Oldambt as well. From the city's point of view, the canals had improved the connections to such an extent that the Oldambt villagers no longer had an excuse for not bringing their goods to the Groningen market.

Relations between Groningen and Oldambt were further aggravated by new taxes on peat (in 1628) and beer (in 1637). An increase in the land tax in 1637 was complicated by a new measurement system that was particularly disadvantageous for the Oldambt. A major political dispute arose, however, when the *volmachten* of Oldambt claimed the right to participate in the diet. They cited historical precedents during the period of Habsburg rule, but Groningen adamantly opposed such rights, claiming that they owned seigneurial, thus in their view sovereign, rights over the territory (Blécourt 1935, 361). Supported by the other rural representatives in the Ommelanden, the dispute was brought before the States General. A verdict was finally issued in 1640 that declared that Groningen was not sovereign over Oldambt, but it left the question of representation in the diet unresolved.

The First Phase of the Revolt: Reaction

In this context the digging of new canals was sure to arouse concern in the Oldambt. Thus a group of landowners went to Groningen to oppose a new canal connecting the new lands in some villages to the larger drainage network in the area. Aside from the considerable duties that had to be paid, the new canal—the Koediep—meant that the water drained from the peateries was to be added to an already overburdened system. Also, as dikes were built along the new canals for shipping purposes, former drainage routes had to be guided under ground through costly culverts and pumps. And because the new sluice at the village of Zuidbroek was badly regulated, farmers saw their lands flooded. An alternative canal was proposed (Oud Archief Groningen 812 r–b: December 31, 1641, Memorie van questien).

As the city turned a deaf ear, the complaints turned into action. The parishioners' initial reactions consisted of simple rejection and refusals to cooperate, perhaps the most traditional forms within the repertoire of contention. Many farmers refused to pay the heavier levies, and shippers and wagoners refused to pay the new tolls. At several points the canal, dug by hired laborers, was filled in overnight by local adversaries. Another part of the traditional repertoire was the formulation of an official complaint to the city, which anyone had a legal right to do. Five landowners who had not been compensated for the ground lost through the digging of the canal put forward such a request in 1637, demanding proper restitution. The request was, of course, polite, as was expected in such an official document. But the burgomasters and Council of the city reacted in a most austere and uncompromising way: Instead of entering into a dialogue, the city put the five complainants, along with their lawyer, in prison when they came to present their request. They were released only on the payment of substantial fines (amounting to as much as 1,100 guilders per person, which was a year's salary for a high civil servant) without any further process.

Irritated by the spread of such public contention, the magistrates issued an *Acte van Souverainiteyt* on July 17, 1639, declaring that Groningen held the sovereign power over the Oldambt. This act had to be signed by the *volmachten* and "other" inhabitants of the villages, and anyone refusing was to be punished. It was this decree that precipitated the revolt. Sebo Huninga, the principal complainant of the five landowners, managed to rally widespread support from all the villages in the Oldambt. Within two weeks it was obvious that all Oldambt *volmachten* would refuse to sign. A more formal response to the *Acte van Souverainiteyt* was the *Procuratie* of August 10, 1639, in which about 200 signatories from fifteen villages (some of whom signed as *volmacht* of a village) declared they had always been free subjects.[3] To defend their freedom, they pledged to back one another up *in raedt ende daedt* (in word and deed). Three of them—Sebo Huninga from Beerta, Wirtjo Matthiae from Eexta, and Doedo Edzens from Noordbroek—were assigned the task of defending the general interest of the Oldambt and were elected as the general *volmachten* of the Oldambt (Huninga, Edsens, and Matthiae 1640).

The city reiterated its claim of sovereignty on October 26, 1639. But when their *drost* (district judge) traveled around, he could find only a few city tenants willing to sign. Huninga, Matthiae, and Edzens were sued, but when they refused to appear before the city court the city did not succeed in arresting them either. In November 1639 the city had Huninga condemned for treason for having revolted against the lawful sovereign power. The sentence was death, although the sentence was later reduced to banishment from the province along with confiscation of his goods and property. But the city had clearly overreached its authority, since the verdict could not be executed, apart from the seizure of property in the city itself. The rural representatives of the Ommelanden in the provincial diet also decided to draw up a strong protest against Groningen, declaring that the city had no right whatsoever to condemn someone to banishment from the province because the city's authority would never extend beyond its borders. The persecuted men were even put under protection of the Ommelanden (Aitzema 1638, 18:347–48).

Escalation and Innovation

At this point the conflict began to escalate. The *drost* had to be accompanied by an armed escort, Oldambters obstructed the inspection of dikes and roads, and the tax for the major drainage board was resisted on a wide scale. In the nearby Sappemeer peateries, local farmers clashed violently with those who had rented the plots from the city. Measures and weights (instruments used for tax purposes) were not properly calibrated, and the new sluice at Zuid-broek, regarded as harmful for the drainage of the arable lands, was smashed to pieces. Dikes along the canal to Zuidbroek were cut in order to obstruct shipping. The Oldambt *volmachten* began to rent out "their" church lands to new farmers, to announce new rules, and to levy their own taxes.[4]

For the time being the outlook was favorable for the Oldambt. In February 1640 the States General ordered that the city should stop the prosecution of Huninga, who was placed under the protection of the States General itself. On the other hand, the Oldambters were told to refrain from keeping men under arms. More significant was the verdict of the States General of July 1640 that explicitly declared that the city was not sovereign over the Oldambt, although it did share the sovereignty with the Ommelanden through the provincial diet (Aitzema 1640, 20:116–21). Thus the first phase of the revolt ended with inconclusive bargaining before the States General. Popular con-tention had mainly been reactive, yet innovations were emerging. The city's harsh response, in particular, had awakened a new consciousness in the whole region, fueled by the verdict of the States General in July 1640 (which was promising for the Oldambt) and by the support of the Ommelanden. With these two powerful external allies, the Oldambt *volmachten* even began drafting their own laws. On October 14, 1640, the rebels issued an act of inde-pendence that started out with the phrase "*De Ingesetenen der Oud-Ampten, doen te weten . . .*" [The residents of Oldambt hereby declare . . .]," which was parallel to the usual formulation for any sovereign power (pamphlet collec-tion, Rijksarchief in Groningen).

But the support of the States General had been limited to the resolution of July 1640. In fact, later in the year, as insurrectionary action spread, the States General began to side with the city. According to the verdict of De-cember 11 and 12, 1640, the arrest of Huninga should now be executed, Oldambters had to pay the taxes and repair the dikes and sluices, and by no means were they allowed to make their own laws or to hire troops.[5] It proved impossible, however, to arrest Huninga with the whole region so belligerent. Meanwhile the Oldambters tried to gain admission to each diet and were re-peatedly rejected by the city. This issue exploded in 1643 when Groningen de-cided to use republican troops to prevent Oldambters and some Ommelander *jonkers* from attending the meeting. The *jonkers* were furious, and for a couple of years the whole provincial administration was threatened, as these rep-resentatives from the countryside refused to enter the city for meetings of the diet. To restore the situation the States General decided in favor of the Ommelanden in the 1643 case, and the city had to give in.

Although the Ommelanden acted as a "distant" ally (the *jonkers* were not that anxious to share their power with ordinary farmers),[6] their position in the provincial government resulted in a vacuum of power and encouraged the Oldambters to continue. It was of great practical importance that the *jonkers* could prevent the city from sending republican soldiers to the Oldambt. A new Oldambt declaration of independence on October 24, 1643 stated that no inhabitant was required to appear before a city court any more: The Oldambt declared its own jurisdiction. Several taxes were collected by Oldambt receivers, and the rents from former monastic goods were appropriated. Tax farmers from the city were hindered by armed Oldambters under the command of a certain Lieutenant Lichthart.[7]

In the meantime the States General was sitting in judgment over the controversies of the area. Ad hoc committees, expanded to include members of the prestigious Court of Holland and sometimes the *Stadhouder,* were created to hear the delegates from both sides. The city tried to find a way out of the legal proceedings by asserting that the issue was an internal affair only. Generally there was little sympathy for the rebels because, above all, Their High Mightinesses (the title of the delegates in the States General) maintained that law and order should be restored as quickly as possible. But the States General could not simply decide in favor of the city. Here the support of the Ommelander *jonkers* mattered. As long as the Ommelanden refused to convene a regular diet (1643–47), they even threatened the very constitutional foundation of the Union—that is, provincial government and provincial sovereignty.

The Final Phase: The Independent *Landschap*

While delegates in The Hague tried to promote the cause of the Oldambt before the States General, popular contention had come to encompass the whole region by the summer of 1647, and an independent administration was formed. As an autonomous *landschap* (territory), the Oldambt claimed all the revenue from church properties and taxation. An *Oldambster Manifest* was issued, which stressed that the Oldambt was entitled to *Self-reddinghe* (self defense), which allowed for independent action after one of the two parties had breached a contract.[8] On March 28, 1648, the city proposed in the provincial government to send republican troops to the Oldambt, but this move was blocked by the *jonkers* of the Ommelanden.[9] The city did secretly send soldiers four days later, on Easter night, but the Oldambters met these troops with a well-trained militia that far outnumbered the city's troops.[10] One soldier of the city was severely wounded and died the next day; several others were captured and interrogated by the Oldambt courts. The others were disarmed and chased back to the city, together with the *drost*.

From then on, regular law sessions were held under the leadership of the new judge, Fokko Menninga, who had replaced the *drost*. Obviously, the repertoire of contention had been extended to include the formation of an independent *landschap*. By now both sides were preparing for war. According to one account, the militia of the Oldambt numbered 2,560 men, excluding 200 mercenaries (Archief van de Staten Generaal 12548.278.2). For their part, the magistrates of Groningen called on the States General to send troops, but their demand was not met by Their High Mightinesses. Instead, official delegates (including the *Stadhouder*) were sent to negotiate a settlement, but their provisional solutions were in vain.

The Oldambters were more confident than ever that the States General would be sympathetic to their cause. In a declaration before the highest authority of the Republic they stressed the rights of their newborn *landschap*. The main issues were the autonomy of the district, the right to representation in the provincial diet, the authority over church properties, and the levying of taxes within the district. The city had violated their freedom when they had sent the armed forces at Easter. According to the rebels, the dispute was by no means a private matter between the city and the Oldambt; its essence concerned the whole constitution of the free Republic of the United Netherlands, in which the legitimate rights of a district were put at risk by unjustified claims of seigneurial prerogative.[11]

The rebels' trust in the legitimacy of their legal claims was enormous. In late May 1648 the news spread that the delegates at the States General, Wirtjo Matthiae and the lawyer Lucas Harckens, were making much progress. The mood was exuberant: "They think they have won everything," a city spy in the Oldambt reported. Companies of militia marched through the villages, firing celebratory rounds (Oud Archief Groningen 812 r–b [PP May 28, 1648]). When the States General finally reached a verdict on August 7, 1649, however, the judgment was positive for the rebels only with regard to several minor issues. With regard to the contested digging of the Koediep, the opening of the road to Kropswolde, the freedom from tolls for shipping peat, and compensation for some of their lands, among other issues, the Oldambters were victorious. New borders between the parishes in the peateries were also settled. But on the more important matters, such as the autonomy of the district, representation in the diet, and the installation of an independent judicial system, the States General's ruling favored Groningen. In the end, the main shortcoming of the Oldambters' case proved to be their failure to produce the necessary original documents to support their claims, documents that had been kept within the city. Only copies could be shown, which did not satisfy the judges of the States General. And although Their High Mightinesses did not recall the verdict of 1640 (which had denied the city sovereignty over the area) the technical problem of the missing documents was sufficient to defeat the claims of the rebels.

Remarkably, no open conflict or bloodshed followed this decision. In fact, with respect to all deeds committed during the revolt, the States General declared an amnesty: No one was to be punished, although some sums were specified for compensation. One notable compensation was 5,000 guilders to be paid by the city to the landowners who had lost their lands by the digging of the Koediep. This was the very issue that had sparked off the revolt in the first place (Aitzema 1649, 29:853–57). Thus the verdict of the States General brought an almost immediate end to the Oldambt revolt. The Oldambt leaders had committed themselves so steadfastly to the formal rules of the judgment of the States General that they could not deny the legitimacy of the verdict. Although the Oldambters had developed new elements within their repertoire of contention—introducing especially the notion of a sovereign *landschap* within the Union—the repertoire of institutionalized bargaining at the highest level of the Republic overshadowed all others.

The Outcome

The question remains as to why this specific verdict was pronounced by the States General. Since the evidence was inconclusive (Modderman 1816, 9; Blécourt 1935, 157), the judicial process could just as well have yielded at least some confirmation of Oldambt's independence by allowing it representation in the provincial diet. Why did the rural representatives of the Ommelanden, or those of the other provinces, not stand up in the defense of their countrymen?

First of all, the States General was characterized by a strong bias toward cities (Hart 1994). For example, in the dispute over the staple of Groningen in 1595, it was said that "the security of the United Provinces did not depend upon ten, twenty or thirty inhabitants of the countryside, but mainly upon the well populated and well fortified frontier cities" (Bos 1904, 339). At some points the representatives from the countryside in the States General proved to be more hesitant to condemn the Oldambt rebels whereas the representatives from the urbanized provinces were quickly convinced by Groningen.

Yet the *jonkers* could not stand up against the powerful cities from the province of Holland, whose wealth was indispensable for the maintenance of the Republic (Hart 1993).

On the crucial point of representation in the diet, the Ommelanden failed to give the Oldambt the unequivocal support it needed in 1648–49 (Blécourt 1935, 119). In this respect, the voting procedures in the diet suggest the reason for their ambivalent attitude. As I noted earlier, the provincial diet consisted of two estates, each with one vote: one for the city and one for the Ommelanden. Participation in the diet was necessarily tied to association with one of the two. The *jonkers* were, in fact, willing to support the claim of the Oldambt for representation as part of the city's vote, but not as part of their own delegation. The Ommelanden itself consisted of four districts, whose representatives jealously guarded their own prerogatives in the diet. Disputes among them had been frequent on this issue (Pauw 1956), and a fifth district would clearly require them to revise their existing agreements. When the solution moved in the direction of having the Oldambters represented as part of the Ommelanden, then, the *jonkers* quickly backed out. Another disadvantage for the Oldambt was that it was a movement from below. Only in the tiny province of Drenthe did landowners have an independent representation in the provincial diet next to the gentry. In all other provinces, as in the Ommelanden, the delegation from the countryside was dominated by the nobility and the gentry.

The Revolt in European Perspective

Within the wider perspective of Europe, the Oldambt revolt was hardly an isolated occurrence. The late sixteenth century and the early seventeenth century were above all periods of territorial consolidation during which peripheries became attractive assets to European state makers. In reaction, of course, peasant movements developed elsewhere as well. Peter Blickle has noticed that with the growing intensification of state domination (above all instigated by taxation), the political rights of the peasantry, which had been quite fluid and poorly defined up to the late Middle Ages, were becoming major issues (Blickle 1973, 435; see also Trossbach 1993, 80; Mousnier 1971). For the city of Groningen, the ancient ideal of a city-state resonated with their attempt to create a consolidated territory, stretching all the way to the border with East Frisia. For a long time control over the courts alone had been sufficient for the city's ambitions in the Oldambt, but in the seventeenth century additional power was considered necessary, particularly with regard to the commercial exploitation of peateries as a means of shoring up the city's finances. In fact Gerding (1995, 360) noted that no other political entity in the Netherlands profited as much from the peat industry as Groningen. By systematizing exploitation for the market and shifting the infrastructural costs (especially of canal building) onto others, the city had seen important new revenues pour into its treasury.

The ideal of an autonomous *landschap* was another feature of the revolt that it shared with other regions, above all with the Frisian territories in Germany. Whereas in the Ommelanden the idea of peasant or farmer representation had been preempted by the *jonkers,* in neighboring East Frisia the peasants became an independent estate around 1600. They claimed and obtained a formal representation through their *volmachten* in the *Landschaft* and appointed their own *syndic* (secretary). Their first official warrant to the diet dated from 1620 (Wiemann 1982, 48–49). It was remarkable that this aspect of representation was not rooted in the past. In previous centuries representative functions had been quite rudimentary, and the farmers' political claims as an independent estate within the *Landschaft* had been vague. Apparently, such issues had not always seemed so important (Wiemann 1982, 13–21), but by the end of the sixteenth century, with the ongoing process of state formation and territorial consolidation, the fiscal demands of the German Empire had grown considerably. Dike maintenance, in addition, had to be organized on a wider scale, and as a result the *Landschaft* and the rights of its inhabitants became a major political concern.

Still, peasant representation in estates was quite exceptional in European history. It was known to exist for more than a few decades only in areas of Sweden, Switzerland, South Germany, East Frisia, and Drenthe. Generally these areas were characterized by a peripheral position and the absence of nobility. Personal liberty and strong property rights, together with early commercialization, were also advantageous for these forms of popular representation (Blickle 1989, 25–27, 30; Trossbach 1993, 82, 85). Some of these factors were also vital in the case of the Oldambt. Bogs and the danger of floods added significantly to the Oldambt's marginality. There was also a strong identification with the "Frisian" tradition, in particular in the affirmation of personal liberty and property rights.

In any case, the popular movement for political independence in the Oldambt demonstrated an enormous degree of local solidarity. The absence of nobles and the constant necessity of dike maintenance may have contributed to this sense of solidarity, but the disputes over taxation, drainage networks, canals, and peateries all added to the consciousness of having one

common enemy: the city of Groningen. The inflexibility of the urban magistrates, unyielding with respect to any of their claims and unwilling to enter
into negotiations with the Oldambters, clearly crystalized the choices. It facilitated both an impressive popular mobilization, partly through an existing
milita network, and the easy acceptance of a new system of self-governance.

Another element in the political culture of the new Dutch Republic should
be stressed in particular. The strong sense of legitimacy in the revolt was
linked to a sense of the sanctity of contracts. All contracts should be established through mutual agreements, and the alteration of a contract also had to
be accepted by both sides. In the event that a contract was violated by the ruler,
the people were entitled to *self-reddinge,* the right of self-defense or of resistance. This rather pragmatic model of social and political order was exceptionally strong in neighboring East Frisia, too. The people themselves enjoyed
a great deal of independence vis-à-vis the ruler, a political culture that was, in
part, the legacy of Johannes Althusius, the *syndic* of Emden. In East Frisia a
prince was not regarded as ruling by some divine right (as he was regarded
in most of the German territories) but as representing the people, who were
organized through the Estates (Hughes 1988, 69; Schilling 1991, 90).

In this broader comparative context, then, the Oldambt revolt shows how
repertoires of contention are gradually transformed in the course of political
conflict and ongoing interaction. As a long-simmering conflict escalated, both
the tactics and the claims of the rebels broadened, climaxing in the establishment of an independent *landschap.* In several other regions of Europe a similar tendency was noted as a reaction to ongoing territorial consolidation from
above. In the specific context of the Dutch Republic, however, this contentious novelty was tempered by a strong commitment to the rules of institutionalized consultation. To be sure, the ability to appeal to the States General
and the potential allies among the *jonkers* of the Ommelanden represented
the extraordinary political opportunities available to the Oldambt peasants.
Still, both the commitment to legal processes and the emphasis on the contract (Groningen was said to have breached its contract with the Oldambt)
pointed to the strong influence of convention in the repertoire. Enormous
sums were spent by the rebels on famous lawyers to represent their cause before the judges of the States General (Blécourt 1935, 197). The lengthy decla-
rations and statements that fill the archives were indissoluble from the political culture. For the Oldambt rebels, even amid the innovations of the revolt,
the rules of institutionalized bargaining, which both opened up opportunities
and imposed limitations, had ultimately to be obeyed.

Notes

I am thankful to Michiel Gerding, Otto Knottnerus, Richard Paping, and Wayne te Brake for their suggestions and inspiration. This article is based mainly upon findings from the General Archives in The Hague and the Municipal and Provincial Archives in Groningen; I am indebted to the staff of these institutions for their help. Peter Hoppenbrouwers lent invaluable support in the analysis of the signatories of the Procuratie.

1. The dichotomy was enhanced by a cultural/ethnic division. The city was *Drents* (that is, originally part of the province bordering on the south) and "Saxon," altogether different from the "Frisian" tradition of the countryside (Hofstee 1937, 25–37).

2. Bit by bit Groningen managed to undo some of these impositions in the years following (Resolutiën der Staten General 1604, 140, 210; 1605, 484; 1606, 703; 1611, 375).

3. Those farmers among the signatories who could be traced back (about 50 percent), generally had above-average holdings. Some who had only a little plot were carpenters, for example. I owe these findings to Peter Hoppenbrouwers. The analysis is distorted, as the most useful register dates from 1660.

4. Archief van Staten van Stad en Lande no. 867, Plakkaat January 10, 1640; see also the verdict of the States General of December 11/12, 1640, in the Archief van de Staten Generaal.

5. Verdict of States General on complaints of the city of Groningen of November 10, 1640, on December 11/12, 1640 (Pamphlet collection Rijksarchief in Groningen). Aitzema is correct, by the way, contrary to Dijkstra's interpretation (Dijkstra 1974, 51).

6. Even the most notable of the *volmachten*, Sebo Huninga and Wirtjo Matthiae, whatever their other business, had been tilling the land themselves for at least a couple of years (Blécourt 1935, 75).

7. Archief van de Staten General 12579.32, 25–8–1641; 10–9–1641; 16–12–1641; Pamphlet collection, Rijksarchief in Groningen: Resolutie of the volmachten of the Oldambten of October 24, 1643.

8. Pamphlet collection, Rijksarchief in Groningen. Still, the declaration did stress that the Oldambt was to remain a faithful member of the United Provinces. See also a list of the civil servants appointed in Archief van de Staten Generaal 12548.278.2.

9. Archief van de Staten van Stad en Lande 475, December 21, 1647; see also Sommair debat 1648 of the city in the Pamphlet collection, Rijksarchief in Groningen. The declaration of March 29, 1648, is found in full length in Dijkstra 1974, 55–56.

10. In the countryside the villages had their own militia (Fockema Andreae 1904). Even the Mennonites were said to have taken up arms for the defense of the Oldambt during the revolt.

11. Ommelander Archief, Rijksarchief in Groningen 1310: Omlander Schrift June 13, 1648; Omlander Schrift July 3, 1648. See also Oldambster jurisdictie 1648, in the Pamphlet collection, Rijksarchief in Groningen.

Archival Sources

Algemeen Rijksarchief (ARA), The Hague

Archief van de Staten Generaal (1.01.06): nos. 12548.254; 12548.278.1–3; 1257.32: Stukken betreffende het proces over Oldambten 1641–49

Gemeente Archief (GAG), Groningen

Oud Archief: Resoluties van de regering der stad Groningen; nos. 812 r–b and 826 r (Stukken Oldambt rebellie)

Rijksarchief in Groningen (RAG)

Archief van Staten van Stad en Lande: no. 867 (Stukken Oldambten ca.1640–50); no. 475 (Plakkaten)

Ommelander Archief: nos. 871 and 1310 (Stukken betreffende Stad-Oldambt, 1639–49)

Pamphlet collection

Koninklijke Bibliotheek (KB), The Hague

Pamphlet collection

Chapter 14

Capitalists, Immigrants, and Populists: The Impact of Social Conflict and the State on the Origins of World War I

Carl Strikwerda

It is only natural, perhaps, that we want to believe that great changes had equally great causes. World War I was undoubtedly a watershed in world history: The Great Depression, Nazism, communism, World War II, and the Cold War are unthinkable without it. Determining the underlying causes of this great event, however, presents a daunting challenge. In searching for an underlying cause of the war, industrialization with all its attendant ripple effects would seem to be the prime candidate. Yet the relationship between the long-term social transformation of industrialization and the outbreak of the short-term but equally momentous upheaval of World War I has only been intermittently explored by scholars. As Michael Mann has argued, social historians and sociologists have generally focused on trends that transcend political boundaries or that appear to have had little impact on foreign policy, trends such as migration, the rise of the working class, and the origins of the welfare state. Even when dealing with the impact of social change on politics, sociologists have often studied social movements within the sphere of domestic politics without examining how they affected the state's diplomatic or military power. As political scientist R. B. J. Walker put it: "To place the two terms 'social movements' and 'world politics' into conjunction is to invite serious conceptual trouble" (Walker 1994, 669). Meanwhile historians have asserted that political elites in 1914 reflected the views of those who held economic power. In other words, the idea that the short-term political decisions that began the war somehow had roots in long-term social and economic changes is implicit in many scholars' works but has rarely been examined systematically.

This chapter will argue that major social trends had an ambiguous impact on international relations, and not necessarily the impact many historians have suggested. Social and economic trends in many ways made war less likely rather than more likely. When war broke out, leaders of states in certain ways acted *against* social and economic trends. In other words, they were often not acting clearly in the interests of economic leaders. Meanwhile social movements exploded in size and influence in the years before the Great War, but their impact was a complicated one. Some movements pressured governments to have aggressive foreign policies and thus made war more likely. The influence of others tended to make war less likely: Socialists opposed militarism, while big business, Catholic, and reformist organizations created international ties that undercut aggressive nationalism or militarism. Yet unless certain breakthroughs had been made in communications and constitutionalism, such movements often had little ability to shape actual policies.

In order to examine the relationship between social change and politics, it is useful to concentrate on three crucial groups: first, big business; second, immigrant workers and the labor movements who sought to organize them; and third, lower-middle-class propagandists, who can be defined loosely as populists. Their actions and interests clashed before 1914 and set off two contradictory forces. On the one hand, business investments and labor migration increased international ties between nation-states before 1914. On the other hand, there were, partially in reaction to this growing internationalism, increasing numbers of populist voices supporting nationalism. The populists criticized a wide variety of targets, but they did attack internationalism and advocate a conservative brand of nationalism in order to criticize what they saw as the negative aspects of industrialization. On balance, big business, labor migration, and even some of the Catholic populist movements, I would argue, made the outbreak of war less likely. Populist agitation had a powerful effect on governments, but in advocating nationalist policies such agitation was more frustrated than successful. Popular conservative nationalism by itself did not, on balance, make war imminent, but it did provide a possible constituency for political leaders casting about for support. When war did come, it came in part because leaders of major states—especially Germany, Austria-Hungary, and France—chose to react against the currents of internationalism set off by industrialization. In doing so, political leaders were not clearly acting in line with the interests of big business. Instead, they were aligning themselves with a brand of conservative nationalism espoused before 1914 primarily by one strand of populism.

Industrialization was a critical source for the domestic pressures that political leaders faced in 1914. But social conflicts did not dictate the choices that these leaders made in foreign policy. In Kenneth Dyson's terms, modern states have depended on three supports: law, legitimacy, and power (Dyson 1980, 101–32). On the eve of the war, almost all Western states had come to depend on the rule of law and some kind of claim to popular legitimacy. The greatest ongoing battle in domestic politics was to determine whether legitimacy included the provision of a minimum of social justice. But the rulers of almost every European state still clung to control of military and foreign policy as their own jealous preserve. The explosion of social movements in the late nineteenth century challenged the status quo in profound ways but, paradoxically, barely touched the elite's grasp on the tools of war. I would argue that this reveals several points: the crucial ability of the state to act in foreign policy in ways opposed to the logic of industrialization, the ability of interest groups and social movements to pursue apparently contradictory policies, the powerful role played by the lower middle class, and the complex ways in which social movements interacted with the political realm.

To make this argument, this chapter will first review the interpretations that scholars have offered on the causes of World War I. Second, it will examine big business, labor, and the lower middle class as examples of social actors before 1914 and look at the impact that these groups had on the conflict between nationalism and internationalism. Third, it will examine the press and constitutional control over foreign policy as the crucial links between domestic politics and international relations. Finally, it will suggest some lessons that the immediate pre–World War I situation offers for social and political theory.

The Causes of the Great War

In reading the various works on the causes of World War I, one might feel that historians and political scientists are writing past each other. Most political scientists who deal with the outbreak of the war attribute its causes to the same source as that of most wars: rivalries between states. Realists and neorealists from Hans Morgenthau on have argued that the inherent warlikeness in the international system has changed little from earlier centuries through to the twentieth. "The texture of international politics remains highly constant; patterns recur, and events repeat themselves endlessly," Kenneth Waltz (1989, 66) argues. Surprisingly, the conclusions of the realists and neorealists, who adopt an essentially narrative methodology, differ little from those of political scientists who use quantitative methods. The scholars involved in the well-known Correlates of War Project believe that they have established "the constancy and timelessness of basic interstate relations.

Technology has changed; objectives, motives, and methods of states remain the same." (Gochman and Moaz 1990, 221).

Most historians, by contrast, argue that fundamentally new forces caused the war. Since the 1960s, Fritz Fischer and Hans Ulrich Wehler have made domestic politics the key to understanding the outbreak of the war—the so-called *primat der Innenpolitik* (the primacy of internal politics). In Germany, building a navy tempted workers away from socialism and bought support from industrialists for the aggressive policies of aristocratic *Junkers*. According to this perspective: "The fear of socialism led not only to an alliance between large industry and large agriculture, but also solidarity of preindustrial lower classes, artisans, small farmers, shopkeepers, and petty bureaucrats with the established order" (Iggers 1984, 28).

Similar alliances emerged in Austria-Hungary, France, and virtually all of Europe (Mayer 1981). The chauvinist nationalism backing these alliances made war more likely because, as Michael Howard argues, "this nationalism was almost invariably characterized by militarism"(Howard 1983, 26). The result was to check liberal and socialist forces that might have worked for peace and to make war eventually inevitable (Joll 1992).

How can we reconcile the apparent continuity of great power politics that political scientists see and the disjunction created by an alliance of capitalists, aristocrats, and the lower middle class noted by historians? One crucial area to examine is the degree to which the newly mobilizing interest groups and social movements were pulled toward a nationalist or internationalist perspective and, thus, whether their actions had the potential to make war more or less likely.

The World of Capital

In order to understand the internationalist tendencies of big business, we must revise our notions of the world economy in which it thrived (Strikwerda 1993b). The years before 1914 were the last time, and perhaps the only time, the larger part of the globe formed a relatively open world economy. As U.S. Federal Reserve Board Vice Chairman Alan Blinder has observed: "To a significant extent, the industrialized nations of the world only recently reattained the levels of economic integration that they had reached at the eve of World War I" ("Back to the Thrilling Trades of Yesteryear," *New York Times,* March 12, 1995, E5). Tariffs were lower than they would be until the 1960s, international trade was at an all-time high and increased steadily before World War I and foreign investment and migration flowed freely (Ashworth 1974; Poidevin 1969). Three of the six largest Ruhr members of the German steel cartel, the *Stahlwerksverband*—Gelsenkirchener, Deutsch-Luxemburg, and Thyssen—had become heavily committed to investments in France, Belgium, or other countries, while French, Belgian, and Luxemburg capital owned almost 20 percent of the cartel's production (Tübben 1930, 38). Even Krupp, the German armaments maker that writers have seen as the quintessential nationalist firm, in 1914 had subsidiaries in Russia and Spain, joint ventures with British and French firms, and investments in Brazil, Africa, and the South Pacific. Belgian, Swiss, and German chemical firms had operations throughout Europe (Hohenberg 1966, 36–47; Haber 1958, 9–180). Despite all the arguments about economic nationalism, the economies of France, Germany, and Britain were becoming more integrated, and at a faster rate, than they would at any other time in history until the 1960s (Craig and Fisher 1991).

This internationalization of capital changes our perspective of prewar domestic politics. Big business only allied with aristocratic elites or nationalist conservatives on certain issues. In France, the general strike called by the Confédération générale du travail in 1906 and the railroad strike of 1910 created a strong coalition around the "party of order" (Mayeur and Rebérioux 1984, 244–85). With Alfred Hugenberg's machinations to guide them, the Ruhr industrialists supported the nationalist Pan-Germans as a way to fight socialism (Kaelble 1967, 146–63; Chickering 1984, 227–30). At the same time, business was skeptical of if not simply opposed to calls for an aggressive foreign policy. When Heinrich Class, leader of the Pan-Germans, tried to interest the iron and steel magnate Hugo Stinnes in supporting expansionism, Stinnes cut him off by declaring: "Let us have three to four years of peaceful development, and Germany will be the undisputed economic master of Europe" (Class 1932, 217). Government, industry, and the miliary often quarreled over the German navy (Epkenhans 1991). In France, the very nationalists who conservative politicians wanted to unite with big business to form a bloc against socialism were often critics of high finance and suspicious of economic "cosmopolitanism" (Freedeman 1993, 58–82). Even some socialists thought that big business, in pursuing its own interests, would lessen the chances for war: After the Franco-German accord over Morocco in 1911, Jean Jaurès told the Chamber of Deputies: "There is another force of peace in the world today, it is modern capitalism in the organized state" (Becqué 1912, 408).

Migration and Labor Internationalism

Labor internationalism before World War I is, of course, another subject on which many scholars have reached a concensus. In short, it was an ignominious failure. The international labor union federations and the Socialist Second International failed to influence any diplomatic confrontation and, more devastating, had scant effect on popular nationalism. The focus in this literature has been twofold: There was a lack of connections at the top, between leaders of the various national movements, and any internationalism among workers in the rank-and-file was extremely weak (Drachkovitch 1953; Haupt 1972; van der Linden 1988). If we look at the ties between movements where their common interests touched, however, I believe a new perspective emerges. We have to see labor internationalism as much at the "middle" as at the top or bottom. The sector where the interests of labor in different countries touched most clearly was immigrant labor. If we examine how powerful a role migration played before the Great War, we can also understand the importance of ties between movements and the new role of international labor regulation.

Just as business moved easily, so too, in the years before World War I, did workers move between states increasingly freely until, for the only time in modern history, much of the world formed virtually a single labor market (Hoerder 1985; Moch 1992). States never gave up the right to expel foreigners for a variety of offenses, but by comparison with earlier centuries and the later decades of the twentieth century, the relative freedom of labor to move is striking (Caestecker 1994). The one major exception was German restrictions on Polish workers from outside the *Reich,* but even here the demand for labor eventually forced the Germans to encourage Poles to come (Nichtweiss 1959). The multinational firms in heavy industry expanded on the Continent precisely along with the growth of labor migration. In Normandy in 1911, Dutch and German companies employed Greeks, Italians, Spaniards, and Algerians (Pawlowski 1911, 239). At a French-owned mine in Germany an observer noted: "Very few of the workers are Germans; one finds a mélange of Poles, Hungarians, Belgians, Dutch, Italians, and Swiss" (Cambon 1914, 25). Nor was this foreign labor cheap, since during the economic boom before the war the United States and Argentina were often competing for the same workers. French labor contractors were outraged when a trainload of Italians whom they had hired stopped en route in Metz, in German Lorraine, and German recruiters lured away the entire contingent (Vignes 1913, 684).

Migration and multinational business led to international ties between labor. By 1910 German labor union leaders were organizing Dutch, Italian, and Scandinavian immigrants (Forberg 1987). The ties between heavy industry across borders encouraged international labor organizing. The German Christian coal miners organized the miners in the Dutch province of Limburg (Jurriens 1981, 137–39). German socialist metallurgists worked with French and Italian unionists to organize Italian immigrant iron and steelworkers in Luxemburg. French and Belgian unions sometimes cooperated along their countries' borders, as did British, Belgian, and Dutch longshoremen who struck together in the summer of 1911 (Boezee 1991, 188; Strikwerda 1993a, 121). Labor migration and ties between labor movements helped labor to have an effect on government policy for immigrant workers. The International Association for Labor Legislation and its close ally, the Association internationale pour la lutte contre le chômage, encouraged Germany, Denmark, Italy, Belgium, France, the Netherlands, Britain, and Austria-Hungary to sign agreements guaranteeing reciprocity for accident insurance (Herren 1992, 133–72; Lowe 1935; Mahaim 1933).

At the same time, the increase in labor migration that this international framework made possible also posed difficult problems that threatened governments. In certain ways, migration was a more difficult problem than the challenge posed by socialism in domestic politics. Socialism could be combated by conventional means, that is, by a variety of alliances between non-socialist parties, small concessions, and diversionary tactics. But curtailing or controlling migration was very difficult, since the most powerful interest groups, both big business and large agricultural landlords, demanded it. The rise in industrial wages in particular meant that large farmers had to tap ever more distant places to find laborers. In eastern Germany, the flow of German citizens, both German- and Polish-speaking, to the Ruhr in the west meant that large agricultural landlords came to depend increasingly on Polish and Ukrainian workers from Russia. The Germans tried to recruit laborers from their ally Austria-Hungary, but landlords and the government in Austria-Hungary protested, since migration to Germany drove up the price of agricultural labor. The tensions between Germany, Russia, and Austria-Hungary over the migrant laborers was one of the contributing factors to the tensions of the summer of 1914. The German government chose in the end to resolve the tension not by negotiation with both of its neighbors but by placating Austria-Hungary and threatening Russia (Olsson 1996).

Populists and Nationalism

Perhaps the most complex relationships between social movements and the state before the Great War involved the lower middle class, particularly shopkeepers and artisans. Every European society saw an explosion of new organizations among the lower middle class. Between 1906 and 1913 the number of buying cooperatives, mutual insurance societies, and trade associations among small business people in Belgium, for example, grew from 100 to 689 (Kurgan–van Hentenryk 1992, 24). Although its economic grievances propelled it to organize, the lower middle class has almost always been seen as inherently right-wing in its politics (Lipset 1967; Bechhofer and Elliott 1981). Like the *Junkers* and Pan-Germans in Imperial Germany, the *Action française* in France tried to appeal to the petty bourgeoisie, warning that "German-Jewish" espionage threatened France's control over its own economy and that socialists and traditional conservatives were dupes for foreign enemies (Daudet 1913, 298–300). The movements of the lower middle class could better be called "populist" in the sense that they represented a challenge to upper-class powerholders in the name of the "people" without necessarily accepting either authoritarian or collectivist solutions (Barkin 1970). "The social conservatism within the petty bourgeoisie," writes David Blackbourn, "was coupled with a resentful and vengeful political radicalism whose precise form was unpredictable" (Blackbourn 1984, 51). Leaders of various interest groups competed for lower-middle-class support. Jakob Riesser, president of the commercially oriented *Hansabund* and chair of the German banking association, and Leopold Müsselmann, a propagandist for the more heavy industry–dominated *Centralverband Deutscher Industrieller,* tried to convince lower-middle-class associations to ally with their organizations (Riesser 1912; Müsselmann 1912).

Was not nationalism the crucial force pushing elites into war? As with the international economy, every textbook and virtually every leading historian of the period tells us that the pre–World War I era was one of conservative nationalism. The 1880s saw the rise of a "new nationalism" of the right that tried to equate all of nationalism with its reactionary program. Yet this conservative nationalism had to coexist with a much broader patriotism that did not have close political identification with one position (Giradet 1966, 20–32). Studying French Lorraine, William Serman found that the elections of 1911 and 1912 "confirm that, in this frontier department, in the eyes of the local elected representatives and citizens, the right had not managed to gain the monopoly on patriotism" (1991, 133). At the same time, both nationalist separatists and nationalist chauvinists in the major states often faced major obstacles. Rather than transfer to France, many French nationalists and Alsatian separatists expected that recognition of German-held Alsace-Lorraine as a self-governing *Land* within the German empire was the most likely solution for the thorniest issue in Franco-German relations (Silverman 1972, 151). On Germany's eastern frontier, the ultranationalist *Ostmarkenverein* failed to get even its erstwhile allies, the noble *Junkers* organized in the Conservative

Party, to support buying out Polish farmers and replacing them with German settlers (Hagen 1980, 253–85). The Pan-Germans and the *Action française* were much smaller than most economic interest associations. The German pro–free trade league, the *Hansabund,* had over 200,000 members, the Pan-Germans only 20,000 (Peters 1992, 24–51; Kaelble 1967, 182). Similarly, imperialism within domestic politics before 1914 was only intermittently successful as an ideology. It had articulate and powerfully placed spokespersons and was able to win state support for acquiring colonies. But only during occasional crises, such as Britain's Boer War or the "Hottentot revolt" in German southwest Africa, did a significant body of public opinion support spending large amounts of money on empire. Imperialist propagandists found that "public opinion in Britain and France proved more difficult to conquer than their respective empires" (August 1985, 163). The French public accepted the cost of the empire after 1900 as a "fait accompli."(Girardet 1972, 96).

Catholic social movements represent one of the best examples of how populist organizations fit awkwardly into attempts to form conservative nationalist coalitions. Most Catholic parties drew support from a variety of classes—farmers, workers, the lower middle class, and upper classes—and created a web of international ties. Catholics from Belgium, the Netherlands, Austria, France, Switzerland, Italy, Luxemburg, and Germany met in international congresses, created organizations to help the lower middle class, and began an international Catholic peace movement (Lambrechts 1912, 80–103; Nord 1986, 472–73; Chickering 1975, 380–82; Vanderpol).

Social Movements, the Press, and Public Opinion

If there were significant groups in pre–1914 Europe that were not pushing for war or were less than strong supporters of militarism, why did not the social movements of the era have more of an effect on the governments? Or why did governments not have to worry more that their military or foreign policies might lack support? Scholars studying social movements emphasize that movements depend for their success on the resources they acquire, the solidarity and cohesion of their supporters, and the opportunities for repression provided by the powerholders they wish to influence. Organized labor and the lower middle class had acquired some substantial resources although ethnic, religious, and political rivalries divided both groups. Big business as an interest group not only had enormous resources but acted in some ways as a movement with numerous organizations engaged in lobbying. What problems and opportunities did these groups face?

Rather than studying groups such as these, which had substantial resources but less power than they felt they deserved, social movement theorists have focused largely on "collective actors who are excluded or marginalized in the political order" (Jenkins 1995, 15). This has meant studying movements of "protest": usually left-wing or radical movements more often than moderate or right-wing ones, but also movements that engage in overt, public displays such as demonstrations, strikes, rallies, and boycotts (Birnbaum 1979; Gamson [1975]1990; Tarrow 1994). The keys to the late-nineteenth-century rise of mass politics, however, were the vast expansion of the suffrage and the number of new political actions that evolved. Besides elections, the political action repertoire included not just the rally and the strike but the newspaper editorial, the pamphlet, the letter-writing campaign, and, most critical of all in some ways, the fund-raising drive. The common distinction between highly organized, militant movements typified by socialism and the more fluid, informally organized "new social movements" of the late twentieth century is unhelpful. Most European movements of the late nineteenth century actually more resembled today's "new social movements." Many of the lower-middle-class, nationalist, and populist organizations had a well-organized core of members, but otherwise they had only a penumbra of loosely affiliated individuals around them. Outside the socialist and labor movements, the typical new movement of the late nineteenth century was obvious not in the streets but in voting booths and at the newspaper stand.

The apparent quietude of the late nineteenth century can mask what a profound change the press, especially, brought about in popular politics. E. H. Carr believed that one major reason the Great War came about was because diplomats felt little pressure from the public, which was largely uninterested in foreign issues. He claimed that "down to 1914, the conduct of international relations was the concern of persons professionally engaged in it" (Carr 1946, 1). A cursory look at the reams of newspaper print devoted to international affairs shows this to be false. When asked "What sells a newspaper?," Kennedy Jones, the great editor of the *Daily Mail,* responded: "War." "The Franco-Prussian War brought into existence the modern evening daily" (Jones 1920, 198–99). Within a few short years, journalism changed from a preserve of a literate elite who got old news in expensive editions to a major business providing up-to-date information for a mass audience. Permanent correspondents were established in foreign capitals, the major wire services could send copy between countries, and linotype and pulp paper allowed a huge increase in circulation and a drop in price. By 1912 a French writer was able to conclude: "Of all the modern phenomena, the most remarkable may be the extraordinary development of the press. The daily reading of newspapers has become a habit of the majority of civilized people" (Levy 1912, 235).

The expansion of the press virtually created the populist and nationalist movements of the late nineteenth century. As a recent historian of the German League has noted: "Propaganda was the *sine qua non* of the Army League's existence; it acted as a lifeline between the national association and local affiliates and between potential members and diehard supporters" (Shevin-Coetzee 1990, 13). Even the smallest organization had its tiny, often ephemeral newspaper as well as pamphlets that gave it its identity. By 1914 Germany had about 4,000 daily and weekly newspapers with a total circulation of over 16 million, while the Catholic *Volksverein für das Katholische Deutschland* had produced a staggering 200 million pieces of printed material (Heitzer 1992, 111).

Yet this era of press freedom and freedom of association had only recently emerged. In Germany, hundreds of cases were brought against socialists for associational and press offences even in the 1890s (Goldstein 1983, 39). In contrast to the explosion of communications and political movements, the actual mechanisms for connecting people and foreign affairs were still rudimentary. No European government ever faced the scrutiny of anything like the U.S. Senate Committee on Foreign Relations. Governments were not required to bring even basic information about diplomatic commitments and military preparations to the representatives of the people (Chow 1920, 283–91). Even in Britain, the "most democratically governed country" in Europe, wrote Arthur Ponsonby, "the people have no voice in controlling foreign policy" (Ponsonby 1915, 6–7). The arguments that states needed colonies in order to ensure prosperity were sometimes greeted with skepticism, but the information needed to assess these claims was often difficult to obtain. The level of "economic literacy" was not high. As late as 1912 former general August Keim could miscalculate the size of the population of France by over 10 million and have his calculations widely repeated as accurate in the German press (Shevin-Coetzee 1990, 27–28). The reactionary nationalist Paul Pilant claimed that there were no less than 600,000 Germans in France—a figure about a half million off (Pilant [1912?], 95).

What social scientists may need to consider is the degree to which the late nineteenth century formed a distinctive chapter in the development of collective action. Almost all the movements that have enriched and torn apart twentieth-century society emerged within the short span of a few decades— socialism, anarchism, racial anti-Semitism, radical nationalism, and democratic Catholicism. Justifiably, most social movement theorists see the era of democratic revolutions, the period from the late eighteenth to the mid-nineteenth century, as the major breakthrough in popular politics. As Jürgen Habermas argues, a "public sphere" in which individuals could debate and reconceptualize their own society only emerged when middle-class leaders divorced themselves from traditional categories (Habermas 1989, 67–102). States in the Western world began to redefine themselves as dependent on the people or at least minimally accountable to the public. The newspaper editorial, voting, strikes, the election rally, the petition drive, and the demonstration all emerged as means by which people could express their will. Yet, again like Habermas, most social movement scholars then jump from the early and mid-nineteenth century to the problems of the mid-twentieth century, when bureaucratization and mass consumer culture challenge the survival of a genuine public sphere. To the extent that the late nineteenth century is dealt with, it is seen as the seedbed of bureaucratization and mass consumer culture (Cohen and Arato 1992, 210–31; Habermas 1989, 141–210). Yet the late nineteenth century was also crucial in actually making the promise of the democratic revolutions a reality. As late as the 1860s there were virtually no national organizations of any kind, nor was there a large-circulation press anywhere on the Continent. The creation of the French Radical, German National Liberal, and Catholic *Zentrum* Parties and the rise of mass circulation newspapers were fundamental developments whose implications were complicated and drawn out.

For the press to have any real impact on foreign policy, there had to be an ongoing debate at the national level. This required a number of large-circulation papers that conveyed both news and opinion to people over most of the country. Yet outside Britain, a real national press barely existed. In Britain, the *Daily Mail* had 700,000 subscribers, the *Daily News* had between 500,000 and 600,000, and the *Times* usually had 200,000 (Hale 1940, 15–23). Although France boasted *Le Petit Parisien,* which claimed the world's largest circulation at 1,636,485 in 1913, few French newspapers had circulations above 100,000 (Chambure 1914, 129–31). In Germany, which had a population almost two-thirds larger than either Britain or France, probably only four papers had circulations of 150,000 or more, and only one, the *Berliner Tageblatt,* with a circulation of 215,000, cut across party lines and influenced government policy. Almost all other papers were local advertising sheets (known as *Generalanzeigner* with no political impact or small, highly partisan political mouthpieces. As a result the government had few publications that it had to take into account as representing public opinion (Rieger 1957, 87). What almost fatally weakened the French press as a constituent element of public control over the government was its dependence on cash payments and subsidies. Even the most respected papers, such as *Le Temps* and *Le Matin,* accepted huge sums from the czarist government, from Krupp, from the Brazilian and Argentinian governments, from Swiss and Belgian businessmen, and from the French sugar cartel (*L'abominable venalité de la presse* 1931, xiii, 16, 70–71, 210–14). Thus in Germany it was the very large number of limited circulation papers reaching only a small group that kept a larger public voice from emerging, whereas in France the financial weakness of the press weakened the emergence of a genuine "public sphere" (Carroll 1939, 8–14).

Interest in foreign affairs among the public was high, but investigative journalism of military or foreign policy was virtually nonexistent. Again, Britain is the exception that proves the rule. Using almost exclusively newspapers and published public documents, the crusading journalists Robert Blatchford, Noel Brailsford, Herbert Massingham, and E. D. Morel produced biting critiques of British foreign policy (Jones 1920, 251–54; Leventhal 1974; Morel 1912). It would be difficult to imagine this in France or Germany. Less information was available to the public, governments were not forced to defend themselves in parliaments as much, and the press had not evolved to the point where, collectively, newspapers provided an alternative authoritative voice in foreign policy.

The result was that by 1914 governments still had an impressive degree of autonomy over foreign and military policy. Interest groups and social movements pushed for their agendas in domestic policy, but in diplomatic issues the public was as often misled or manipulated as it was informed. Governments on the Continent before 1914 could actually use the expansion of the press as a means to dissimulate and mislead simply by withholding information and allowing partial and self-serving information to be multiplied a hundredfold in the press, which was hungry for copy. Both in Germany, to win support for a hard line in the Moroccan Crisis of 1911, and in France, to push through the new three-year conscription bill in 1913, governments manipulated public opinion. The results heightened international tensions and made it virtually impossible for politicians and the public to discuss foreign policy with any detachment (Krumeich 1984; Rieger 1957, 97–100; Mommsen 1981, 377).

Conclusion: Social Conflict and the State

Historians have tried to connect the paths of social change and social movements resulting from the Industrial Revolution with the growth in military power and diplomatic competition that led to World War I. The relations are in fact complex and difficult to unravel. Big business and the lower middle class were not always allies of governments that were devoted to conservative nationalism. Important sectors of big business had internationalist interests. Lower-middle-class populism could be diverse in its political tendencies. Nationalism was not yet, as it was to be after World War I, clearly the privileged domain of the reactionary right, nor was popular conservative nationalism so strong that it pushed governments to act. Finally, labor movements in recruiting immigrant workers, in organizing in industries that had significant connections across borders, and in shaping international labor policy did have the basis for genuine internationalism. One reason why social change did not have a greater impact on the decisions reached in the July crisis is that social movements often had much greater power in domestic politics than in influencing foreign policy. The press had exploded as a force in popular politics, but it had only begun to develop as a national forum in which issues of national security could be debated.

At the same time, the view generated by political scientists of the outbreak of World War I may also be questioned. The names and the diplomatic repertoires were the same, but the states that went to war were not those that had fought in previous conflicts. Profound changes were going on in European society, which created a radically different world in which diplomats and generals struggled to maintain their old autonomy. The tragedy of 1914, in some ways, was that elites acted as they had for centuries even though the world around them had changed to make war a much more damaging crime to inflict on society.

Yet the leaders of states retained a surprising degree of autonomy that allowed them to act against the internationalizing currents in their own societies. As Michael Mann has argued, in 1914 economic power, popular political power, and state power had all expanded enormously, but reconciling the private control of economic power with the political power of the representatives of the people was an ongoing battle. The equally momentous challenge of civilizing state power had barely begun (Mann 1993, 723–99). As a result, several confrontations in domestic politics had fateful consequences. The alliance of big business and conservative elites against labor in domestic politics made it much easier for the state to remain autonomous in its control of foreign and military policy. The deep and multiple divisions between liberals, Catholics, and socialists made progressive alliances to tame big business unlikely. Yet if the social question was not ameliorated, domestic politics was too chaotic to permit politicians or the public to challenge elite control over foreign and military policy. Tragically, it took total war, in some cases two world wars, and the fear of fascism and communism before contending social groups could reach a truce and learn the dangers of unchecked state power (Strikwerda 1998). The great crises of the twentieth century were linked to the great changes of the previous century in what could be considered small ways: the creation of national public opinion, the institution of constitutional controls on the government, the formation of compromises in domestic politics. Yet understanding and securing these small changes has proved an enduringly great task.

Chapter 15

Fishnets, Internets, and Catnets: Globalization and Transnational Collective Action

Sidney Tarrow

A Fishy Story

Hidden behind the headlines on the savage war in the former Yugoslavia in the summer of 1994, a conflict was roiling the waters of the Bay of Biscay.[1] It pitted Spanish fishermen against their French and British competitors over fishing rights, with environmental issues and questions of national sovereignty in the background. As *The European* described it:

> Spanish tuna fishermen sailed home . . . after a two-day battle with their French counterparts some 700 km. off Spain's northwestern coast of Galicia. The Spanish brought back a captured boat [the *Gabrielle*] they claim will support allegations that the French violate fishing quotas and methods.[2]

The conflict was one that was becoming familiar in these days of depleted stocks of Atlantic fish: The Spanish *boniteros* (tuna men) accused the French of using nets bigger than those permitted by European Union (EU) regulations, the French insisted that their nets were legal, and environmentalists wrung their hands at the growing threat to the world's oceans. In Paris the government demanded the restitution of the *Gabrielle* and sent its navy to capture a Spanish ship and tow it to a French port.[3] As the ships of the two nations maneuvered dangerously on troubled waters, a war of words heated up between their capitals. In Madrid the government—tongue in cheek—wrung its hands at its uncontrollable fishermen and protested the state piracy carried out by the French.

Whatever its legal basis, the French maneuver seemed to work. In Galicia the *boniteros* who had made off with the *Gabrielle* were convinced by their authorities to return it, and in Brussels Spain's agriculture and fisheries minister met with his French counterpart, who agreed that EU inspectors would henceforth be allowed to check French nets.[4] By the end of the month the French had agreed to limit the length of their nets to the 2.5 km. set down in the European Commission's regulations. The tuna war seemed to be over.[5]

But now a new storm blew up over the Bay of Biscay. Not trusting their government's willingness to defend their interests, an armada of *boniteros* blockaded the ferries of the Cantabrian coast, and—just for good measure— they blocked the French port of Hendaye, too.[6] In early August they were back on the high seas, this time hacking off the nets of two British boats and an Irish boat with their propellers. Like the French boats, the British and the Irish ones were accused of using nets that were longer than the EU's statutory limit of 2.5 km.[7] (With typical British phlegm, Whitehall claimed that *their* nets were environmentally friendly: Though longer than 2.5 km. limit set by the EU, they made up for it with huge holes designed to let the dolphin through while the apparently less intelligent tuna were caught.)[8]

At this point the environmental organization Greenpeace jumped into the fray, sending a ship to inspect the British and French nets. The French—who have had a long and violent relationship with this transnational movement— attacked its vessel with water cannon and a stun grenade, accusing it of attempting to cut the nets of French trawlers. The Greenpeace activists denied it, claiming that they were only trying to record whether the French ships were taking endangered species, such as dolphins.

Six months later Spanish fishermen were back in the news, fishing for halibut across the Atlantic outside Canada's self-declared 200-mile limit. The Canadians had called for a ban on fishing off the Grand Banks to allow badly depleted fish stocks to be renewed, but the Spanish paid them no heed. Finding a Spanish vessel just outside the 200-mile limit, the Canadian navy seized it, towing it into the harbor of St. John's, to the cheers and rotten tomatoes of the assembled fisherfolk. The Spanish responded by sending warships to the area, and the EU voted to break off all political contacts with Canada and threatened trade sanctions if the Canadians did not desist.[9]

Given coverage in the national media of Canada, Spain, France, and Britain, the story of the tuna wars was redolent with folkloric images of sputtering French officials, archaic Spanish ships, tight-lipped British sailors, and jeering "Fundy" fishermen. But beneath the folkloric surface of the tuna war, serious issues were at stake: the preservation of dwindling sea stocks, the protection of a Spanish industry that directly or indirectly employs 800,000 people, the power of a supranational institution—the European Commission—

to interfere in people's lives, and the apparent helplessness of national governments to protect their own nationals.

Globalization and Social Movements

For students of collective action and social movements, episodes like the one just described raise important questions. On the one hand, the tale is reminiscent of the great tradition of social movements in the West in its repertoires, in the role of preexisting social networks, and in the targeting of institutions:

1. Though the site of the conflict was the high seas, the Spanish sailors used a well-known tactic from the modern repertoire of contention—sequestering another social actor to force action to be taken to accomodate their claims.

2. Like the narratives of most social movements, the story involved previously organized networks of social actors within professional and territorial categories—"catnets," in Charles Tilly's words (1978c).

3. The Spanish used the strategy of targeting political institutions to advance their claims against other social actors. At least since the rising parliamentarization of protest in Britain in the late eighteenth century, states have been the central fulcrums of collective action, even when claim makers were making demands against other social actors (Tilly 1995b, ch. 2).

But alongside these tried and true artifacts of social movement theory, there is a new and disconcerting aspect to episodes like the tuna war: The conflict between private citizens of the four countries crossed national boundaries and was triggered by the acts of an international institution. Not only that: The struggle was also a *performance*—albeit an unusual one—for the benefit of an international audience. It was an example of what some observers think is becoming a fixture of collective action as the world approaches the year 2000: *transnational collective action*.[10]

But there is a puzzle in the relationships described in the story: Although collective action crossed national lines, it was mainly *domestic* actors and *national* associations that began the cycle of conflict and national *states* whose efforts were needed to end it. Although the conflict was resolved in the framework of the EU, it was the Spanish, French, and British governments agreeing to allow EU inspectors onto their boats that accomplished the resolution. Transnational movements? Or the extension into transnational public space of actions triggered by national collective actors?

Whatever the meaning of events like these, students of social movements have become increasingly aware of them. This is no mere scholarly enthusiasm: On the outcome of the debate hinges more than a new wrinkle in the history of collective action and international relations theory. If transnational movements are taking shape, they challenge the continued autonomy, sovereignty, and control by the national state over its own territory and the potential of citizens to construct fields of action outside their political communities. It is toward contributing to this debate and toward bringing together the usually distinct perspectives of social movement and international relations theories that this chapter is aimed.

Globalizing Conflict

What are the forces that support the thesis of transnational collective action? The first part of this thesis relates to the globalization of the world economy and its attendant system of global communications, the second has to do with the possibilities that these changes open up for transnational collective action; the third addresses the possibility that—knit together by international institutions and transnational social movements—something resembling a global civil society is developing.

The Sources of Globalization

In the popular version of the theory of transnational social movements, sometime around the end of World War II a global economy began to develop, assisted by the liberalization of international trade and the appearance of a new economic hegemony. Its most basic aspect, wrote Kevin Robins, was a shift to a world "in which all aspects of the economy—raw materials, labour information and transportation, finances, distribution, marketing—are integrated or interdependent on a global scale." Moreover, "they are so on an almost instantaneous basis . . . The forces of globalization thereby tend to erode the integrity and autonomy of national economies" (1995, 345).

Robins's insistence on the "instantaneous" expression of integration and interdependence takes us to the second element of the thesis: the appearance of global communications structures that weave core and periphery of the world system closer together. Decentralized and private communications technologies accelerate this growth, providing individuals and groups with independent means of communication (Frederick 1993; Ganley 1992).

The result of this growth in worldwide economics and global communications is that citizens of the north and west have been brought closer to those of the east and south, making the former more cosmopolitan and the latter more aware of their inequality. The most spectacular expression of this cognitive and physical integration is the widespread immigration from the east and south to the west and north, with the consequence that global cities have developed into microcosms "in which to observe the growing dualism between the world's rich and poor and the encounter of global cultures" (Robins 1995, 345; Castells 1994). But it has also made it possible for Western environmentalists and human rights advocates to speak the same language and to work toward the same goals as their counterparts in the Third World.

These structural changes have a cultural concomitant: that we live in a culturally more unified universe, one in which young people dress the same, ride the same skateboards, play the same computer games, and listen to the same rock music. One result is to "destroy the cultural isolation in which misunderstanding ferments but, often at the same time, intensifies perceptions of difference that increase social antagonisms and promote social fragmentation" (O'Neil 1993, 68). Another is to create perceived chains of economic and social impact between different parts of the globe. And this takes us to the second part of the thesis: transnational collective action.

Transnational Collective Action

In his summary of the rapidly burgeoning literature on the effects of globalization, Robins claims only that it tends to erode the boundaries of national *economies,* but others have seen it eroding the power of the national state too. In the age of globalization, the thesis continues, it is not only images of contentious politics that are transmitted instantaneously from country to country; so are people and their conflicts. Cheap airline tickets and porous national boundaries make it possible for movement missionaries and their potential followers to diffuse movements as diverse as environmentalism and Muslim fundamentalism around the world.

Partly in response to global economic trends since World War II, international organizations and institutions have proliferated. Many—like the World Bank—have become targets for social movement protest (Kowalewski 1989; Walton 1989). Others—like the European Union—are also targeted, but in addition they deliberately encourage nongovernmental groups with subsidies and opportunities to attend conferences, and they offer information and advice (Mazey and Richardson 1993a, 1993b; Dalton 1994). As a result a host of nongovernmental organizations have clustered around them (Smith 1994, 419). Like the national state that grew in the nineteenth century, international institutions provide new and alternative opportunities for collective action to a host of social actors, but these are opportunities for action at a higher level. This takes us to the strong thesis of transnational social movements.

Transnational Social Movements: The Strong Thesis

The thesis of transnational social movements, which I have aggregated from a number of sources, has four general characteristics.

First, in the age of global television, whirring fax machines, and electronic mail, the national political opportunity structures that used to be needed to mount collective action may be giving way to transnational structures (Pagnucco and Atwood 1994, 411).[11] When insurgency mounted in central Europe in 1989, it was not primarily because local opportunities were opening up. It succeeded largely because an international regime—the Helsinki Accords (Thomas 1997)—offered a framework of opportunities for activism and because Mikhail Gorbachev signaled to the ruling Communist Parties of the region that they could no longer depend on the Red Army to defend them (Bunce 1991). The growth of political opportunities outside the national state is the first reason for the expansion of transnational collective action.

Second, the strong thesis holds that the national state—incubator and fulcrum of social movements in the past—may no longer be able to constrain social movements the way it used to. In part this is because of the declining capacity of governments to disguise what is going on from their own citizens. But in part it is because the integration of the international economy weakens states' capacity to cope with global economic trends. As determined a scholar of state building as Charles Tilly could write in 1991: "The increasing fluidity of capital, labor, commodities, money and cultural practices undermines the capacity of any particular state to control events within its boundaries" (1).

Third, as the capacity of the state to control global economic forces declines, individuals and groups have gained access to new kinds of resources to mount collective action (Rosenau 1990). Where electronic communication becomes a means for the propagation of movement information, there is a low-risk empowerment of passive people all over the world—what we may call "easy riding on the Internet." And where international organizations and institutions share responsibility for certain policy areas with national and subnational authorities, movement entrepreneurs can engage in "venue shopping"—choosing the level in a "layered structure" that provides them with the greatest opportunities and imposes the least constraints.[12]

Fourth, the furthest extension of the thesis holds that, rising from the growth of a global economy and its attendant communications revolution, wound around the latticework of international organizations and institutions, and powered by transnational social movements, something resembling a transnational civil society may be developing (Frederick 1993; O'Neil 1993). According to one version of this thesis:

> Movements are changing from fairly coherent national organizations into transnational networks, with highly fragmented and specialized nodes composed of organizations and less organized mobilizations, all of which are linked through new technologies of communication. (Garner 1994, 431)

The Weakness of the Strong Thesis

This thesis is bold and exciting but problematic. To begin with, few of its advocates employ a rigorous or consistent definition of social movements. If we define all forms of transnational nongovernmental activity as social movement activity, then of course we will find much evidence of it in the world today. But if "social movement" is used to signify sustained sequences of collective action mounted by organized collective actors in interaction with elites, authorities, and other actors in the name of their claims or the claims of those they represent,[13] then the structural and cultural conditions associated with globalization may not be sufficient on their own to produce transnational social movements.

Second, many of the properties that advocates of the thesis associate with the global economy of the 1990s predate it—in some cases by a century or more. In the first place, although the world economy has become increasingly integrated in recent decades, the phenomenon of economic integration itself is hardly new. In the last quarter of the nineteenth century, the telegraph linked Europe, the Americas, and Europe's overseas colonies with instant communications, and long-distance transportation became available to many (Hobsbawm 1987, 13). Railroads were both reducing space and exploding traditional notions of time long before cheap air travel, fax machines, and television were knitting people together in a global village.[14]

In the second place, even before the age of empire social movements in very similar forms and with similar goals were diffused across boundaries through word of mouth, immigration, proselytism, and transnational movement organizations. Antislavery—perhaps the first successful modern transnational movement—began in Britain in the late eighteenth century and spread in the early nineteenth through the unlikely combination of movement missionaries, colonial administrators, and the British navy (Sikkink 1995; Drescher 1987).

Lessons from Social Movement Theory

These historical examples are reinforced by what the past three decades of social movement research have taught us about the conditions in which social movements form. That is, it is not only when the macrostructural or cultural conditions are conducive to mobilization but also where indigenous resources and opportunities come together that interests and incentives turn into concerted collective action. In particular, research has shown that movements take root among preexisting social networks in which relations of trust, reciprocity, and cultural learning are stored and out of which collective identities are shaped.[15]

This is the thesis that Charles Tilly developed when he placed "organization" in a triangular relationship with interest and collective action in his "mobilization model" (1978c, 57). In examining the kinds of groups that are likely to mobilize, he paid attention both to the *categories* of people who recognize their common characteristics and to *networks* of people who are more linked to each other by a specific interpersonal bond than by a formal organization (62). The resulting idea of "catnets," which Tilly adopts from Harrison White (n.d.), stresses a group's inclusiveness as "the main aspect of group structure which affects the ability to mobilize" (Tilly 1978c, 64). Doug McAdam advanced a similar idea when he showed how the recruitment of Freedom Summer volunteers grew out of their participation in preexisting social networks (1988a). Social networks provide the interpersonal trust, the collective identities, and the social communication of political opportunities that are needed to galvanize individuals into collective action and to coordinate it into a social movement.

The importance of interpersonal networks in movement mobilization has obvious implications for the "strong" version of the transnational thesis. Objective conditions like economic interdependence, north–south relative deprivation, immigration, and a global media community may produce the structural and cultural preconditions for the appearance of similar movements in a variety of countries. But even with such structural preconditions, the transaction costs of linking the indigenous groups of a variety of countries into integrated transnational networks would be difficult for any social movement to overcome.

Contemporary Cautions

When we turn to contemporary movements, especially in the Third World, there are three additional reasons to be cautious about the strong transnational movement thesis.

1. Not all prospective movements have the resources to respond to transnational forces with proportional activism. Consider the labor movement. Even in Western Europe, where the EU encourages transnational cooperation, organized labor has not been able to match the rate of multinational business growth with cooperation across national boundaries.[16]

2. Depending on movement organizations from advanced industrial countries is not the best way for activists in the South to build sustained social movements. For one thing, their links with international activists are often fragile or intermittent (Macdonald, n.d.). Like the Greenpeace activists in the tuna war, the international activists can go home to warm hearths while the local activists are left to fend for themselves.

3. Global communications can be dangerously deceptive tools for social movements to depend upon too. Recall how double edged dependence on the media was for the antiwar movement in the United States in the 1960s (Gitlin 1980). The media allowed the movement to grow more rapidly than it could have if it had depended only on its own organizational fabric, but dependency on the media left it without the incentive to build permanent organizations when—as soon occurred—the media chose to transmit less-favorable images of the movement. For all these reasons, we should seek a more cautious and more differentiated model of transnational activism than the sweeping model of transnational social movements.

A Typology of Transnational Interactions

I do not wish to argue that there are no important forms of transnational collective action linked to the globalization of the world economy and fed by the communications revolution. For example, where institutions like the EU link social actors across boundaries and produce incentives to collective action, transnational social movements may be developing (Imig and Tarrow 1996, 1997). But many of the phenomena often catalogued as *structurally transnational* are really cases of transnational diffusion; others are more profoundly transnational but are less sustained, less unified, and less integrated into grassroots social networks than are true social movements; and still others—though they may be domestically integrated—are temporary mechanisms of transnational political exchange between pairs of domestic political actors in different countries. This is why a more differentiated version of the transnational collective action thesis is a more promising route for research and theory.

Let us begin with two of the dimensions that have emerged from the dis-

Figure 15.1 A Typology of Transnational Collective Action

| | | Integration in Domestic Social Networks | |
		Nonintegrated	Integrated
Time Frame	Temporary	Cross-border diffusion	Political exchange
	Sustained	Transnational issue networks	Transnational social movements

cussion above: first, the degree to which a transnational interaction is either temporary or sustained; and second, the extent to which transnational actors are integrated within indigenous social networks. The intersection of these two dimensions produces the fourfold typology of transnational collective action illustrated in Figure 15.1.

Temporary Transnationalism I: Cross-Border Diffusion

Most of the examples we have of transnational collective action are cases of the diffusion either of specific forms of collective action or of entire movements from one country to others. This is perhaps the oldest form of transnational politics. We see it in the movements of Protestant "saints" in the Reformation and in the diffusion of the French Revolution—albeit on French bayonets. By the nineteenth century social movements were less dependent on the movement of missionaries or arms. Research on the 1848 revolutions has shown how particular forms of collective action—like the barricade and the mass demonstration—were adopted in virtually every country touched by these upheavals (Godechot 1971; Tarrow 1998). With more long-term results, by the second half of the century, eastern European immigrants were building workers' movements in the New World, from the Lower East Side of Manhattan to Chile and Argentina.[17] But once established, each national movement struck indigenous roots—drew upon already existing indigenous roots—and became largely independent of the others. The most impressive exception, the Second Socialist International, was also the most colossal failure when, in 1914, virtually every European Socialist Party broke ranks to support their national governments' war efforts.

Contemporary collective action may be diffused more rapidly than these nineteenth-century movements, but it follows similar trajectories and intersections with domestic networks and cultures. Consider the Chinese students who organized a resistance movement in June 1989 so massive that it took an army to suppress them. On radio and television, through fax and videotape players, they had learned of the collapse of communism in eastern

Europe. If dissidents in Budapest could overthrow a regime by celebrating a reburial, why could Chinese students not do the same thing following the death of Hu Yaobang? Even the symbols they used, like the Goddess of Democracy that was rolled out onto Tiananmen Square, was designed, in part, to appeal to a global media market (Tarrow 1998).

But this would not have occurred if there had been no purely domestic sources and no opportunities to fuel the Chinese students' rebellion. On the contrary: Not only were their grievances rooted in the Chinese university system and in the tradition of Chinese political theater, but the reform of the Chinese state and economy had eroded the mechanisms of social control that traditionally kept student rebellion in check. What is certainly true, however, is that the transnational media signaled to the Chinese students the opportunity to use forms of collective action that were succeeding elsewhere and gave them the chance to communicate their claims to an international audience.

Temporary Transnationalism II: Political Exchange

Like transnational diffusion, political exchange across boundaries generally involves actors from different countries with ideological affinities, each of whom has something to gain from the relationship and offers something to the other. Needless to say, "gains" and "losses" should not be interpreted narrowly and materially. For example, whereas Brazilian rubber tappers about to lose their land desperately needed material support, the North American environmentalists who came to their assistance in the late 1980s had purposive and ideological incentives to do so.

These ideological convergences are not permanent arrangements. Although the groups involved have ideological affinities with one another, their alliance is generally organized around a specific issue or campaign; when that issue is resolved or the campaign ends, the alliance becomes latent but the national groups remain. Why? Because each national group has its own indigenous constituencies and continuing incentives for collective action within their national settings. Their existence does not depend on their transnational relationship. But because cooperation is issue based and is not lodged in a permanent organization, transnational political exchange is hardly more stable than the diffusion of collective action across national boundaries.

Sustained Transnationalism I: Transnational Issue Networks

But what, it may be objected, of the hundreds of transnational nongovernmental associations that link citizens across the world in environmental, human rights, women's, peace, and indigenous people's groups? The term "movement" is often attached to these linkages, but it seems more accurate to classify them, with Margaret Keck and Kathryn Sikkink (1995, 1998), as "transnational issue networks":

> A transnational issue network includes the set of relevant actors working internationally on an issue who are bound together by shared values, a common discourse, and dense exchanges of information and services. Such networks are most prevalent in issue areas characterized by high value content and informational uncertainty. They involve actors from non-governmental, governmental and intergovernmental organizations, and are increasingly present in such issue areas as human rights, women's rights, and the environment. (Keck and Sikkink 1998, 2)

How do these networks differ from true social movements and why are they often confused with movements? Part of the confusion results from two different uses of the term "network": for issue networks and for social networks. Though some scholars are coming to believe that cyberspace provides the resources for networks to form across wide distances (Frederick 1993), there would seem to be a clear difference between Keck's and Sikkink's concept of *issue* networks and the interpersonal *social* networks that social movement researchers have detected at the foundation of domestic social movements.[18]

Keck's and Sikkink's issue networks are primarily discursive in content, "distinguishable largely by the centrality of principled ideas or values in motivating their formation," and "at the core of the relationship [among their components] is information exchange." "They mobilize information strategically so as to gain leverage over much more powerful organizations and governments" (Keck and Sikkink 1995, 1). Issue networks lack the categorical basis, the continual interpersonal relations, and the exposure to similar opportunities and constraints that social movement scholars have found in domestic social networks. They are closer to the "epistemic communities" detected by students of international relations and the policy networks studied by specialists in U.S. politics than to sustained social movements.

Sustained Transnationalism II: True Transnational Social Movements

These remarks are not meant to deny that there are such phenomena as transnational social movement organizations. We saw an example of one of the most successful of them—Greenpeace—in the tuna war mentioned at the outset of this discussion. The European and U.S. peace movement of the

1980s was a second such phenomenon. Islamic fundamentalism is a third. But it is hard to find, combined in the same movement, the conditions necessary to produce a social movement that is, at once, integrated within several societies, unified in its goals, and capable of sustained interaction with a variety of political authorities.

Greenpeace developed out of a congeries of domestic movements that were similarly motivated and had a few highly visible targets, such as companies that engaged in oceanic pollution or states that threatened the planet with nuclear testing. Similarly, the peace movement of the 1980s grew out of an international issue that had produced an unusual degree of transnational consensus against the policies of a U.S. president who appeared to be threatening the planet with his administration's arms buildup. And Islamic fundamentalism is rooted in one of the oldest transnational institutions in the world, with domestic networks of religious schools and mosques in which to root itself. These were special conditions that provided activists with unusual opportunities and incentives for integrated mobilization and sustained contentious politics in a number of different opportunity structures. But they are not reproduced each time a transnational interaction occurs among nongovernmental actors.

Was the collapse of communism in eastern Europe in 1989 not a transnational movement? Certainly its near simultaneity in many countries indicates that organized collective actors were taking sustained action against similar regimes in the name of similar sets of goals. Aided by the Human Rights protocol in the Helsinki Accords, some of the dissidents had developed ties across national borders in the preceding years (Thomas 1997). But the phenomenon was more a case of rapid cross-border diffusion based in part on the development of a transnational issue network than an integrated social movement. Its simultaneity and the similar forms it took owed as much to the uniformity of the Stalinist regimes in eastern Europe and their integration in an empire as it did to the mutual contacts and collective action frames developed by its activists. Transnational state socialist regimes with a single center of power in Moscow or elsewhere are not likely to appear very often.

Is There a Transnational Dynamic?

That there are many transnational cases of diffusion, political exchange, issue networks, and movements growing out of the globalization of the world economy and the thickening of transnational ties should be obvious from the wealth of examples presented above. But before concluding that a transnational civil

society is being constructed, we need to look more closely at the *kinds* of linkages that are developing across boundaries and whether they are cumulative
and dynamic. For example, the growing web of e-mail networks that are
traversing the world may excite the attention of those with easy access to
computers because of their obvious capacity to reduce transaction costs and
transmit information quickly across national lines, but they do not promise
the same degree of crystallization, of mutual trust and collective identity, as
do the interpersonal ties in social networks. Whether they will produce enduring social movements it is too soon to tell.

The trends that some have seen creating a world of transnational movements are only in their infancy and may be cumulative. So I want to close
not with a conclusion but with a few questions that students of transnational
collective action will need to confront about the dynamics of transnational collective action.

First, does the new technology of global communication and cheap international travel change the *forms* of movement diffusion or only the speed of
its transmission, compared to the movements of the past? Before concluding
that the world is entering an unprecedented age of global movements, we will
need to look at movements in the past—and this is where comparative historical studies come in. Otherwise, as Pizzorno once wrote: "At every upstart
of a wave of conflict we shall be induced to think that we are at the verge of a
revolution; and when the downswing appears, we shall predict the end of class
conflict" (1978, 291).

Second, can it be said that integrated social movements can span continents in the absence of an integrated interpersonal community at both ends
of the transnational chain? And—an even stronger claim—that such communities can be *created* with resources borrowed from abroad? In the course of
the nineteenth century and most of the twentieth, local social networks were
the essential armature of social movements. Although we have examples of
immigrant chains creating new movements where immigrants arrived, these
movements soon grew roots in their adopted soil and cut themselves off from
their origins in Europe. Those who are convinced of the strong thesis will
need to show that impersonal cyberspace networks or travel between countries can not only stimulate new movements (for example, transnational diffusion) but will also maintain the transnational tie as part of their underlying
social network.[19]

Third, will the new power of international movements lead to benevolent
forms of "people's power," as writers like Michael O'Neil seem to think (1993,
ch. 4)? Or will it lead to the violent forms that Benedict Anderson and others

have seen in the potential of "long-distance nationalism" (1992). It is worth re-
calling that the most powerful global movement of the early 1990s was made
up not of Western environmentalists or human rights activists linked benevo-
lently to indigenous people's movements in the Third World but of radical
Islamic fundamentalists who murdered folk singers and beat up women who
went around unveiled.

Fourth, is there a cumulative dynamic developing from the two weaker
forms just sketched into the two stronger ones? And although it might seem
logical for transnational issue networks to evolve into unified movements,
there is anecdotal evidence that they are to some extent *alternatives* to mobilization; that they are what former movement activists do when their domestic movements have passed their peak *instead of* domestic mobilization.[20]

Finally, what is the role of the national state in all of this? We should re-
member that modern states developed in a strategic dialogue with social
movements, ceding them the autonomy and opportunities to organize when
they had to and when it was useful to do so, and that they reclaimed that territory whenever these movements faded (Piven and Cloward 1993). Why
would states be any more supine when faced by transnational diffusion, exchange issue networks, or even social movements than they were against
domestic movements in the nineteenth century?[21]

States have already evolved transnational strategies and transnational organizations to ferret out the most dangerous sources of international turbulence. And states are encouraging some movements—such as the European
environmental movement—to take their claims to transnational institutions
like the EU (Dalton 1994); at the same time, states inhibit the EU from dealing with others, such as the antinuclear movement. States in the late twentieth century can do more than make war; they can create transnational organizations and institutions to combat and control social movements. If this is
the case, then the national state and the national social movement will be with
us for a long time to come.

Notes

The original version of this paper was first delivered at the Tenth Anniversary Conference of
the Historical Studies Program of the New School for Social Research, March 1995. This
version was first delivered to the Seminar on Social Movements and Social Change in a
Globalizing World, University of Michigan. I am grateful to David Blatt for suggesting the
current title. For comments on one or another of the three versions, I wish to thank Giovanni
Arrighi, David Blatt, Matt Evangelista, Doug Imig, Peter Katzenstein, Michael Kennedy,
Bert Klandermans, Mark Lichbach, Frances Fox Piven, Beverly Silver, Chuck Tilly, Dan
Thomas, Deborah Yashar, and Mayer Zald. I am also grateful to Margaret Keck and Katherine

Sikkink, with whom my exchanges of views have, I hope, sharpened the argument presented here.

1. I draw here upon the narrative of this episode in my "Europeanisation of Conflict: Reflections from a Social Movement Perspective" (1995, 225–28).

2. "Spanish Fishermen Seize French Boat in Tuna War," *The European,* July 22–28, 1994, 6.

3. See "La armada francesa captura un barco de España en repesalia por el conflicto pesquero," *El País,* July 25, 1994, 20, for the Spanish side of the story.

4. Alberta Sbragia points out that the decision to allow EU inspectors to monitor net sizes was an important extension of the European Commission's authority. This politically sensitive step may have been taken because the dispute occurred (and can be expected to recur) outside of the territorial jurisdiction of any one country. I am grateful to Professor Sbragia for her comments on this episode.

5. See "Le conflit entre pêcheurs espagnols et français semble s'apaiser," *Le Monde,* July 22, 1994, 13; "L'accord entre les professionnels de l'île d'Yeu et Jean Puech n'a pas calmé les courroux des pêcheurs espanols," *Le Monde,* July 28, 1994, 17.

6. "Atun contra Europa," *El País,* August 1, 1994, 8; "Des chalutiers espagnols bloquent le port d'Hendaye," *Le Monde,* July 27, 1994, 17.

7. See "Navy Moves In to Stop Tuna War 'wolf packs,'" *London Times,* August 5, 1994, 1; "Los boniteros espanoles rompen redes ilegales a barcos britànicos e irlandeses," *El País,* August 8, 1994, 21.

8. See "Navy Moves In to Stop Tuna War "wolf packs.'"

9. See "Canada Fishing Dispute Grows," *Manchester Guardian Weekly,* March 19, 1995, 1; "Canadians Cut the Nets of Spain Ship," *New York Times,* March 28, 1995, A13; "When They Talk About Fish, the Mellow Canadians Bellow," *New York Times,* March 31, 1995, A11.

10. An introduction to the recent literature on transnational movements would have to begin with Rosenau 1990 and include Anderson 1992; Arrighi 1991; Brysk 1993; Featherstone 1990; Keck and Sikkink 1995, 1998; O'Neil 1993; Pagnucco and Atwood 1994; Pagnucco and Smith 1993; Risse-Kappen and Schmitz 1995; Smith 1994; Thomas 1997; Wapner 1995, 1996; and Yashar 1998.

11. The literature on political opportunity structures has grown too large to summarize easily. For an attempted theoretical synthesis, see chapter 5 of my *Power in Movement* (1998). For an interesting application to the international peace movement, see Pagnucco and Smith 1993.

12. As Bert Klandermans noted, commenting on an earlier version of this paper: "With the increasing number of political layers involved in the definition and implementation of a policy, the choice of one's adversaries becomes less obvious and therefore more a matter of social construction" (1995, 5).

13. This is a synthesis of the definitions proposed by Kriesi et al. 1995; McAdam, McCarthy, and Zald 1996; Tarrow 1998; and Tilly 1995b.

14. Hobsbawm gives one illustration: In 1879, almost 1 million tourists visited Switzerland, 200,000 of them Americans; this is the equivalent of more than one in twenty of the entire U.S. population as of its first census (1987, 14).

15. The most accessible sources on the centrality of social networks to movement mobilization are Emirbayer and Goodwin 1994; Fernandez and McAdam 1989; Gould 1991, 1995b; Jackson 1960; Knoke 1990; McAdam 1982, 1988a, 1988b; Oberschall 1973; Pinard 1971; Rosenthal et al. 1985; and Wellman et al. 1988.

16. See Turner forthcoming. For a more optimistic view of European labor's integrative potential, see Visser and Ebbinghaus 1992.

17. Two classical studies trace the transfer of the eastern European labor movement experience to the United States: Isaac Hourwich's *Immigration and Labor* (1969) and Steven Fraser's *Labor Will Rule* (1991). For the influence of immigrants on the Argentine labor movement, see del Campo 1973; Godio and Palomino 1988. On the immigrant origins of the Chilean movement, see Ansell 1972; Barria Seron 1967.

18. I believe that this is so even though Keck and Sikkink derive their definition of the term "network" from the work of J. Clyde Mitchell, who was writing about domestic networks (1973, 23). Clearly, more clearing of conceptual underbrush needs to be carried out among scholars of social networks and issue networks.

19. There was evidence for interpersonal diffusion in the 1960s when a largely peaceful protest repertoire spread to West Germany from the U.S. New Left. Doug McAdam and Dieter Rucht (1993) saw as agents of this transition a group of West German students who had studied in the United States and carried the message *personally* back to Europe in 1968. But once founded, the West German New Left went off in directions radically different from the movements of the 1960s in the United States.

20. Margaret Keck doubts that the networks that she and Kathryn Sikkink have studied are in the act of producing transnational social movements. Referring to activists in environmental nongovernmental organizations in Brazil in the 1990s, she observes: "These are longtime activists and organizers—people who know what mobilization is about and *that's not what they're doing*" (personal communication to the author, September 8, 1995, quoted with permission [emphasis added]).

21. Needless to say, they may react differently to each, which is one reason that we need to proceed with a more differential analysis than the strong thesis provides. For example, even repressive regimes may respond less repressively to transnational issue networks than they do to transnational movements, since the former are less likely to provide resources to domestic dissident groups.

Bibliography

L' abominable venalité de la presse, d' apres les documents des archives russes (1897–1917).
1931. Paris: Librairie du travail.

Agulhon, Maurice. 1982. *The Republic in the Village: The People of the Var from the French Revolution to the Second Republic.* Translated by Janet Lloyd. New York: Cambridge University Press.

Ahlgren, Gillian T. W. 1995. "Negotiating Sanctity: Holy Women in Sixteenth-Century Spain." *Church History* 64, no. 3: 373–88.

Aitzema, Lieuwe van. 1655–71. *Historie of verhael van saken van staet en oorlogh, in ende omtrent de Vereenigde Nederlanden.* Vols. 18–29 (1638–1649). The Hague: Veely.

Alapuro, R. 1988. *State and Revolution in Finland.* Berkeley: University of California Press.

———. 1994. *Suomen synty paikallisena ilmiönä 1890–1933* (Formation of Finland 1890–1933 in a local perspective). Helsinki: Hanki ja Jää.

Alvarez, Sonia E. 1990. *Engendering Democracy in Brazil.* Princeton: Princeton University Press.

Anderson, Benedict R. O'G. 1992. "Long-Distance Nationalism: World Capitalism and the Rise of Identity Politics." The Wertheim Lecture, Centre for Asian Studies, Amsterdam.

Angstmann, Else. 1928. *Der Henker in der Volksmeinung: Seine Namen und sein Vorkommen in der mündlichen Volksüberlieferung.* Bonn: Fritz Klopp Verlag.

Ansell, Alan. 1972. *Politics and the Labour Movement in Chile.* New York and Oxford: Oxford University Press.

Apolito, Paolo. 1990. *"Dice che hanno visto la Madonna": Un caso di apparizioni in Campania.* Bologna: Il Mulino.

———. 1992. *Il Cielo in terra: Construzioni simboliche di un'apparizione mariana.* Bologna: Il Mulino.

Arato, Andrew. 1981. "Civil Society against the State: Poland, 1980–81." *Telos* 47 (Spring): 23–47.

Arrighi, Giovanni. 1991. "World Income Inequalities and the Future of Socialism." *New Left Review* 189: 39–65.

Ashworth, W. 1974. "Industrialization and the Economic Integration of Nineteenth Century Europe." *European Studies Review* 4: 291–314.

August, Thomas G. 1985. *The Selling of the Empire: British and French Imperialist Propaganda, 1890–1940.* Westport, Conn.: Greenwood Press.

Axon, William E. A. 1870. *The Black Knight of Ashton.* Manchester, Eng.: John Heywood.

Aya, R. 1990. *Rethinking Revolutions and Collective Violence: Studies on Concept, Theory, and Method.* Amsterdam: Het Spinhuis.

Bächtold-Stäubli, Hanns ed. 1929–30 "Dieb, Diebstahl." In *Handwörterbuch des deutschen Aberglauben,* vol. 2: 229–31. Berlin and Leipzig: Walter de Gruyter Verlag.

Baines, Edward. 1824. *History, Directory, and Gazetteer of the County Palantine of Lancashire.* 2 vols. Liverpool, Eng.: Wm. Wales and Co.

———. [1835.] 1966. *History of the Cotton Manufacture in Great Britain.* London: Frank Cass.

Bakhtin, Mikhail. 1984. *Rabelais and His World.* Translated by Helene Iswolsky. Bloomington: Indiana University Press.

———. 1986. "The Problem of Speech Genres." In *Speech Genres and Other Essays,* by M. M. Bakhtin, 60–102. Austin: University of Texas Press.

———. 1992. "Discourse in the Novel." In *The Dialogic Imagination,* by M. M. Bakhtin, 259–422. Austin: University of Texas Press.

Baldwin, Leland. 1939. *Whiskey Rebels: The Story of a Frontier Uprising.* Pittsburgh, Pa.: University of Pittsburgh Press.

Bamford, Samuel [1841] 1967. *The Autobiography of Samuel Bamford.* 2 vols. Edited with an Introduction by W. H. Chaloner. London: Frank Cass.

Barkey, Karen. 1994. *Bandits and Bureaucrats: The Ottoman Route to State Centralization.* Ithaca, N.Y.: Cornell University Press.

Barkin, Kenneth. 1970. "A Case Study in Comparative History: Populism in Germany and America." In *The State of American History,* edited by Herbert Bass, 374–404. Chicago: Quadrangle.

Barria Seron, Jorge. 1967. *Breve historia del sindicalismo chileno.* Santiago: INSORA.

Bart, Jean. 1996. *La Révolution française en Bourgogne.* Clermont-Ferrand.

Bartlett, David L. 1995. "Losing the Political Initiative: The Impact of Financial Liberalization in Hungary." In *The Waning of the Communist State: Economic Origins of Political Decline in China and Hungary,* edited by Andrew G. Walder, 114–50. Berkeley: University of California Press.

Bax, Mart. 1995. *Medjugorje: Religion, Politics, and Violence in Rural Bosnia.* Amsterdam: VU Uitgeverij.

Bearak, Barry. 1989. "Visions of Holiness in Lubbock: Divine or Imagined?" *Los Angeles Times,* April 9, pp. 1, 36–38, 40.

Bearman, Peter S. 1994. *Relations into Rhetorics: Local Elite Social Structure in Norfolk, England, 1540–1640.* New Brunswick, N.J.: Rutgers University Press.

Bechhofer, Frank, and Brian Elliott, eds. 1981. *The Petite Bourgeoisie: Comparative Studies of the Uneasy Stratum.* London: Macmillan.

Becqué, Emile. 1912. *L'internationalisation des capitaux.* Montpellier: Imprimerie générale du Midi.

Belmont, Nicole. 1981. "Fonction de la derision et symbolisme du bruit dans le charivari." In *Le Charivari,* edited by Jacques Le Goff and Jean-Claude Schmitt, 15–22. Paris: Ecole des Hautes Etudes en Sciences Sociales.

Benford, Robert D., and Scott A. Hunt. 1992. "Dramaturgy and Social Movements: The Social Construction and Communication of Power," *Sociological Inquiry* 62: 35–55.

Bernhardt, Kathryn. 1992. *Rents, Taxes, and Peasant Resistance: The Lower Yangzi Region, 1840–1950.* Stanford, Calif.: Stanford University Press.

Bianco, Lucien. 1986. "Peasant Movements," In *Cambridge History of China,* edited by John Fairbank and Albert Feuerwerker, vol. 13: 270–328. Cambridge: Cambridge University Press.

Bielby, William T., and James N. Baron. 1986. "Men and Women at Work: Sex Segregation and Statistical Discrimination." *American Journal of Sociology* 91, no. 1 (January): 781.

Bilinkoff, Jodi. 1992. "A Spanish Prophetess and Her Patrons: The Case of María de Santo Domingo." *Sixteenth Century Journal* 23: 17–30.

Birnbaum, Pierre. 1979. *Collective Action and the State*. Cambridge: Cambridge University Press.

Blackbourn, David. 1984. "Between Resignation and Volatility: The German Petite Bourgeoisie in the Nineteenth Century." In *Shopkeepers and Master Artisans in Nineteenth Century Europe,* edited by Geoffrey Crossick and Heinz-Gerhard Haupt, 35–61. London: Methuen.

———. 1993. *Marpingen: Apparitions of the Virgin Mary in Bismarckian Germany*. Oxford: Clarendon Press.

Blázquez Miguel, Juan. 1987. *Sueños y procesos de Lucrecia de León*. Madrid: Tecnos.

Blécourt, A. S. de. 1935. *Oldambt en de Ommelanden*. Assen, Netherlands: Van Gorcum.

Blewett, Mary. 1992. "Traditions and Customs of Lancashire Popular Radicalism in Late Nineteenth-Century America." *International Labor and Working Class History* 42: 5–19.

———. 1993. "Deference and Defiance: Labor Politics and the Meanings of Masculinity in the Mid-Nineteenth-Century New England Textile Industry." *Gender and History* 5: 398–415.

Blickle, Peter. 1973. *Landschaften im Alten Reich*. Munich: Beck.

———. 1989. *Studien zur geschichtlichen Bedeutung des deutschen Bauernstandes*. Stuttgart: Gustav Fischer.

Blok, Anton. 1995. *De Bokkerijders: Roversbenden en geheime genootschappen in de Landen van Overmaas, 1730–1778*. Rev. ed. Amsterdam: Bert Bakker/Prometheus.

Boezee, Frank. 1991. "Militancy and Pragmatism: An International Perspective on Maritime Labour, 1870–1914." *International Review of Social History* 36: 165–200.

Bohstedt, John. 1983. *Riots and Community Politics in England and Wales, 1790–1810*. Cambridge: Harvard University Press.

———. 1988. "Gender, Household, and Community Politics: Women in English Riots, 1790–1810." *Past and Present* 120: 88–123.

Bonachea, Rolando E. and Nelson P. Valdés, eds. 1972. *Revolutionary Struggle (1947–1958)*. Vol. I of *Selected Works of Fidel Castro*. Cambridge: MIT Press.

Bos, P. G. 1904. *Het Groningsche Gild- en Stapelrecht tot de Reductie in 1594*. Groningen, Netherlands: Wolters.

Bowman, Winifred M. 1960. *England in Ashton-under-Lyne*. London: John Sherratt and Son.

Brackenridge, Henry M. 1859. *History of the Western Insurrection in Pennsylvania*. Pittsburgh, Pa.: W. S. Haven.

———. [1796] 1972. *Incidents of the Insurrection*. Edited by Daniel Marder. Pittsburgh, Pa.: University of Pittsburgh Press.

Braude, Ann. 1989. *Radical Spirits: Spiritualism and Women's Rights in Nineteenth-Century America*. Boston: Beacon Press.

Braudel, Fernand. 1973. *The Mediterranean and the Mediterranean World in the Age of Philip II*. 2 vols. Translated by Sian Reynolds. New York: Harper and Row.

Brazil. 1995. *Tribunal Superior Eleitoral*. Brasilia: Tribunal Superior Eleitoral.

Bristol, Michael D. 1985. *Carnival and Theater: Plebeian Culture and the Structure of Authority in Renaissance England*. New York: Methuen.

Brødsgaard, Kjeld Erik. 1992. "Civil Society and Democratization in China." In *From Leninism to Freedom,* edited by Margaret L. Nugent, 231–57. Boulder, Colo.: Westview.

Brovkin, Vladimir. 1990. "Revolution from Below: Informal Political Association in Russia, 1988–1989." *Soviet Studies* 42 (April): 233–57.

Brubaker, Rogers. 1993. "East European, Soviet, and Post-Soviet Nationalisms: A Framework for Analysis." *Research on Democracy and Society* 1: 353–78.

Bruszt, László. 1991. "The Negotiated Revolution in Hungary." *Social Research* 57: 365–87.

Brysk, Alison. 1993. "Acting Globally: Indian Rights and International Politics in Latin America." In *Indigenous Peoples and Democracy in Latin America,* edited by D. L. Van Cott, 29–51. New York: St. Martin's Press.

Buechler, Steven M. 1993. "Beyond Resource Mobilization? Emerging Trends in Social Movement Theory." *Sociological Quarterly* 34: 217–35.

Bunce, Valerie. 1991. "Democracy, Stalinism, and the Management of Uncertainty." In *Democracy and Political Transformation,* edited by G. Szoboszlai, 138–64. Budapest: Hungarian Political Science Association.

Burguera y Serrano, Amado de Cristo. 1934. *Los Hechos de Ezquioga ante la razón y la fe.* Valladolid, Mexico: Imprenta y Librería Casa Martín.

Burke, Peter. 1978. *Popular Culture in Early Modern Europe.* New York: Harper and Row.

Bushaway, Bob. 1982. *By Rite: Ceremony and Custom in England, 1700–1880.* London: Junction.

Butterworth, Edwin. 1842. *An Historical Account of the Towns of Ashton-under-Lyne, Staly-bridge, and Dukinfield.* Ashton, Eng.: A. Phillips.

Caballero, J. 1972. "Corazón de Jesús." *Diccionario de historia ecclesiástica de España* 1: 612–14.

Cadoret-Abeles, Anne. 1981. "Les apparitions du Palmar de Troya: Analyse antropologique d'un phénomène religieux." *Mélanges de la Casa de Velazquez* 17: 369–91.

Caestecker, Frank. 1994. "Alien Policy in Belgium, 1830–1940: The Creation of Guest Workers, Refugees, and Illegal Immigrants." 2 vols. Ph.D. diss., European University Institute.

Calhoun, C. 1983. "Industrialization and Social Radicalism: British and French Workers' Movements and the Mid-Nineteenth-Century Crises." *Theory and Society* 12: 485–504.

———. 1991. "The Problem of Identity in Collective Action." In *Macro-Micro Linkages in Sociology,* edited by Joan Huber. Newbury Park, Calif.: Sage.

———. 1993a. "Nationalism and Ethnicity." *Annual Review of Sociology* 19: 211–39.

———. 1993b. "'New Social Movements' of the Early Nineteenth Century." *Social Science History* 17: 385–428.

Cambon, Victor. 1914. *Les derniers progres de l'Allemagne.* Paris: P. Roger.

Carr, E. H. 1946. *The Twenty Years' Crisis: 1919–1939.* 2nd ed. London: Macmillan.

Carroll, E. Malcolm. 1939. *Germany and the Great Powers, 1866–1914.* New York: Prentice-Hall.

Castells, Manuel. 1994. "European Cities, the Informational Society, and the Global Economy." *New Left Review* 204: 18–32.

Catling, Harold. 1970. *The Spinning Mule.* Newton Abbot, Eng.: David and Charles.

Chambure, A. de. 1914. *A Travers la Presse.* 5th ed. Paris: T. Fert, Albony, et cie.

Chickering, Roger. 1975. *Imperial Germany and a World without War: The Peace Movement and German Society, 1892–1916.* Princeton: Princeton University Press.

———. 1984. *We Men Who Feel Most German: A Cultural Study of the Pan-German League, 1886–1914.* Boston: Allen and Unwin.

Childs, John. 1982. *Armies and Warfare in Europe, 1648–1789.* Manchester, Eng.: Manchester University Press.

Chow, S. R. 1920. *Le contrôle parlementaire de la politigue étrangère en Angleterre, en France, et au Etats-Unis.* Paris: Sagot.

Christian, William A., Jr. 1984. "Religious Apparitions and the Cold War in Southern Europe." In *Religion, Power, and Protest in Local Communities: The Northern Shore of the Mediterranean,* edited by Eric R. Wolf, 239–66. Berlin: Mouton.

———. 1989. "Francisco Martínez quiere ser santero: Nuevas imágenes milagrosas y su control en la España del siglo XVIII." *El Folklore Andaluz* 4: 103–14.

———. 1990a. *Apariciones en Castilla y Cataluña (siglos XIV–XVI)*. Translated by Eloy Fuente. Madrid: Nerea.

———. 1990b. "The Delimitation of Sacred Space and the Visions of Ezquioga, 1931–1987." In *Luoghi sacri e spazi della santità*, edited by Sofia Boesch Gajano and Lucetta Scaraffia, 85–103. Turin, Italy: Rosenberg and Sellier.

———. 1991. *Religiosidad local en la España de Felipe II*. Translated by Javier Calzada and José Luis Gil Aristu. Madrid: Nerea.

———. 1992. *Moving Crucifixes in Modern Spain*. Princeton: Princeton University Press.

———. 1996. *Visionaries: The Spanish Republic and the Reign of Christ*. Berkeley: University of California Press.

Clark, Anna. 1992. "The Rhetoric of Chartist Domesticity: Gender, Language, and Class in the 1830s and 1840s." *Journal of British Studies* 31: 62–88.

———. 1995. *The Battle for the Breeches: The Making of the British Working Class, 1780–1850*. Berkeley: University of California Press.

Class, Heinrich. 1932. *Wider den Strom: Vom Werden und Wachsen der nationalen Opposition im alten Reich*. Leipzig, Germany: Koehler.

Clegg, H. A., Alan Fox, and A. F. Thompson. 1964. *A History of British Trade Unions since 1889*. Vol. 1. Oxford: Oxford University Press.

Cobb, Richard. 1972. "La bande d'Orgères, 1790–1799." *In Reactions to the French Revolution*, by Richard Cobb, 181–215. London: Oxford University Press.

Cobbett, William. 1829. *The Poor Man's Friend, or Essays on the Rights and Duties of the Poor*. London: Author. Reprinted in 1977, Fairfield, N.J.: Augustus M. Kelley.

———. 1933. *The Autobiography of William Cobbett: The Progress of a Plough-boy to a Seat in Parliament*. Edited by William Reitzel. London: Faber and Faber.

———. [1830] 1967. *Rural Rides*. Edited by George Woodcock. Harmondsworth, Eng.: Penguin.

Cohen, Jean L. 1985. "Strategy or Identity: New Theoretical Paradigms and Contemporary Social Movements." *Social Research* 52, no. 4: 663–716.

Cohen, Jean L., and Andrew Arato. 1992. *Civil Society and Political Theory*. Cambridge: MIT Press.

Cohen, Sande. 1988. *Historical Culture: On the Recoding of an Academic Discipline*. Berkeley: University of California Press.

Colley, Linda. 1992. *Britons: Forging the Nation, 1707–1837*. New Haven: Yale University Press.

Colombet, Albert. 1936. "Une justice seigneuriale à la fin de l'ancien régime: Vantoux et ses grands jours." *Mémoires de la société pour l'Histoire du Droit et des Institutions des anciens pays bourguignons, comtois, et romands* 3: 195–207.

Comaroff, Jean. 1985. *Body of Power, Spirit of Resistance: The Culture and History of a South African People*. Chicago: University of Chicago Press.

Cooke, Jacob. 1963. "The Whiskey Insurrection: A Re-evaluation." *Pennsylvania History* 30: 316–46.

Cosmos, Georgia. 1992. "The Singing Angels and Prophesying Children: Religious Cultures of Protestants in Southern France after the Revocation of the Edict of Nantes, 1685–1689." Master's thesis, Department of History, La Trobe University, Melbourne.

Cotton, Nicolas. 1977. "Popular Movements in Ashton–under-Lyne and Stalybridge before 1832." M.Litt. thesis in history, University of Birmingham.

Coulthart, John Ross. 1844. *A Report on the Sanitary Condition of the Town of Ashton-under-Lyne; with Remarks on the Existing Evils, and Suggestions for Improving the Health, Comfort, and Longevity of the Inhabitants*. Ashton-under-Lyne, Eng.: Luke Swallow.

Craig, Lee, and Douglas Fisher. 1991. "Integration of the European Business Cycle,

1870–1910." Working paper no. 163, Department of Economics and Business, North Carolina State University.

Creigh, Alfred. 1870. *History of Washington County*. Philadelphia: Everts.

Cresswell, Timothy. 1994. "Putting Women in Their Place: The Carnival at Greenham Common." *Antipode* 26: 35–58.

Crumrine, Boyd. 1882. *History of Washington County, Pennsylvania*. Philadelphia: L. H. Evarts.

Dalton, Russell. 1994. *The Green Rainbow: Environmental Groups in Western Europe*. Princeton: Princeton University Press.

Danckert, Werner. 1963. *Unehrliche leute: Die verfehmten Berufe*. Bern and Munich: Francke Verlag.

Darnton, Robert. 1984. *The Great Cat Massacre and Other Episodes in French Cultural History*. New York: Basic Books.

Daudet, Léon. 1910. "Arthur Jaures et Jean Meyer." In *Une campagne d'action française*, by Léon Daudet 296–300. Paris: Nouvelle librairie nationale.

———. 1913. *L'avant-guerre: Etudes et documents sur l'espionage juif-allemande*. Paris: Nouvelle librarie nationale.

Davis, Natalie Zemon. 1975. *Society and Culture in Early Modern France*. Stanford, Calif.: Stanford University Press.

Davis, Susan G. 1986. *Parades and Power: Street Theatre in Nineteenth-Century Philadelphia*. Philadelphia: Temple University Press.

De Avelar, Sonia. 1987. "Women's Work in Latin America." Report, International Labour Office, Oficina Regional para America Latina y el Caribe, Lima.

———. 1993. "Engendering Development in Latin America?" Paper presented at the Sixth International Forum of the Association for Women in Development/AWID, Washington, D.C.

del Campo, Hugo. 1973. "Los origines del movimiento obrero argentino." *Historia del movimiento obrero* (Buenos Aires: Centro Editor de America Latina) 25.

Diamond, Larry, Juan J. Linz, and Seymour Martin Lipset. 1989. *Democracy in Developing Countries*. Vol. 4: *Latin America*. Boulder, Colo.: Lynne Rienner Publishers.

Dijkstra, C. E. 1974. "De Oldambten tegen de stad . . . een vruchteloze strijd," Groningsche Volksalmanak. *Historisch Jaarboek voor Groningen*, 1974–75: 39–58.

Dinzelbacher, Peter. 1981. *Vision und Visionliteratur um Mittelalter*. Stuttgart: Anton Hiersemann.

Dix, Robert H. 1984. "Why Revolutions Succeed and Fail." *Polity* 16: 423–46.

Dobson, C. R. 1980. *Master and Servant: A Prehistory of Industrial Relations, 1717–1800*. London: Croom Helm.

Doherty, John. 1829. *A Report of the Proceedings of a Delegate Meeting of the Operative Spinners of England, Ireland, and Scotland, Assembled at Ramsey, Isle of Man, on Saturday, December 5, 1829, and Three Following Days*. Manchester, Eng.: M. Wardle.

Domínguez, Jorge I. 1978. *Cuba: Order and Revolution*. Cambridge: Harvard University Press.

Drachkovitch, Milorad M. 1953. *Les socialismes français et allemand et le problème de la guerre, 1870–1914*. Geneva: Droz.

Drescher, Seymour. 1987. *Capitalism and Antislavery: British Mobilization in Comparative Perspective*. Oxford and New York: Oxford University Press.

Duyvendak, Jan Willem. 1995. *The Power of Politics: New Social Movements*. Boulder, Colo.: Westview Press.

Dyck, Ian. 1992. *William Cobbett and Rural Popular Culture*. Cambridge: Cambridge University Press.

———. 1993. "William Cobbett and the Rural Radical Platform." *Social History* 18: 185–204.

Dyson, Kenneth H. F. 1980. *The State Tradition in Western Europe.* Oxford: Oxford University Press.

Edelman, Nicole. 1995.*Voyantes, guérisseuses, et visionnaires en France, 1785–1914.* Paris: Albin Michel.

Elerie, J. N. H., and P. C. M. Hoppenbrouwers, eds. 1991. *Het Oldambt.* Vol. 2, *Nieuwe visies op geschiedenis en actuele problemen.* Groningen, Netherlands: Nederlands-Agronomisch Historisch Instituut.

Emirbayer, Mustafa, and Jeff Goodwin. 1994. "Network Analysis, Culture, and the Problem of Agency." *American Journal of Sociology* 99: 1411–54.

———. 1995. "Symbols, Positions, Objects: Toward a New Theory of Revolutions and Collective Action." Working Paper Series, no. 223, Center for Studies of Social Change, New School for Social Research, New York.

Engels, Friedrich. 1968. "Preface to the American Edition of 1887." In *The Condition of the Working Class in England,* appendix 3. Stanford, Calif.: Stanford University Press.

Epkenhans, Michael. 1991. *Die wilhelminische Flottenrüstung, 1908–1914.* Munich: Oldenbourg.

Epstein, Barbara. 1991. *Political Protest and Cultural Revolution: Nonviolent Direct Action in the 1970s and 1980s.* Berkeley: University of California Press.

Epstein, James. 1990. "The Constitutional Idiom: Radical Reasoning, Rhetoric, and Action in Early Nineteenth Century England." *Journal of Social History* 23: 553–74.

Esherick, Joseph W. 1990. "Xi'an Spring." *The Australian Journal of Chinese Affairs* 24 (July): 209–35.

Esherick, Joseph W., and Jeffrey Wasserstrom. 1990. "Acting Out Democracy: Political Theater in Modern China." *Journal of Asian Studies* 49 (November): 835–65.

Fattorini, Emma. 1994. "In Viaggio dalla Madonna." In *Donne e Fede: Santità e Vita Religiosa in Italia,* edited by Lucetta Scaraffia and Gabriella Zarri, 495–515. Rome and Bari: Laterza.

Featherstone, Mike. 1990. *Global Culture: Nationalism, Globalization, and Modernity.* London and Newbury Park, Calif.: Sage.

Feith, H. O. 1856. *Register van het Archief van Groningen.* Vol. 4. Groningen, Netherlands: Scholtens.

Felkin, William. 1844. *Parliamentary Gazetteer of England and Wales, Adapted to the New Poor-Law. Franchise, Municipal, and Ecclesiastical Arrangements, and Compiled with Special Reference to the Lines of Railroad and Canal Communication, as Existing in 1842–3.* London: A. Fullarton.

Ferguson, Russell. 1938. *Early Western Pennsylvania Politics.* Pittsburgh, Pa.: University of Pittsburgh Press.

Fernandez, Roberto M., and Doug McAdam. 1989. "Multiorganizational Fields and Recruitment to Social Movements." In *International Social Movement Research,* edited by Bert Klandermans, vol. 2: 315–43.

Ferrand, Renaud. 1989. "Le vol dans les églises en Lyonnais et en Beaujolais (1679–1789): Le sacrilège des exclus." *Bulletin du Centre d'Histoire Economique et Sociale de la Région Lyonnaise* 2: 43–76.

Findley, William. 1796. *History of the Insurrection in the Four Western Counties of Pennsylvania.* Philadelphia: Smith.

Firth, Raymond. 1973. *Symbols Public and Private.* London: Allen and Unwin.

Fockema Andreae, S. J. 1904. *Groninger Plakaatboek* Groningen, Netherlands: Noordhoff.

Forberg, Martin. 1987. "Gewerkschaftsbewegung und Arbeitsimmigranten: Agitationsstrategien und Organisierungsversuche der Freien Gewerkschaften in Deutschland 1890–1914." In *Internationale Tagung der Historiker der Arbeiterbewegung: 22 Linz Konferenz 1986,* edited by Gabriella Hauch, 97–104. Vienna: Europa Verlag.

Ford, Caroline. 1990. "Religion and the Politics of Cultural Change in Provincial France: The Resistance of 1902 in Lower Brittany." *Journal of Modern History* 62: 1–33.

Formsma, W. J. 1976. "Staatsinstellingen." In *Historie van Groningen,* edited by W. J. Formsma, 277–92. Groningen, Netherlands: Wolters-Noordhoff.

Fortunet, Françoise, Marcel Fossier, et al. 1981. *Pouvoir municipal et communauté rurale à l'époque révolutionnaire en Côte d'Or (1789–an IV).* Dijon, France.

Foucault, Michel. 1977. *Discipline and Punish. The Birth of the Prison.* Translated by Alan Sheridan. New York: Pantheon Books.

———. 1980. "Two Lectures." In *Power/Knowledge: Selected Interviews and Other Writings, 1972–1977,* by M. Foucault, edited by Colin Gordon, 78–108. New York: Pantheon Press.

Fraser, Steven. 1991. *Labor Will Rule: Sidney Hillman and the Rise of American Labor.* New York: Free Press.

Frederick, Howard H. 1993. "Computer Networks and the Emergence of Global Civil Society." In *Global Networks,* edited by Linda M. Harasim, 283–95. Cambridge: MIT Press.

Freedeman, Charles E. 1993. *The Triumph of Corporate Capitalism in France, 1867–1914.* Rochester, N.Y.: University of Rochester Press.

Freifeld, Mary. 1986. "Technological Change and the Self-Acting Mule: A Study of Skill and the Sexual Division of Labour." *Social History* 11: 319–43.

Frijhoff, Willem. 1995. *Wegen van Evert Willemsz: Een Hollands weeskind op zoek naar zichzelf, 1607–1647.* Nijmegen, Netherlands: SUN.

Furet, François. 1981. *Interpreting the French Revolution.* Cambridge: Cambridge University Press.

Gallini, Clara. 1983. *La Sonnambula meravigliosa: Magnetismo e ipnotismo nell'Ottocento italiano.* Milan: Feltrinelli.

Gamson, William A. 1965. *Power and Discontent.* Homewood, Ill.: Dorsey Press.

———. 1975. *The Strategy of Social Protest.* Homewood, Ill.: Dorsey Press.

———. [1975] 1990. *The Strategy of Social Protest.* 2nd ed. Belmont, Calif.: Wadsworth.

———. 1992. *Talking Politics.* Cambridge: Cambridge University Press.

Gamson, William A., Bruce Fireman, and Steven Rytina. 1982. *Encounters with Unjust Authority.* Homewood, Ill.: Dorsey Press.

Gamson, William A., and David S. Meyer. 1996. "Framing Political Opportunities." In *Comparative Perspectives on Social Movements: Political Opportunities, Mobilizing Structures, and Cultural Framing,* edited by Doug McAdam, John McCarthy, and Mayer Zald. New York: Cambridge University Press.

Ganley, Gladys D. 1992. *The Exploding Political Power of Personal Media.* Norwood, N.J.: Ablex.

Garlock, Jonathan. 1974. "A Structural Analysis of the Knights of Labor." Ph.D. diss., University of Rochester.

Garner, Roberta. 1994. "Transnational Movements in Postmodern Society." *Peace Review* 6: 427–33.

Gerding, M. A. W. 1994. "(Wildervanck), Adriaan Geerts." In *Vierhonderd jaar Groninger Veenkoloniën in biografische schetsen,* 260–65. Groningen, Netherlands: Regio-Projekt.

———. (1995), *Vier eeuwen turfwinning: De verveningen in Groningen, Friesland, Drenthe en Overijssel tussen 1550 en 1950.* Wageningen, Netherlands: A.A.G. Bijdragen no. 35.

Gilmore, David D. 1987. *Aggression and Community: Paradoxes of Andalusian Culture.* New Haven: Yale University Press.

Girardet. Raoul. 1972. *L'idée coloniale en France de 1871 à 1962.* Paris: La Table Ronde.

———. 1983. *Le nationalisme français.* Paris: Colin.

Gitlin, Todd. 1980. *The Whole World Is Watching: Mass Media in the Making and Unmaking of the New Left.* Berkeley and Los Angeles. University of California Press.

Gochman, Charles S., and Zeev Moaz. 1990. "Militarized Interstate Disputes, 1816–1976." In *Measuring the Correlates of War*, edited by J.David Singer and Paul F. Diehl, 193–221. Ann Arbor: University of Michigan Press.

Godechot, Jacques. 1971. *Les révolutions de 1848.* Paris: Albin Michel.

Godio, Julio, and Héctor Palomino. 1988. *El movimiento sindical argentino hoi.* Buenos Aires: Fundación Friedrich Ebert.

Goffman, Erving. [1956] 1967 "The Nature of Deference and Demeanor." In: *Interaction Ritual*, by Erving Goffman, 47–95. New York: Pantheon Books.

Goldstein, Robert. 1983. *Political Repression in Nineteenth Century Europe.* London: Croom Helm.

Goodwin, J. 1994. "Toward a New Sociology of Revolutions." *Theory and Society* 23, no. 6: 731–66.

Goodwin, J., and Theda Skocpol. 1989. "Explaining Revolutions in the Contemporary Third World." *Politics and Society* 17: 489–509.

Gottdiener, Mark. 1985. *The Social Production of Urban Space.* Austin: University of Texas Press.

Gould, Roger. 1991. "Multiple Networks and Mobilization in the Paris Commune, 1871." *American Sociological Review* 56: 716–29.

———. 1993. "Trade Cohesion, Class Unity, and Urban Insurrection: Artisanal Activism in the Paris Commune." *American Journal of Sociology* 98: 721–54.

———. 1995a. *Insurgent Identities: Class, Community, and Protest in Paris from 1848 to the Commune.* Chicago: University of Chicago Press.

———. 1995b. "Networks, Identities, and Protest in the Whiskey Rebellion." Paper presented to the Conference on Structure, Identity, and Power: The Past and Future of Collective Action, Amsterdam, June.

———. 1996. "Patron-Client Ties, State Centralization, and the Whiskey Rebellion." *American Journal of Sociology* 102: 400–429.

Granovetter, Mark, and Charles Tilly. 1986. "Inequality and Labor Process." (Working Paper Series, no. 29, Center for Studies of Social Change, New School for Social Research, New York.

Guitton, Jean. 1985. *Portrait de Marthe Robin.* Paris: Bernard Grasset.

Guojia jiaowei sixiang zhengzhi gongzuo si (Political-Ideological Work Office of the State Education Commission), ed. 1989. *Jingxin dongpo de 56 tian* (A soul-stirring fifty-six days). Beijing: Dadi chubanshe.

Gurevich, Aron. 1988. *Medieval Popular Culture: Problems of Belief and Perception* (Problemi srednevekovoy kulturi [1981]). Translated by János M. Bak and Paul A. Hollingsworth. Cambridge: Cambridge University Press.

Gutmann, Myron P. 1980. *War and Rural Life in the Early Modern Low Countries.* Princeton: Princeton University Press.

Haapala, P. 1986. *Tehtaan valossa: Teollistuminen ja työväestön muodostuminen Tampereella 1820–1920* (In the light of the factory: Industrialisation and the formation of the working class in Tampere, Finland, 1820–1920, with an English summary). Helsinki: Suomen Historiallinen Seura.

Haapala, P., and M. Hyrkkänen. 1988. "Suomen yhteiskunta, työväenluokka ja -liike 1859–1918" (Society, working class, and worker movement in Finland, 1850–1918). *Työväentutkimus*, no. 2: 3–10.

Haas, J. A. K. 1978. *De verdeling van de Landen van Overmaas, 1644–1662.* Assen, Netherlands: Van Gorcum.

Haber, E. 1958. *The Chemical Industry in the Nineteenth Century.* Oxford: Oxford University Press.

Habermas, Jürgen. 1989. *The Structural Transformation of the Public Sphere.* Cambridge: MIT Press.

Hagen, William. 1980. *Germans, Poles, and Jews: The Nationality Conflict in the Prussian East, 1772–1914.* Chicago: University of Chicago Press.

Hahner, June. 1976. *Women in Latin American History: Their Lives and Views.* Los Angeles: UCLA Latin American Center.

Hale, Oron J. 1940. *Publicity and Diplomacy with Special Reference to England and Germany, 1890–1914.* New York: Appleton-Century.

Hall, Catherine. 1992. *White, Male, and Middle Class: Explorations in Feminism and History.* London: Routledge.

Hall, Robert. n.d. "'The Most Holy Cause': Technology, the State, Chartism, and the Defense of the Family." Unpublished manuscript.

Hamashima Atsutoshi. 1982. *Mindai Kōnan nōson shakai no kenkyū* (Rural society in Jiangnan during the Ming dynasty). Tokyo: Tokyo University Press.

Harland, John, and T. T. Wilkinson. 1882. *Lancashire Folk-Lore.* Manchester, Eng.: John Heywood.

Harper, R. Eugene. 1991. *The Transformation of Western Pennsylvania, 1770–1800.* Pittsburgh, Pa.: University of Pittsburgh Press.

Hart, Marjolein C. 't. 1993. *The Making of a Bourgeois State: War, Politics, and Finance during the Dutch Revolt.* Manchester, Eng.: Manchester University Press.

———. 1994. "Intercity Rivalries and the Making of the Dutch State." In *Cities and the Rise of States in Europe, A.D. 1000 to 1800,* edited by Charles Tilly and Wim P. Blockmans, 196–217. Boulder, Colo.: Westview Press.

Harvey, David. 1986. *Consciousness and the Urban Experience: Studies in the History and Theory of Capitalist Urbanization.* Baltimore: Johns Hopkins University Press.

———. 1989. *The Condition of Postmodernity.* Oxford: Blackwell.

Hattam, Victoria C. 1993. *Labor Visions and State Power: The Origin of Business Unionism in the United States.* Princeton: Princeton University Press.

Haupt, Georges. 1972. *Socialism and the Great War.* Oxford: Oxford University Press.

Hável, Vaclav, et al. 1985. *The Power of the Powerless: Citizens against the State in Eastern Europe.* Armonk, N.Y.: M. E. Sharpe.

Heitzer, Horst Walter. 1992. "Katholische Volksbewegungen in Deutschland." In *Een Kantelend Tijdperk: De Wending van de Kerk near het volk in Noord-West-Europa/Ein Zeitalter im Umbruch. Die Wende der Kirche zum volk im nordwestlichen Europa (1890–1910),* edited by Emiel Lambert, 91–123. Leuven, Netherlands: University Press.

Herren, Madeleine. 1993. *Internationale Sozialpolitik vor dem Ersten Weltkrieg.* Berlin: Duncker and Humblot.

Hjerppe, R. 1981. "Käsityöläiset uuden yhteiskunnan murroksessa" (The artisans at the dawn of the new society, with an English summary). In *Kun yhteiskunta muuttuu* (The society in change), edited by Y. Kaukiainen, P. Schybergson, H. Soikkanen, and T. Mauranen, 213–35. Helsinki: Suomen Historiallinen Seura.

Hobsbawm, Eric. 1964a. "General Labour Unions in Britain, 1889–1914." In *Labouring Men: Studies in the History of Labour,* 179–203. London: Weidenfeld and Nicolson.

———. 1964b. "Economic Fluctuations and Social Movements since 1800." In *Labouring Men: Studies in the History of Labour,* 126–57. London: Weidenfeld and Nicolson.

———. 1984a. "The "New Unionism" in Perspective." In *Workers: Worlds of Labor,* by E. Hobsbawm, 152–75. New York: Pantheon.

———. 1984b. "The Making of the Working Class, 1870–1914." In *Workers: Worlds of Labor,* by E. Hobsbawm, 194–213. New York: Pantheon.

———. 1987. *The Age of Empire, 1875–1914.* New York: Random House.

Hobsbawm, Eric, and Terence Ranger, eds. 1983. *The Invention of Tradition.* Cambridge: Cambridge University Press.

Hobsbawm, Eric, and Joan Wallach Scott. 1980. "Political Shoemakers." *Past and Present* 89: 86–114.

Hoerder, Dirk. 1985. "An Introduction to Labor Migration in the Atlantic Economies: 1815–1914. In *Labor Migration in the Atlantic Economies: The European and North American Working Classes During the Period of Industrialization,* edited by Dirk Hoerder, 1–21. Westport, Conn: Greenwood Press.

Hofstee, E. W. 1937. *Het Oldambt: Een sociografie.* Vol. 1, *Vormende krachten.* Groningen, Netherlands: Wolters.

Hohenberg, Paul. 1966. *Chemicals in Western Europe.* Baltimore: Johns Hopkins University Press.

Holt, James, 1977. "Trade Unionism in the British and U.S. Steel Industries, 1880–1914: A Comparative Study." In *The Labor History Reader,* edited by Daniel Leach, 166–96. Urbana: University of Illinois Press.

Hone, William. 1827. *The Everyday Book; or, Everlasting Calender of Popular Amusements, Sports, Pastimes, Ceremonies, Manners, Customs, and Events, Incident to Each of the Three Hundred and Sixty Five Days, in Past and Present Times.* vol. 2. London: William Hone.

Hoppenbrouwers, Peter. 1988. "Demographische Entwicklung und Besitzverhältnisse im Wold-Oldambt (Provinz Gronigen) (ca. 1630–1730): Die Quellen und ihre Probleme." In *Bevölkerungsgeschichte im Vergleich: Studien zu den Niederlanden und Nordwestdeutschland,* edited by Ernst Hinrichs und Henk van Zon, 9–26. Aurich, Germany: Ostfriesische Landschaft.

———. 1991. "Grondgebruik en agrarische bedrijfstructuur in het Oldambt na de vroegste inpolderingen (ca. 1630–ca. 1720)." *Historia Agriculturae* 22: 73–94.

Hourwich, Isaac. 1969. *Immigration and Labor: The Economic Aspects of European Immigration to the United States.* New York: Arno.

Howard, Michael. 1983. *The Causes of Wars.* London: T. Smith.

Hsiao Kung–chuan. 1960. *Rural China: Imperial Control in the Nineteenth Century.* Seattle: University of Washington Press.

Hughes, Michael. 1988. *Law and Politics in Eighteenth Century Germany* London: Boydell.

Huninga, Sebo, Dodo Edsens, and Wirtjo Matthiae. 1640. *Procuratie ende daer op gevolgde remonstrantien ende protest* [. . .]. The Hague: KB Pamflet.

Hunt, E. H. 1981. *British Labour History, 1815–1914.* Atlantic Highlands, N.J.: Humanities Press.

Hunt, Lynn. 1984. *Politics, Culture, and Class in the French Revolution.* Berkeley: University of California Press.

Iggers, George. 1984. Introduction to *The Social History of Politics,* edited by George Iggers, 1–48. Leamington Spa, Eng.: Berg.

Imbert-Gourbeyre, A. 1873. *Les stigmatisés.* Paris: Victor Palmé.

Imig, Doug, and Sidney Tarrow. 1995. "The Europeanization of Movements? Contentious Politics and the European Union, October 1983–March 1995." Paper presented to the ECSA Annual Conference at Charleston, S.C., and the Conference on Globalization and Social Movements in Mt. Pélérin, Switzerland.

———. 1996. "The Europeanization of Movements? Contentious Politics and the European Union, October 1983–March 1995." Working paper no. 96.3, Institute for European Studies. Ithaca N.Y.: Cornell University.

———. 1997. "From Strike to Eurostike: The Europeanization of Social Movements and the Development of a Euro-Polity." Working paper no. 97–10, Center for International Studies. Cambridge: Harvard University Press.

Inter-American Commission of Women, OAS. 1990. "Non-Governmental Women's Organizations and National Machinery for Improving the Status of Women: A Directory for the Caribbean Region." Washington, D.C.: Organization of American States.

———. 1992. *Regional Statistical Bulletin on Women*. Vol. 6. Washington, D.C.: Organization of American States.

Inter-Parliamentary Union [IPU]. 1991. *Distribution of Seats between Men and Women in National Parliaments: Statistical Data from 1945 to 30 June 1991*. Reports and Documents Series, no. 18. Geneva: IPU.

———. 1993. *Women in Parliament as of 30 June 1993*. Geneva: IPU.

———. 1995a. *Women in Parliaments 1945–1995: A World Statistical Survey*. Reports and Documents Series, no. 23.

———. 1995b. *Women in Parliament as of 30 June 1995*. Geneva: IPU.

Jackson, Maurice. 1960. "The Failure of an Incipient Social Movement," *Pacific Sociological Review* 3: 35–40.

Jacoby, Sanford. 1991. "American Exceptionalism Revisited: The Importance of Management." In *Masters to Managers: Historical and Comparative Perspectives on American Employers*, edited by S. Jacoby, 173–200. New York: Columbia University Press.

Jaeger, Hans. 1967. *Unternehmer in der deutschen Politik (1890–1914)*. Bonn: Rohrscheid.

James, Alfred. 1950. "A Political Interpretation of the Whiskey Insurrection." *Western Pennsylvania Historical Magazine*, Sept.–Dec., 90–101.

Janssen de Limpens, K. J. Th. 1982. "Genealogische en biografische geschiedenis van het geslacht De Limpens." *Publications* 118: 9–53.

Jaquette, Jane S., ed. 1991. *The Women's Movement in Latin America: Feminism and the Transition to Democracy*. Boulder, Colo.: Westview Press.

Jelly, Frederick. 1993. "Discerning the Miraculous: Norms for Judging Apparitions and Private Revelations." *Marian Studies* 44: 41–55.

Jenkins, J. Craig. 1995. "Social Movements, Political Representation, and the State: An Agenda and Comparative Framework." In *The Politics of Social Protest: Comparative Perspectives on States and Social Movements*, edited by J. Craig Jenkins and Bert Klandermans, 14–35. Minneapolis: University of Minnesota Press.

Jennings, Kent. 1990. "Women in Party Politics." In *Women, Politics, and Change*, edited by Louise Tilly and Patricia Gurin, 223. New York: Russell Sage Foundation.

Jessenne, Jean-Pierre. 1987. *Pouvoir au village et révolution: Artois, 1760–1848*. Lille, France.

Jingji ribao, ed. 1989. *Jieyan ling fabu zhiqian: 4.15–5.20 dongluan dashi ji* (Before martial law was declared: Major events during the turmoil of April 15 to May 20). Beijing: Jingji ribao chubanshe.

Johnson, Hank M., and Bert Klandermans, eds. 1995. *Social Movements and Culture*. Minneapolis: University of Minnesota Press,.

Johnston, Hank, and Bert Klandermans, 1995. "The Cultural Analysis of Social Movements." In *Social Movements and Culture*, edited by Hank Johnston and Bert Klandermans, 3–24. Minneapolis: University of Minnesota Press.

Joll, James. 1992. *The Origins of the First World War*. 2nd ed. London: Longman.

Jones, Kennedy. 1920. *Fleet Street and Downing Street*. London: Hutchinson.

Jones, P. M. 1985. *Politics and Rural Society: The Southern Massif Central c 1750–1880*. Cambridge: Cambridge University Press.

Jones, Susan Mann, and Philip Kuhn. 1978. "Dynastic Decline and the Roots of Rebellion." In *Cambridge History of China*, edited by John Fairbank, vol. 10: 107–62. Cambridge: Cambridge University Press.

Joset, Camille-Jean. 1981a. *André Marie Charue: 27e évêque de Namur (1941–1974) reconnaît les apparitions. Documents*. Beauraing, Belgium: Pro Maria.

————. 1981b. *Thomas-Louis Heylen: 26e évêque de Namur (1899–1941) confronté aux apparitions de Beauraing*. Beauraing, Belgium: Pro Maria.

————. 1982. "Sources et documents primitifs inédits antérieurs à la mi-mars 1933." In *Dossiers de Beauraing 4*. Beauraing, Belgium: Pro Maria.

Joyce, Patrick. 1980. *Work, Society, and Politics*. London: Methuen.

Jurriens, R. 1981. "The Miners' General Strike in the Dutch Province of Limburg (21 June– 2 July 1917)." *The Low Countries History Yearbook*, no. 14: 124–53.

Kaelble, Harmut. 1967. *Industrielle Interessenpolitik in der wilhelminischen Gesellschaft: Centralverband Deutscher Industrieller 1895–1914*. Berlin: De Gruyter.

Kagan, Richard L. 1990. *Lucrecia's Dreams: Politics and Prophecy in Sixteenth-Century Spain*. Berkeley: University of California Press.

Kanbe Teruo. 1972. "Shindai goki Santosho ni okeru danhi to nōson mondai" (The *tuanfei* in late Qing Shandong and village problems). *Shirin* 55, no. 4: 61–98.

Kang Yong Qian shiqi chengxiang renmin fankang douzheng ziliao (Materials on people's resistance and struggles in the Kangxi, Yongzheng, and Qianlong reigns). 1979. Edited by Zhongguo renmin daxue, Qingshi yanjiu suo, and Dangan xi Zhongguo zhengzhi zhidu shi jiaoyan shi. Beijing: Zhonghua.

Katznelson, Ira. 1985. "Working-Class Formation and the State: Nineteenth-Century England in American Perspective." In *Bringing the State Back In,* edited by Peter Evans, Dietrich Ruesmeyer, and Theda Skocpol, 257–84. New York: Cambridge University Press.

Katznelson, Ira, and Aristide R. Zolberg, eds. 1986. *Working-Class Formation: Nineteenth-Century Patterns in Western Europe and the United States*. Princeton: Princeton University Press.

Keck, Margaret E. and Kathryn Sikkink. 1998. *Activists beyond Borders: Transnational Advocacy Networks in International Politics*. Ithaca, N.Y.: Cornell University Press.

————. 1995. "Transnational Issue Networks in International Politics." Paper presented to the Annual Conference of the American Political Science Association, Chicago.

Kertzer, David. 1988. *Ritual, Politics, and Power*. New Haven: Yale University Press.

Kettunen, P. 1986. *Poliittinen liike ja sosiaalinen kollektiivisuus: Tutkimus sosialidemokratiasta ja ammattiyhdistysliikkeestä Suomessa 1918–1930* (Politische Bewegung und soziale Kollektivität: Eine Untersuchung über die Sozialdemokratie und die Gewerkschaftsbewegung in Finnland, 1918–1930, with a German summary). Helsinki: Suomen Historiallinen Seura.

Keuning, H. J. 1933. *De Groninger veenkoloniën: Een sociaal-geografische studie*. Amsterdam: Paris.

Kiberd, Declan. 1988. "The War against the Past." In *The Uses of the Past: Essays in Irish Culture,* edited by Audrey S. Eyler and Robert F. Garratt, 24–54. Newark: University of Delaware Press.

Kirby, R. G., and A. E. Musson. 1975. *The Voice of the People: John Doherty, 1798–1854*. Manchester, Eng.: Manchester University Press.

Kirk, Neville. 1985. *The Growth of Working-Class Reformism in Mid-Victorian England*. London: Croom Helm.

Klandermans, Bert. 1995. "Protest and Contention in Layered Structures." Comments prepared for the Conference on Structure, Identity, and Power: The Past and Future of Collective Action, Amsterdam, 2–4, 1995.

Klandermans, Bert, and Sidney Tarrow. 1988. "Mobilization into Social Movements: Synthesizing European and American Approaches." *International Social Movement Research* 1: 1–38.

Knight, Alan. 1992. "Revisionism and Revolution: Mexico Compared to England and France." *Past and Present* 134: 159–99.

Knoke, David. 1990. *Political Networks: The Structural Perspective*. Cambridge: Cambridge University Press.
————. 1991. "Land Kanaän aan de Noordzee: Een vergeten hoofdstuk." *Historia Agriculturae* 22: 25–72.
Kobayashi Kazumi. 1973. "Koso, koryo to sono kanta: Kaso seikatsusha no omoi to seijiteki shukyoteki jiritsu no michi." *Shisō* 2: 228–47. Translated by Cynthia Brokow and Timothy Brook, "The Other Side of Rent and Tax Resistance Struggles: Ideology and the Road to Rebellion." In *State and Society in China: Japanese Perspectives on Ming-Qing Social and Economic History,* edited by Linda Grove and Christian Daniels, 215–44. Tokyo: University of Tokyo Press.
Kojima Shinji. 1978. *Taihei tenkoku kakumei no rekishi to shisō* (The history and thought of the Taiping revolution). Tokyo: Yamamoto Shoten.
Konrád, George. 1984. *Antipolitics.* Translated by Richard E. Allen. San Diego: Harcourt, Brace, Jovanovich.
Kooper, J. 1939. *Het waterstaatsverleden van de provincie Groningen.* Groningen, Netherlands: Wolters.
Kowalewski, David. 1989. "Global Debt Crises in Structural-Cyclical Perspective." In *Markets, Politics, and Change in the Global Political Economy,* edited by W. P. Avery and D. P. Rapkin, 357–84. Boulder, Colo.: Lynne Rienner.
Kriesi, Hanspeter, et al. 1995. *The Politics of New Social Movements in Western Europe.* Minneapolis and St. Paul: University of Minnesota Press.
Kriesi, Hanspeter, Ruud Koopmans, Jan Willem Duyvendak, and Marco G. Giugni, 1995. *New Social Movements in Western Europe: A Comparative Analysis.* Minneapolis: University of Minnesota Press.
Krumeich, Gerd. 1984. *Armaments and Politics in France on the Eve of the First World War: The Introduction of Three-Year Conscription, 1913–1914.* Leamington Spa, Eng.: Berg.
Kselman, Thomas A. 1983. *Miracles and Prophecies in Nineteenth-Century France.* New Brunswick, N.J.: Rutgers University Press.
Kselman, Thomas A., and Stephen Avella. 1986. "Marian Piety and the Cold War in the United States." *The Catholic Historical Review* 73: 403–424.
Kuhn, Philip. 1970. *Rebellion and Its Enemies in Late Imperial China.* Cambridge: Harvard University Council on East Asian Studies.
————. 1975. "Local Self-Government under the Republic: Problems of Control, Autonomy, and Mobilization." In *Conflict and Control in Late Imperial China,* edited by Frederic Wakeman, Jr. and Carolyn Grant, 257–98. Berkeley: University of California Press.
Kurgan-van Hentenryk, Ginette. 1992. "Une classe oubliée: La petite bourgeoisie de 1850 à 1914." In *Aux frontieres des classes movennes: La petite bourgeoisie belge avant 1914,* edited by Ginette Kurgan-van Hentenryk and Serge Jaumain, 15–28. Brussels: Editions de l'Université de Bruxelles.
LaCapra, Dominick. 1983. *Rethinking Intellectual History: Texts, Contexts, Language.* Ithaca, N.Y.: Cornell University Press.
Laclau, Ernesto. 1990. *New Reflections on the Revolution of Our Time.* London: Verso.
————. 1992. "Democratic Politics Today." Preface to *Dimensions of Radical Democracy: Pluralism, Citizenship, and Community,* edited by Chantal Mouffe, 1–16. London:Verso.
La Fontaine, Jean. 1985. *Initiation.* Manchester, Eng.: Manchester University Press.
Lambrechts, Hector. 1912. *Les grands magasins et les cooperatives de consommation au pont de vue des classes moyennes.* Paris: Rousseau.
Langbein, John H. 1974. *Prosecuting Crime in the Renaissance: England, Germany, France.* Cambridge: Harvard University Press.
Langlois, Claude. 1984. *Le Catholicisme au feminin: Les congrégations françaises à supérieure générale au XIXᵉ siècle.* Paris: Les Editions du Cerf.

Laqueur, Thomas. 1989. "Crowds, Carnival, and the State in English Executions, 1604–1868." In *The First Modern Society,* edited by A. L. Beier, David Cannadine, and James M. Rosenheim. Cambridge: Cambridge University Press.

Larana, Enrique, Hank Johnston, and Joseph R. Gusfield, eds. 1994. *New Social Movements: From Ideology to Identity.* Philadelphia: Temple University Press.

Lazonick, William. 1979. "Industrial Relations and Technical Change: The Case of the Self-Acting Mule." *Cambridge Journal of Economics* 3: 231–62.

Leach, E. R. 1964. "Anthropological Aspects of Language: Animal Categories and Verbal Abuse." In *New Directions in the Study of Language,* edited by E. H. Lenneberg, 23–63. Cambridge: MIT Press.

———. 1966. "Ritualization in Man in Relation to Conceptual and Social Development." In *A Discussion on Ritualization of Behaviour in Animals and Man,* edited by Julian Huxley, 403–8. Transactions of the Royal Society of London, Series B, vol. 251. London: Royal Society.

———. 1976. Culture and communication. Cambridge: Cambridge University Press.

Lefebvre, Henri. 1991. *The Production of Space.* Translated by Donald Nicholson-Smith. Oxford: Basil Blackwell.

Leon, Magdalena, ed. 1994. *Mujeres y participación política: Avances y desafíos en América Latina.* Bogotá: Tercer Mundo Editores.

Le Roy Ladurie, Emmanuel. 1979. *Carnival in Romans.* Translated by Mary Feeney. New York: George Braziller.

Levack, Brian P. 1987. *The Witch-Hunt in Early Modern Europe.* London and New York: Longman.

Leventhal, F. M. 1974. "H. N. Brailsford and the Search for a New International Order." In *Edwardian Radicalism, 1900–1914,* edited by A. J. A. Morris, 202–17. London: Routledge.

Levi, Giovanni. 1989. *Inheriting Power: The Story of an Exorcist.* Translated by Lydia G. Cochrane. Chicago and London: University of Chicago Press.

Levy, Raphael-Georges. 1912. "La 'Gazette de Francfort.'" *Journal des Economistes* 39, no. 2: 235–52.

Lincoln, Bruce. 1985. "Revolutionary Exhumations in Spain, July 1936." *Comparative Studies in Society and History* 27: 241–60.

Linebaugh, Peter. 1975. "The Tyburn Riot against the Surgeons." In Albion's *Fatal Tree: Crime and Society in Eighteenth-Century England,* edited by Douglas Hay et al., 65–117. New York: Pantheon Books.

———. 1992. *The London Hanged: Crime and Civil Society in the Eighteenth Century.* Cambridge: Cambridge University Press.

Link, Eugene. 1942. *Democratic-Republican Societies, 1790–1800.* New York: Columbia University Press.

Link, Perry. 1994. "The Old Man's New China," *New York Review of Books* 41, no. 11: 31–36.

Lipset, Seymour Martin. 1967. *Political Man.* Garden City, N.Y.: Doubleday Anchor.

Li Yun et al., eds. 1989. *Diankuang de shenian zhi xia* (The tumultuous summer of the year of the snake). Beijing: Guofang keji daxue chubanshe.

Lovenduski, Joni. 1993. "The Dynamics of Gender and Party." Introduction to *Gender and Party Politics,* edited by Joni Lovenduski and Pippa Norris, 1–15. Thousand Oaks, Calif.: Sage.

Lowe, Boutelle Ellsworth. 1935. *The International Protection of Labor.* 2nd ed. New York: Macmillan.

Luria, Keith, and Romulo Gandolfo. 1986. "Carlo Ginzburg: An Interview." *Radical History Review* 35: 89–111.

Macdonald, Ted. N.d. "Indigenous Peoples and Environmentalists: Where's the Link?"

Unpublished paper, Cultural Survival Project, Center for International Affairs, Harvard University.

Mack, Phyllis. 1992. *Visionary Women: Ecstatic Prophecy in Seventeenth-Century England.* Berkeley: University of California Press.

Mahaim, Ernest. 1933. "The Principles of International Labor Legislation." *Annals of the American Academy of Political and Social Science* 166: 11–13.

Mann, Michael. 1993. *The Sources of Social Power.* Vol. 2, *The Rise of Classes and Nation-States, 1760–1914.* Cambridge: Cambridge University Press.

Mann, Susan. 1987. *Local Merchants and the Chinese Bureaucracy, 1750–1950.* Stanford, Calif.: Stanford University Press.

Margadant, T. W. 1979. "French Rural Society in the Nineteenth Century: A Review Essay." *Agricultural History* 53: 196–213.

———. 1984. "Tradition and Modernity in Rural France in the Nineteenth Century." *Journal of Modern History* 56: 668–97.

Marks, Gary. 1989. *Unions in Politics: Britain, Germany, and the United States in the Nineteenth and Early Twentieth Centuries.* Princeton: Princeton University Press.

Marston, Sallie A. 1989. "Public Rituals and Community Power: St. Patrick's Day Parades in Lowell, Massachusetts, 1841–1874." *Political Geography Quarterly* 8: 255–69.

Marx, Anthony. 1995. "Contested Citizenship: The Dynamics of Racial Identity and Social Movements." *International Review of Social History,* supplement 3: 159–84.

Mastnak, Tomaz. 1990. "Civil Society in Slovenia: From Opposition to Power." *Studies in Comparative Communism* 23 (Autumn/Winter): 305–17.

Matthey, I. B. M. 1975. "Op fiscaal compas," In *Westeremden, Het verleden van een Gronings terpdorp,* edited by I. B. M. Matthey, 195–360. Groningen, Netherlands: Rijksarchief.

Mauss, Marcel. [1903] 1972. *A General Theory of Magic.* Translated by Robert Brain. London: Routledge.

Mayer, Arno. 1981. *The Persistence of the Old Regime: Europe to the Great War.* New York: Pantheon.

Mayeur, Jean-Marie, and Madeleine Rebérioux. 1984. *The Third Republic from Its Origins to the Great War, 1871–1914.* Cambridge: Cambridge Unviersity Press.

Mazey, Sonia, and Jeremy Richardson. 1993a. "Environmental Groups and the EC: Challenges and Opportunities." In *A Green Dimension for the European Community,* edited by David Judge, 109–28. London: Cass.

———. 1993b. *Lobbying in the European Community.* Oxford: Oxford University Press.

McAdam, Doug. 1982. *The Political Process and the Development of Black Insurgency.* Chicago: University of Chicago Press.

———. 1988a. *Freedom Summer.* Chicago: University of Chicago Press.

———. 1988b. "Micromobilization Contexts and Recruitment to Activism." *International Social Movement Research* 2: 125–54.

———. 1995. "'Initiator' and 'Derivative' Movements: Diffusion Processes in Protest Cycles." In *Repertoires and Cycles of Collective Action,* edited by Mark Traugott. Durham, N.C.: Duke University Press.

———. 1996. "Conceptual Origins, Current Problems, Future Directions." In *Comparative Perspectives on Social Movements: Political Opportunities, Mobilizing Structures, and Cultural Framings,* edited by Doug McAdam, John D. McCarthy, and Mayer N. Zald, 23–40. Cambridge: Cambridge University Press.

McAdam, Doug, John McCarthy, and Mayer N. Zald, eds. 1996. *Comparative Perspectives on Social Movements: Political Opportunities, Mobilizing Structures, and Cultural Framing.* New York and Cambridge: Cambridge University Press.

McAdam, Doug, and Dieter Rucht. 1993. "The Cross-National Diffusion of Movement Ideas." *Annals of the American Academy of Political and Social Science* 528: 56–74.

McAdam, Doug, Sidney Tarrow, and Charles Tilly. 1996. "Towards a Comparative Synthesis on Social Movements and Revolution." Paper presented to the Conference on Comparative Politics, Brown University, May 4–6.

McCalman, Iain. 1989. *Radical Underworld: Prophets, Revolutionaries, and Pornographers in London, 1795–1840.* Cambridge: Cambridge University Press.

McCarthy, John D., David W. Britt, and Mark Wolfson. 1991. "The Institutional Channeling of Social Movements in the Modern State." *Research in Social Movements* 13: 4–76.

McCarthy, John D., and Mayer N. Zald. 1973. *The Trend of Social Movements in America: Professionalization and Resource Mobilization.* Morristown, N.H.: General Learning Press.

McDaniel, Tim. 1994. "Response to Goodwin." *Theory and Society* 23: 789–93.

McFarland, Joseph. 1910. *Twentieth-Century History of Washington and Washington County, Pennsylvania.* Chicago: Richmond and Arnold.

Mcgowan, John. 1991. *Postmodernism and Its Critics.* Ithaca, N.Y.: Cornell University Press.

McPhee, Peter. 1978. "Popular Culture, Symbolism, and Rural Radicalism in Nineteenth-Century France." *Journal of Peasant Studies* 5: 235–53.

———. 1992. *A Social History of France, 1780–1880.* New York: Routledge.

Meihuizen, L. S. 1976. "Sociaal-economische geschiedenis van het Groningerland." In *Historie van Groningen,* edited by W. J. Formsma, 293–330. Groningen, Netherlands: Wolters-Noordhoff.

Melucci, Alberto. 1989. *Nomads of the Present: Social Movements and Individual Needs in Contemporary Society.* Philadelphia: Temple University Press.

Mengels, Winand.[1773] 1887. "Memorie of Kronyckboek, etc." *Publications* 24: 167–297.

Merriman, John M. 1975. "The *Demoiselles* of the Ariège, 1829–1831." In *1830 in France,* edited by John M. Merriman, 87–118. New York: New Viewpoints.

———. 1978. *Agony of the Republic: The Repression of the Left in Revolutionary France, 1848–51.* New Haven: Yale University Press.

Meuli, Karl. 1975. "Über einige alte Rechtsbräuche/Charivari." In *Gesammelte Schriften,* by Karl Meuli, vol. 1. Basel, Switzerland: Schwabe and Co. Verlag.

Meyer, David S., and Suzanne Staggenborg. 1996. "Movements, Countermovements, and the Structure of Political Opportunity." *American Journal of Sociology* 101: 1628–60.

Midlarsky, Manus I., and Kenneth Roberts. 1985. "Class, State, and Revolution in Central America." *Journal of Conflict Resolution* 29: 163–93.

Mitchell, J. Clyde. 1973. "Networks, Norms, and Institutions." In *Network Analysis,* edited by Jeremy Boissevain and J. Clyde Mitchell, 1–23. The Hague: Mouton.

Moch, Leslie Page. 1992. *Moving Europeans.* Bloomington: Indiana University Press.

Modderman, J. R. 1816. *Iets over de door de stad Groningen opnieuw over het Oldambt (. . .) gepraetendeerde superioriteit.* Groningen, Netherlands: KB Pamflet.

Mommsen, Wolfgang. 1981. "Nationalism, Imperialism, and Official Press Policy in Wilhemine Germany, 1850–1914." In *Opinion publique et politique exterieure, 1870–1914,* 367–83. Rome.

Monter, William. 1990. *Frontiers of Heresy: The Spanish Inquisition from the Basque Lands to Sicily.* Cambridge: Cambridge University Press.

———. 1993. "Les enfants au sabbat: Bilan provisoire." In *Le Sabbat des sorciers, xve–xviiie siècles,* edited by N. Jacques-Chaquin and M. Préaud, 383–88. Grenoble, France: Jérome Millon.

Moore Jr., B. 1978. *Injustice: The Social Bases of Obedience and Revolt.* London: Macmillan.

Morel, E. D. 1912. *Morocco in Diplomacy.* London: Smith and Elder.

Morgan, Carol E. 1992. "Women, Work, and Consciousness in the Mid-Nineteenth-Century English Cotton Industry." *Social History* 17: 23–41.

Mouffe, Chantal. 1992. "Democratic Politics Today." Preface to *Dimensions of Radical Democracy: Pluralism, Citizenship, and Community,* edited by Chantal Mouffe, 1–16. London: Verso.

Mousnier, Roland. 1971. *Peasant Uprisings in Seventeenth-Century France, Russia, and China.* London: Allen and Unwin.

Mueller, Carol McClurg. 1992. "Building Social Movement Theory." In *Frontiers in Social Movement Theory,* edited by Aldon D. Morris and Carol McClurg Mueller, 3–25. New Haven: Yale University Press.

Müsselmann, Leo. 1912. *Die Wirtschaftlichen Verbände.* Leipsig, Germany: Göschen'sche Verlagshandlung.

Niccoli, Ottavia. 1990. *Prophecy and People in Renaissance Italy.* Translated by Lydia G. Cochrane. Princeton: Princeton University Press.

Nichtweiss, J. 1959. *Die auslandische Saisonarbeiter in der Landwirtschaft der ostlichen und mittleren Gebiete des Deutschen Reiches 1890–1914.* Berlin: Rutten und Loening.

Nord, Philip. 1986. *Paris Shopkeepers and the Politics of Resentment.* Princeton: Princeton University Press.

Oberschall, Anthony. 1973. *Social Conflict and Social Movements.* Englewood Cliffs, N.J.: Prentice-Hall.

O'Donnell, Guillermo, P. Schmitter, and L. Whitehead, eds. 1986. *Transitions from Authoritarian Rule: Prospects for Democracy.* Baltimore: Johns Hopkins University Press.

O'Gorman, Frank. 1982. *The Emergence of the British Two-Party System, 1760–1832.* London: Arnold.

———. 1984. "Electoral Deference in 'Unreformed' England: 1760–1832." *Journal of Modern History* 56: 391–429.

———. 1989. *Voters, Patrons, and Parties: The Unreformed Electoral System of Hanoverian England, 1734–1832.* Oxford: Clarendon Press.

———. 1992. "Campaign Rituals and Ceremonies: The Social Meanings of Elections in England, 1780–1860." *Past and Present* 135: 79–115.

Olsson, Lars. 1996. "Labor Migration as a Prelude to World War I." *International Migration Review* 30, no. 4: 875–900.

O'Neil, Michael J. 1993. *The Roar of the Crowd: How Television and People Power Are Changing the World.* New York: Times Books.

Orr, Shepley. 1995. "Language, Values, and Structural Sociology: On Meaning and the Micro-Macro Link in Network Analysis." Paper presented at the ASA annual meeting.

Ost, David. 1990. *Solidarity and the Politics of Antipolitics.* Philadelphia: Temple University Press.

Otsuki Yushi. 1983. "Chūgoku minshu hanran shiron" (The history of popular disturbances in China). In *Zoku Chūgokuminshu hanran no sekai,* edited by Seinen Chūgoku kenkyūsha kaigi, 553–83. Tokyo: Kyuko shoin.

Owen, Alex. 1989. *The Darkened Room: Women, Power, and Spiritualism in Late Victorian England.* London: Virago.

Paasikivi, J. K. 1957. *Paasikiven muistelmia sortovuosilta* (Paasikivi's memoirs from the years of oppression). Vol. 1. Helsinki and Porvoo: WSOY.

Padgett, John F., and Christopher K. Ansell. 1993. "Robust Action and the Rise of the Medici, 1400–1434." *American Journal of Sociology* 98: 1259–1319.

Pagnucco, Ron, and David Atwood. 1994. "Global Strategies for Peace and Justice." *Peace Review* 6: 411–18.

Pagnucco, Ron, and Jackie Smith, 1993. "Democracy and Foreign Policy: Political Opportunity and the U.S. Peace Movement," *Peace and Change* 18: 157–81.

Paige, Karen, and Jeffrey Paige. 1981. *The Politics of Reproductive Ritual.* Berkeley: University of California Press.

Parlamento Latino-Americano. 1995. "Declaración del PARLATINO," 5ª Reunión de la Comisión Especial de la Mujer del PARLATINO, São Paulo, July 29, 1995.

Paterson, Thomas G. 1994. *Contesting Castro: The United States and the Triumph of the Cuban Revolution.* New York: Oxford University Press.

Pauw, C. 1956. *Strubbelingen in Stad en Lande.* Groningen, Netherlands: Wolters.

Pawlowski, Auguste. 1911. "Le nouveau bassin minier de la basse-normandie." *Journal des économistes* 32, no. 2: 221–40.

Peng Zeyi. 1983. *Shijiu shiji houban qi de zhongguo caizheng yu jingjz* (Chinese fiscal administration and economy in the second half of the nineteenth century). Beijing: Renmin.

Pennsylvania Archives. N.d. Philadelphia: Commonwealth of Pennsylvania.

Pérez Jr., Louis A. 1976. *Army Politics in Cuba, 1898–1958.* Pittsburgh, Pa.: University of Pittsburgh Press.

Pérez-Stable, Marifeli. 1993. *The Cuban Revolution: Origins, Course, and Legacy.* New York: Oxford University Press.

Perry, Elizabeth. 1980. *Rebels and Revolutionaries in North China, 1845–1945.* Stanford, Calif.: Stanford University Press.

———. 1984. "Collective Violence in China, 1880–1980." *Theory and Society* 13, no. 3: 427–54.

———. 1985. "Tax Revolt in Late Qing China: The Small Swords Society of Shanghai and Liu Depei of Shandong." *Late Imperial China* 6, no. 1 (June): 83–111.

Peters, Michael. 1992. *Der alldeutsche Verband am Vorabend des Ersten Weltkrieges (1908–1914).* Frankfurt: Lang.

Phillips, John A. 1982. *Electoral Behavior in Unreformed England: Plumpers, Splitters, and Straights.* Princeton: Princeton University Press.

———. 1990. "Municipal Politics in Later Eighteenth-Century Maidstone: Electoral Polarization in the Reign of George III." In *The Transformation of Political Culture: England and Germany in the Late Eighteenth Century,* edited by Eckhart Hellmuth. London: German Historical Institute and Oxford University Press.

———. 1992. *The Great Reform Bill in the Boroughs: English Electoral Behaviour, 1818–1841.* Oxford: Clarendon Press.

Pilant, Paul. [1912?] *Le péril allemand.* Paris: Editions et librarie.

Pinard, Maurice, et al. 1971. "Process of Recruitment in the Sit-In Movement." In *The Black Revolt,* edited by James A. Geschwender, 184–97. Englewood Cliffs, N.J.: Prentice-Hall.

Piven, Frances Fox, and Richard Cloward. 1993. *Regulating the Poor.* 2nd ed. New York: Vintage.

Pizzorno, Alessandro. 1978. "Political Exchange and Collective Identity in Industrial Conflict." In *The Resurgence of Class Conflict in Western Europe,* edited by Colin Crouch and Alessandro Pizzorno, vol. 2: 277–98. London: Macmillan.

Poidevin, Raymond. 1969. *Les relations économiques et financières entre la France et l'Allemagne de 1898 à 1914.* Paris: Colin.

Polachek, James. 1975. "Gentry Hegemony: Soochow in the T'ung-chih Restoration." In *Conflict and Local Control in Late Imperial China,* edited by Frederic Wakeman, Jr. and Carolyn Grant, 211–56. Berkeley and Los Angeles: University of California Press.

Ponsonby, Arthur. 1915. *Democracy and Diplomacy.* London: Methuen.

Population Crisis Committee. 1988. "Country Ranking of the Status of Women: Poor, Powerless, and Pregnant." Briefing paper, Washington, D.C.: Population Crisis Committee.

Prazniak, Roxann. 1981. "Community and Protest in Rural China: Tax Resistance and County-Village Politics on the Eve of the 1911 Revolution." Ph.D. diss., University of California, Davis.

Pred, Alan. 1990. *Making Histories and Constructing Geographies: The Local Transformation of Practice, Power Relations, and Consciousness.* Boulder, Colo.: Westview Press.

Price, John. 1972. "A History of the Outcaste: Untouchability in Japan." In *Japan's Invisible Race,* edited by George De Vos and Hiroshi Wagatsuma, 6–32. Berkeley and Los Angeles: University of California Press.

Prosperi, Adriano. 1986. "Dalle 'divine madri' ai 'padri spirituali.'" In *Women and Men in Spiritual Culture, XIV–XVII Centuries: A Meeting of South and North, Studiën Nederlands Instituut te Rome, VIII,* edited by Elisja Schulte van Kessel, 71–90. The Hague: Staatsuitgeverij.

Przeworski, Adam. 1991. *Democracy and the Market: Political and Economic Reforms in Eastern Europe and Latin America.* London: Cambridge University Press.

Radbruch, Gustav, ed. 1960. *Die peinliche Gerichtsordnung Karls V. von 1532 (Carolina).* Stuttgart: Reclam.

Rancière, Jacques.[1992] 1994. *The Names of History: On the Poetics of Knowledge.* Minneapolis: University of Minnesota Press.

Rasila, V., E. Jutikkala, and K. Kulha. 1976. *Suomen poliittinen historia* (The political history of Finland). Vol. 2. Helsinki and Porvoo: WSOY.

Raun, T. 1984. "The Revolution of 1905 in the Baltic Provinces and Finland." *Slavic Review* 43: 453–67.

Reddy, William. 1987. *Money and Liberty in Modern Europe: A Critique of Historical Understanding.* Cambridge: Cambridge University Press.

Rentola, K. 1992. "Toinen kirja" (The second book). In *Karkkilan eli Högforsin ja Pyhäjärven entisen Pahajärven ihmisten historia* (The history of the people in Karkkila or Högfors and Pyhäjärvi, former Pahajärvi), edited by S. Aalto and K. Rentola, 247–877. Jyväskylä, Finland: Gummerus.

Resolutiën der Staten Generaal (RSG). 1604–1624. Edition Rijks Geschiedkundige Publicatiën The Hague: Nijhoff.

Rev, Istvan. 1987. "The Advantages of Being Atomized: How Hungarian Peasants Coped with Collectivization." *Dissent* (Summer): 336–50.

Rieger, Isolde. 1957. *Die wilhelminische Presse im überlick, 1888–1918.* Munich: Pohl.

Riesser, Jakob. 1912. *Der Hansabund.* Jena: Diederichs.

Risse-Kappen, Thomas, and Hans Peter Schmitz. 1995. "Principled Ideas, International Institutions, and Domestic Political Change in the Human Rights Area: Insights from African Cases." Paper presented to the Annual Meeting of the American Political Science Association, Chicago.

Robert D. Benford. 1986. "Frame Alignment Processes, Micromobilization, and Movement Participation." *American Sociological Review* 51: 464–81.

Robins, Kevin. 1995. "Globalization." In *Social Science Encyclopedia,* edited by Adam Kuper and Jessica Kuper, 345–46. London: Routledge.

Roma, Josefina. 1991. "Les Dones i el fenòmen aparicionista."

Root, Hilton. 1987. *Peasants and King in Burgundy: Agrarian Foundations of French Absolutism.* Berkeley: University of California Press.

Rose, Sonya O. 1992. *Limited Livelihoods: Gender and Class in Nineteenth-Century England.* Berkeley: University of California Press.

———. 1993. "Respectable Men, Disorderly Others: The Language of Gender and the Lancashire Weavers' Strike of 1878 in Britain." *Gender and History* 5: 382–97.

Rosenau, James. 1990. *Turbulence in World Politics.* Princeton: Princeton University Press.

Rosenberg, Harriet. 1988. A Negotiated World. Toronto: University of Toronto Press.

Rosenthal, Naomi, et al. 1985. "Social Movements and Network Analysis: A Case Study of Nineteenth-Century Women's Reform in New York State." *American Journal of Sociology* 90: 1022–54.

Ross, Kristin. 1988. *The Emergence of Social Space: Rimbaud and the Paris Commune.* Minneapolis: University of Minnesota Press.

Rupp, Jan C. C. 1992. "Michel Foucault, Body Politics, and the Rise and Expansion of Modern Anatomy." *Journal of Historical Sociology* 5: 31–60.

Russo, Mary. 1986. "Female Grotesques: Carnival and Theory." In *Feminist Studies/Critical Studies,* edited by Teresa de Lauretis, 213–29. Bloomington: Indiana University Press.

Ryan, Mary. 1989. "The American Parade: Representations of the Nineteenth-Century Order." In *The New Cultural History,* edited by Lynn Hunt, 131–53. Berkeley: University of California Press.

———. 1990. *Women in Public: Between Banners and Ballots, 1825–1880.* Baltimore: Johns Hopkins University Press.

Saint Jacob, Pierre de. 1960. *Les paysans de la Bourgogne du nord au dernier siècle de l'Ancien Régime.* Paris: Belles Lettres.

Sasaki Masaya. 1963. "Kanpo ninen Ginken no koryo bodo" (The tax resistance uprising in Yin county in 1852). *Kindai Chūgoku kenkyū* (Studies on modern China) (Tokyo University) 5: 185–299.

Saville, John. 1974. "Trade Unions and Free Labour: The Background to the Taff Vale Decision." In *Essays in Social History,* edited by M. W. Flinn and T. C. Smout, 251–76. Oxford: Clarendon Press.

Scaraffia, Lucetta. 1994. "'Il Cristianesimo l'ha fatta libera, collocandola nella famiglia accanto all'uomo' (dal 1850 alla 'Mulieris Dignitatem')." In *Donna e fede: Santità e vita religiosa in Italia,* edited by Lucetta Scaraffia and Gabriella Zarri, 441–93. Rome and Bari: Laterza.

Schilling, Heinz. 1991. *Civic Calvinism in Northwestern Germany and the Netherlands: Sixteenth to Twentieth Centuries.* Kirksville, Miss.: Sixteenth Century Journal Publishers.

Schneider, Robert A. 1995. *The Ceremonial City: Toulouse Observed, 1738–1780.* Princeton: Princeton University Press.

Schuitema Meijer, A. T. 1977. *Historie van het archief der stad Groningen.* Groningen, Netherlands: Gemeentearchief.

Scott, James. 1985. *Weapons of the Weak: Everyday Forms of Peasant Resistance.* New Haven: Yale University Press.

———.1990. *Domination and the Arts of Resistance: Hidden Transcripts.* New Haven, Conn.: Yale University Press.

Serman, William. 1991. "The Nationalists of Meurthe-et-Moselle, 1888–1912." In *Nationhood and Nationalism in France: From Boulangism to the Great War, 1889–1918,* edited by Robert Tombs, 121–35. London: HarperCollins.

Sewell, William Jr. 1994. "Collective Violence and Collective Loyalties in France: What the French Revolution Made a Difference." *Politics and Society* 18: 527–52.

Shevin-Coetzee, Marilyn. 1990. *The German Army League: Popular Nationalism in Wilhelmine Germany.* Oxford: Oxford University Press.

Shields, Rob. 1991. *Places on the Margin: Alternative Geographies of Modernity.* London: Routledge.

Shugart, Mathew Sobert. 1989. "Patterns of Revolution." *Theory and Society.* 18: 249–71.

Siim, Birte. 1991. "Welfare State, Gender Politics, and Equality Policies." In *Equality, Politics, and Gender,* edited by Elizabeth Meehan and Selma Sevenhuijsen, 175–92. London: Sage Publications.

———. 1994. "Gender, Power, and Democracy." Paper presented at the sixteenth World Congress of the International Political Science Association, Berlin, August 21–25, 1994.

Sikkink, Kathryn. 1995. "Historical Precursors to Modern Transnational Issue Networks: Campaigns against Slavery, Footbinding, and Female Circumcision." Paper presented at the Annual Conference of the American Political Science Association, Chicago.

Silverman, Dan. 1972. *Reluctant Union: Alsace-Lorraine and Imperial Germany, 1871–1914.* College Station: Pennsylvania State University.

Silverman, David, and Brian Torode. 1980. *The Material Word: Some Theories of Language and Its Limits.* London: Routledge and Kegan Paul.

Simmel, Georg. 1950. "The Secret Society" [1908]. In *The Sociology of Georg Simmel.* Translated by Kurt H. Wolff, 345–76. Glencoe, Ill.: Free Press.

Skocpol, T. 1979. *States and Social Revolutions: A Comparative Analysis of France, Russia, and China.* Cambridge: Cambridge University Press.

Slaughter, Thomas P. 1986. *The Whiskey Rebellion: Frontier Epilogue to the American Revolution.* New York: Oxford University Press.

Sleinada, S. J. P. [1779] 1972. *Oorsprong, oorzaeke, bewys en ondekkinge van een godlooze bezwoorne bende nachtdieven en knevelaers binnen de Landen van Overmaeze en aenpaelende landtstreeken ontdekt, etc.* Maastricht, Netherlands: Schrijen.

Smith, A. J. 1901. "Het eiland Ulsda." *Groninger Volksalmanak* 1901–1902: 196–224

Smith, Jackie. 1994. "Organizing Global Action." *Peace Review* 6: 419–26.

Snow, David A., E. Burke Rochford Jr., Steven K. Worden, and Robert D. Benford. 1986. "Frame Alignment Processes, Micromobilization, and Movement Participation." *American Sociological Review* 51: 464–81.

Snow, David A., and Robert D. Benford. 1988. "Ideology, Frame Resonance, and Participant Mobilization." In *From Structure to Action: Social Movement Participation across Cultures,* edited by Bert Klandermans, Hanspeter Kriesi, and Sidney Tarrow, 197–217, Greenwich, Conn.: JAI Press.

Snyder, Richard. 1992. "Explaining Transitions from Neopatrimonial Dictatorships." *Comparative Politics* 24: 379–99.

Soikkanen, H. 1967. "Miksi revisionismi ei saanut kannatusta Suomen vanhassa työväenliikkeessä?" (Why had revisionism no support in the old worker movement in Finland?) In *Oman ajan historia ja politiikan tutkimus* (Contemporary history and politology) edited by L. Hyvämäki et al., 183–99. Helsinki: Otava.

Soja, Edward. 1985. "The Spatiality of Social Life: Towards a Transformative Retheorisation." In *Social Relations and Spatial Structures,* edited by Derek Gregory and John Urry, 90–127. New York: St. Martin's Press.

———. 1989. *Postmodern Geographies.* London: Verso.

Spater, George. 1982. *William Cobbett: The Poor Man's Friend.* 2 vols. Cambridge: Cambridge University Press.

Spierenburg, Pieter. 1984. *The Spectacle of Suffering: Executions and the Evolution of Repression. From a Preindustrial Metropolis to the European Experience.* Cambridge: Cambridge University Press.

Squires, Judith. 1994. "Engendering Participation: Citizenship and Plurality." Paper presented at the sixteenth World Congress of the International Political Science Association, Berlin, August 21–25.

Staehlin, Carlos María. 1954. *Apariciones: Ensayo crítico.* Madrid: Razón y Fe.

Stallybrass, Peter. 1985. "'Drunk with the Cup of Liberty': Robin Hood, the Carnivalesque, and the Rhetoric of Violence in Early Modern England." *Semiotica* 54: 113–45.

Stallybrass, Peter, and Allon White. 1986. *The Politics and Poetics of Transgression.* Ithaca, N.Y.: Cornell University Press.

Stenius, H. 1987. *Frivilligt, jämlikt, samfällt: Föreningsväsendets utveckling i Finland fram till 1900– talets början med speciell hänsyn till massorganisationsprincipens genombrott* (Voluntarily, equally, mutually: A history of voluntary associations in Finland until the early twentieth century with special regard to the principles of mass organization, with an English summary). Helsingfors, Finland: Svenska Litteratursällskapet i Finland.

Strand, David. 1990. "Protest in Beijing: Civil Society and the Public Sphere in China." *Problems of Communism* (May–June): 1–19.

Strikwerda, Carl. 1993a. "France and the Belgian Immigration of the Nineteenth Century." In *The Politics of Immigrant Workers: Labor Activism and Migration in the World Economy since 1830,* edited by Camille Guerin-Gonzales and Carl Strikwerda, 101–31. New York: Holmes and Meier.

———. 1993b. "The Troubled Origins of European Economic Integration: International Iron and Steel and Labor Migration in the Era of World War I." *American Historical Review* 98, no. 4: 1106–29.

———. 1998. "Reinterpreting the History of European Integration: Business, Labor, and Social Citizenship in Twentieth Century Europe." In *European Integration in Social and Historical Perspective, 1850 to the Present,* edited by Jytte Klausen and Louise Tilly. Lanham, Md.: Rowman and Littlefield.

Sullivan, Larry. 1990. "The Emergence of Civil Society in China, Spring 1989." In *The Chinese People's Movement: Perspectives on Spring 1989,* edited by Tony Saich, Armonk, N.Y.: M. E. Sharpe.

Suzuki Chusei. 1952. *Shincho chukishi kenkyū* (Studies of mid-Qing history). Tokyo: Ryōgen shobo.

———. 1958. "Shinmatsu no zaisei to kanryo no seikaku" (Late Qing fiscal administration and the character of officials). *Kindai Chugoku kenkyu* 2: 190–281.

Swidler, Ann. 1995. "Cultural Power and Social Movements." In *Social Movements and Culture,* edited by Hank Johnston and Bert Klandermans, 25–40. Minneapolis: University of Minnesota Press.

Sykes, Robert A. 1982. "Popular Politics and Trade Unionism in Southeast Lancashire, 1829–1842." Vol. 1. Ph.D. diss. in History, University of Manchester.

Szelényi, Ivan. 1988. *Socialist Entrepreneurs: Embourgeoisement in Rural Hungary.* Madison: University of Wisconsin Press.

Tambiah, S. J. 1985. *Culture, Thought, and Social Action. An Anthropological Perspective.* Cambridge: Harvard University Press.

Tarrow, Sidney. 1989. *Struggles, Politics, and Reform: Collective Action, Social Movements, and Cycles of Protest.* Cornell Western Societies Paper no. 2. Ithaca, N.Y.: Center for International Studies.

———. 1992. "Mentalities, Political Cultures, and Collective Action Frames: Constructing Meaning through Action," in *Frontiers in Social Movement Theory.* eds. Aldon D. Morris & Carol McClurg Mueller. New Haven: Yale University Press, 1992. pp. 174–202.

———. 1994. *Power in Movement: Social Movements, Collective Action and Politics.* Cambridge: Cambridge University Press.

———. 1995. "The Europeanization of Conflict: Reflections from a Social Movement Perspective." *West European Politics* 18: 223–51.

———. 1997. "Social Movements and Contentious Politics: A Review Article." *American Political Science Review.*

———. 1998. *Power in Movement: Social Movements and Contentious Politics.* 2nd, rev. ed. New York and Cambridge: Cambridge University Press.

Thomas, Dan. 1997. "Norms, Politics, and Human Rights: The Helsinki Process and Decline of Communism in Eastern Europe." Ph.D. diss., Cornell University Department of Government.

Thomas, E. Bruce. 1938. "Political Tendencies in Pennsylvania, 1783–1794." Ph.D. diss., Temple University.

Thomas, Hugh. 1971. *Cuba: The Pursuit of Freedom.* New York: Harper and Row.

Thomis, Malcolm I., and Jennifer Grimmett. 1982. *Women in Protest, 1800–1850.* London: Croom Helm.

Thompson, Dorothy. 1984. *The Chartists: Popular Politics in the Industrial Revolution.* New York: Pantheon.

Thompson, E. P. 1971. "The Moral Economy of the English Crowd in the Eighteenth Century." *Past and Present* 50: 76–136.

———.1974. "Patrician Society, Plebeian Culture." *Journal of Social History* 7: 382–405.

———.1978. "Folklore, Anthroplogy, and Social History." *Indian Historical Review* 3: 247–66.

———. 1981. "'Rough music' et charivari. Quelques reflexions complimentaires." In *Le charivari,* edited by Jacques Le Goff and Jean-Claude Schmitt, 273–84. Paris: Ecole des Hautes Etudes en Sciences Sociales.

———. 1991. *Customs in Common: Studies in Traditional Popular Culture.* New York: New Press.

Thurlings, Th. J. M., and A. A. P. Van Drunen. 1960. "Sociaal–economische geschiedenis." *Limburgs verleden* 1: 191–47.

Thurston, Herbert. 1952. *The Physical Phenomena of Mysticism.* Chicago: H. Regnery.

Tilly, Charles. 1964. *The Vendée.* Cambridge: Harvard University Press.

———. 1972. "How Protest Modernized in France, 1845–1855." In *The Dimensions of Quantitative Research in History,* edited by William O. Aydelotte, Alan G. Bogue, and Robert William Fogel, 192–255. Princeton: Princeton University Press.

———. 1978a. "Anthropology, History, and the Annales." *Review* 1, nos. 3/4: 207–13.

———. 1978b. "Changing Forms of Collective Actions." In *From Mobilization to Revolution,* chap. 5. Reading, Mass.: Addison-Wesley.

———. 1978c. *From Mobilization to Revolution.* Englewood Cliffs, N.J.: Prentice-Hall.

———. 1979. "Did the Cake of Custom Break?" In *Consciousness and Class Experience in Nineteenth-Century Europe,* edited by John Merriman, 17–41. New York: Holmes and Meier.

———. 1981. "Britain Creates the Social Movement." Center for Research on Social Organizations working paper no. 232, University of Michigan.

———. 1982. "Britain Creates the Social Movement." In *Social Conflict and Political Order in Modern Britain,* edited by James Cronin and Jonathan Schneer, 21–51. New Brunswick, N.J.: Rutgers University Press.

———. 1983a. "Charivaris, Repertoires, and Urban Politics." In *French Cities in the Nineteenth Century,* edited by John Merriman, 73–91. New York: Holmes and Meier.

———. 1983b. "Speaking Your Mind, Without Elections, Surveys, or Social Movements." Center for Research on Social Organization working paper no. 298, University of Michigan.

———. 1985. "War Making and State Making as Organized Crime." In *Bringing the State Back In,* edited by Peter Evans, Dietrich Rueschemeyer, and Theda Skocpol, 169–91. Cambridge: Cambridge University Press.

———. 1986a. *The Contentious French.* Cambridge, Mass.: Belknap.

———. 1986b. "European Violence and Collective Action since 1700." *Social Research* 53: 159–84.

———. 1990a. *Coercion, Capital, and European States, A.D. 990–1990.* Cambridge: Blackwell.

———. 1990b. "Where Do Rights Come From?" (Working Paper Series, no. 98, Center for Studies of Social Change, New School for Social Research, New York.

———. 1991. "Prisoners of the State." Working Paper Series, no. 129, Center for Studies of Social Change.

———. 1992. "How to Detect, Describe, and Explain Repertoires of Contention." Working Paper Series, no. 150, Center for Studies of Social Change, New School for Social Research, New York.

————. 1993a. "Contentious Repertoires in Great Britain, 1758–1834." *Social Science History* 17: 253–80.

————. 1993b. *European Revolutions, 1492–1992.* Oxford: Blackwell.

————. 1994a. "Democracy Is a Lake." Working Paper Series, no. 185, Center for Studies of Social Change, New School for Social Research, New York.

————. 1994b. "Social Movements as Historically Specific Clusters of Political Performances." *Berkeley Journal of Sociology* 38: 1–30.

————. 1995a. "Political Identities." Working Paper Series, no. 212, Center for Studies of Social Change, New School for Social Research, New York.

————. 1995b. *Popular Contention in Great Britain, 1758–1834.* Cambridge: Harvard University Press.

Tilly, Charles, and Louise Tilly, eds. 1981. *Class Conflict and Collective Action.* Beverly Hills, Calif.: Sage Publications.

Tilly, Charles, Louise Tilly, and Richard Tilly. 1975. *The Rebellious Century, 1830–1930.* Cambridge: Harvard University Press.

Tilly, Louise, and Patricia Gurin. 1990. "Women, Politics, and Change." In *Women, Politics, and Change,* edited by Louise Tilly and Patricia Gurin, 3–32. New York: Russell Sage Foundation.

Touraine, Alain. 1988. *Return of the Actor: Social Theory in Postindustrial Society.* Minneapolis: University of Minnesota Press.

Trexler, Richard C. 1981. *Public Life in Renaissance Florence.* New York: Academic Press.

Trossbach, Werner. 1993. *Bauern, 1648–1806.* Munich: Oldenbourg.

Tübben, Willi. 1930. "Die nationale und internationale Verbandspolitik der Schwerindustrie vor und nach dem Kriege." Diss., University of Heidelberg, Würzburg.

Tufnell, Edward C. 1834. *Character, Object, and Effects of Trades' Unions; with Some Remarks on the Law Concerning Them.* London: James Ridgway and Sons.

Turner, Lowell. Forthcoming. "Beyond National Unionism?" In *The Shifting Boundaries of Labor Politics,* edited by Richard Locke and Kathleen Thelen. Cambridge: MIT Press.

Turner, Victor. 1969. *The Ritual Process: Structure and Anti-Structure.* Ithaca, N.Y.: Cornell University Press.

————. 1977. "Variations on a Theme of Liminality." In *Secular Ritual,* edited by Sally E. Moore and Barbara G. Myerhoff, 36–52. Assen and Amsterdam: Van Gorcum.

United Nations. 1991. *The World's Women, 1970–1990: Trends and Statistics.* Social Statistics and Indicators, series K, no. 12. New York: United Nations.

United Nations. 1995. *The World's Women, 1995: Trends and Statistics.* New York: United Nations.

United Nations Centre for Social Development and Humanitarian Affairs. 1988. *Directory of National Machinery for the Advancement of Women.* Vienna: United Nations.

————. 1991. *Women in Decision-Making: Case Study on Costa Rica.* New York: United Nations.

————. 1992. Women in Politics and Decision-Making in the Late Twentieth Century. Dordrecht, Netherlands: Martinus Nijhoff.

United Nations Department for Policy Coordination and Sustainable Development. 1995. *Women in a Changing Global Economy: 1994 World Survey on the Role of Women in Development.* Publication N.E.95.IV.1. New York: United Nations.

United Nations Development Programme. 1993. *Human Development Report 1993.* New York: Oxford University Press.

United Nations ECLAC. 1989. *Women and Politics in Latin America and the Caribbean.* Santiago de Chile: Serie Mujer y Desarrollo.

————. 1992. *Major Changes and Crisis: The Impact on Women in Latin America and the*

Caribbean. Santiago de Chile: United Nations, Economic Commission for Latin America and the Caribbean.

Valdes, Teresa, and Enrique Gomariz, eds. 1995. *Latin American Women: Compared Figures.* Santiago de Chile: Instituto de la Mujer, Ministério de Asuntos Sociales de España and FLACSO Sede Chile.

Valverde, Marianna. 1988. "'Giving the Female a Domestic Turn': The Social, Legal, and Moral Regulation of Women's Work in British Cotton Mills, 1820–1850." *Journal of Social History* 21: 619–34.

van der Linden, Marcel. 1988. "The National Integration of European Working Classes (1871–1914)." *International Review of Social History* 33: 285–311.

Vanderpol, A. 1914. *La propagande catholique pour la Paix.* Brussels: Goemaere.

Vardi, Liana. 1993. *The Land and the Loom: Peasants and Profit in Northern France.* Durham, N.C.: Duke University Press.

Vauchez, André. 1987. "Jeanne d'Arc et le prophétisme féminin des xive et xve siècles." In *Les Laïcs au moyen âge, pratiques et expériences religieuses.* 277–86. Paris: Cerf.

Verba, Sidney. 1990. "Women in American Politics." In *Women, Politics, and Change,* edited by Louise Tilly and Patricia Gurin, 555–72. New York: Russell Sage Foundation.

Vignes, Maurice. 1913. "Le bassin de Briey et la politique de ses entreprises siderurgiques ou minières." *Revue d'économie politique* 27: 578–600.

Vignier, Françoise. 1962. "La justice de Magny-sur-Tille (XVe–XVIIIe siècles)." *Mémoires de la société pour l'Histoire du Droit et des Institutions des anciens pays bourguignons, comtois et romands* 23: 278–88.

Viikki, R. 1989. *Suur-Huittisten historia* (The history of the greater Huittinen). Vol. 3. Jyväskylä, Finland: Gummerus.

Visser, Jelle, and Bernhard Ebbinghaus. 1992. "Making the Most of Diversity: European Integration and the Transnational Organization of Labor." In *Organized Interests and the European Community,* edited by Justin Greenwood, Jurgen Grote, and Karsten Ronit, 230–37. London: Sage.

Voss, Kim. 1993. *The Making of American Exceptionalism: The Knights of Labor and Class Formation in the Nineteenth Century.* Ithaca, N.Y.: Cornell University Press.

———. 1996. "The Collapse of a Social Movement: The Interplay of Mobilizing Structures, Framing, and Political Opportunities in the Knights of Labor." In *Comparative Perspectives on Social Movements: Political Opportunities, Mobilizing Structures, and Cultural Framing,* edited by Doug McAdam, John McCarthy, and Mayer Zald, 227–258. New York and Cambridge: Cambridge University Press.

Walder, Andrew G. 1989a. "The Political Sociology of the Beijing Upheaval of 1989." *Problems of Communism* (Sept.–Oct.): 30–40.

———. 1989b. "Factory and Manager in an Era of Reform." *China Quarterly* 118 (June): 242–64.

———. 1991. "Workers, Managers, and the State: The Reform Era and the Political Crisis of 1989." *China Quarterly* 127 (September): 467–92.

———. 1992. "Popular Protest in the 1989 Democracy Movement: The Pattern of Grass Roots Organization." USC Seminar Series, no. 8. Hong Kong: Institute of Asia-Pacific Studies, Chinese University of Hong Kong.

Walder, Andrew G., and Gong Xiaoxia. 1993. "Workers in the Tiananmen Protests: The Politics of the Beijing Workers' Autonomous Federation." *Australian Journal of Chinese Affairs* 29 (January): 1–29.

Walker, R. B. J. 1994. "Social Movements/World Politics." *Millenium: Journal of International Studies* 23, no. 2: 669–700.

Wallerstein, Immanuel. 1974. *The Modern World-System.* New York: Academic Press.

Walton, John. 1989. "Debt, Protest, and the State in Latin America." In *Power and Popular*

Protest: Latin American Social Movements, edited by Susan Eckstein, 299–328. Berkeley and Los Angeles: University of California Press.

Waltz, Kenneth. 1979. *Theory of International Politics.* Reading, Mass.: Addison-Wesley.

Wang, Yeh-chien. 1973. *Land Taxation in Imperial China, 1750–1911.* Cambridge: Harvard University Press.

Wapner, Paul. 1995. "Politics beyond the State: Environmental Activism and World Civic Politics," *World Politics* 47: 311–40.

———. 1996. *Environmental Activism and World Civic Politics.* Albany, N.Y.: State University of New York Press.

Ware, Norman J. 1929. *The Labor Movement in the United States, 1860–1895: A Study in Democracy.* New York: D. Appleton.

Warner, Shelley. 1990. "Shanghai's Response to the Deluge." *The Australian Journal of Chinese Affairs* 23 (January): 121–32.

Waterbolk, E. H. 1976. "Staatkundige geschiedenis." In *Historie van Groningen,* edited by W. J. Formsma, 235–76. Groningen, Netherlands: Wolters-Noordhoff.

Waylen, Georgina. 1994. "Women and Democratization: Conceptualizing Gender Relations in Transition Politics." *World Politics* 46, no. 3 (April): 327–54.

Weber, Eugen. 1976. *Peasants into Frenchmen: The Modernization of Rural France, 1870–1914.* Stanford, Calif.: Stanford University Press.

Weiss, Richard. 1946. *Volkskunde der Schweiz: Grundriss.* Erlenbach-Zürich: Eugen Rentsch Verlag.

Wellman, Barry. 1971. "Social Identities in Black and White." *Sociological Inquiry* 41: 57–66.

———. 1988. "Structural Analysis: From Method and Metaphor to Theory and Substance." In *Social Structures: A Network Approach,* edited by B. Wellman and S. D. Berkowitz, 19–61. New York and Cambridge: Cambridge University Press.

Wellman, Barry, et al. 1988. "Networks and Personal Communities." In *Social Structures: A Network Approach,* edited by B. Wellman and S. D. Berkowitz, 130–84. New York and Cambridge: Cambridge University Press.

Wellman, Kathleen. 1992. *La Mettrie: Medicine, Philosophy, and Enlightenment.* Durham, N.C., and London: Duke University Press.

Wendt, Alexander E. 1994. "Collective Identity Formation and the International State." *American Political Science Review* 88: 384–98.

Weschler, Lawrence. 1982. *Solidarity: Poland in the Season of Its Passion.* New York: Simon and Schuster.

White, Harrison. n.d. "Notes on the Constituents of Social Structure." Unpublished paper, Harvard University.

Whitten, David. 1975. "An Economic Inquiry into the Whiskey Rebellion of 1794." *Agricultural History* (July): 591–604.

Wichers, A. J. 1965. *De oude plattelandsbeschaving: Een sociologische bewustwording van de "overherigheid."* Assen, Netherlands: Van Gorcum.

Wickham-Crowley, Timothy P. 1992. *Guerrillas and Revolutions in Latin America: A Comparative Study of Insurgents and Regimes since 1956.* Princeton: Princeton University Press.

———. 1994. "States and Societies in Revolution: Two Steps Forward, Perhaps One Step Back?" *Theory and Society* 23: 777–83.

Wiemann, Harm. 1982. *Materialien zur Geschichte der Ostfriesischen Landschaft.* Aurich: Ostfriesische Landschaft.

Wiley, Richard. 1912. *The Whiskey Insurrection: A General View.* Elizabeth, Pa.: Herald.

Will, Pierre-Etienne. 1990. *Bureaucracy and Famine in Eighteenth-Century China.* Translated by Elborg Forster. Stanford, Calif.: Stanford University Press.

Will, Pierre-Etienne, and R. Bin Wong. 1991. *Nourish the People: The State Civilian Granary*

System in China, 1650–1850. Ann Arbor: University of Michigan Center for Chinese Studies.

Winter, P. J. van. 1948. *Westerwolde generaliteitsland.* Assen, Netherlands: Van Gorcum.

Woloch, Isser. 1994. *The New Regime: Transformations of the French Civic Order, 1789–1820s.* New York: Norton.

Wong, R. Bin. 1982. "Food Riots in the Qing Dynasty." *Journal of Asian Studies* 41, no. 4: 767–88.

Workers' Party. 1995. *Workers' Party Newsletter.* São Paulo, Brazil: Workers' Party.

Wouters, H.H.E. 1970. *Grensland en bruggehoofd: Historische studies met betrekking tot het Limburgse Maasdal en, meer in het bijzonder, de stad Maastricht.* Assen, Netherlands: Van Gorcum.

Wu Mouren et al., eds. 1989. *Bajiu zhongguo minyun jishi* (A record of the 1989 Chinese democracy movement). New York: n.p.

Xu Dalin. 1950. *Qingdai juanna zhidu* (The system of purchasing offices by contributions during the Qing period). Beijing: Yanjing University.

Yashar, Deborah J. 1998. "Indigenous Protest and Democracy in Latin America." In *Constructing Democratic Governance,* edited by Jorge I. Domínguez and Abraham Lowenthal, 87–105. Baltimore and London: Johns Hopkins University Press.

Yokoyama Suguru. 1955. "Chūgoku ni okeru nōmin undo no ichi keitai" (One form of the peasant movement in China: The tax resistance movement before the Taiping Rebellion). *Hiroshima daigaku bungakubu kiyo* (Bulletin of the Faculty of Letters, Hiroshima University) 7: 311–49.

———. 1972. *Chūgoku kindaika no keizai kōzō* (The economic structure of China's modernization). Tokyo: Aki Shobo.

Zald, Mayer N. 1996. "Culture, Ideology, and Strategic Framing." In *Comparative Perspectives on Social Movements: Political Opportunities, Mobilizing Structures, and Cultural Framing,* edited by Doug McAdam, John McCarthy, and Mayer Zald, 261–74. New York: Cambridge University Press.

Zimdars-Swartz, Sandra. 1989a. "Popular Devotion to the Virgin: The Marian Phenomena at Melleray, Republic of Ireland." *Archives de sciences sociales des religions* 67: 125–44.

———. 1989b. "Religious Experience and Public Cult: The Case of Mary Ann Van Hoof." *The Journal of Religion and Health* 28: 36–57.

———. 1991. *Encountering Mary: From La Salette to Medjugorje.* Princeton: Princeton University Press.

Zolberg, A. R. 1986. "How Many Exceptionalisms?" In *Working-Class Formation: Nineteenth-Century Patterns in Western Europe and the United States,* edited by I. Katznelson and A. R. Zolberg, 397–455. Princeton: Princeton University Press.

Zongzheng wenhua bu zhengwen bangongshi, ed. 1989. *Jieyan yiri (shangji)* (A day of martial law, vol. 1). Beijing: Jiefang jun wenyi chubanshe.

Contributors

Risto Alapuro is professor of sociology at the University of Helsinki. His works include *State and Revolution in Finland* (1988). He has been a visiting scholar at the University of Michigan, the University of Paris III, and the Institute of Sociology at the Academy of Sciences in Moscow.

Anton Blok is professor of cultural anthropology at the University of Amsterdam and the Amsterdam School for Social Science Research. He has conducted ethnographic fieldwork in Sicily and archival research in the Netherlands. He previously taught at the University of Nijmegen and held visiting positions at the University of Michigan; the University of California, Berkeley; Yale University; and the Université de Provence at Aix-en-Provence. His publications include *The Mafia of a Sicilian Village, 1860–1960* (1975) and *The Bokkerijders: Roversbenden en geheime genootschappen in de Landen van Overmaas, 1730–1774* (1995).

William A. Christian Jr. is the author of *Apparitions in Late Medieval and Renaissance Spain* (1981), *Moving Crucifixes in Modern Spain* (1992), and *Visionaries: The Spanish Republic and the Reign of Christ* (1996). An independent scholar, he lives much of the time in Spain.

Sonia De Avelar, a political scientist and currently a consultant for international development organizations, has researched Brazilian labor history, women in development issues, and gender inequalities in access to power resources in Latin America and the Caribbean. Recent publications include, with Gina Zabludovsky, "Women's Leadership and Glass Ceiling Barriers in

Brazil and Mexico," in *Women's Leadership in a Changing World*, for the United Nations Development Fund for Women (1996).

Roger V. Gould teaches in the sociology department at the University of Chicago. He has published articles on social networks and collective action and a book on protest in nineteenth-century Paris entitled *Insurgent Identities*. His current research focuses on feuding.

Michael P. Hanagan teaches nineteenth- and twentieth-century European social history and comparative history at the New School for Social Research. He is the author of *The Logic of Solidarity: Artisans and Industrial Workers in Three French Towns, 1871–1914* (1980) and *Nascent Proletarians: Class Formation in Pre-Revolutionary France, 1840–1880* (1989). With Miriam Cohen, he is currently completing a book-length study on the relationship between families, reformers, and the state in the emergence of the welfare state in Europe and the United States from 1870 to 1950.

Marjolein 't Hart teaches social and economic history at the University of Amsterdam. She has been a Vera List Fellow at the Center for Studies of Social Change at the New School for Social Research. Her book on Dutch state formation, *The Making of a Bourgeois State: War, Politics, and Finance during the Dutch Revolt*, was published in 1993.

Leslie Page Moch teaches European social history and migration history at Michigan State University. She is the author of *Moving Europeans: Migration in Western Europe since 1650* (1992) and *Paths to the City: Regional Migration in Nineteenth-Century France* (1983). She is currently at work on a study of Bretons in Paris, 1880–1940.

Marifeli Pérez-Stable is a professor of sociology at the State University of New York at Old Westbury. She is the author of *The Cuban Revolution: Origins, Course, and Legacy* (1993). Her research interests include the dynamics of change and stability in state socialism, the origins of Latin American revolutions, development paths in the Spanish-speaking Caribbean, and the impact of U.S. intervention on national and state formation in the Caribbean and Central America.

Robert M. Schwartz teaches history at Mount Holyoke College in South Hadley, Massachusetts. He is the author of *History and Statistics: The Case of*

Witchcraft in Early Modern Europe and New England (1992) and *Policing the Poor in Eighteenth-Century France* (1988), which received the 1989 David H. Pinkney Prize from the Society for French Historical Studies and the 1990 First Book Prize from the Phi Alpha Theta honorary society in history. He is currently writing a book that examines the social and political evolution of rural communities in Burgundy during the eighteenth and nineteenth centuries.

Marc W. Steinberg is an assistant professor at Smith College. He has published a number of articles on the role of discourse in class formation and collective action in nineteenth-century England. His book *Fighting Words: Working-Class Formation, Collective Action, and Discourse in Early Nineteenth-Century England* will be published in 1999.

Carl Strikwerda is an associate professor of history and chair of European studies at the University of Kansas. He received his Ph.D. at the University of Michigan after studying with Louise Tilly and Charles Tilly. He is the author of *A House Divided: Catholics, Socialists, and Flemish Nationalists in Nineteenth Century Belgium* and a coeditor of *The Politics of Immigrant Workers: Labor Activism and Migration in the World Economy since 1830* (with Camille Guerin-Gonzales) and *Consumers against Capitalism? Consumer Cooperation in Europe, North America, and Japan, 1840–1990* (with Ellen Furlough).

Sidney Tarrow is Maxwell Upson Professor of Government at Cornell. He is the author of *Power in Movement* (1998) and an associate editor of the University of Minnesota Press series Social Movement, Protest, and Contention. He is currently collaborating with Doug McAdam and Charles Tilly in a study on the dynamics of contention.

Wayne te Brake teaches late medieval and early modern European history at Purchase College, State University of New York. His publications include *Regents and Rebels: The Revolutionary World of an Eighteenth-Century Dutch City* (1989) and *Shaping History: Ordinary People in European Politics, 1500–1700* (1998). His current research is a comparative study of the accommodation of religious differences following the religious wars of the sixteenth and seventeenth centuries.

Charles Tilly, who teaches sociology, history, and political science at Columbia University, has been studying contentious politics, chiefly European, since 1954.

Kim Voss is associate professor of sociology at the University of California, Berkeley. She is the author of *The Making of American Exceptionalism: The Knights of Labor and Class Formation in the Nineteenth Century* (1993) and coauthor of *Inequality by Design: Cracking the Bell Curve Myth* (1996). Her current research interests include the role of defeat frames in social movements and new organizing initiatives in contemporary U.S. unions.

Andrew G. Walder is professor of sociology and senior fellow at the Institute of International Studies, Stanford University. He has previously taught at Columbia University, Harvard University, and the Hong Kong University of Science and Technology. He is the author of *Communist Neo-Traditionalism: Work and Authority in Chinese Industry* (1986) and the editor of *The Waning of the Communist State* (1995), *China's Transitional Economy* (1996), and *Zouping in Transition* (1998). He is currently engaged in research on Beijing's Red Guard movement of 1966–67.

R. Bin Wong, professor of history and social sciences at the University of California, Irvine, has recently written *China Transformed: Historical Change and the Limits of European Experience* (1997) and coedited *Culture and State in Chinese History: Conventions, Accommodations, and Critiques* (1997). His current research projects include books on Chinese political economy and Chinese economic history.

Index